Third Canadian Edition

Essentials of Early Childhood Education

Third Canadian Edition

Essentials of Early Childhood Education

Carol Gestwicki
Central Piedmont Community College

Jane Bertrand
Centre for Early Child Development, George Brown College

Australia Canada Mexico Singapore Spain United Kingdom United States

Essentials of Early Childhood Education, Third Canadian Edition

by Carol Gestwicki and Jane Bertrand

Associate Vice President, Editorial Director:
Evelyn Veitch

Editor-in-Chief, Higher Education:
Anne Williams

Senior Marketing Manager:
David Ward

Senior Developmental Editor:
Alwynn Pinard

Senior Content Production Manager:
Natalia Denesiuk Harris

Production Service:
International Typesetting and Composition

Copy Editor:
Kim Ward

Proofreader:
Martha Ghent

Production Coordinator:
Ferial Suleman

Design Director:
Ken Phipps

Interior Design:
Opus House

Cover Design:
Johanna Liburd

Cover Image:
Graeme Montgomery/Getty Images

Compositor:
International Typesetting and Composition

Printer:
Thomson/West

Adapted from *The Essentials of Early Education* by Carol Gestwicki, published by Delmar. Copyright 1997 by Delmar.

Printed and bound in the United States
1 2 3 4 10 09 08 07

For more information contact Nelson, 1120 Birchmount Road, Toronto, Ontario, M1K 5G4. Or you can visit our internet site at http://www.nelson.com

Library and Archives Canada Cataloguing in Publication

Gestwicki, Carol, 1940–

Essentials of early childhood education / Carol Gestwicki, Jane Bertrand. — 3rd Canadian ed.

First Canadian ed. published under title: The essentials of early education.
Includes bibliographical references and index.

ISBN-13: 978-0-17-625271-7
ISBN-10: 0-17-625271-1

1. Early childhood education—Canada—Textbooks. 2. Early childhood teachers—Canada. 3. Teaching—Vocational guidance—Canada. I. Bertrand, Jane, 1951– II. Title.

LB1775.6.G47 2007 372.210971
C2006-906603-5

CONTENTS

Section Two

The Early Childhood Workforce ... 111

CHAPTER FOUR

Early Childhood Educators ... 113

CHAPTER FIVE

Becoming an Early Childhood Educator ... 129

CHAPTER SIX

The Work Environment ... 154

Section Three

The Early Childhood Workforce Comes of Age ... 175

CHAPTER SEVEN

The Roots of Early Child Development Programs in Canada ... 177

CHAPTER EIGHT

CHAPTER NINE

PREFACE

> Research shows us that the first years of life and early brain development are critical for later learning, health, and well-being. During those early years, children need adults—parents, other family members, teachers, and others—who support their healthy growth and development in many important ways. A competent early child development workforce that is able to work with children, parents and communities is critical to integrate and build on the early years programs now scattered across communities (McCain & Mustard, 1999).

The Early Years Study (McCain & Mustard, 1999) recognized that competent early child development program staff are crucial to implementing programs that are sensitive to the needs of young children and their families. Such a workforce will be a powerful agent in breaking down the barriers (professional, regulatory, and funding) that exist between staff now working in child care centres, family child care settings, nursery schools, parenting centres, family resource programs, and kindergarten.

It is a wonderful time to be entering the early childhood workforce. Since the release of the Early Years Study in 1999, public interest in early child development programs has exploded. Policymakers have responded. Investment has increased. The silos do continue and Canada is far from having a comprehensive early child development system but the public and policymakers recognize the central role of early childhood educators. You will have an opportunity to help build the system that will emerge over the next couple of decades.

Why Was This Book Written?

This book is written from the authors' strong convictions that the care and education of children in their earliest years must go beyond rhetoric, to provide optimum experiences and environments for real children in our very real world. Those who enter the early childhood workforce find both enormous challenges and immense gratification as they nurture the healthy development of children and families. As child development research continues to discover the importance of the experiences, interactions, and environments that support children in the first years of their lives, it becomes increasingly clear that the adults responsible for children's care must be prepared to provide the best opportunities for children. As the need and demand for early child development programs for children from birth through the elementary school years continues to expand in unprecedented dimensions, so too does the need for educated early childhood professionals.

This demand is related to a second strong conviction from which this book grows: not just anyone can, or should, work with young children, and moreover, young children do not need "just anyone." They need particular people, with specific characteristics, knowledge, skills, and attitudes, who have thoughtfully and deliberately prepared to enter into caring relationships with young children and their families. They need people who have committed themselves to following career paths in early childhood education, and who understand and accept the realities of the profession as it has evolved to this point. They need people who have decided to touch young lives and are willing to stay the course.

Two Main Themes

These are the two main themes of this book: (1) that early childhood educators do important, meaningful, valuable work, supporting children and families during the most critical period of development; and (2) that only persons who are willing to accept the need for thoughtful and careful professional preparation will be able to help children reach their full potential. This book, then, proposes to examine the world of early child development and to assist the process of professional growth for those who are considering it as their future, a future that impacts generations to come. It is assumed that students will use this text in a course that introduces them to concepts of early child development, near the beginning of their professional education, whether in a two- or four-year program. Because the text is designed for students who will continue with other courses in an ECE college program, the specifics of theoretical perspectives, curriculum ideas and activities, and program management are left for those later courses.

Since the intention of the text is to help students begin active construction of themselves as early childhood educators, the style is both informative, so that students may truly understand the current field, and introspective, so that students may actively juxtapose their personal knowledge, goals, and experiences to consider the professional roles and possibilities of working with young children. So, however you as a student came to study the essentials of early childhood education, you are invited to reflect on the profession.

Coverage

The *Introduction* outlines the social and political context for early child development programs in Canada.

Section One, *Early Child Development Programs Today*, introduces you to the field in Canada.

Chapter 1, *Early Child Development Programs*, defines the parameters of the field and explores the diversity of program structures, age groups that early childhood educators work with, special population groups, and program sponsors.

Chapter 2, *Early Child Development Pedagogy and Curriculum*, discusses different approaches to organizing early childhood environments for young children.

Chapter 3, *Quality in Early Child Development Programs*, describes the central elements of quality in early childhood settings.

The second section of the book, *The Early Childhood Workforce*, introduces the roles and responsibilities of early childhood educators.

Chapter 4, *Early Childhood Educators*, explores the various roles of early childhood educators who work with children and families in a wide spectrum of settings.

Chapter 5, *Becoming an Early Childhood Educator*, demonstrates that good early childhood educators are not born but grow actively, with much personal effort and thought. It considers the characteristics, skills, knowledge, and experiences that are important in creating oneself as an early childhood practitioner.

Chapter 6, *The Work Environment*, discusses the career opportunities now open to early childhood educators. It also examines some of the current challenges you will face as you enter the early childhood workforce.

Section Three is entitled *The Early Childhood Workforce Comes of Age*. As we enter the twenty-first century, early child development is at an exciting time. The combination of a seemingly unending need for early childhood educators, clear knowledge about what contributes to quality programs, and demands for professional standards and acceptance offers us positive directions for the future.

Chapter 7, *The Roots of Early Child Development Programs in Canada*, describes the history of early child development. In this chapter, you will see the multiple traditions and various philosophies and historic/social influences that have shaped the modern world of early child development. Many of the names and events that you will read on the historical Timeline will appear in this chapter to describe our historical roots.

Chapter 8, *The Modern Profession*, considers the current emphasis on professionalism, which will shape your introduction to joining the early childhood workforce.

Chapter 9, *Advocacy*, considers the role of advocacy for early childhood educators, both within early childhood settings and in the world at large. It leaves you with the challenge to become an early childhood educator and advocate for young children and their families, early child development programs, and the early childhood workforce.

Changes from the Second Canadian Edition

This is the third Canadian edition of *The Essentials of Early Childhood Education*. The changes in the third edition reflect increased public interest in early child development and the expanding opportunities open to ECE graduates.

Throughout the text there are updated statistics and references to new Canadian studies. Recent research and policy reports makes possible to provide a more complete picture of the Canadian situation. This edition continues to update American research with Canadian findings.

There appears to be growing consensus on the use of the term 'early childhood educator'—similar to 'nurse' or 'teacher'—which describes a professional occupation and implies appropriate professional education. Early childhood educators may practise their profession in many different settings, including child care centres, family resource programs, or kindergartens. Some of these settings require early childhood educators (for example, regulated child care centres).

Chapter 1 includes an expanded section on integrated delivery models that combine existing kindergarten, child care, and family support programs. Chapter 2 offers more detailed coverage of various pedagogical approaches and curriculum models. Chapter 3 updates what we know from research about quality in early childhood settings. Section Two has been reorganized to present a fuller picture of the opportunities now open to ECE graduates and to the work environment that is evolving across the country. Chapter 9 examines many of the challenges facing the early childhood sector in advancing to a more comprehensive system of early child development.

Features

Each chapter features objectives, review questions, study activities, and suggested readings. The key terms are defined at the end of each chapter.

Enjoy early childhood facts that spark discussion and thought, as they appear in a *Timeline* in the margin of the pages throughout the book.

Watch for the *Research into Practice* feature, which highlights examples of evidence-based practice and practice-based evidence that guide early child development policies and practices. The *Making It Happen* boxes feature early child development programs from across the country. *Meet the Early Childhood Workforce* boxes feature early childhood educators who began with studies in early childhood education.

Most of the photographs were taken on location at child care centres, family child care homes, schools, and hospitals, and feature children who responded spontaneously, in order to provide accurate "snapshots" of real world early childhood education.

We welcome you to consider studies in early childhood education. We hope that you and your fellow students will discuss the topics and issues in depth and work through some of the additional readings and assignments at the end of each chapter. There are specific activities that will encourage you to explore the Nelson ECE Resource Centre Web site that accompanies this book: www.ece.nelson.com. The Web site is a wonderful resource that contains free downloadable activities and a wide variety of ECE-related Web links.

We need and want you to stay. Early childhood educators, families, and communities can join together to nurture, stimulate and educate young children. At no time in the history of Canada have children and families needed more the support, care, and expertise that early childhood education has to offer. Together we can prepare today's youngest Canadians for a rapidly changing and diverse world. The future may be uncertain and world tensions overwhelming, but we can be certain that a strong start is the best foundation for life.

Acknowledgments

Over the years we have heard the stories of many students, early childhood educators, and colleagues who have made their own discoveries of the essential truths and pleasures of working with young children. This book is dedicated to them with thanks for their friendship along the way.

This Canadian edition is indebted to the generous permissions I received to reprint materials. Thanks to Canadian Child Care Federation, Early Childhood Educators of British Columbia, Childcare Resource and Research Unit, *IDEAS Journal*, SpeciaLink, and the Early Childhood Education program at Red River College.

Since I completed the first Canadian edition of this book, I have had the privilege of continuing to work with J. Fraser Mustard to move the early years' agenda forward in Canada and internationally.

In addition, I appreciate the efforts and responses of the editorial and production staff at Thomson Nelson, and the helpful comments and suggestions of reviewers: Gail Hunter, George Brown College; Dale Long, Seneca College; Laila Shah, Seneca College; and Beverly Snell, Red River College.

INTRODUCTION

Early childhood education is a field of study that prepares individuals to work with young children and their families.

Framework of Understanding Takes Hold

> What we envision will be a first "tier" program for early child development, as important as the elementary and secondary school system and the post secondary education system. (McCain & Mustard, 1999, 23.)

In 1999, Dr. Fraser Mustard and the Hon. Margaret McCain delivered a landmark report, *The Early Years Study: Reversing the Real Brain Drain*, to the Ontario government. The report marshals the knowledge from science, communities, practitioners, and families. **Early childhood development** is understood as a critical period of human growth that sets the foundation for lifelong learning, behaviour, and health. Children live in families and families live in communities. The recommendations call for significant investment in the early years and the establishment of a new system for early child development and parenting.

The timely report established a new framework of understanding about early child development. Almost a decade later, that understanding is a guide to early childhood educators and early child development programs in Canada and in much of the world.

Public Awareness Is Shifting

Public interest in the early years of life exploded in the late 1990s and at the turn of the century. Newspaper headlines, magazine articles, websites, and television newscasts blasted out messages such as "the first years last forever" or "Canada's future prosperity lies in today's cribs." Pamphlets and guidebooks about why the early years are important and what parents and others can do to support healthy child development proliferated. Corporate business leaders joined early childhood educators (Bay Street meets *Sesame Street*) to raise public awareness about what our youngest children need. Local, provincial/territorial, and federal governments implemented public policies to increase the resources available for the early years.

An interesting constellation of events focused the spotlight on early child development in Canada and elsewhere in the world. North American media reports of revolutionary new brain research (that confirmed what nurturing parents and early childhood educators have always known) pointed to hard evidence that early experiences influenced early brain development. Educators and employers were alarmed about poor youth literacy rates and Canada's ability to compete in a competitive world economy.

The new framework of understanding reinforced the idea that experiences and environments shape the course of early brain development in the minds of Canadians. Therefore, early child development programs and strategies that support young children and their families must be wise investments and simply the right thing to do. Public awareness quickly accepted that early child development was important and that families were the most important influence on that development.

Provincial/territorial and federal governments began to see budget surpluses after years of fighting deficits and cutting back on spending. The time seemed ripe to increase the availability of early child development programs. A proliferation of new initiatives with a focus on healthy child development and supports to parents and families popped up across Canada in the late 1990s and at the beginning of the 21st century.

At the same time, more and more Canadian parents with young children were working outside the home and needed to find regular, nonparental care arrangements. The numbers of child care spaces grew—dramatically in Quebec but only slightly in the rest of Canada. While the public's awareness in early child development increased and the need for nonparental care increased, the public seemed to see child care as taking care of children while parents worked (EKOS, 1997). Now that perception seems to be shifting. The public debate about child care in the past three years has dominated two federal elections. The public's perception of child care and what its primary purpose is, has shifted from child care as child minding to child care as a developmental program that supports children's early learning, while it supports families' ability to earn a living (EKOS, 2005; Environics, 2006).

Now the Canadian public places a high value on child care programs and the importance of affordable child care to the fabric of society. Most regard the lack of affordable child care to be a serious problem, and there is a need for governments to play a role in helping parents meet their child care needs. There is now a public consensus that child care programs are beneficial both in terms of the benefits they provide to children in early development and in preparing them for school, as well as in helping parents, particularly those with lower incomes, participate in the work force (Environics, 2006). This is most definitely a shift in public opinion over the past ten years.

As you look at the Timeline, you will see there have been various forms of early child development programs in Canada over the past two centuries. The earliest public expenditures on children included funds for schools to teach primary academic skills. Public schools then expanded to include kindergartens, which began as products of a particular philosophy of early childhood. With their inclusion in the public schools, kindergartens have undergone changes in philosophy and format, and the debate about these changes is ongoing. The first child care centres sprung up at the end of the nineteenth century to provide care and protection for poor mothers seeking employment. The nursery schools that middle-class Canadian children began attending in the 1920s reflected both the societal value of early education and the cultural acceptance of the importance of childhood.

Canada does not yet have a cohesive policy of support for the early years, but most Canadians believe that the healthy development of young children is key to our future. There is consensus that the early years agenda is an important one. The agenda is supported by the science of early child development, concern about economic prosperity, and changing demographics and families. Child care has shifted from being a private family matter to a matter of broad public interest and debate. Momentum is growing to create a first "tier" system that includes child care. It is an exciting time to enter the **early childhood workforce**.

Spotlight on Quality, Curriculum, and Pedagogy

The science of early child development draws together research from biology, psychology, sociology, medicine, anthropology, and neuroscience. The findings from all disciplines point to the impact of early experiences on the development of children's brains and on their lifelong health, well-being, competence, and abilities to cope (Doherty, 1997; Keating & Hertzman, 1999; Shonkoff & Phillips, 2000; Bertrand, 2001). Development does continue across middle childhood, adolescence, and into adulthood. "Early brain and child development sets a foundation for health, well-being, behaviour and learning but later development plays a significant role in building on the base" (Bertrand, 2001, p. 17). What children experience in early life becomes embedded in their biological and developmental pathways. New experiences, opportunities, and challenges will certainly affect later development, but they will always interact with the pathways laid down by past experience.

The evidence from animal and human studies in biological studies and the social sciences is consistent: the effects of the social and physical environment in the early years of human development affect our risk for physical and mental health problems in adult life. This is coupled with a growing body of evidence that the early period of child development affects cognition, learning, and behaviour in the later stages of life. The converging evidence creates a broad consensus about the fundamental importance of the early years of development and points to the importance of the quality of early child development programs.

The practice of early child development is very much concerned with the quality of programs for young children and their families. Different communities and societies often have different perceptions about children, childhood, and the purposes of early child development programs. They produce significant variations in ideas about quality in those programs, but communities and countries with varying histories and circumstances share many common ideas. The core elements of quality seem to cross cultural, community, and country borders (Friendly & Beach, 2005) and begin with a clear understanding of the purpose and goals of the program (Moss, 2004).

Across Canada, early childhood educators and others are in agreement that early child development programs need an educational philosophy and framework to support practice in programs. *Educational* means pedagogy which can be translated as education-in-its-broadest-sense (Friendly & Beach, 2005). Curriculum is the content of early childhood programs and is organized to support the purpose, goals, and pedagogy. Program standards—child-staff ratios, staff training qualifications, physical environment and parent participation—support the pedagogy and curriculum.

The recent review of early learning and child care programs (including kindergarten, child care centres, preschool, and nursery schools), by an international team of experts, pointed to the need for improving quality in Canadian programs, and the need to pay more attention to pedagogy and curriculum. Several provincial governments are developing guidelines to support more attention to how programs are organized for young children. Parents, who are now more aware of the potential educative value of early child development programs, want to know more about how programs will promote their children's early learning. The practice of childhood education is now into a more public spotlight. Early childhood educators have opportunities to be explicit about why, what, and how they work with young children and families.

Canada's economy and society are undergoing significant change as we shift to a "knowledge-based" economy, which depends on ideas and innovation rather than natural resources or manufacturing. To be successful in the global market, Canada must have a competent, well-educated workforce. Success in school is much more likely when children enter school ready and motivated to learn—physically, emotionally, socially, and cognitively. Quality early child development programs contribute to readiness for school learning and school success (Doherty, 1997).

Recognizing the need for a competent workforce, public attention turns to reports of school achievement and academic testing. Now government and business leaders are starting to understand the connection between how well children are doing when they enter school and later school success. Children who are able to take turns, wait to have their needs met, listen to storybooks, and play for extended periods of time find it easier to adapt to school environments and are more likely to do well at school. Early childhood settings help to develop these critical skills so children can get along with other children and adults.

Changing Demographics

Demography is the study of human population trends. One of the greatest influences on trends in early child development programs is the demographic data that portray changing patterns of family life and employment. In the past thirty years, two interrelated social patterns have appeared.

- The number of single-parent families has increased owing to rising divorce rates and to the increase in the number of children born to single parents.
- Census data reveal that the majority of all parents, whether in one- or two-parent families, are in the workforce. The need of these families for some form of supplemental child care for children from birth on is changing the face of early childhood care and education.

One of the most obvious effects of the changing demographics of families and the workplace has been the enormous increase in the amount of nonparental care needed. Various family supports are recognized as necessary for the well-being of children, families, and communities. Schools and child care programs are increasingly being asked to assume helping roles for parents by providing social support as well as education. Early years programs are now seen as a necessity both for the support of family needs and for the care and early education of young children. Early childhood educators are in a vital position to provide this community support in a time of changing social patterns.

Looking forward, the demand for full-time, full-year options in early child development programs to support parents who are working will probably continue to increase, although the number of children from birth to twelve years will not change much over the next decade. The participation rates of mothers in the labour force continue to increase, although the increases are smaller than those over the past three decades.

Families' needs for full-time, full-year options and their awareness of the value of early child development programs are also likely to increase. Public awareness of

FIGURE 1.1

Working Mothers with Children under Six Years in Canada

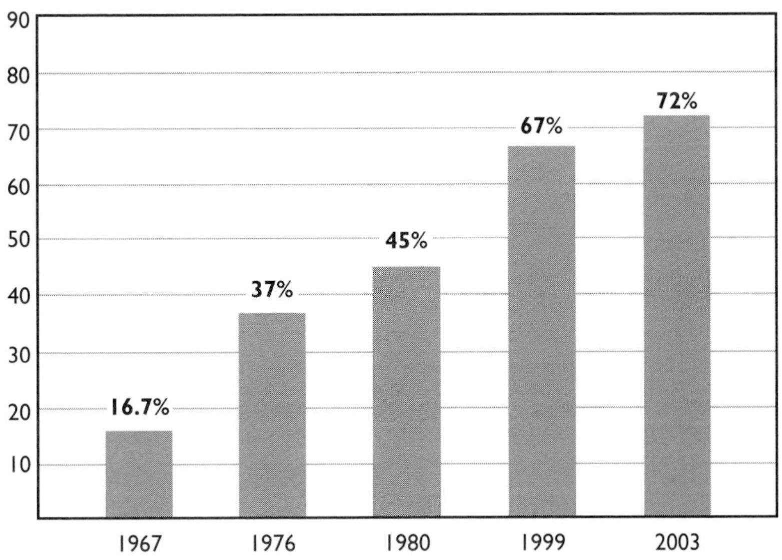

Sources: Beach et al, 2004; Beach & Friendly, 2005; Beach, Bertrand & Cleveland, 1998; Johnson, Lero & Rooney, 2001.

the importance of development in the early years is creating recognition of, and demand for, a variety of early child development programs that combine early education, care, and support to families.

The other major development in the demographics of Canada is the growing cultural-ethnic and linguistic diversity of its population.

- Growing numbers of newcomers from around the world continue to arrive in Canada annually.
- In 2001, 16 percent of all children and youth under twenty-five years are members of a visible minority group (Statistics Canada, 2005). It is estimated that by 2017, one in every five people in Canada will be a member of a visible minority group (Canadian Council on Social Development, 2006).
- Canada's Aboriginal population is growing faster than its non-aboriginal population. The birth rate for the Aboriginal population is higher than for the rest of Canada and Aboriginal children represent a higher proportion of the Aboriginal population compared to Canadian children overall (Statistics Canada, 2003). One in every three Aboriginal people is under fifteen years compared to only one in every five people in the overall Canadian population.

Today's families come in all sizes and shapes.

How Are Canadian Children Doing?

Are children who enter Grade One in September, 2007, doing better—healthier, more ready for school, more outgoing, and co-operative—than children were fifty years earlier in 1957?

We know that children are born healthier and are less likely to die from disease or injury today than they were fifty years ago. But we don't know if the numbers of children with difficult behaviour or emotional problems have increased or decreased. There are more reported child abuse incidents, but this may reflect greater public awareness and less tolerance.

Parents, teachers, child welfare workers, and doctors often report that children have more behaviour and emotional difficulties today than in the past. But we cannot verify the anecdotes with evidence, because this kind of information was not collected for the whole population fifty years ago. We do know that not all children are doing well even though we live in an affluent country. We also know that some children are doing much better than others and the gap is evident well before school starts.

RESEARCH INTO PRACTICE

Monitoring Children's Development

Today researchers and governments are collecting more information and we can draw a detailed picture about Canada's children—how they are doing and what their lives are like (Ross, Scott, & Kelly, 1996; Ross, Roberts, & Scott, 2000; Canadian Council on Social Development, 2006).

- Most children (85 percent) live in two-parent families.
- Most children seem to enter school with the competencies and skills needed to be successful, but as many as 25 percent do not.
- About 20 percent of all children seem to have a behaviour or emotional problem.
- More than 15 percent of children live in relative poverty.

Debate About Public Investment in Early Child Development

"The development of human capital at an early age is central to a thriving economy. It's a smarter path to take" (Charles Coffey, Executive Vice-President, Government & Community Affairs, RBC. www.bizniagara.ca/champions/charlescoffey.htm.). Early learning and care supports the formation of human and social capital—now and in the future. It is vital to the prosperity of the City [Niagara] and the country.

- Children who participate in high quality early learning and care programs are more likely to succeed in school than those who experience custodial and mediocre non-parental child care (Shonkoff & Phillips, 2000; Peisner-Feinberg et al., 2001).

- Economic vitality is directly linked to social cohesion. Early learning and care programs that support young children and their families are shared spaces that welcome newcomers and support the participation of all families into their community (Beauvais & Jenson, 2003).
- Parents who are secure in the arrangements they have for their young children while they work are better able to focus on their work, have less absenteeism, and are more likely to accept promotions (Akyeampong, 1998; Duxbury & Higgins, 2001).

The costs of doing nothing about early child development are significant:

- Investment in early childhood initiatives also yields a cost-benefit. In the United States, the Perry Preschool Project estimated that each $1 invested in its early childhood education programs for children in low-income families yielded an avoidance of over $7 in later special education, justice, and welfare spending.
- In Canada, economists Cleveland and Krashinsky (1998) modeled a cost-benefit study for non-targeted service provision concluding that for every dollar invested in high quality child care, there is a two dollar benefit to children, parents, and society. The return on investment in early childhood is greater than the return on investments made later in life. Early investments in a young child's daily experiences set trajectories for success and compounded benefits. Children who are successful at school entry benefit more from the public investment in education while needing fewer of the more expensive remedial supports.

Rights of Childhood

"Action now will put our children and our future on a firmer foundation for the future. This action is necessary, not only to keep a reasonable standard of living, but also because it is the right thing to do for our young children" (McCain & Mustard, 1999, p. 2).

The Convention of the Rights of the Child was adopted by the United Nations in 1989. It includes the idea that children are citizens with rights and are entitled to resources. The child's individual rights to resources should be respected, quite apart from the child's value as an asset to society.

Canada supported both drafting the Convention and mobilizing the world's nations to sign it. The fifty-four clauses of the Convention include children's rights that have direct implications for early child development programs (Friendly, 2000). The Convention states that all children have the right to child care services while their parents work, and to education opportunities that will prepare them to participate in society. Early child development programs are critical if we value children and respect their rights to their share of our resources.

Implications for Early Childhood Educators

In Canada, a continuum of early child development programs evolved from earlier early childhood education programs, child care arrangements, kindergarten, and family support programs. It includes a broad range of interconnected programs and services to support children's optimal development and families' child-rearing skills. Educators who make up the early childhood workforce are equipped to work with young children in all of these settings.

On September 11, 2000, the first ministers (provincial and territorial premiers and the prime minister) signed the federal/provincial/territorial Early Child Development Agreement and committed $2.2 billion to be used for expanded early child development programs. In 2003, the federal/provincial/territorial governments signed the Multilateral Agreement on Early Learning and Child Care and the federal government committed another $1 billion (over 5 years) to child care programs. The sector is expanding.

Early child development programs are entering a new period of development in Canada. There is much work to do and not all new initiatives will best serve the interests of young children and their families. But the overall direction is unmistakable—early child development programs and related opportunities for early childhood educators are expanding. Canada's young children and families come in all sizes and shapes, so early child development programs must be sensitive to ethnic, linguistic, and religious diversity. The early child development programs that grow up in the 21st century will differ tremendously and will be dependent on an equally diverse early childhood workforce.

SUGGESTED READINGS

Bertrand, J. (2001). *Summary of research findings on children's developmental health.* Ottawa: Canadian Institute of Child Health & Canadian Child Care Federation.

Johnson, K., Lero, D. & Rooney, J. (2001). *Work-life compendium 2001: 150 Canadian statistics on work, family and well-being.* Guelph: Centre for Families, Work and Well-Being, University of Guelph.

McCain, M. & Mustard, J.F. (1999). *Early years study.* Toronto: Ontario Children's Secretariat.

Mustard, J.F. (in press). *Revised early years study.* Toronto: Council on Early Child Development.

United Nations. (1989). *Convention on the rights of the child.* Ottawa: Human Rights Program Department of Canadian Heritage.

Section One

Early Child Development Programs Today

In this section, you are introduced to the field of early child development in Canada. Chapter 1 will define early child development programs in Canada, and Chapter 2 considers how early childhood settings are organized to provide both care and education to young children. Chapter 3 will explore the issue of quality from the perspective of children, parents, early childhood educators, and society, and will discuss specific components of quality in early child development programs.

A Professional and Life Choice

GANDINI ➤ It seems that you made a choice to dedicate your life to the education and care of young children. When did you make this life choice?

MALAGUZZI ➤ I could just avoid answering, as others have done before, by saying that when you don't ask me I know, but when you ask me, I do not know the answer anymore. There are some choices that you know are coming upon you only when they are just about to explode. But there are other choices that insinuate themselves into you and become apparent with a kind of obstinate lightness, that seem to have slowly grown within you during the happenings of your life because of a mixing of molecules and thoughts. It must have happened this latter way. But also World War II, or any war, in its tragic absurdity might have been the kind of experience that pushes a person toward the job of educating, as a way to start anew and live and work for the future. This desire strikes a person, as the war finally ends and the symbols of life reappear with a violence equal to that of the time of destruction.

I do not know for sure. But I think that is where to look for a beginning. Right after the war I felt a pact, an alliance, with children, adults, veterans from prison camps, partisans of the Resistance, and the sufferers of a devastated world. Yet all that suffering was pushed away by a day in spring, when ideas and feelings turned toward the future, seemed so much stronger than those that called one to halt and focus upon the present. It seemed that difficulties did not exist, and that obstacles were no longer insurmountable.

It was a powerful experience emerging out of a thick web of emotions and from a complex matrix of knowledge and values, promising new creativity of which I was only becoming aware. Since those days I have often reassessed my position, and yet I have always remained in my niche. I have never regretted my choices or what I gave up for them (Edwards, Gandini, & Forman, 1994, p. 49).

CHAPTER ONE
Early Child Development Programs

OBJECTIVES

After studying this chapter, students will be able to

- define early child development programs,
- identify different types of settings that provide early child development programs, and
- discuss and compare the availability of early child development programs found in different regions across Canada.

Each day almost 1.5 million children, from **infants** to **school-age children,** are cared for and educated by people other than their families, outside the regular school system. As they climb onto buses, streetcars, and trains, are strapped into car seats and strollers, or wave goodbye as their parents leave home, these children will be cared for and educated by adults who are designated as "teachers" or "caregivers." Some children will go to **child care centres** or after-school programs, which might be located in school buildings, work sites, community centres, or churches. Other children will be cared for and educated in home settings, either the child's own home or the caregiver's home. Some children will spend only a few hours a week in early childhood settings, whereas others will be there for most of their waking hours.

Other programs help parents and other family members to participate fully in their young children's early learning and development. Young children and their mothers, fathers, grandparents, uncles, aunts, or older brothers and sisters may attend play groups or drop-in centres together. Child care centres offer parents opportunities to learn about their children's new interests and achievements and other community resources, as well as access information about child development. Prenatal and postnatal programs offer support and resources to expectant and new parents.

All of these children and their families participate in situations that fall into our definition of **early child development programs. Early childhood educators,** individuals with specific qualifications in early childhood education, can choose to work in a variety of settings and with children in several different developmental phases. Early childhood educators also work with parents and other family caregivers to better understand each family's values and strengths and to offer support. In this chapter we shall examine the many facets and faces of early child development programs.

Early Child Development Defined

Early child development is the most critical phase of human development and extends from conception through middle childhood. Early child development programs include:

- prenatal and postnatal programs that support healthy pregnancy, birth, and infancy;
- parenting and family support programs;
- **early childhood education and care or early learning and child care** programs; and
- comprehensive community-based initiatives.

Early child development programs include programs that care for and educate young children, and support parenting, families, and communities. The provinces and territories have allocated federal early child development funding to a variety of programs and initiatives for young children and their parents. (The Government of Quebec does not participate in the agreement, but is receiving its share of funding and expanding early child development programs in that province.)

MAKING IT HAPPEN

Early Child Development Programs

- Ayesha lives in downtown Toronto. She goes to kindergarten in the local public school every morning and goes home at lunch with a neighbour, a regulated family child care provider, who cares for five children in the afternoon. Her mother or father picks her up around 5:30 p.m.
- Carmen is four months old. She lives in a small village outside Halifax. Her mother receives maternity/parental leave benefits and is staying at home to care for Carmen for six months. Carmen and her mother meet other parents and infants in a local church basement every Friday morning. The group grew out of a prenatal support group offered by the local public health department; each Friday, the parents set up a floor play space for the infants, with equipment and play materials provided by public health.
- Simon lives in Calgary. He is three years old and goes to a nursery school three mornings a week. His father works a night shift and his mother works at the shopping mall on Friday nights and all day Saturdays. One parent is at home with Simon all of the time except for Friday night when he stays with his Grandma.
- Carla is twelve months old and goes to a child care centre at the university where her dad works. She is often there by 8:00 a.m. and goes home with her dad around 5:00 p.m.
- Elisheva is a four-year-old who is severely brain damaged. She can sit only with support, cannot speak, and needs to be fed. For a year, she has been in a municipally-operated child care centre where a specially trained Resource Teacher provides the extra help that allows her to be part of her group. Her mother and father are in the labour force.
- Ian's parents are both professionals working full-time. Almost every day, Ian goes to a community-based child care centre run by a parent board. His special group of friends includes Tyson, whose mom is struggling to move from welfare to work, Katie, whose parents are both autoworkers, and Liam, a psychiatrist's son.

- Jessica, who is two and a half, goes with her mother and younger brother to a family resource program two or three mornings a week. Sometimes her mother stays and sometimes she will leave for a couple of hours and then come back for Jessica and her brother.

Ayesha, Simon, Carla, Ian, Elisheva, Carmen, and Jessica are all in early child development settings. Although the funding, management and administration of the programs differ, their daily activities are similar. If the settings are of high quality, the children are exploring rich social and physical environments that support their healthy development.

In each of these settings, the physical environment is set up for children. Carla's infant room has a large open play area with lots of soft cushions and pillows. The wall is lined with a cruising rail for beginning walkers and there are low shelves with several bright toys for shaking, poking, pushing, and pulling. Jessica's favourite time at the family resource program is the circle time, when one of the staff or a parent reads stories from picture books, and all the children and parents join in songs and child-centred activities. Ayesha's kindergarten, Simon's nursery school, Ian's and Elisheva's child care, and Carla's infant room have a circle time too. Simon often plays in the dramatic play centre at his nursery school; there are dress-up clothes and lots of dishes and pots and pans. Simon likes to pretend he is a busy chef at a big restaurant. Ayesha's kindergarten looks a lot like Simon's nursery school. Her favourite place is the art easel with its fresh pots of paint each day.

In each of these settings, there are adults who both educate and care for each child as they build relationships that are both responsive and respectful to children's growing competence and abilities to cope. They make sure their needs for food, physical safety, sleep, and toileting are met. These adults know that children are not isolated individuals but are part of families, and support to those families is critically important. There are also other children to play with in each of these settings and adults who play a role in setting the stage and encouraging the play among the children.

Children do not come to an early childhood setting merely to do their "learning." Rather, they "live" in these settings for several hours each week. Just as they are learning at home when they discover how the flusher on the toilet works or how to use simple tools to fix things or how soothing it is to hear dad's voice sing them to sleep, each hour in an early childhood setting is filled with new information and experiences.

Source: Reprinted with permission from Beach & Bertrand (2000), *More than the sum of the parts,* Childcare Resource & Research Unit, pp. 7–8.

All of the children described in the box "Early Child Development Programs" participate in early childhood settings that are guided by early childhood educators—adults who have studied **Early Childhood Education (ECE)** or have a combination of equivalent education and experience. Even the parent-run Friday drop-in program that grew out of a public health prenatal support program has access to an early childhood educator who offers suggestions and resources. If the settings are of high quality, the children are exploring rich social and physical environments that support their healthy development. Although the funding, management, and administration of the programs differ, their daily activities are similar.

Early child development programs support children's early development, learning, care, and families' capacity to participate fully in their children's early development. Early child development programs include all forms of nonparental care and early education programs (with the exception of the formal education system that

Children have opportunities to play together at early child development programs.

starts at Grade One in Canada) for children from infancy through middle childhood, programs that support pregnancy and early infancy, parenting, families, and communities. High-quality early child development programs ensure that the programs are geared toward young children, families, and communities and involve the participation of early childhood educators. Quality programs must be responsive to each child's individual development, each family's values and child-rearing practices, and each community's cultural context.

This definition gives us a sense of the variety of settings that early child development programs encompass. The definition conveys the concept that early child development programs include various structures that meet individual needs for different families. It is obviously important to include both care and education concepts in the definition. Early child development programs expand the definition to include programs that specifically support and nurture families' active participation in their children's early development and promote communities' capacity for early child development.

In this chapter, we will explore different types of early child development programs. In later chapters, we will uncover the historical roots of early childhood programs that were derived from education, social welfare, recreation, and health concerns and that defined a need for young children to receive care and education outside their families. All good settings for young children provide educational activities to encourage children's competence, as well as care to support children's development of coping skills and their overall well-being. Good programs for children

1628
John Comenius, a Czech educator, writes *The School of Infancy*, referring to the "School of the mother's lap," in which a child from birth through age six would achieve the rudiments of all learning.

provide opportunities for learning, assistance with personal routines in safe, healthy, and nurturing environments, and, most important, positive relationships with adults and other children. Therefore, the joint functions of care and education are included in the term "early child development." Good programs also recognize that families have the most powerful influence on early learning and development. By increasing the capacity of family caregivers to nurture and stimulate children, we amplify our efforts. But we can support families only when we begin with full respect for individual childrearing values and practices and the strengths that each family has.

Prenatal, Postnatal, and Infant Programs

Federal, provincial, and local governments in Canada invest in a range of programs, services, and information campaigns to promote healthy pregnancy, birth, and infancy. Some programs are directed at reducing risks that are associated with exposure to alcohol and tobacco. Others provide information and support to promote healthy births and infancy.

Early childhood educators work with families, many of which may expand as parents have more children. Prenatal, postnatal, and early infancy programs may be delivered in conjunction with other types of early child development programs. Knowing about what prenatal, postnatal, and early infancy programs exist in communities expands your ability to support young children and families.

Early Childhood Education and Care

There are almost 5 million children from newborn to eleven years of age in Canada. Nearly 2 million children under twelve years of age are involved in some form of nonparental care (outside kindergarten and elementary school programs) while their parents are at work or school (Canadian Council on Social Development, 2006). Over 500 000 preschool children attend school kindergarten programs, and 300 000 children, with at least one parent or guardian not in the paid labour force, attend early child development programs outside the home or school environment. There are also more than 14 000 children who participate in provincial or territorial early intervention programs.

The need for nonparental care arrangements while parents are working or attending school often determines the type of **early childhood education and care (ECEC)** programs families choose. Some programs, such as child care centres, are designed to accommodate the needs of working parents and promote children's early development and learning. Other types of nonparental care arrangements often incorporate activities that support early child development. In many instances, children will participate in more than one setting. For instance, a child who is cared for in family child care may attend a local playgroup, family resource centre, or kindergarten. Because there are so many different types of programs and no organized system for early child development, it is difficult to determine exactly how many children and families are participating. However, Table 1.1 offers a broad overview of how many children participate in various early child development programs and/or nonparental care arrangements. Keep in mind that one-third of all children whose

TABLE 1.1

Early Childhood Education and Care Arrangements for Newborns to Eleven-Year-Olds in Canada

Arrangements Related to Parents' Employment	*Children Attending*
Centre-based program*	612 000
Kindergarten	470 000
Regulated family child care	134 000
Unregulated family child care**	750 000
In-home care***	400 000
Self/sibling care	345 000
Aboriginal Head Start	12 000
Provincial/territorial Early Intervention Programs	15 000

* Includes regular full-time or part-time participation in nursery schools, child care centres, preschool centres, and after-school programs.

** Includes both relative and nonrelative home-based nonparental care arrangements.

*** Some of the children in the arrangements not necessarily related to employment may also be in another arrangement related to parents' employment.

Unregulated family child care is the most common form of nonparental child care used by families in Canada.

Sources: Adapted from Johnson, Lero, & Rooney (2001); Beach, Bertrand, Michal, Forer, & Tougas (2004); Friendly & Beach (2005)

Parents who work often require full-day care for their children.

parents are working are in more than one early childhood education and care arrangement (Johnson, Lero, & Rooney, 2001).

Table 1.2 gives an overview of seven different categories of early childhood education and care programs. Some programs could be included in more than one category or overlap with other types of early child development programs. We need to understand the terms and concepts used to describe each type of program, as well as each program's potential in meeting the needs of young children and their families. As early childhood educators entering the field, you can gain a better understanding of potential career opportunities by becoming familiar with early child development programs available across Canada.

Child Care Centres

Child care centres include group or centre-based programs outside regular schooling for children from as young as three months to those up to twelve years of age. Most child care programs offer **full-day programs** five days a week (although some children may attend **part-day programs**), as well as programs before and after school and during school holidays for school-age children. The majority of child care centres in Canada offer service for preschool children two to five years of age.

TABLE 1.2

Early Childhood Education and Care

Centre-based child care	Full-day early child development programs for groups of children under school age or for school-age children during out-of-school hours. Organized to provide stimulating, nurturing programs for children that accommodate parents' work schedules.
Preschool/nursery school	Part-day, often part-week, early child development programs for children between the ages of approximately 2 1/2 and five years. Usually less than four hours per day.
Family child care	Nonparental care for small groups of children from newborn to twelve years in a caregiver's home. May incorporate early child development activities.
In-home care	Care provided by a caregiver or nanny in the child's own home. May incorporate early child development activities.
Early childhood intervention	Early child development programs and activities available to young children and families who have developmental challenges or who are at risk of developmental delays.
Recreation and leisure	Early child development programs that are organized around specific physical or creative activities for young children.
Kindergarten	Early child development program available to all five-year-old children through the education system. In some parts of Canada, kindergarten is also available to four-year-old children.

Child care centres serve the needs of parents who are working outside the home or who are pursuing further education or training and, thus, need supplemental care for their children for eight or more hours a day. Many full-day programs operate from early morning (for example, from 7:00 or 7:30 a.m.) until 6:00 p.m. or later, to allow parents time to drop off their children, put in a full work or study day, and return to the centre to pick up the children. Child care centres usually have staff scheduled to work at staggered times, to provide adequate coverage over the full period.

Some child care centres that serve particular corporations, health care institutions, or businesses offer several shifts of child care to accommodate the needs of parents who work during the evening or night. However, most programs offer regular daytime care only. Child care centres may accept children on a part-time basis, but seasonal or emergency care or services for parents who work shifts and irregular hours are scarce across the country.

Child care programs are regulated by provincial and territorial governments' child care legislation. Each province has established its own approach to organizing and licensing child care and preschool or nursery school programs, and it is difficult to make direct comparisons among the different jurisdictions. However, Table 1.3 provides an overview of what types of services are regulated, how many children attend, and what the different services are called. The regulated services are the anchor of Canada's early child development programs, although less than 15 percent of all Canadian children are enrolled in these programs.

TABLE 1.3

Regulated Child Care Programs

Province/Territory	*Regulated Programs*	*Children Attending (2003/04)*
Newfoundland and Labrador	Child care centres (full-time & part-time)	4 103
	School-age child care	578
	Regulated family child care	240
Prince Edward Island	Early childhood centres (full-time & part-time, including kindergarten, nursery school, & child care centre)	3 365
	School-age child care centres	695
	Family day care homes	40
Nova Scotia	Child care centres (full-time & part-time, including nursery schools, preschools, child development centres & school age)	12 600
	Family day care homes	159
New Brunswick	Day care centres & school-age programs (full-time & part-time)	11 474
	Community day homes	150
Quebec	Centres de la petite enfance (full-time & part-time centre & family child care)	97 711
	Milieu scolaire (school-age child care)	141 977
	Milieu familial (family child care)	82 044
Ontario	Child care centres (full-time & part-time, including nursery schools)	124 292
	School-age child care	62 613
	Supervised private home day care	19 838
Manitoba	Day care centres (full-time & part-time, including nursery schools)	13 104
	School-age child care centres	6 126
	Family day care homes	4 209
Saskatchewan	Child day care agencies (full-time)	4 666
	School-age child care centres	874
	Family child care homes	2 370
Alberta	Day care centres (full-time & part-time, including nursery schools, parent co-ops, kindergartens in regulated centres & drop-in)	41 405
	School-age child care centres	17 767
	Family day homes	6 554
British Columbia	Group day care centres (full-time & part-time including preschools)	39 769
	Out-of-school care	23 089
	Family child care	17 372

Province/Territory	*Regulated Programs*	*Children Attending (2003/04)*
Northwest Territories	Day care centres (full-time & part-time, including nursery schools)	802
	After-school care	161
	Family day homes	256
Nunavut	Day care centres	919
	School-age child care	95
Yukon	Child care centres (full-time & part-time)	743
	School-age child care	243
	Family day homes	383

Note: Regulated group programs and family child care may have different names and age categories in various parts of the country, but they share a number of commonalities in the care and education they provide.

Source: Adapted from Friendly & Beach, 2005

Specific requirements may concern staff qualifications, **adult-child ratios** (the maximum number of children allowed for every staff member), maximum number of children, physical space regulations, including the minimum amount of space necessary for each child, daily care routines, and program activities. We will examine these requirements in more detail in Chapter 3.

In Canada, regulated child care programs may be operated by nonprofit organizations, commercial or independent operators, and public organizations (such as local government).

Most child care centres in Canada are **nonprofit;** they are operated for the primary purpose of supporting child and family needs and well-being. A nonprofit centre might be a stand-alone organization with a voluntary board of directors, which can include parents, community members, and individuals with child care expertise. Or it might be operated by a larger agency or institution. The YMCA in Canada, for instance, operates over seventy-five centres. Approximately eighty community colleges directly operate child care centres, which also provide model sites for ECE students (Beach, Bertrand, & Cleveland, 1998).

Commercial child care centres, also called proprietary or for-profit centres, are privately owned businesses. About 23 percent of Canada's child care centres operate as commercial businesses, ranging from small, owner-operated programs to large chains (Childcare Research and Resource Unit, 2000). In Newfoundland and Alberta, most child care centres are proprietary, whereas other provinces or territories, such as Manitoba, have no commercial child care centres.

Nonprofit, government-operated child care centres, which are directly operated by a government, are less common in Canada. Ontario municipalities do operate close to 100 child care centres, and some Alberta municipalities operate school-age child care programs. In Quebec, the provincial department of education administers school-age child care centres, which are located in elementary schools.

Parents' fees, which may be eligible for government subsidies, pay for the majority of the costs of child care centres. In some jurisdictions, provincial or territorial governments provide grants directly to child care centres. These funds may include operating, start-up, and capital funding, funding for children with **special needs,** and funds to enhance wages. Chapter 3 examines the funding of regulated child care centres in more detail.

Nursery schools. Nursery schools offer two- to three-hour care for preschool children (two to six years old) during the school year (September to June). These programs may not function during a full week (for example, a group of three-year-olds might attend classes from nine until noon, on Monday, Wednesday, and Friday mornings). The usual purpose of these programs is to offer stimulation, activities, and group experiences to help the children develop optimally. Many of these programs have their roots in early nursery school or kindergarten education (see Chapter 7). Today, in some parts of Canada, nursery schools are called "preschools" or "preschool programs."

In most provincial/territorial jurisdictions, nursery schools are regulated through the same legislation as child care centres and must meet similar structural, funding, and organizational requirements. However, nursery schools in Saskatchewan and Quebec are not covered by child care legislation. Nursery schools and preschool programs may be nonprofit or commercial operations, or they may be publicly run.

1815
The first Maternal Association is established by a group of ministers' wives in Portland, Maine, to encourage the moral and religious training of children.

There are no statistics available on how many children attend nursery school programs or how many programs exist. Some provinces and territories include nursery schools in their report of regulated child care centre spaces, whereas others exclude them. Sometimes nursery schools are considered part-time child care centre programs and are combined with school-age child care programs.

We do know that 300 000 children whose mothers are not in the paid labour force are in centre-based early child development programs (Statistics Canada, 1992). It is quite likely that at least half of these children are attending nursery school or preschool programs. Some of the children whose parents participate in the paid labour force or in training and education programs also attend nursery school programs. Parents might use nursery school services in combination with other nonparental child care arrangements, or they might juggle their work and study responsibilities around the nursery school hours.

Family Child Care

Family child care refers to the small groups of children that a child care provider cares for in a private residence. The residence is usually the home of the provider. Family child care may be regulated through provincial/territorial legislation or may operate outside licensing requirements.

Government regulations, policies, and funding shape the organization of regulated family child care services in each province or territory. Each jurisdiction sets out the maximum number of children who may be cared for by an individual in a regulated or unregulated home setting. If there are additional children, the program must meet the province or territory's requirements for regulated child care centres. The provincial and territorial governments either license and regulate caregivers or license a family child care agency that supervises individual family child care programs.

Unregulated family child care is the most common type of remunerated child care arrangement in Canada; it is also the least visible and most variable model of child care. It can be an early childhood education and care program, in which an early childhood educator who has access to resources and support in her community provides nurturing care and stimulating education to children in a home setting. It also includes custodial child care arrangements, in which children are left in the care of an individual who "keeps an eye on the kids" while carrying out other housekeeping tasks.

The structure and organization of family child care varies among the provinces and territories (Beach, Bertrand, Forer, Michal, & Tougas, 2004; Friendly & Beach, 2005).

Newfoundland: In 1999, the *Child Care Services Act* regulated family home child care. The province extends financial support to family resource programs that support family home child care. Up to four children (including the caregiver's own children under seven years) are permitted.

Prince Edward Island: Regulated family child care homes are licensed and monitored by the provincial government. Caregivers are allowed up to seven children (including the caregiver's own, under ten years of age), with a maximum of three children under two years of age in regulated homes. In unregulated family child care settings, a total of five children, including the caregiver's own preschool children, are allowed, with a maximum of two children under two years or a maximum of three children if all three children are under two years of age.

Nova Scotia: Regulated family child care homes are supervised by licensed agencies. Six children, including the caregiver's own preschool children, are permitted in either regulated or unregulated family child care. If all the children, including the caregiver's own, are school-age, eight children are allowed.

New Brunswick: Regulated family child care homes are licensed and regulated by the provincial government. Regulated caregivers are permitted to care for one of the following groups of children: a maximum of three infants, five children between two and five years of age, nine school-age children, or a mixed-age group of six children, including the caregiver's own children under twelve years. An unregulated family child care home is allowed a maximum of four children, including the caregiver's own children under twelve years, and a maximum of two children under two years.

Quebec: Regulated family child care settings are supervised by early childhood agencies (centres de la petite enfance) that also offer centre-based programs and are licensed by the provincial government. Caregivers in regulated and unregulated family child care are permitted to care for up to six children, including the caregiver's own children under twelve years. If the caregiver is assisted by another adult, he or she may care for a maximum of nine children.

Ontario: The province licenses private home day care agencies, which supervise family child care homes. Care for a maximum of five children up to twelve years of age is permitted in a home that is supervised by a licensed agency. No more than two of the children may be under two years, and no more than three of the children may be under three years, including the caregiver's own children under six years. An unregulated caregiver is allowed to care for up to five children, not including her own.

Manitoba: Regulated family child care homes are directly licensed by the province. One licensed caregiver may care for up to eight children under twelve

1816 Robert Owen establishes an infant school providing care for children of mill workers in Lancaster, England.

years, including her own children under twelve years. No more than five children may be under six years, and no more than three children may be under two years. Unregulated caregivers are permitted to care for up to four children, including the caregiver's own children, and no more than two children may be under two years.

Saskatchewan: Regulated programs are licensed and monitored by the provincial government. A regulated caregiver is permitted to care for up to eight children between six weeks and twelve years, including her own children under thirteen years. Only five of the children may be younger than six years, and only two may be younger than thirty months. Unregulated caregivers are allowed to care for up to eight children, including the caregiver's own children, under thirteen years.

Alberta: The provincial government does not license family child care homes or agencies but does enter into contracts with agencies to approve and monitor caregivers according to provincial standards. Regulated caregivers are permitted to care for up to six children under eleven years, including the caregiver's own children under eleven years. A maximum of three children may be under three years, and no more than two children may be under two years. In unregulated homes, a caregiver is allowed to care for up to six children, including her own children under twelve years. A maximum of three children may be under three years.

British Columbia: Family child care homes are individually licensed by the provincial government and are permitted to care for up to seven children under two years, including the children living in the home. Of the seven children, there may be no more than five **preschoolers** and two school-age children, no more than three children under three years of age, and no more than one child under twelve months. Unregulated caregivers are permitted to care for two children, not including the caregiver's own children.

Northwest Territories: Regulated family child care homes are individually licensed by the territorial government. A maximum of eight children under twelve years, including the caregiver's own children, is permitted. No more than six of the eight children may be five years or under, no more than three children may be under three years, and no more than two children may be under two years. An unregulated caregiver may care for up to four children, including her own children under twelve years.

Nunavut: Regulated homes are individually licensed by the territorial government. Caregivers may care for a maximum of eight children under age 12, including the caregiver's own children. No more than six children may be age five or younger and no more than two children may be under two years.

Yukon Territory: Regulated homes are individually licensed by the territorial government. Regulated caregivers may care for up to eight children, including the caregiver's own children under six years. No more than three infants are permitted if there are also three preschool or school-age children. If there are two caregivers, an additional four school-age children are permitted. Unregulated caregivers may care for up to three children, not including the caregiver's own children.

Six provinces (Newfoundland, Quebec, Manitoba, Saskatchewan, Alberta, and British Columbia) and the Yukon require family caregivers to have some training.

Family child care is delivered in different ways in Canada. There are distinctions between regulated and unregulated family child care, and between supervised and unsupervised, and supported and non-supported settings. Family child care delivery models include

- licensed family day care agencies;
- licensed family day care providers;
- registration of family day care providers;
- resource-supported, regulated family day care providers;
- resource-supported, unregulated family day care providers; and,
- unsupported, unregulated family day care providers (Canadian Child Care Federation, 1991).

Regulated or unregulated, family child care programs can often be adapted to meet the needs of working parents and diverse families in isolated rural and urban settings. Also, these programs can accommodate an individual child or a small mixed-age grouping from infancy to early adolescence.

In-Home Child Care

In-home child care arrangements include nannies and caregivers who provide care and education in the child's own home. They may live in the child's home, or they may live elsewhere and come for designated work periods. Live-in caregivers are typically called "nannies" in Canada (Kaiser & Rasminsky, 1991). Many families specifically seek out early childhood educators to provide in-home child care, hoping to ensure nurturing and safe care and stimulating experiences for their children.

In-home child care can provide greater flexibility for parents who commute long distances or work long hours. Children remain in their own home and have the constant care of one individual in their parents' absence. In many instances, children will also participate in other early child development programs, including nursery schools, family resource programs, and kindergarten.

Parents often find someone to provide in-home child care in their local communities through family resource programs, community information services, or postsecondary services. Alternatively, parents might purchase the services of an agency that selects candidates to provide in-home child care. In Canada there are no governmental regulations or requirements for such agencies, although in British Columbia, Ontario, and Quebec, the agencies must obtain a licence to operate.

Many live-in nannies are from other countries and are able to move to Canada through the Live-in Caregiver Program. This is a federal immigration program that allows future employers to sponsor immigrants who wish to enter Canada to provide in-home child care. The nanny must live in the family's home for a two-year period; at the end of the period, she may apply for landed immigrant status. These arrangements are usually conducted through an agency.

Early Childhood Intervention

Specific public policies, programs, and activities have been designed to meet the needs of young children and their families with specialized needs in order to promote healthy development during early childhood (Shonkoff & Meisels, 2000). These initiatives are included under the broad term "early intervention." Early childhood intervention draws on the knowledge and expertise of early childhood education, child

2000
1950
1900
1850
1819
Johann Pesalozzi, a Swiss educator, becomes the first recognized early childhood teacher in Yverdon, Switzerland.
1800
1750
1700
1650

and family development, education, health, and **social services.** Early childhood intervention services include a wide range of programs and approaches offered to families with children who have developmental challenges or who are at risk of developmental delays owing to disability or negative environmental conditions.

> An early childhood intervention service refers to "any non-medical, non-protection service, primarily developmental, that is used to assist a young child and his family. Thus attendance in an appropriate nursery school or daycare program can be seen as an early intervention" (Irwin, 1995, p. vii).

In Canada, early childhood intervention services include the following:

- **Inclusive early childhood programs** are "programs that include children with disabilities in the same programs they would attend if they did not have disabilities" (Irwin, 1995, p. vii). Inclusive programs encourage and facilitate the full participation of children with disabilities or special needs, not only their physical presence (Irwin, 1995). We will discuss the curriculum elements and challenges of inclusive early childhood education and programs in Chapter 2.
- **Compensatory programs** are designed for children up to six years who have developmental delays or who are at risk, or likely to be at risk, of developmental delays because of environmental conditions.
- **Early Intervention (EI)** programs support families whose children up to three or six years have special needs or are at risk of developmental delays owing to disability or psychological or social factors (Irwin, 1995).

1822 Robert Owen moves to New Harmony, Indiana, and establishes an infant school and day care centre as part of the community.

Early Intervention programs may be discrete services or integrated into another health, social service, or education program. These other early childhood education and care programs include centre-based programs, family child care services, nursery schools, and family support programs.

As you can see, the delivery of early intervention programs varies. But the provision of early intervention programs does follow two basic principles. They are interdisciplinary, meaning that they include services and strategies from more than one field. They are also family-centred, which means that the family is the primary focus of the services, rather than an individual child out of the context of her or his family (Meisels & Shonkoff, 1990).

Compensatory programs. These programs are designed to support families whose children's development is delayed or at risk because of environmental conditions, particularly conditions related to economic disadvantage and poverty. **At risk** means there are concerns about developmental delays, learning abilities, or challenging behaviours. Compensatory programs provide specific interventions to families to reduce the child's vulnerabilities and to increase the likelihood of success in formal schooling. While this intervention may include a high-quality early childhood education and care program that stimulates and supports preschool children's development, it also offers specific supports and services to other family members.

Canada has a number of early childhood intervention services that are compensatory programs. In some instances, they provide an early child development program for preschool children that also involves their parents and a number of other health and social services. These programs may be identified as **Head Start** programs. (Head Start programs originated in the United States during the 1960s; we will learn more about them in Chapter 7.) The following compensatory programs focus on improving parents' and other family members' abilities to nurture and stimulate their children:

- *Community Action Program for Children (CAP-C).* This federal initiative involves community coalitions, which deliver health and community services, including early education, to children up to six years of age who are living in conditions of risk. Project initiatives include home visits, Head Start programs, parent training, nutrition education, counselling, collective kitchens, and traditional Aboriginal healing programs. There are approximately 500 CAP-C initiatives in over 300 communities across Canada. Over 100 000 children, parents, and other caregivers visited CAP-C projects in 2001 (Johnson et al., 2001) and as many as 28 000 of them visit each week (Guy, 1997).
- *The Aboriginal Head Start program.* This program is another federal government early intervention initiative that was developed to "provide comprehensive experiences for Indian, Metis and Inuit children and their families . . . based on caring, creativity and pride flowing from the knowledge of their traditional beliefs within a holistic and safe environment" (Childcare Resource & Research Unit, 2000). Aboriginal Head Start began in 1994 with a focus on Aboriginal families living off-reserve in cities and large northern communities (Beach, Bertrand, & Cleveland, 1998). In 1998, Aboriginal Head Start was extended to First Nations communities (Childcare Resource & Research Unit, 2000). First Nations Head Start is an early childhood intervention program intended to prepare children for their school years and to establish early child development programs that are created and controlled by First Nations (on-reserve) communities. In 2001, there were 168 First Nations Head Start programs serving 305 communities and 114 Aboriginal Head Start programs off-reserve (Johnson, Lero, & Rooney, 2001).

Early Intervention programs are directed to children with developmental challenges.

Early Intervention (EI) programs. These programs deliver services to children (from birth to age three or six, depending on the province or territory) who have developmental challenges or who are at risk because of a disability or psychological/social factors. EI programs usually include a home-based component, early identification assessment, program planning (family service plans and individual program plans), and specialized equipment. The programs may also offer family support and early childhood services such as family resource programs, parent/caregiver support groups, nursery schools, and toy-lending libraries.

EI programs, like regulated child care programs, lie within provincial/territorial jurisdiction. Each province and territory organizes the structure of the EI services and determines how they are funded. Some provinces refer to these services as Infant Development Programs or Direct Home Services (Irwin, 1995). There are over 170 specific EI programs across Canada, although, in some instances, a single EI program is province-wide with several separate delivery sites (Beach, Bertrand & Cleveland, 1998).

MAKING IT HAPPEN

Moncton Headstart Inc.

In 1974, Moncton Headstart began in a small apartment on Fleet Street in Moncton. The program offered free day care for a few children with parents who could not afford outside care and who were unskilled in their parenting role. Its initial goal was to help prepare children of low-income families for success in Grade One of the public school system. In 1992, Moncton Headstart Inc. adopted the following mission statement:

> to provide socially, emotionally, and educationally disadvantaged parents and preschool children with a professional, non-threatening and accessible learning environment that will enable the family to become whole, self-sufficient, and contributing members of the community.

The Children's Program

The children's program seeks to foster age-appropriate self-help, motor, cognitive, and communication skills; to expose the child to the outside world; to stimulate thinking and problem-solving skills; to develop the child's sense of security, personal control, and personal worth, and to foster feelings of being loved, of belonging, and of being capable.

Activity centres engage children in both cognitive and motor activities. A loft provides a quiet area, a family centre encourages sociodramatic play, a circle area is used for group activities, and a playground provides for healthy outdoor play. Good nutrition and positive experiences in the larger community, through planned outings and activities, are emphasized.

Family Activities

Family outings and special events give parents an opportunity to enjoy recreation and learning experiences with their children. A growing sense of community with other families is a potential benefit.

Periodic family meetings are held at the centre, with van transportation provided. During these meetings, children spend time in the classroom with the assistant teacher while the parents meet with the head teacher and group leader to set and make plans to meet goals.

Participation of the parents in both the child development program and in their own development program is mandatory. It involves a weekend retreat, two "Days In" per month (participating in the children's program), parent sessions, and workshops.

Moncton Headstart Adjunct Programs

Moncton Headstart is founded on the belief that basic physical needs (food, shelter, and safety) must be met before one can deal with concepts of self-development. This program offers the following services:

- Adult Literacy Initiative;
- Mapleton Teaching Kitchen. This special education program for families looks at basic nutrition, economic food provision, and home management skills;
- Lorne Preston Educational Fund. The fund awards scholarships to assist Headstart parents and former Headstart children to attend college or university;
- Future Horizons. This service offers subsidized housing to integrate economically disadvantaged Headstart families in stable neighbourhoods; and

- Moncton Headstart Recycles Inc.This small-business initiative offers education and support to people who depend primarily on government social programs.Through working in the recycling business, participants acquire employment and other skills. Used clothing is channelled in two directions: wearable clothing is exported to developing countries' markets for sale, and discards are converted to cotton rags.

Too often, children and families who are caught up in the cycle of generational poverty experience exclusion and segregation within their community.The programs of Moncton Headstart are designed to teach skills that promote inclusion and participation. Caring for others is the main message.

Source: Adapted from Bradshaw (1997).

Recreation and Leisure Programs

You are probably familiar with recreation and leisure programs in your community—from swimming classes at the community centres, to preschool storytime at the local library, to T-Ball baseball leagues at the local park. Most Canadian neighbourhoods offer physical and creative activities to young children and their families. Public libraries, children's museums, and out-of-school recreation programs are three examples of recreation and leisure programs.

Public libraries encourage children to enjoy books and learning to read from an early age. Collections include a designated children's section that features children's picture books, easy-to-read books, first novels, video and audio tapes, and computer activities. Many offer regular parent/caregiver and child storytimes.

Children's museums are interactive displays designed to engage children in displays about a particular topic or concept. They may be part of larger museums or may be established as separate museums for children.

Out-of-school recreation programs offer a variety of regular physical activities to school-age children. They may be organized to accommodate parents' work and provide regular nonparental care arrangements.

Recreation and leisure programs include many activities that support early development. What kinds of programs are available in your community and how do they complement other early child development programs?

Adult and child music programs and storytimes help parents and other caregivers participate in their children's early learning.

Kindergartens

In all provinces and territories most **kindergarten** programs are offered through the public school system and are operated under provincial/territorial education legislation. In Prince Edward Island, publicly funded kindergarten programs are provided by community early childhood education and care programs. Some kindergarten programs operate outside the public school system on a fee-for-service basis, either as private schools or as part of licensed child care programs.

2000 1950 1900 1850 1800 1750 1700 1650

Provincial/territorial education legislation sets out requirements for children's minimum age, the number of instructional days and hours, and teacher qualifications. There may also be specific adult-child ratio and maximum group size requirements.

Most kindergarten is offered on a part-time basis, either half days (morning or afternoon) or two to three full days (school days) per week, although there are some full-time, full-day kindergarten programs that operate within public schools. Half-day programs are usually two to three hours in length, and full-day kindergarten programs are four to five hours in length (excluding lunch programs). In New Brunswick, Quebec, and Nova Scotia, kindergarten for five-year-olds comprises full days. In all jurisdictions except New Brunswick, attendance is voluntary. Families are not required to pay fees for their children's participation in publicly funded kindergarten.

Age limits for attending kindergarten programs vary slightly across provincial/territorial jurisdictions but most require children to be at least four years and eight months old in September (five years by December 31) to attend kindergarten or senior kindergarten programs, and at least three years and eight months old in September (four years by December 31) to attend junior kindergarten programs.

1826 Friedrich Froebel writes *Education of Man*, describing the Kindergarten system.

Ontario has **junior kindergarten** programs for four-year-old children and **senior kindergarten** programs for five-year-old children. Kindergarten programs in other jurisdictions are generally available only to five-year-old children, although there are growing numbers of **prekindergarten** programs for four-year-old children in Quebec, Winnipeg, Saskatchewan, Nova Scotia, and British Columbia. There are approximately 383 000 children attending public education kindergarten or senior kindergarten programs and 121 000 children attending junior kindergarten or prekindergarten programs in Canada.

Kindergarten programs often intersect with child care services. Many four- and five-year-old children who attend public kindergarten programs also attend licensed child care programs or informal family child care, or they are cared for by an in-home caregiver. Licensed child care programs are often located in public school buildings. Kindergarten programs are intended to provide educational and social experiences for young children in preparation for formal schooling. At the same time, many Canadian families use kindergarten programs as part of a child care package. Kindergarten programs and other early childhood services for young children often share many of the values and assumptions that underlie curriculum approaches. There are a number of initiatives between child care and kindergarten programs that have attempted to coordinate these programs, including school board policies and practices to encourage increased collaboration, shared physical space, and common curriculum planning and professional development opportunities.

Kindergarten programs also intersect with early intervention services and family support programs, particularly as provincial and territorial governments explore options for integrated children's services.

Full day or half-day kindergarten? What does the research say? Most provinces and territories offer only half-day kindergarten programs for five-year-olds (Friendly & Beach, 2005). Nova Scotia, New Brunswick, and Quebec offer full-day programs. Some school districts in other provinces also offer full-day programs targeted to specific populations. Ontario's Francophone school boards often offer full-day kindergarten to five-year-olds and four-year-olds. The introduction of full-day kindergarten is discussed from time to time in the provinces of Alberta and Ontario.

The rapid growth in expansion of full-day kindergarten programs in the United States has encouraged many U.S. studies. In 1969, in the U.S., kindergartners usually attended short half-day programs. Only 11 percent were in full-day programs (more than four hours, but usually closer to six). By 2000, the percentage enrolled in full-day programs had grown to 60 percent (U.S. Census Bureau, 2001).

American research confirms that attendance in full-day kindergarten results in academic and social benefits for students, at least in the primary grades. Cryan et al. (1992) found that children who participated in full-day kindergarten had better school performance in later grades. After comparing similar half-day and full-day programs in a statewide longitudinal study, Cryan et al. found that full-day kindergartners were more independent learners, more likely to be involved in classroom activities, were productive with peers, and more reflective than half-day kindergartners. They were also more likely to approach the teacher and they expressed less withdrawal, anger, shyness, and blaming behaviour than half-day kindergartners. In general, children in full-day programs exhibited more positive behaviours than pupils in half-day or alternate-day programs. Similar results have been found in other U.S. studies (Humphrey, 1983; Holmes and McConnell, 1990; Karweit, 1992; Elicker & Mathur, 1997; Weiss & Offenberg, 2002; Welsh, 2002).

Full-day programs seem to provide a relaxed, unhurried school day with more time for a variety of experiences, for assessment opportunities, and for quality interaction between adults and children (Herman, 1984). Parents pointed out a number of advantages: no more shuttling children from school to an afternoon babysitter or worrying about whether their child had been safely picked up. Full-day kindergarten allows children and teachers time to explore topics in-depth, reduces the ratio of transition time to class time, provides for greater continuity of day-to-day activities, and provides an environment that favours a child-centered, developmentally appropriate approach.

Full-day kindergarten in the U.S. has also been spurred by the introduction of the National Educational Goals focusing on math and literacy competencies in the early grades. This has also led experts to warn teachers, administrators, and parents to resist the temptation to provide full-day programs that are didactic rather than intellectually engaging in tone. Seat work, worksheets, and early instruction in reading or other academic subjects are largely inappropriate in kindergarten. By contrast, developmentally appropriate, child-centered all-day kindergarten programs need to:

- integrate new learning with past experiences through project work and through mixed ability and mixed age groupings in an unhurried setting (Drew & Law, 1990; Katz, 1995);
- involve children in first-hand experience and informal interaction with objects, other children, and adults (Housden & Kam, 1992);
- emphasize language development and appropriate preliteracy experiences;
- work with parents to share information about their children, build understanding of parent and teacher roles, emphasize reading to children in school and at home, and set the stage for later parent-teacher partnerships;

- offer a balance of small group, large group, and individual activities (Katz, 1995);
- assess students' progress through close teacher observation and systematic collection and examination of students' work; and
- develop children's social skills, including conflict resolution strategies.

The Caledon study of kindergarten and child care in four provinces found that three-quarters of parents supported the idea of a full-day integrated program (Johnson & Mathien, 1998). A report for the Calgary Board of Education, summarizing previous research on full-day kindergarten programs, concluded that:

> All studies indicated a positive relation between participation in full-day kindergarten and subsequent school performance. Higher achievement in academic development as well as greater growth in social and behavioural development is consistently reported . . . All studies reviewed here suggest that a full-day developmentally appropriate kindergarten program is especially beneficial to children from low socioeconomic levels and/or educationally disadvantaged backgrounds. (Blades, 2002)

Results from fifteen full-day kindergarten programs in Edmonton showed that children who began kindergarten with lower levels of reading and writing skills were able to catch up to the other children who attended only half-day kindergarten (da Costa & Bell, 2003). The Northern Lights School Division, at the beginning of the full-day kindergarten program, found 24 percent of students were identified as having special needs. By Grade One, teachers only identified nine percent of the students as needing special assistance to meet the Grade One goals (Colley, 2005).

Family Support Programs

The category of family support programs is a broad one that includes a variety of services, strategies, and activities. Family support programs complement and sometimes enrich a family's existing strengths and resources. These programs may address existing problems or aim to prevent potential problems and also be considered as early childhood intervention. Three specific types of family support programs are found in most parts of Canada today: family resource programs, home-visiting, and family literacy. They may be offered as separate programs or in combination with each other or with other early child development programs.

Family resource programs are family-focused; that is, they offer activities that are directed to young children and to parents or other caregivers. There are approximately 2 000 such programs across Canada, with representation in each province and territory (Beach et al., 1998). They offer a range of services in diverse physical settings and with different types of funding and sponsorship. Nevertheless, family resource programs can be identified by common principles, functions, and types of activities.

Family resource programs share the following set of principles:

- an ecological approach to services for children, families, and communities;
- an emphasis on prevention and wellness of families;
- a recognition of the need for social networks to support families;
- an emphasis on interdependence in families' needs and abilities to give and receive support;

MAKING IT HAPPEN

Family Literacy in British Columbia

The family literacy movement in B.C is growing; Literacy BC identified more than 80 family literacy programs/services in that province in 2000. There has been a significant increase in the number of schools, libraries, family resource programs, social service agencies, health boards, and government organizations that have contacted Literacy BC for information, consultation, and support regarding family literacy program development, educator training, and resources.

These groups are rapidly becoming more aware of the value and benefits of family literacy programs and services, and are looking for leadership, partnership, and direction.

Literacy BC's annual **Family Literacy Day/Week Campaign** raises awareness and builds partnerships and capacity for family literacy. In fact, staff report that they can barely keep up with the requests for information, resources, funding, and offers of partnerships for the next year's events!

Other family literacy activities supported by Literacy BC include

- support to new and existing family literacy initiatives through consultation, referral, and provision of resources;
- ongoing development of a provincial family literacy resource collection and provision of on-loan access;
- maintenance of the family literacy directory of programs and services in B.C., including the B.C. component of the national family literacy online directory;
- facilitation of the family literacy electronic conference in order to provide online support and training to family literacy educators and groups in B.C.;
- encouragement of good practice in the family literacy field through the distribution and promotion of the B.C. Framework of Principles and Standards of Good Practice in Family Literacy; and
- designing and delivering a one-day training workshop for family literacy educators.

Source: J. Rasmussen (2000). Personal communication.

- a view of parenthood as an important stage of adulthood;
- an acceptance of cultural diversity in approaches to childrearing; and
- a recognition that play is essential to optimum child development (Kellerman, 1995).

Based on these principles, family resource programs provide services that have voluntary attendance and involve the entire family, including nonfamily caregivers (Kyle & Kellerman, 1998). Parents and program staff work together to determine which services will be offered. Family resource programs encourage peer support groups among mothers, fathers, other family members, and caregivers. Family resource programs are multidisciplinary; programs cut across health, social services, education, recreation, and child care service categories. Program staff bring experience and credentials from different disciplines, and programs establish working links with other community services. Family resource programs may direct specific services toward problems, but the overall approach is to provide support with the realization that all families experience difficulties from time to time and that their strengths can be used to work through the difficulties.

1830s
Infant schools are introduced in Halifax by factory owners.

1836
Massachusetts passes the first child labour law (seldom enforced) in the United States, prohibiting children under fifteen from working in factory mills unless they had three months of schooling in the previous year.

Most family resource programs focus on children up to six years of age, their families, and their caregivers. The programs may serve a number of functions, including

- parent support and education;
- support to in-home and family child care providers;
- promotion of optimal child development;
- material support (such as food or clothing) to families;
- support to high-need families (such as parents of children with special needs, recent immigrant or refugee families, or parents with substance abuse problems);
- resources for early childhood educators and social service professionals;
- support and resources for informal social networks; and
- community development, planning, and advocacy (Kellerman, 1995).

As you can see, this is an overwhelming list of functions that could be carried out in many types of specific services. In practice, most family resource programs focus on a few primary functions and then develop activities that will best carry out the function in the community (Kellerman, 1995). For instance, parent support may take the form of a parenting course, or parents may observe and interact with other parents and program staff as part of a drop-in program. Some activities serve several functions. Toy-lending libraries promote optimal child development, provide material support, draw parents together to encourage informal social networks, and provide adaptive play materials and activities for children with disabilities and their families.

Family and in-home child care providers are the main users of over half of the family resource programs in Canada. Support to this group of users may include in-service training such as workshops, drop-in programs, child care information and referral services, and toy-lending libraries.

A 1994 survey of family resource programs in Canada found that the most common family resource program activities are

- playgroups and drop-in programs;
- parent support groups;
- parenting, caregiver, and early educator courses and workshops;
- toy-lending libraries;
- special events for children and families;
- child care information and referral services;
- respite care for parents and caregivers and child care while parents/caregivers participate in other family resource program activities;
- "warm-lines" (noncrisis telephone support or electronic discussion group);
- crisis intervention and counselling (including informal and peer counselling);
- early childhood intervention services for families and their children with developmental challenges or at risk of developmental delays;
- services and support programs to meet specific needs, such as prenatal and postnatal support for teen mothers and fathers, support groups for survivors of violence, ESL classes, life-skills courses, and literacy programs; and
- community development initiatives, including planning and advocacy for children's and family services (Kellerman, 1995).

Family resource programs offer program activities that best serve their own mandate, primary functions, and community. Think about how a family resource program could best support families with young children in your community. What would be the program's primary function? What types of activities should be included? Can you identify the role of early childhood educator as part of the program staff?

Not only do the program activities vary from one family resource program to another but also are found in a variety of settings and under different sponsorship and funding across Canada. A 1994 survey noted that almost two-thirds of the programs are not-for-profit organizations, governed by boards of directors (Kellerman, 1995). Almost a quarter of the programs are part of other community, recreation, health, or social service organizations such as community centres, YMCAs or YWCAs, public libraries, and community health centres. About 8 percent are offered in conjunction with other types of ECEC programs, including child care centres and/or regulated family child care, and another 7 percent are operated by social service agencies, such as child welfare or children's aid associations.

There are also variations in the way family resource programs are defined and organized in each province or territory (Kellerman, 1995). Programs that focus on support to caregivers in unregulated child care are more likely to be recognized as family resource programs in Ontario than they are in British Columbia. In Alberta, programs offering support to parents of school-age children are considered family resource programs. Nevertheless, the broad definition of family resource programs we have used in this book is typical of the direction of the family resource program network across Canada.

In Ontario, some family resource programs receive funding from the provincial government to provide support for unregulated family child care providers. Provincial funding is made available to over half of the family resource programs. In Newfoundland, family resource programs are funded to support both regulated and unregulated family child care.

In British Columbia, a separate system of family resource programs, called child care support programs, is funded by the provincial government to support caregivers by offering services such as child care registries and family child care training courses. The government of British Columbia also funds another group of family resource programs, known as Family Places, which focus on services to families with young children. A Family Place typically offers drop-in and playgroups services, which are not offered by the child care support programs. Although the programs are intended for parents, other caregivers often participate (Kellerman, 1995).

The federal Community Action Program for Children (CAP-C), discussed earlier in this chapter, provides funding support to high-risk families with young children. Many family resource programs across Canada are part of CAP-C projects.

Family literacy initiatives "recognize the influence of the family on the literacy development of family members and try to support families in literacy activity and in accessing literacy resources" (Thomas, 1998, p. 6). Specific family literacy programs and activities include storytelling and music circles for young children and parents or caregivers, adult education using family experiences, book bags for infants and young children and their parents, and the creation and use of play materials that encourage the acquisition of skills necessary to support literacy.

Home-visiting is a family support program that bring expertise and resources to the homes of families with young children. Many home-visiting programs are

2000
1950
1900
1850
1800
1750
1700
1650

1837
First public normal school is established at Lexington, Massachusetts.

Friedrich Froebel establishes the first kindergarten (children's garden) for children ages three to six years in Blankenburg, Germany.

1846
Common School Act is passed in Canada West (later Ontario) and brings about curriculum standardization.

offered as early childhood intervention strategies and are part of early intervention programs for children with developmental difficulties or compensatory programs. Home-visiting has a long tradition in early childhood programming, including single visits by public health nurses to smooth the transition to parenting and single visits by kindergarten teachers to smooth transition to school. Over the last decade and a half, home-visiting has been included in a number of more intensive and focused prevention programs and has also been used as an adjunct to other forms of programming including Early Head Start (Love et al., 2002) and Parent Child Centres (Johnson & Walker, 1991).

A small-scale, rigorous home-visiting research study in Elmira, New York (Olds, Henderson, Chamberlin, & Tatelbaum, 1986) sparked an early rush of enthusiasm for home-visiting approaches based on good evidence of success. The Elmira project focused on Nurse Family Practitioners supporting the mother-child relationship and prevention of abuse in high-needs families with very intensive visiting over the early years.

Other home visiting programs span a variety of aims. For example, the HIPPY program aims at literacy and other child development goals and early successes were reported for this program (Hebrew University of Jerusalem, 1993).

Home-visiting combined with centre-based programs appears to work better than home-visiting alone, and better than centre-based programs alone. For example, in the evaluation of Early Head Start (Love et al., 2002), "Mixed programs" combining home visits and centre-based programs had broader impacts on children than either approach alone. Researchers suggest that the combination offered more flexible options for engaging a variety of families, a reminder that "one-size" rarely "fits all."

In Canada, several provinces have initiated home-visiting programs. Most are delivered through public health departments and build on universal visits or telephone calls to all families with newborns. In Ontario, Healthy Babies, Healthy Children is delivered by the province's 37 public health units. The program offers all families with new babies information on parent and child development and delivers extra help and support to families who are experiencing difficulties. Healthy Babies, Healthy Children screens families for any risks to healthy child development during the mother's pregnancy, at birth, and anytime up to age six. All new parents who consent receive a phone call after the birth of a baby and are offered a home-visit from the local public health nurse. Home-visits from peer or family home visitors (experienced mothers who live in the community) as well as from public health nurses are offered to young children who are at risk of developmental problems.

Comprehensive Community-Based Programs

Many communities are trying to draw together and integrate different early child development programs to support young children and their families. Both public awareness and the overall number of early child development programs are growing.

Across Canada, many communities are taking advantage of the climate of opportunity and experimenting with community-based early child development models. Some of these initiatives grow out of CAP-C collaborations (mentioned earlier in the section on compensatory programs).

While each community-wide early child development program is unique and efforts reflect local context and provincial/territorial policies, two main strategies stand out:

- community-wide mobilization to improve environments for all young children; and
- weaving together of different types of early child development programs to create a seamless early child development program to meet the needs of young children and their families.

MAKING IT HAPPEN

Better Beginnings Better Futures

Better Beginnings, Better Futures, located in Ontario, is a unique community-based early child development project. The project focus is on children up to eight years of age living in eight low-income communities in Ontario. The communities themselves have defined what services they need to promote their children's development and to alleviate the impact of economic disadvantage. Each Better Beginnings, Better Futures community is unique, but most offer early childhood intervention services, such as home visits, family support programs, and school and child care centre enrichment, which are coordinated with other early child development services in each community. Better Beginnings has an exciting research component, whereby the impact on children, families, and communities is monitored and a group of children and families will be followed for twenty years to measure the long-term effects of the program. Short-term outcomes reported that "where programs for children 0–4 were sustained from infancy (home visiting) through the preschool period, with parent-child playgroups and quality child care, children started school with less anxiety, fewer behavioural problems, and more ready to learn" (Peters, 2001, p.3).

Understanding the Early Years—Building Community Capacity for Early Child Development

Understanding the Early Years (UEY) is a national research initiative. It is based on the belief that communities will use community-specific research to make the case to allocate resources to provide opportunities for young children. Developed by the Applied Research Branch (ARB) of Human Resources Development Canada (HRDC), *Understanding the Early Years* project emerged in response to a growing recognition that (1) increasing our understanding of the factors that help or hinder child development, and (2) increasing community tracking of how well children are developing are crucial to ensuring the best possible start for Canada's children.

One of the main purposes of UEY is to help determine the extent and nature of community influences on child development and how this might vary from child to child. Data is collected in the community about what resources are available, children's readiness to learn at school entry (using the Early Development Instrument) and child, family, and community context using the National Longitudinal Survey of Children and Youth. The three independent but complementary data collection components allow for more detailed monitoring and reporting at the community level. Together, this information helps fill gaps in our understanding of the community factors that affect early child development and the ways a community can best support the growing needs of young children and their parents.

Putting together the information collected from these three components provides a framework for analysis that will not only tell us more about *what* is working well, or less well, but also will give some indication as to

(cont'd)

Better Beginnings Better Futures (cont'd)

why services and neighbourhood resources work the way they do. This analysis will also provide the basis for community-wide discussions on how to develop community strategies and allocate resources with the goal of optimizing child development outcomes.

The thirteen communities in Canada involved in this initiative are Abbotsford, British Columbia; Saskatoon, Saskatchewan; South Eastman, Manitoba; Niagara Falls, Ontario; Montreal, Quebec; Hampton, New Brunswick; Mississauga, Ontario; Coquitlam, British Columbia; Prince Albert, Saskatchewan; Winnipeg, Manitoba; Prince Edward Island (province-wide); southwestern Newfoundland; and north Toronto, Ontario. In each of the communities, there is a coalition of individuals and organizations who want to make changes that will improve outcomes for children. They are hoping to use the information as a tool to help them both reallocate and increase investment in their communities that will benefit young children.

Sources: Janus & Offord (2000), Human Resources Development Canada (2001).

Coordination, Collaboration, and Integration

The Canadian OECD review, completed in 2004, focused attention on the problems created by the two solitudes: education and child care. The OECD review team stressed the need to heal the rift between kindergarten programs and child care and emphasized the need to "Build bridges between child care and kindergarten education, with the aim of integrating ECEC [early childhood education and care] both at ground level and at policy and management levels" (OECD, 2004 p.7).

Across Canada, new policy and program initiatives recommend alignment and coordination of programs and other initiatives and promote consolidation of existing programs. For example:

- The Child and Youth Officer for British Columbia (2005) has recommended a neighbourhood hub approach that will encourage local child care, family support, family health, and early intervention programs to coordinate efforts, possibly co-locating in primary school space. The report stipulates that regulated child care should be a central component of the hubs and that a funding envelope with appropriate accountability mechanisms should be given to community tables for planning and program delivery.
- A community-research project conducted from 2003 to 2004 found promising practices in three groups of First Nations in Canada that are working to coordinate early child development programs. The findings suggest a model of early learning and child care that views the programs as a hook for mobilizing community involvement in strategies to support young children and families and as a hub for organizing coordinated, intersectoral service delivery (Ball, 2005).
- In 2004, La Commission nationale des parents francophones conducted a pan-Canadian tour to determine the early child development-related needs of its members and their communities. The tour identified strong support for an integrated services model, summarized as universal access to high quality, affordable services within a community structure managed by parents

(Lafreniere-Davis, 2005). Similar conclusions had been reached in multiple stakeholder consultations among francophones in Ontario (Deloitte & Touche, 2000).

- Toronto First Duty has expanded the concept to include the transformation of kindergarten, child care and family support programs, and funding into a new delivery model. Toronto First Duty is an early learning and care initiative for *every child* that supports the healthy development from conception to entry to Grade One *at the same time* as it supports parents to work or study, and in their parenting roles. Toronto First Duty is a single, accessible program delivery platform that is located in primary schools and coordinated with early intervention and family health services.

RESEARCH INTO PRACTICE

Toronto First Duty

Next Steps and Lesson Learned

Toronto First Duty pioneered the integration of child care, kindergarten, and family support services into a single quality program offering flexible enrollment options for families.

The development phase of Toronto First Duty concluded in June 2005 as the partners prepared to make integrated service delivery the operational standard for Toronto's children's service system. Four of the five original Toronto First Duty sites will not receive specialized funding beyond August 2006. One site, the Bruce WoodGreen Early Learning Centre (BWELC), continues to operate, with designated funding for an additional three years. The site will be a prototype that furthers the integration process and continues to inform the implementation of the Best Start Strategy in Toronto and across Ontario.

Lessons from the Bruce WoodGreen Early Learning Centre

While each site provided unique insights, BWELC moved furthest along the integration continuum. A number of factors fuelled the integration process at the site and provide lessons for future policy and program development.

Community Motivation: The impetus for early childhood program integration came from the school itself. Bruce School was one of many Toronto inner schools slated for closure under a revised provincial funding formula. The Atkinson Charitable Foundation (ACF) agreed to fund a leading-edge early years model on condition that the school was kept open. The school's staff, parent council, and school board administrators recognized the continued existence of the school depended on the successful development of the new model.

A Vision Informed by Research: The design of BWELC drew on relevant research, particularly the Royal Commission on Learning (1994) and its recommendation for a seamless program of education and care for young children, staffed by teachers and ECEs, and the McCain-Mustard *Early Years Study* that proposed the creation of child and parenting centres through the consolidation of existing community programs. These inputs combined to produce the program vision. Motivation, expertise, and clear direction provided momentum.

Building on Existing Assets: The school's early years' programs included junior and senior kindergarten classes, a literacy specialist, a Family Literacy Centre, and a breakfast and lunch program. Missing was the capacity to extend the activities beyond the school day or school year. WoodGreen Community Services is an established multi-service agency operating child care programs in schools throughout the community.

(cont'd)

Toronto First Duty (cont'd)

WoodGreen's leadership embraced the vision and came on board, not to develop a child care program per se, but to complement the school's existing services to create a full day/full year flexible program. Specifically, WoodGreen provided the ECE staff and a manager who would both lead the development of the centre and directly supervise the ECEs.

"Volunteerism" or Willing Staff: Early childhood educators joined BWELC knowing they would be working in a non-traditional environment. Teachers, parenting workers, and education assistants at the school were given the opportunity to transfer. New staff requested the positions aware of the expectations. All new applicants were interviewed by representatives of the partners.

The expectations and support of the site leadership, joint professional development, and designated time for program planning led to the development of a "staff team" rather than a group of collaborative individuals with distinct roles.

Maximizing Resources: No designated space was allocated for the new programming. The playground, kindergarten, and parenting centre rooms were organized to meet provincial legislative standards for child care. The school kitchen revamped its menu to comply with regulations. The program has access to all the school's facilities and equipment including the library, gym, and specialized staff. No additional *project* staff was hired. The program manager and school principal jointly provide leadership. Staffing numbers are the same as would be required to operate parallel kindergarten/child care/parenting programs. The staff team draws on all the partners for professional development and specialized supports.

Improved Quality: The program for four- and five-year-olds meets the kindergarten curriculum expectations of the Ministry of Education; the health, safety, and staffing standards of the Day Nurseries Act; and the parent engagement approach of the Toronto District School Board's parenting programs. For example, a child/staff ratio of 10:1 is maintained throughout the day—considerably below the 20:1 guideline set by the education ministry.

Sharing Evidence: Critical to the program's development was the gathering of evidence. Research was incorporated from the beginning. Evaluations indicate enhanced program quality and better parent engagement and suggest improved child outcomes based on direct testing and staff reports. Sharing the findings with staff maintained commitment and further informed all facets of program development.

Accessible Service Provision: The service design responds to changing family needs and provides parents with choice among the flexible arrangements. It begins with a parent-child focus for infants and toddlers and merges into a more child-centred program during the preschool years. Children requiring additional supports are linked to specialized services through the centre. A family's first contact is most frequently made through the free parent-child drop-in. Children two and a half years and up are eligible for a half-day program at no cost. Parents who want a full (9:00 a.m. to 3:00 p.m.) or extended day program (7:30 a.m. to 6:00 p.m.) pay $7 to $14/day respectively. The low fee, about one-third that for traditional child care, is a draw for parents. Also unlike traditional child care, parents pay only for the amount of time the child is enrolled. The design means the centre is used by a representative cross section of families in the community including at-home, working parents, and caregivers. The program's popularity with parents has resulted in considerable unmet demand.

Sustainability

BWELC re-allocated resources and test-drove the First Duty model. The lessons from their experience are:

- Integrating early childhood services requires clear goals and expectations. These should be contained within a new provincial framework for early learning, child care and parenting supports outlining the vision, policy and practice.

- Successful systems change involves the meaningful engagement of stakeholders at all levels informed by expert knowledge.
- A new policy framework must be accompanied by an infrastructure to support program and professional development.
- Integration promotes more intensive use of existing community assets and facilities but does not negate the need for service expansion.
- New investments should further integration by complementing existing resources rather than adding new program layers.
- Service integration can be accomplished within current staffing requirements but requires a realignment of job responsibilities.
- Building parent/public support for systems change requires the development of programming which is accessible and responsive to their needs.
- Regular assessment and evaluation provide accountability. Shared with practitioners they support program quality and improve child outcomes.
- Integrated early child development models can benefit children, parents, early childhood educators and other staff members and communities.

Source: Adapted from Corter, C., et al. (2006) *Toronto First Duty Phase I Summary: Evidence-based Understanding of Integrated Foundations for Early Childhood.* Toronto: Atkinson Centre at OISE/UT.

SUMMARY

The definition of early child development programs includes a wide variety of programs serving children from birth through age six and from six through twelve in out-of-school programs. These programs also serve the children's families. Early child development programs include full- and part-day programs; nonprofit, commercial, and public enterprises; and centres located in schools, communities, and workplaces. Home-based child care arrangements may be early child development programs that encourage children's optimal development and early learning and seek out opportunities for children to play with other children.

In some communities, early child development programs are reaching out and connecting up with each other. Models of integration include First Duty and neighbourhood hubs.

REVIEW QUESTIONS

1. Define early childhood development programs and early childhood education and care.
2. Describe what is meant by each of the following terms: full-day care; part-day care; commercial centres; nonprofit centres; family child care; special needs; early childhood intervention; and Head Start.
3. Compare similarities and differences in early childhood education and care programs in the provinces and territories.

STUDY ACTIVITIES

1. Read one of the following books for insight into working with a particular age group or in a particular setting. See the references at the end of the book for bibliographic information.
   a. Ashton-Warner, Sylvia. *Teacher* (preschoolers in New Zealand).
   b. Ayers, William. *The Good Preschool Teacher* (includes profiles of infant and toddler caregivers, family child care providers, kindergarten teachers, and a teacher of homeless children).
   c. Hillman, Carol. *Teaching Four-Year-Olds: A Personal Journey.*
   d. Kidder, Tracy. *Among Schoolchildren* (elementary school).
   e. Roemer, Joan. *Two to Four from Nine to Five* (family child care).
   f. Wollman, Patti G. *Behind the Playdough Curtain: A Year in My Life as a Preschool Teacher.*
2. Talk with a variety of early childhood educators from various early child development settings. Your instructor may invite some to class. Summarize their responses to the following questions: What contributes to their job satisfaction? Job dissatisfaction? What is their specialized training? What are three or four typical events during their day with the children?
3. Spend some time in the early childhood setting of at least one of the following: infant care, toddler care, a preschool setting, a kindergarten classroom, a classroom of one of the early grades, a family child care home, or a Head Start program. Listen to, and discuss, the reports of others about their visits.
4. Check your phone book to see what child care programs and preschools are located in your community. What types of program do you suppose they are, judging from their advertisements?
5. Find out what prenatal programs are available for pregnant women in your community. Who is eligible to attend? Are there any fees?

KEY TERMS

adult-child ratios: The number of children of a particular age who may legally (by regulation) or optimally (by accreditation standards) be cared for by one adult.
at risk: Used when concerns exist about developmental delay owing to negative environmental or physical conditions.
Canadian Child Care Federation (CCCF): Largest Canadian professional ECEC organization; established in 1987. Current membership is over 10 000 with affiliated provincial/territorial member organizations. Mission is to work within communities to improve the quality of child care for all Canadian children.
child care centre: Programs that provide nonparental care and early education to groups of children in a setting outside the children's home.
commercial: Also called proprietary and for-profit. Early childhood programs established to earn profit for their owners.
compensatory programs: Preschool programs designed to ameliorate the impact of social or economic disadvantage through an enriched environment.
early child development programs: All programs designed for young children, their families, and communities to promote children's healthy development and early learning, and to provide nonparental care.

early childhood education and care (ECEC): Early child development programs that are organized to provide care and learning opportunities for children from infancy through middle childhood.
Early Childhood Education (ECE): Postsecondary education programs to prepare early childhood educators.
early childhood educator: Individual with a combination of ECE credentials and expertise who works with young children and their families in early child development programs.
early intervention (EI): Programs that work with children whose development is delayed or at risk, often offering comprehensive services.
early learning and child care (ELCC): Another term for early childhood education and care programs.
family child care: Arrangements for child care within small groups (often less than six children), usually in the care provider's home.
family literacy: Literacy programs for young children and their parents and caregivers.
family resource program: Family-focused programs that offer activities and services to young children and their families and caregivers.
full-day programs: Programs that provide care for children throughout the day, including meal and sleep arrangements.
Head Start: Established in 1965, an educational program for preschoolers in families below the poverty level. Comprehensive services include education; family support through social services and parent education; and medical, dental, and nutritional services for children.
home-visiting: Brings services and expertise to children's homes. May be directed to children, adults, or both.
inclusive early childhood programs: Early child development programs that facilitate children's full participation, regardless of abilities/disabilities.
infants: Children from birth through the first year to eighteen months of life.
in-home child care: Nonparental child care provided in the child's own home.
junior kindergarten: Half-day programs for four-year-old children operated in Ontario's school system and in some Quebec at-risk communities.
kindergartens: Programs for five-year-olds, now generally operated in every school system, and originated by Friedrich Froebel.
nonprofit: Early childhood programs subsidized by government or agency funds, in which any surplus funds are used for program improvement.
part-day programs: Programs for children that operate for only a half-day, or for only several days a week.
preschoolers: Generally children aged three to five.
school-age children: Children in grades one through six.
senior kindergarten: Half- or full-day programs for five-year-old children operated in most Canadian school systems (except Prince Edward Island).
social services: The branch of professional services that helps provide for basic needs for families and individuals.
special needs: When development and learning do not follow typical patterns, individuals are said to have special needs requiring intervention through modifications in the environment or teaching techniques to help them develop optimally.

toddlers: Children from the time they become independently mobile (about age one) through to their third year (age three).

SUGGESTED READINGS

Assembly of First Nations. (1995). *National overview of First Nations child care in Canada.* Ottawa: Assembly of First Nations.

Beach, J. & Bertrand, J. (2000). *More than the sum of the parts: An early child development system for Canada.* Occasional Paper No. 12. Toronto: Childcare Resource and Research Unit, University of Toronto.

Canadian Council on Social Development. (2006). *Growing Up in North America.* Ottawa: CCSD.

Cleveland, G. & Krashinsky, M. (1998). *The benefits and costs of good child care: The economic rationale for public investment in young children.* Toronto: Childcare Resource & Research Unit.

Corter, C., Bertrand, J., Pelletier, J., Griffen, T., McKay, D., Patel, S., Ioannone, P. (2006). *Toronto First Duty phase 1 summary: Evidence-based understanding of integrated foundations for early childhood.* Toronto: Atkinson Centre at OISE/UT. http://www.toronto.ca/first duty.

Friendly, M. & Beach, J. (2005). *Early childhood education and care in Canada 2004.* Toronto: Childcare Resource & Research Unit, University of Toronto.

Health Canada, Human Resources Development Canada, and Indian & Northern Affairs Canada (2005). *Federal/Provincial/Territorial early childhood development agreement: Report on government of Canada activities and expenditures 2003-2004.* Ottawa: Minister of Public Works and Government Services Canada.

Kyle, I. & Kellerman, M. (1998). *Case studies of Canadian family resource programs: Supporting families, children and communities.* Ottawa: Canadian Association of Family Resource Programs.

Ontario Coalition for Better Child Care. (2000). *A guide to child care in Ontario.* Toronto: OCBCC.

CHAPTER TWO

Early Child Development Pedagogy and Curriculum

OBJECTIVES

After studying this chapter, students will be able to

- connect theories and knowledge about child development to ideas about how best to structure daily experiences for young children in early child development programs;
- identify different curriculum and pedagogical approaches used in early child development programs;
- discuss common concerns regarding early academics, readiness, and achievement testing;
- identify what is meant by inclusion and discuss the benefits for all children and adults involved;
- discuss the concepts that lie behind antibias curriculum;
- describe some of the benefits of mixed-age groupings in early education settings; and
- discuss some ideas regarding the use of technology in early child development programs.

Looking back at our definition of early child development, we can see that it also takes into account what children actually do while taking part in a program. A program's organization, or its **pedagogy** and **curriculum,** in early child development includes all that the child experiences. *Pedagogy* refers to how we deliberately cultivate children's development (National Science Council, 2001). It is education in its broadest sense (Moss, 2004). *Curriculum* is what we include in the environment and embed in children's experiences. This chapter considers different pedagogical and curriculum approaches and how you can begin to identify what approaches best suit your understanding about how children develop and learn. This chapter also introduces some of the current issues facing early childhood educators in their day-to-day implementation of curriculum in family child care settings, child care centres, nursery schools, family support programs, early childhood intervention initiatives, and kindergartens.

Early child development pedagogy and curriculum begins with a **philosophy** about how children learn and development and what is most important to know. An early child development philosophy is developmental rather than custodial (Doxey, 1990).

It is based on knowledge about child development and beliefs and goals that are geared to the optimal development of the whole child, in contrast to a philosophy that concentrates on intellectual development for academic achievement.

Pedagogy and curriculum, in early child development, include both the care and the learning that occur when the child participates in an early child development setting. It is everything that is part of a child's day or hours spent in a home- or centre-based program. Pedagogy and curriculum include daily schedules and routines, the physical environment, play materials, learning experiences, and, most importantly, the people who are part of the early child development setting. This chapter will examine a few specific early child development curriculum models to give you an idea of the many different ways that early child development programs can provide care and education to young children and their families.

Knowledge and Understanding of Child Development

Just as there are many forms or models of early child development programs, there are a number of curriculum and pedagogical approaches that can be adapted to different types of settings for children of varying ages. Curriculum and pedagogical approaches begin with our values and beliefs about children. Cultural values and beliefs shape our understanding of what is worth knowing. Child development theories build on values and beliefs and shape a program's philosophy, pedagogy, and curriculum. Early child development programs are social settings that guide children in learning about the world around them. Early childhood pedagogy and curriculum models reflect differences in culture.

You will learn more about the history of educational and psychological theories (or theories of human development) in your other early child development studies. Chapter 7 offers you a brief history about several child development theories. The summary in this chapter will introduce you to the major child development theories influencing early child development curriculum and pedagogy.

A theory is an organized, coherent set of ideas that helps explain data and information and make predictions. A theory of child development is an integrated set of ideas that describes, explains, and predicts human behaviour. Each one has its own ideas or images of the child and childhood and begins with a set of values and beliefs about children. Theories of human development explore how development occurs. Theories pose questions for research studies. At the same time, findings or results from research reinforce (validate) or refute theories. Theories do not exist apart from a particular social context. They are influenced by prevailing cultural values and daily practices. Theories are an often mysterious blend of hunches, intuition, beliefs and supporting *facts* from experiments and observations. Theories are often seen to be ultimate truths but usually are trends which fit a particular period of time and enjoy a period of popularity.

In North America, three major categories of child development theories emerged in the twentieth century that continue to influence early childhood curriculum and pedagogy.

- Behaviourist theories of child development are based on the assumption that development is a result of learning, which is a long-lasting change in behaviour based on experience or adaptation to the environment.
- Maturationist theories of child development emphasize that our early experiences, particularly those with our parents or other significant individuals, have a major influence on our life-long development. They believe that human growth and development unfolds from within and that children develop at their own pace.
- Constructivist theories of child development view children as active partners with their socio-cultural environment. Children are seen to actively construct their own knowledge as they manipulate, explore, and interact with their world. Social constructivist theories of development view children as competent and connected to adults and other children in their social environment.

Developmental Philosophy

Early childhood curricula and pedagogies begin with a developmental philosophy that recognizes optimal child and family well-being as the most important goal of early child development. You will discover that each philosophy will make different assumptions about how children develop and learn and about what is worth knowing. Philosophies are usually based on educational or psychological theories.

RESEARCH INTO PRACTICE

Quality by Design—Ideas

An early childhood system made up of a series of linked elements is the best way to ensure that high quality early learning and child care (ELCC) programs are the norm rather than the exception, according to research and comparative analysis. These elements include *ideas* about the purpose of programs, and what and how children learn and develop.

A conceptual framework should include

- a clear statement of the values that underpin the system;
- system-level goals for children and families;
- educational philosophy related to the values and goals; and
- curriculum defined as a short general statement.

A high quality ELCC system should begin by articulating the ideas that will define it. The ideas will be contained in a conceptual framework that begins with a statement of the values held by the society and what it wants for its children. The values statement is based on implicit societal values and beliefs about the nature of the child and childhood. It is coloured by the history, circumstances, and context—economic, social, and cultural—in which the society exists.

Different societies often have different perceptions about children, childhood, and the purposes of early learning and child care. While these sometimes produce significant variations in ideas about quality in ELCC

(cont'd)

Quality by Design—Ideas (cont'd)

programs, countries with different histories and circumstances share many common ideas, too. As Debbie Cryer (USA) points out: "the core quality elements . . . appear to cross international borders."

Long-term system-level goals break down the values statement into more detailed pieces. These should include goals for children—what kinds of attitudes, skills, and propensities we want to encourage. These could, for example, include developing respect for diversity, ability to work cooperatively with others, love of learning, self confidence, and creative expression. They should also include goals for families, for example, confident parenting and participation in the workforce; and goals for the community and society, for example, a well-educated citizenry, gender equality, and social inclusion.

The conceptual framework should also include an educational philosophy and framework to support practice at the individual program level. *Educational* is used here to mean what is sometimes called *pedagogy*, which can be translated as " education in its broadest sense." Moss and others have described this as development of the child through active involvement with the environment and with others by exploring, questioning, experimenting, and debating, rather than as a prescriptive plan for instructional activities.

How programs should be organized to support the goals and philosophy is sometimes called a *curriculum*. This should be a short statement that outlines the processes by which the stated outcomes for children are to be achieved; for example, through experiential learning, play-based programming, and involvement with adults and other children.

According to the Organization for Economic Co-operation and Development (OECD), an explicit educational philosophy and general curriculum serves several purposes: (1) promotion of an even level of quality; (2) provision of guidance and support for staff in their daily practice; and (3) facilitation of communication between parents and staff. The educational philosophy and curriculum should be flexible so that it can be adapted at the level of the individual program by well-trained and respected early childhood educators while still being consistent with the broad vision.

Program standards such as child-staff ratios, staff training qualifications, and parent participation support the philosophy and curriculum. Finally, the importance of an ongoing participatory process that includes discussion with a range of stakeholders about the conceptual framework and the other elements of the quality system should not be overlooked.

Source: Excerpt from Friendly, M. & Beach, J. (2005) *Quality by design.* Toronto: Childcare Resource & Research Unit, University of Toronto.

Pedagogy

Different pedagogical approaches relate to different beliefs, values, theories, and philosophies about how children best learn and develop. They range from views that children learn best through child-directed play (sometimes called **free play**) to views that children need **direct instruction** (adult-initiated teaching strategy) from adults. In practice, most early child development programs have elements of both child-directed play and adult-directed instruction but the balance between the two is what varies.

The social context is a critical element to take into account in considering how children learn and development. Family structure, social and economic characteristics, community influences, and ethnic and linguistic backgrounds are part of the social environment and part of learning and development.

Problem-Solving Play

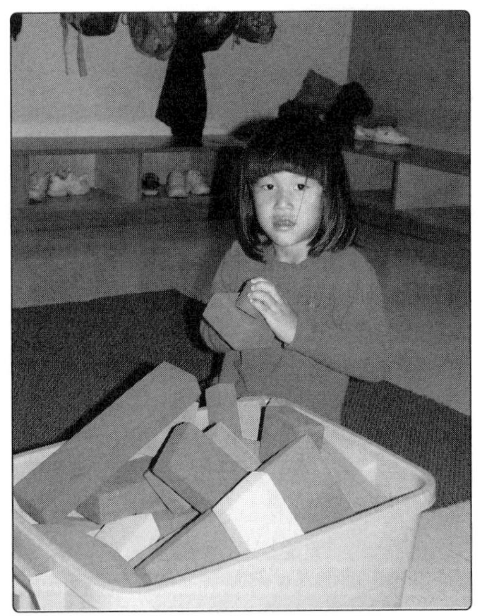

A bucket of blocks is an endless opportunity to arrange and rearrange.

Play is the predominant activity of early child development programs. An understanding of play and its role as an essential part of early child development programs and curricula will be a central component of your studies in early childhood education. Play is difficult to define because it is viewed somewhat differently in different cultural contexts and different early child development curricula contexts.

The Ontario Early Years Study recommended environments for young children that "offer children an array of opportunities to explore, discover and create . . . . Play-based, problem-solving with other children and an adult is an early learning strategy" (McCain & Mustard, 1999, pp. 159–60). Problem-based play is activity that captures and engages children in their quest to understand the world.

Play is the context in which children make sense of the world. Play is children's method of learning. Knowledge and skills become meaningful when used in play, as tools for learning are practiced and concepts become understood. All elements of learning and development are explored and practiced in play. The whole child is unified and supported in environments that support play. A play-based pedagogy is child-directed and purposeful.

In a play-based pedagogy, early childhood educators participate in play and guide children's planning, decision-making, and communication, and extend children's explorations with narrative, novelty, and challenges. Play encourages learning through interaction with objects, people, and information. Early childhood educators establish play that integrates social, emotional, physical, language, and cognitive development that respect diversity and are inclusive. Play is defined as an activity in which children are actively engaged, that is, freely chosen, intrinsically motivated, non-literal, and serves the child's needs for pleasure, emotional release, mastery, or resolution (Johnson, Christie & Wardle, 2005). Play-based pedagogy includes activities organized to facilitate movement, activity, choice, autonomy, communication, and social interaction (Bennett, J. 2004).

Children who thrive in primary school and set trajectories for later academic success are those who enter Grade One with strong communication skills, are confident, able to make friends, persistent and creative in completing tasks and solving problems, and excited to learn. These are the same qualities that children acquire through high quality play during their preschool years (Segal, 2004; Zigler et al., 2004).

Symbolic Play

Symbolic or pretend play is the primary mode of learning during the preschool years and continues to be important into the primary grades. Pretend play means practice in choosing, negotiating, planning, thinking, problem-solving, and taking risks. High quality pretend play means the child is deeply involved and acquiring and practicing skills.

Pretend play helps children take the perspective of others and promotes later abstract thought. Pretense involves mental representation. A child's ability for joint planning and assigning roles during pretend play with other children is related to their level of **theory of mind,** or their ability to understand that others have beliefs, desires, and intentions that are different from one's own. The understanding that what one believes and what others believe may not be the same, is a critical element in the development of theory of mind that is acquired around four years of age (Astington, 1998). Children's development of mental representation is an important cognitive achievement needed for academic skills, such as reading comprehension and use of mathematical symbols.

Pretend play increases how often children practice **self-regulation.** For instance, self-regulating private speech occurs more often than do less complex play settings, and settings with tasks having predetermined goals and greater teacher direction.

Play Builds Literacy, Numeracy, and Inquiry Skills

Play has been a well-established feature of early childhood education. But the increasing emphasis on accountability appears to have led to a corresponding decline in the general understanding of the important contribution that high-quality play—especially pretend play—can make to children's literacy, numeracy, and inquiry skills in the early years. A shift from a focus on play during preschool years to a strong emphasis on formal instruction to learn letters and use phonics can limit children's literacy skills as well as their numeracy and inquiry skills (Frede & Ackerman, 2002; Kraft & Berk, 1998; Barnett et al., 2006; Zigler et al., 2004). High quality play that is mediated by adults who are play partners able to inject judicious direct instruction into the daily play is an effective pedagogy for emergent literacy, numeracy, and science skills.

Play is a pedagogical strategy that takes advantage of children's seemingly natural activity. Effective preschool learning environments embed opportunities for learning in the physical environment and play activities. Play, combined with judicious amounts of direct instruction, creates important learning moments that build children's competencies. Early childhood educators can set up play opportunities that relate to the children's experiences and help them move beyond their current levels of understanding and abilities through a process known as **"scaffolding."** Children learn best when they can play, explore the world, and interact with expert adults and peers. Their explorations require flexibility and inventiveness. Children react to the outcomes of their investigations and create strategies for discovery.

Play is a platform for inquiry and exploration. Play engages children's attention when it offers a challenge that is within the child's capacity to master (McCain & Mustard, 1999; National Research Council, 2001). When adults become involved in children's play, they can help with the difficult spots or sequences in activities in a way that is clearer and reinforces learning (Keating, 1998).

Cognitive research points to the value of pretend play's symbolism in literacy acquisition. Symbolic play requires children to determine task goals and carry them out and provides opportunities for narrative recall and use of complex language (National Science Council, 2001; Bergen, 2002). Children in complex pretend play situations used more elaborative narratives and have higher levels of narrative structure than they do in other situations. The ability to use narrative is an important emerging literacy skill. Numerous studies of literacy skill development through play, which embed literacy materials within play settings in preschool, kindergarten,

RESEARCH INTO PRACTICE

Purposeful Play

Early childhood educators balance opportunities for figuring out how the world works, facing and achieving challenges with the practice necessary to perform skills effortlessly (Gopnik, 2005). Research studies report that purposeful play activities support children's ability to think and to learn.

- A bucket of blocks offers endless opportunities to arrange and rearrange, much like a scientist or mathematician arranging and rearranging ideas to find a solution to a problem and builds the capacity for flexible thinking.
- Storytelling and picture books draw children into fantasy and narratives, and motivate reading and writing skills.
- Guided play with board games using number lines, dots on a die, and small markers (to place on the number line) builds the understanding of numbers that underlies more complex mathematics.
- Make-believe or pretend play with costumes and props is practice in symbolic thought and problem-solving. It extends children's creativity and encourages innovation and adaptability.
- Art-making with paints or crayons and paper mirrors the child's developmental progress.

and multi-age programs, have typically shown increases in children's use of literacy materials and engagement in literacy acts (e.g., Christie & Enz, 1992; Neuman & Roskos, 1992; Stone & Christie, 1996; Einarsdottir, 2000; Roskos & Christie, 2004; Singer & Lythcott, 2004). Pretend play that is supported and sometimes guided by adults develops schemas and scripts as organized mental structures that are applied to understanding print. Pretend play is linked to more advanced uses of language that are linked to reading.

The language of numbers is the ability to see relations that are about quantity and builds on understandings about amount (e.g., more and less) early in life (Griffin & Case, 1998). Rich pretend play opportunities with other children and adults provide counting systems including: counting words; mathematical relationships, one-to-one correspondence; order; and numbers for the size of a set of objects (National Science Council 2001). Typically, children bring together an understanding about quantity differences between objects (e.g., big and little, large and small, etc.) and a continuum of values in between. Play consolidates understandings about numbers and children learn to use a number line for solving number problems that involve addition, subtraction, multiplication, and division. Play that involves games with rules supplements pretend play in mastering and integrating understandings about numbers and number lines.

Scientific reasoning begins in infancy. Babies notice how objects move and behave, gather information, build patterns of expectations about the world around them, and form general categories. Toddlers experiment with tools and learn to manipulate objects. They learn to solve simple problems they encounter in their environment—how to get an object out of reach or how to make their desires understood. Preschool children use methods of science including data collection, predicting, recording, and talking about findings. Problems to be solved emerge in, or can be introduced to, preschool pretend play. Early childhood educators may introduce problems into the environment that engage children's curiosity and provide opportunities for them to apply and reinforce their problem solving skills.

Direct Instruction

Direct instruction is adult-initiated, planned teaching. It may involve one child, a small number of children, or a large number of children, and an early childhood educator or other adult. It may be used to facilitate learning of academic content, physical skills, and social skills. Direct instruction typically starts with clearly stated learning objectives or outcomes. Materials and instructions are carefully sequenced to promote the child's or children's mastery of the content (Beretier, 1972; National Science Council, 2001).

In many early childhood programs, group time or circle time is an opportunity for direct instruction. Early childhood educators may plan specific content and take advantage of the potential efficiency of the simultaneous attention of a group of children (National Science Council, 2001).

Developmentally Appropriate Practice

Developmentally appropriate practice (DAP) is a pedagogical approach based on knowledge of the development of children's abilities and observation of individual differences, including abilities, interests, and culture. It can be applied in settings with children from infancy through middle childhood. The approach considers that all areas of development—physical, social, emotional, and cognitive—are important and that it is the early childhood educator's responsibility to plan an environment and support experiences to enhance all areas of development.

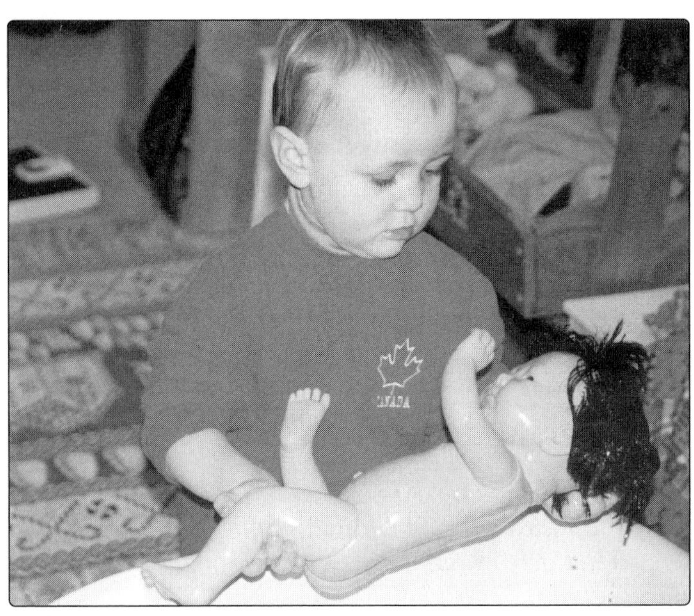
Developmentally appropriate practices influence all domains of the child's development, rather than focusing solely on the cognitive.

Programs designed on developmentally appropriate practice contain a number of common characteristics that can be incorporated into related curriculum approaches. Typically, early childhood educators in a developmentally appropriate program

- support the whole child, that is, all areas of the child's development;
- use observations of children's individual interests and developmental progress to plan the curriculum;
- promote children's active exploration and interactions with others;
- use learning materials and activities that are concrete and part of the lives of young children;
- provide for a wide range of developmental interests that meet the children's individual needs and skills;

- offer increased challenges as children's abilities and skills progress; and
- provide materials and allow time so children can choose activities (Bredekamp, 1987)

The **National Association of the Education for Young Children (NAEYC)** has defined specific standards of developmentally appropriate practice (Bredekamp, 1987). Guidelines are presented that describe how principles of developmental appropriateness can be applied in early childhood settings and set out the framework for developmentally appropriate curricula. You will learn more about these guidelines in Chapter 3, which considers voluntary standards for quality early childhood settings.

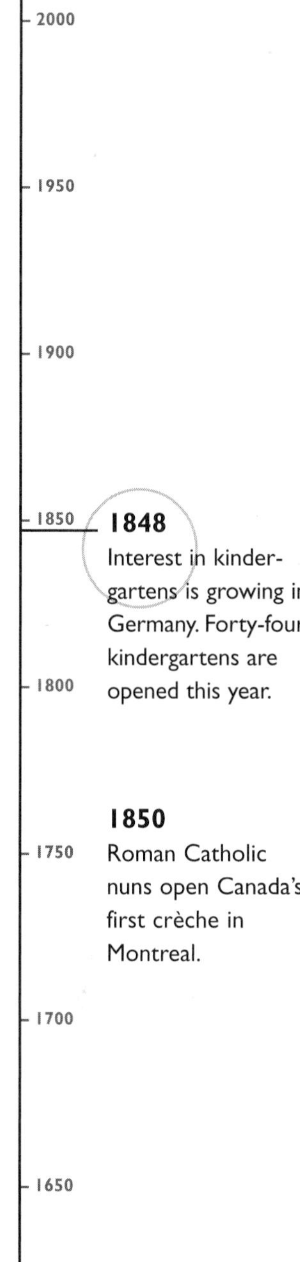

Curriculum Models

Montessori Schools

Montessori schools, following the philosophical approach of Maria Montessori (see Chapter 7), have proliferated in North America since the early 1960s. Montessori schools use unique methods and materials, and hire specially trained teachers. Sequences of prescribed tasks, using **didactic** Montessori materials, are presented to children in a designated order. Montessori teachers, or directresses, have received specialized training in an institution accredited for Montessori teacher training, which emphasizes observing children and presenting in **sequential steps** the directions for activities for which children are ready. The Montessori philosophy includes introducing children to varieties of **practical life skills,** such as washing dishes, sweeping floors, and watering plants. The curriculum also includes sensorial components, which involve providing materials to help children broaden and refine their sensory perceptions, and conceptual components, which means using concrete academic materials to introduce children to reading, writing, mathematics, and social studies.

There are particular terms that help explain the Montessori philosophy. Some of these include **absorbent mind,** Montessori's description of the ease with which young children learn unconsciously from the environment; didactic materials, those that teach children directly by making errors in their use obvious to the child for self-correction; and **sensitive periods,** the periods of learning during which children are particularly sensitive to particular stimuli. One abiding distinction of the Montessori philosophy is the respect for children and their abilities and accomplishments.

Many Montessori schools are for children ages two through six, although in some communities, Montessori education may continue through the elementary grades and beyond. In North America today, there are Montessori schools that strictly follow the original techniques, such as the Association Montessori International (AMI), and others that follow practices adapted to North American culture and current thinking, such as the American Montessori Society (AMS).

High/Scope

Another current model in early childhood education and care programs is the **High/Scope** curriculum. This curriculum has developed under the leadership of David Weikart, who was a founder of the Perry Project, one of the best-known intervention programs of the 1960s (see Timeline, pp. 179). The High/Scope curriculum is based on Jean Piaget's constructivist theories of child development. "The curriculum rests on the fundamental premise that children are active learners, who learn best from activities that they themselves plan, carry out and reflect on" (Epstein, 1993, p. 30). As in most good early childhood programs, children learn in a variety of learning centres with plenty of appropriate materials. Teachers help children actively plan what they will do each day, after which the children carry out their plan during work time for self-selected activities and then review what they have done (**"plan, do, review"**). Early childhood practitioners join in children's play, asking questions to extend their thinking skills. The High/Scope curriculum identifies five ingredients of active learning for young children:

- materials for the child to explore;
- manipulation of materials by the child;
- choices by the child about what to do with the materials;
- language from the child; and
- support from the adult (Epstein, 1993).

Early childhood practitioners may study the High/Scope philosophy in short workshops and training institutes. An important part of the philosophy involves using small groups to help children focus on the following **key experiences,** a set of eight concepts based on Piaget's ideas of preschoolers' cognitive characteristics and learning potential:

- active learning initiated by children and involving sensory and manipulative materials
- use of language
- opportunities to represent their own ideas and experiences
- opportunities for classification
- use of seriation
- use of number concepts
- experience with spatial relationships
- opportunities to understand time concepts

Reggio Emilia

After World War II, preschools opened in the northern Italian town of Reggio Emilia. Today the municipal government supports thirty-five **Reggio Emilia** schools, serving children aged three to six and infants up to age three. About 47 percent of the town's preschool population and 33 percent of its infants attend Reggio Emilia schools (Gestwicki, 2006). This city-run early child development program has captured the attention and imagination of early childhood practitioners in Canada and around the world for several reasons. First, it enjoys a high degree of community support and is viewed as an essential part of a cohesive, healthy, and productive community. Second, the schools' physical beauty and attention to detail are evident to all who visit the program. Third, the program philosophy and curriculum builds on Lev Vygotsky's concept of the social construction of knowledge and skillfully integrates other theoretical concepts, including Jean Piaget's theory of cognitive development, John Dewey's concept of progressive education, Hugh Gardner's theory of multiple intelligences, and Urie Bronfenbrenner's ecological environment theory (Berk & Winsler, 1995).

Loris Malaguzzi was the founder and leader of Reggio Emilia's approach and programs. He based his system of early childhood education on a few key principles:

Emergent curriculum follows and extends children's own interests.

- child-centred programs, which respect children and emphasize the reciprocal adult-child relationship;
- an "environment as teacher" approach, which organizes space to promote relationships, creates aesthetically pleasing surroundings, promotes choices and activities, stimulates all areas of learning, and reflects children's ideas, values, and culture;
- a curriculum centred on children's interests, reflected in projects that are undertaken in considerable depth and detail;
- a spirit of collaboration between early childhood practitioners and young children in facilitating intellectual discovery through social process; and
- the participation of families as an integral part of the educational experience (Gestwicki, 2006).

Many early childhood practitioners are turning to an **emergent curriculum** model that allows them to incorporate some of the principles found in Reggio Emilia programs. However, Reggio Emilia is not a curriculum model that can be transported from its roots in northern Italy to Canadian settings. It is a way of thinking and interpreting the immediate surroundings (natural environment and social community) and following the lead of children and their families to create a unique early childhood setting. Emergent curriculum is an approach that encourages early childhood practitioners to really respond to their immediate surroundings—physical place and people—and guide children's natural curiosity about their environment to encourage learning.

Emergent curriculum first appeared in the 1970s, and Elizabeth Jones coined the term in the introduction to a curriculum book (Jones & Nimmo, 1994). Many North American early childhood practitioners are finding it a useful framework that integrates knowledge about child development and an approach to planning that allows the child's interests to lead (Goulet, 2001).

RESEARCH INTO PRACTICE

Processes of Emergent Curriculum

The Early Childhood Education diploma program and the eight lab centres at George Brown College have adopted an emergent curriculum model. Marie Goulet, ECE faculty member, prepared the following handout for ECE students, which describes how early childhood practitioners can support children's learning and respect their interests and explorations.

Provision

Provide materials and space for children to explore and play. Consider the needs of individuals and group development. Environments should be rich enough for each child to find her interests with opportunities to learn.

Sustain

Learning requires repeated practice to ensure integration and mastery. Provide materials and support to maintain practice at the same level of difficulty (horizontal curriculum). Strategies include: open-ended questions, broadcasting, joint-attention, imitation, parallel play, adding new materials that offer the same practice.

Enrich

Learning involves achievable challenges to extend and elaborate children's skills (vertical curriculum). Extensions involve problem-solving, increased complexity, new combinations, increasing logical thinking. Strategies include: adding materials with open-ended questions—(what can you do with this?), asking predictive questions (what would happen if . . .), asking problem-solving questions (how can you . . .), asking relationship questions (which one rolled further? which ones belong together?)

Documentation and Representation

Document children's explorations and thinking by collecting and displaying the materials that track the growth of children's play. Represent what happened with children's work, photographs, videotapes, audiotapes. Documentation includes descriptions of children's actions and language that are connected to the children's purpose, development, person meaning and identity.

Source: Goulet, Marie (2001). Reprinted with permission.

Sesame Street

Sesame Street is the most successful programme in the history of children's television. It has been broadcast to more than 120 million children in 130 nations and is watched by 77 percent of American preschool children (Gladwell, 2002). Derived directly from the 1967 Public Broadcasting Act, *Sesame Street* began broadcasting on US television in 1969 to promote the intellectual and cultural growth of preschoolers (Carnegie Commission on Educational Television, 1967). Television producer Joan Ganz Cooney, and puppeteer Jim Henson, collaborated to form the Children's Television Workshop and developed the idea of teaching through the perceptual salience of commercial television: quick cuts, animation, and humour with talking puppets and humans posing as narrators.

The historical events and educational policies of the late 1960s shaped *Sesame Street*'s educational goals and audience. One major historical force of the time was the Civil Rights movement. The movement focused attention on the crucial role education would have to play if children from low-income circumstances, including disproportionately large numbers of minority-group members, were to escape the cycle of poverty. Head Start and *Sesame Street* were two outgrowths of broad education policies that recognized that special efforts to stimulate the educational progress of children from low-income backgrounds should include an emphasis on school-readiness skills starting at a very early (preschool) age. A research study of the era, published by Benjamin Bloom (1964) at the University of Chicago, concluded that more than one half of a child's lifetime intellectual capacity is formed by five years of age.

Sesame Street focuses on improving the social and academic skills of disadvantaged children and helping them succeed at school. The educational or instructional design of *Sesame Street* is based on the premise that learning is a process that takes place from the outside in and moves from simple to complex. Learning readiness is related to mastering simple patterns, skills, and concepts in preparation for more complex concepts. The plan also sets out to model pro-social skills and introduce specific information and concepts related to early literacy and numeracy skills.

Sesame Street relies on the insight that "if you can hold the attention of children, you can educate them" (Gladwell, 2002, p. 100). It uses the direct instruction strategies that combine specific learning objectives, carefully sequenced images, and matching dialogue into episodes that are designed to focus the child's attention and master specific content. The high production values and the combination of stable components of the environment (for example, characters such as Big Bird), isolation and repetition of key concepts in each show (such as the number '6' or letter 'c'), and the judicious use of novel or unexpected events are used to directly instruct young children.

The approach of *Sesame Street* in using direct instruction embedded in an entertaining format that engages children can be found in many early child development programs. They are typically organized around specific themes that are relevant to children's daily lives and subject areas such as literacy, math, science, social skills, art and music. Children are encouraged to master specific content such as visual patterns or recognition of colours.

Curriculum Issues

The early child development curriculum models described in the previous section are examples of the kinds of approaches you are likely to find in early childhood education and care programs in your communities. You can see that there are both similarities and differences among the models. Most early childhood practitioners tend to find themselves comfortable in one approach more than another. Many practices—what kinds of materials to make available to children, observing children's interactions with each other, or displaying representations that children have created—are common in a number of curriculum approaches.

The same curriculum issues often challenge early childhood practitioners working in different settings and with different curriculum approaches. What is the best way to organize children's groups—same age or mixed-age groups? Should early childhood education and care programs try to ensure that children are ready to adapt to school settings, or should the schools adapt to children? How can early childhood programs support children who have developmental challenges or identified special needs? How can early childhood settings respect and support all young children (boys and girls) and their families from diverse cultural, linguistic, and religious backgrounds? Does electronic technology have a place in today's early child development programs?

1856
Margarethe Schurz, a student of Froebel's, begins a small German-language kindergarten for six children in her home in Watertown, Wisconsin.

Mixed-Age Groupings

Children in early child development programs are not always organized into groups of the same age and stage of development. In home-based programs it is more common to find children from different ages together in the same setting—similar to a family with siblings of various ages.

Those of you who have listened to grandparents and great-grandparents reminisce about attending one-room schoolhouses will understand that **mixed-age groupings** in education are not a new phenomenon. But the concept is receiving renewed attention in early education programs and has been used successfully not only in Canada but also in England, Sweden, and Italy. Rethinking the concepts of mixed-age groupings allows early childhood educators to capitalize on the differences in the experience, knowledge, and abilities of children (Corson, 2005).

A mixed-age grouping combines children across at least two, preferably three, chronological years. Usually, the grouping remains together for much of the time, with the oldest children moving on each year and new children joining as the youngest in the group. This means that children are in a group for at least two and sometimes three years and remain with the same early childhood practitioner over this time. In regulated group centres, multi-age groupings "refers to the placement of children of different ages together in activity and learning areas for substantial portions of the daily schedule" (Bernhard, Pollard, Eggers-Pierola & Morin, 2000, p. 80). Such an arrangement is more like a typical family or neighbourhood setting than like a classroom that educates children in "litters" of only age-mates.

Such a system has some clear social advantages. One benefit is that, over extended time, children's relationships with one another, and relationships between children, teachers, and parents can develop and provide security and deeper knowledge. Another advantage is that older children have opportunities to exhibit leadership skills with younger children and to assume responsibility. Older children in mixed-age groupings seem to increase their own regulation of their behaviour, perhaps taking seriously their roles as models for the younger children. Their pro-social, caring skills also increase. Younger children benefit by participating in the more complex forms of play developed by the older children and by imitating their behaviours. Cooperative behaviours increase for all children (Katz, Evangelou, & Hartman, 1991).

There are cognitive benefits for children in these groupings, as well. Rigid curricula with age-graded expectations must necessarily be relaxed in mixed-age settings. Children are allowed to develop and learn at their own rates without fear of failure and with less competition. Children's unique needs are more easily identified when teachers are not considering group goals; the curriculum is more likely to be matched to children's needs and skill-learning levels. Children whose knowledge is similar but different stimulate one another's mental growth and thinking. Therefore, **cooperative learning** and peer tutoring situations generally abound in mixed-age settings.

Early childhood educators are key in determining how effectively mixed-age groupings actually work to benefit children. Simply putting children of different ages together does not guarantee these benefits; early childhood practitioners need to carefully structure the environment, plan the curriculum, and play particular roles. As early childhood educators learn about children's interests, abilities, learning styles, and choices for play partners, they can support individual growth. They plan activities that are child-initiated, so that children can find their own place on the developmental ladder. By freeing themselves from the role of director, early childhood educators can step in to facilitate as children need their interaction. Early childhood educators may consciously create opportunities for children to work together, make suggestions about how children can help one another, or frame thought-provoking questions that suggest ways of working with others who are younger or older. Children, with adult guidance, can learn much about democratic practices by jointly solving the problems that naturally arise in a multi-age grouping, such as what to do when the younger ones don't want to listen to the longer books that the older ones love to have read chapter by chapter.

Early childhood educators often resist the move to mixed-age groupings at first, fearing that it will be too difficult to plan for great differences and that individual age-stage behaviours won't mix. However, early childhood educators usually change their opinions after some experience. They discover that they are teaching more responsively and appropriately. They benefit by learning about individual differences in new ways and by questioning their stereotypes and prejudices about behaviours that they may have assumed stemmed from age levels. They discover that the teaching and learning in their classrooms are shared among all participants. Perhaps this innovation will be in your professional future.

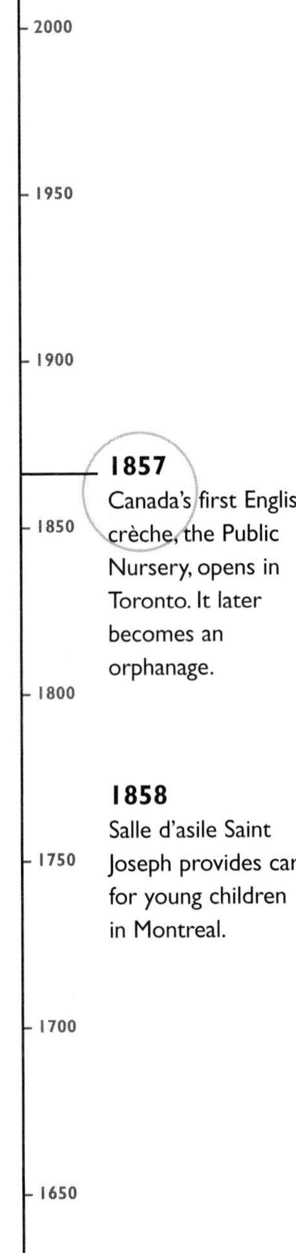

Adult and Child Focus

Early child development curriculum is often oriented to parents or other caregivers and to children. In some instances, parents or other caregivers attend the program with their children some or all of the time. In other early childhood settings that provide nonparental care, parents or caregivers do not participate directly in program activities with their children (except during drop-off and pick-up times or at special events). In either situation, the curriculum can be directed to both parents or other caregivers and children.

A two-pronged approach that is both parent- and child-oriented, recognizes the power of early learning within the family and seeks to support parents' and other caregivers' participation in the children's early development.

MAKING IT HAPPEN

A Place to Grow

Sylvia was pregnant when she emigrated from China to Canada with her two-year-old daughter. Her husband was to follow later. One of the people who lived in the same apartment complex told Sylvia about the Parenting and Family Literacy Centre, run by the Toronto District School Board, located in the local school. [Parenting and Family Literacy Centres offer activities to support children's early learning and provide parenting support, education, and courses. They have both a child and adult curriculum focus.]

They found the center to be a warm and welcoming place, with parents and other caregivers, like grandparents, and young children engaged in activities that help young minds develop through play. There was music and storytelling and games and snacks. At the Centre, Sylvia's little girl found other children who spoke Cantonese, and Sylvia found toys and books in their language to take home. Both of them started to learn English. The center showed Sylvia how to make toys from ordinary household objects. She learned the importance of reading to her toddler. They made friends.

Source: McCain & Mustard. (1999), p. 105. Reprinted with permission.

Readiness for School Learning

Children's coping and competence when they enter formal schooling is related to their academic success—how well they do in school and whether they complete high school and pursue other training and education. There is growing interest in ensuring that all children enter school "ready to learn" as a way of improving academic achievement and social well-being. There is also concern that Canadians' literacy abilities and mathematical achievement fall behind many other countries (Willms, 2000). If the early years set the foundation for later academic achievement (as well as social competence), it makes sense to consider how well prepared children are for school environments. This does not mean that young children should learn to read earlier or that pre-reading, prewriting, or number skills are the only criteria for school **readiness**.

Gillian Doherty, an early childhood research expert, points to five components of readiness for school learning, based on research findings:

- physical well-being and appropriate motor development;
- emotional health and a positive approach to new experiences;
- age-appropriate social knowledge and competence;
- age-appropriate language skills; and
- age-appropriate general knowledge and cognitive skills (1997, p. 18).

The desire to improve children's readiness for school learning sometimes leads to an emphasis on **early academics** or the direct instruction of reading and number skills during the early years. Since the modern era of early childhood education began in the 1960s, one issue has generated a good deal of debate: how much academic content and method is appropriate for children in their early years? Although many professional early childhood practitioners understand and support developmentally appropriate practices for young children, some are less grounded in developmental knowledge. They are more easily influenced by administrators, parents, and policymakers who push for academic experiences for young children, which look a good deal like those presented to older children.

A number of reasons underlie this concern for accelerating young children's acquisition of academic skills.

- Many Canadians believe that the public education system is failing many young children, particularly those from socially and economically disadvantaged backgrounds, who were beginning school unprepared for the rigours of academic learning. Among the many programs that proliferated during the years following this initial concern were some that stressed academics in a highly structured, adult-controlled system.
- The school system operates kindergarten programs for five-year-old children in Canada. In many cases, other early-learning programs for preschool children are established within the school system. School systems are used to dealing with older children's development and learning and, thus, often based these new programs for the youngest ones on a dribbled-down version of what the older ones were doing, rather than recognizing that what is good for older children may be quite different for younger children. Based largely on the work of behavioural learning theorists, these programs for preschools and kindergartens often emphasize helping children learn the specific skills that they would need for later learning. The methods that early childhood practitioners employed in these academically oriented programs look suspiciously like those used in classrooms for much older children, where teachers tended to take on the primary role of instructing, drilling, assigning, directing, and testing for retained knowledge.
- Essentially, proponents of early academics have moved the academic curriculum to begin in earlier grades. What was once taught in Grade One is now frequently expected to be mastered in kindergarten, which means that the preschool years must be spent learning the subskills for reading and math that would bring success at that later stage. In many cases, administrators of school programs were pressured by policymakers to produce evidence of learning, which is more easily measured and quantified in the kinds of academic knowledge that can be drilled and taught by rote. Therefore, educational systems moved to earlier academics to attempt to answer some of the system's own questions about how best to achieve learning results and how to define its role in serving very young children.
- Today many families, unfamiliar with knowledge of early child development programs, are most comfortable in finding a program that resembles their own educational experiences. "What are you teaching them?" they ask. "Do they just play here?" As consumers who want to be assured that they are receiving their full money's worth, they, too, want to see measurable results, which, unfortunately for developmentally appropriate practice, may be more concrete and obvious when a preschooler has a worksheet to take home than when he has spent a productive morning building in the block area. "This assumption has enabled parents to accept the commonly held view that today's children are ready for learning earlier than in past generations" (Gestwicki, 2006, p. 22).

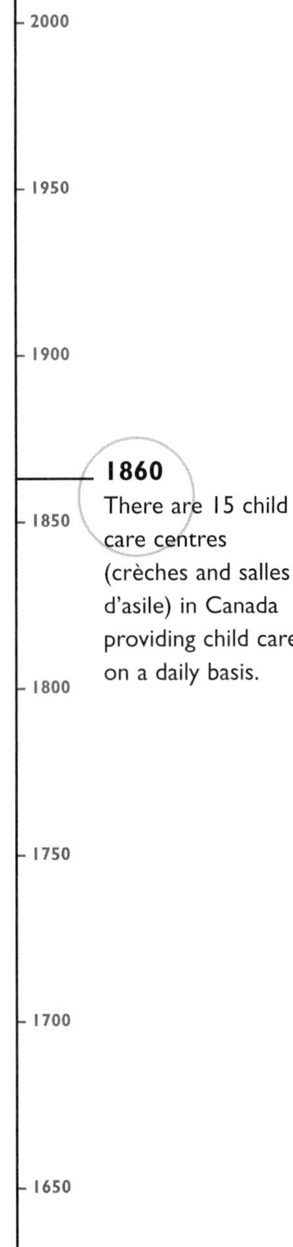

Making marks—with crayons, pencils and paints—is a step along the way to learning to print.

- Parents who are concerned about giving their children the "competitive edge" believe that getting children started off on the right track when they are very young should logically enable their later acceptance into the right school or program. This leaves parents vulnerable to accepting the influence of both professionals and entrepreneurs who promote ideas for early teaching.

Where is the real danger for young children in being caught between the opposite poles of this debate on developmentally appropriate practices and formally structured academic experiences? By ignoring the active nature of the young child's learning style, children's healthy development may be jeopardized.

Infants and young children do not just sit twiddling their thumbs, waiting for adults to teach them to read and do math. They expend a vast amount of time and effort in exploring and understanding their immediate world. Healthy education supports and encourages this spontaneous learning. Early instruction miseducates, not because it attempts to teach, but because it attempts to teach the wrong things at the wrong time. When we ignore what the child has to learn and instead impose what we want to teach, we put infants and young children at risk for no purpose (Elkind, 1988, p. 25).

What sorts of risks do many experts see in prematurely exposing children to academic learning? There are several.

- Children's self-esteem will suffer if they are unable to succeed at the tasks that seem so important to adults. Many children, especially young children, just cannot learn in the ways that academic instruction requires, no matter how hard they try. They cannot sit still, comprehend, or use the material they have learned by rote, or even see its importance. They feel incompetent, as they realize that they have failed to meet adults' standards, without understanding that what they have failed at is alien to their nature and learning style. When these kinds of learning are not meaningful to children, they feel no sense of self-worth, even when they do master some learning.
- Another component of healthy development that is thought to be at risk in academic preschool programs is self-control (Greenberg, 1990). Learning to make good choices is an important part of self-discipline. In a teacher-directed and teacher-managed environment, young children have few opportunities to make choices. The longitudinal studies of the preschool programs in Ypsilanti, Michigan, suggest more positive social and emotional adjustment of adolescents and adults who participated as children in preschool programs that allowed them to choose and initiate their activities (Schweinhart, Weikart, & Larner, 1986).
- Formal instruction often puts excessive and inappropriate demands on young children, which can result in an overload of stress. A number of studies confirm that there is increased stress on children in developmentally inappropriate learning situations (Burts, Charlesworth, & Fleege, 1992).
- Lastly, it seems likely that the long-term effects of rushing children prematurely into formal academics may be less than positive. Frequently, children's attitudes

and dispositions to learning are negatively affected by the stress and circumstances of those first learning experiences. Evidence also suggests that children whose introduction to academic content and methods has been delayed past preschool and kindergarten have had at least equally positive results in later learning, rather than being handicapped when compared with peers whose academics began earlier (Burts et al., 1992). This seems to support the notion that waiting until children are developmentally ready for later kinds of school learning is beneficial.

Early childhood educators are not unanimous in this position. There are those who believe that early and extensive direct instruction enhances children's later academic success, and that the earlier this direct instruction is started, the better (Gersten & Keating, 1990). It will be important for you to immerse yourself in understanding the research and statements of both viewpoints. Only by forming a personal philosophy about appropriate practices for children will early childhood educators be able to adequately defend their position to others.

You will need to be prepared to offer convincing and solid rationales for structuring environments and learning experiences in which children initiate their own active learning through play. These environments and experiences are supported by facilitators who recognize that teaching based on active learning provides opportunities to develop *all* domains of the child's growth, and is more likely to support readiness for all learning and success in school.

Also early childhood educators must recognize that literacy and numeracy are important skill areas. Individual Canadians need these skills to be successful in almost any workplace and to participate fully in a democratic society. These are basic skills to survival in our society as we enter the twenty-first century. Therefore, early childhood educators can understand that families are often anxious that their children acquire the skills necessary for learning to read and compute numbers when they enter formal schooling. We should be concerned too. However, direct instruction in isolated skills such as letter recognition or matching things that are the same and different will not be nearly as effective as other curriculum strategies.

Early childhood educators can provide environments that do prepare children for learning to read and understand mathematics. Early child development environments can be structured in a number of ways that support emergent literacy and emergent numeracy during the early years and then early literacy and numeracy abilities as they develop.

Emergent literacy is the development of children's ability to use print forms of language and includes making marks, scribbling, reciting stories from memory, and printing letters. Writing and reading become meaningful, and children understand their purpose even if they cannot read and write themselves. Literacy develops relationship to oral language, but is a separate ability. Literacy is the symbolic representation of oral language.

We can support emergent literacy by

- understanding that literacy develops in close relationship to oral language;
- speaking with children about things that interest them;
- engaging in reading out loud and storytelling;
- developing a sense of narrative;

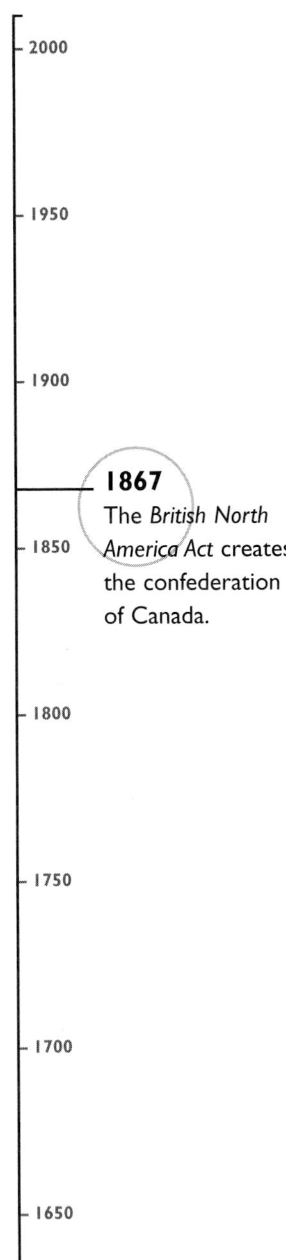

2000
1950
1900
1850
1800
1750
1700
1650

1871
In Ontario, the *School Act* makes schooling compulsory for children aged 7 to 12 for four months of the year. Schools in some boards were open six days a week and eleven months of the year.

- valuing and modeling adult literacy use;
- enriching our environment with books and print;
- encouraging play reading and writing; and
- offering activities that develop visual discrimination, fine motor control, and phonological awareness.

Emergent numeracy is the understanding of numbers and what they represent. It involves both an understanding of quantity (big and little, two comes after three) and quality (more and less, a little bit, and a lot). Understanding of quantity (and numbers) begins very early as children explore objects and their properties.

Monitoring Readiness for School Learning

The concept of readiness for school and learning creates the need to assess how well children are doing when they enter school. If the focus is on moving academic learning earlier into early childhood, the assessment is accomplished by testing young children. If being ready for school means being ready for the academic demands of the primary classroom, children are expected to enter school already knowing what formerly was not taught until Grade One. Now, as schools move to measure the quality of their instruction, it is increasingly important to them that children have achieved particular standards of learning at specific points.

Since **standardized tests** tend to focus on narrowly cognitive tasks, young children's overall development and strengths are not given equal importance in making decisions about readiness. And since young children do not have the requisite skills for successfully taking tests—sitting still, following directions, writing, or making specific marks—the test results are often inadequate measures of what they truly know and who they are. In setting out particular expectations for what children should already know before they enter or progress in school, the concept of readiness really becomes a method of gatekeeping, excluding those children who cannot be expected to adjust to the demands of school (Willer & Bredekamp, 1990).

If the focus on readiness takes into account physical, social, emotional, and cognitive areas of development (as outlined at the beginning of this section), we need a different kind of measurement to monitor how well children are doing during the early years. We need measurement that will tell us how well early child development programs and communities are doing in supporting young children and their families.

The measurement of low birth weight is a universal marker that serves a similar function. It is a measure of maternal health and reflects the conditions surrounding pregnancies. It also points to problems in the physical and social environment and is a point of reference to monitor to see if changes to prenatal supports or social conditions are making a difference.

One point after birth when it is possible to get a measure of the whole population of children is when they enter the school system. A readiness to learn or school readiness measure should be a tool that communities can use to assess how well they are responding to their children's needs. It also is a measure to monitor the impact of initiatives designed to support children during the early years.

The Offord Centre for Child Studies in Hamilton, Ontario, has developed and tested a tool that is a broad measure of children's development or readiness to learn at school entry. Called the Early Development Instrument (EDI) (Janus & Offord, 2000), it is based on the concept of readiness to learn that includes all areas of development. The EDI measures children's ability to be cooperative and attend to the teacher, to benefit from educational activities, and get along with other children. The instrument consists of five domains (or scales): physical health and well-being, social knowledge and competence, emotional maturity, language and cognitive development, and general knowledge and communication skills. Kindergarten teachers complete the EDI for each child, but the results are reported at the population level for individual communities and schools. This means that all of the scores for the children in a kindergarten class are grouped together to give a picture on the overall readiness for school of that group of children living in that community (Kershaw et al, 2006).

The EDI is a tool that allows us to monitor how well children are doing, at the community or neighbourhood level, when they enter school. School readiness, measured by EDI, can be used as an indicator of children's health in a community, because it reflects a broad concept of developmental health and provides a population-level indicator (Janus, 2005). It is also a measure of how well the community is doing to support early development. It is not intended to identify individual children's developmental problems or delays.

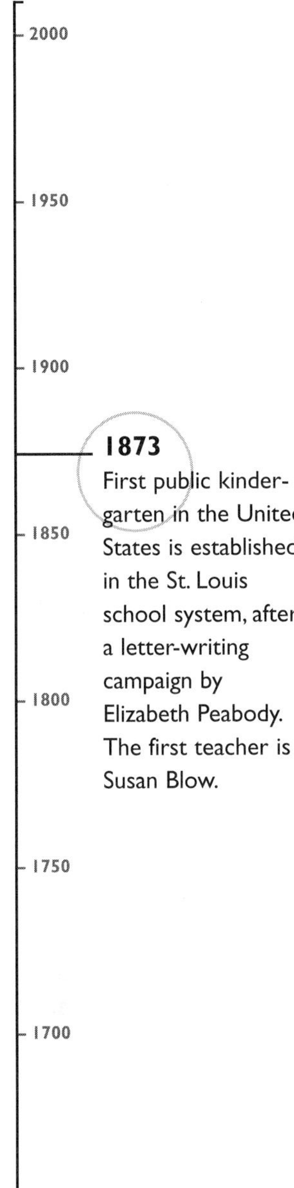

Inclusion in Early Child Development Programs

There likely will be at least one young child with special developmental or learning needs enrolled in the first early child development program you work in as a student or a graduate. Although the **inclusion** (also called integration, and formerly known as **mainstreaming**) of children began in the mid-1970s, only recently have we seen these programs become common in many communities.

Benefits have been identified in these programs for all the children involved, both those whose development follows typical patterns and those who require special supports and adaptations. Research shows that children with disabilities in nonsegregated settings are able to learn and practice many new skills through imitation of their peers. Children with disabilities demonstrate higher levels of social play and initiate more appropriate social interactions with peers than do children in **special education** or segregated preschool settings (Diamond, Hestenes, & O'Connor, 1994). The gains that children in integrated classrooms make in language, cognitive, and motor-skill development are comparable to those of children in special education classrooms. Therefore, they are able to take advantage of the activities that promote development while gaining an advantage in levels of play. More realistic expectations are placed on children with special needs who attend the same programs as children with typical abilities (Chandler, 1994). Children with special needs will be perceived as "less different" if they are not excluded from environments with other children and, thus, may be more easily accepted by family, peers, and community.

Studies also show that children without disabilities benefit when children with special needs are included in preschool classrooms. In addition to making developmental gains equivalent to those that children make in noninclusive classrooms (Diamond et al., 1994), they may gain a more realistic view of people with disabilities and develop positive attitudes instead of prejudices toward others who are different from themselves. In inclusive settings, children are able to develop responsive, helpful behaviours toward others and become sensitive to the needs of others.

Parents of children with and without special needs generally support the concept of inclusion but express concerns about whether the needs of all children within the classroom will be met (Galant & Hanline, 1993). However, after experience in such classrooms, both groups of parents become far more positive about the impact on their children. For parents of children with special needs, their child's integration may help them feel less isolated within the community and more hopeful about their child's future.

1878
The American Froebel Union is established by Elizabeth Peabody. It is the first professional association for those concerned with the education of young children.

What has inclusion been like for early childhood educators who have been trained to work with children whose development follows typical patterns? Initially, early childhood educators react with caution, fear, or negative responses, wondering whether the placement is wise for the child and fair to all the children. But in two studies (Giangreco and Kontos, reported in Diamond et al., 1994), early childhood educators noted that the children had become part of the group, without the disability being identified as their most important characteristic. Early childhood educators who worked in inclusive classrooms reported they had become more confident and flexible in their teaching, reflecting more on the needs of all the children in their class. Three Canadian studies (Irwin, Lero, & Brophy, 2004) on the inclusion of children with special needs found multiple factors related to successful inclusion, including:

- the director's inclusion leadership—modeling commitment, ensuring staff are supported within the centre, acting as an advocate for inclusion, and marshalling resources to support inclusion efforts;
- staff's attitudes and commitment toward inclusion;
- overall program quality; and
- skilled support staff or in-house resource teachers to enhance ratios.

The support and involvement of resource consultants and a range of specialists are also important to help staff develop skills that allow them to promote the development of children with a wide range of special needs, modify existing curricula, and encourage positive peer interactions among children.

There can be barriers to successful inclusion. One is that there are philosophical and methodological differences between early childhood special education and regular early childhood education. The individualized teaching plans of early special education emphasize skill acquisition, structured use of instructional time, a strong behavioural orientation, and more teacher direction than is considered good practice in regular early childhood education. These differences create various issues of turf, with many special educators feeling that they can provide the best education for children with disabilities. However, it has been noted that "cooperation, collaboration, and mutual respect between regular and special education early childhood teachers and therapists was an important component of successful integrated programs" (Diamond et al., 1994, p. 71). When early childhood educators have the support of an intervention team that respects their expertise and their educational approaches, most believe that they can meet the needs of the children with disabilities in their classrooms.

It is most helpful to successful inclusion if specialists provide intervention work within naturally occurring situations in the setting, rather than disrupting the curriculum and routines. So the speech therapist comes in to present a group activity to *all* the children or to interact conversationally or in a game with small groups during free play time, rather than coming in to remove the young child with special language needs for an individual therapy session. So, too, the physical therapist encourages all the children to try rolling on her giant ball, realizing that the participation of children without physical limitations may encourage the child with cerebral palsy to take part. Besides preventing disruption of the program's routine, including all children avoids sending the message to other children that the child is not really a member of their group. The early childhood educator is more likely to feel supported when the members of the special intervention team share the common framework and goals.

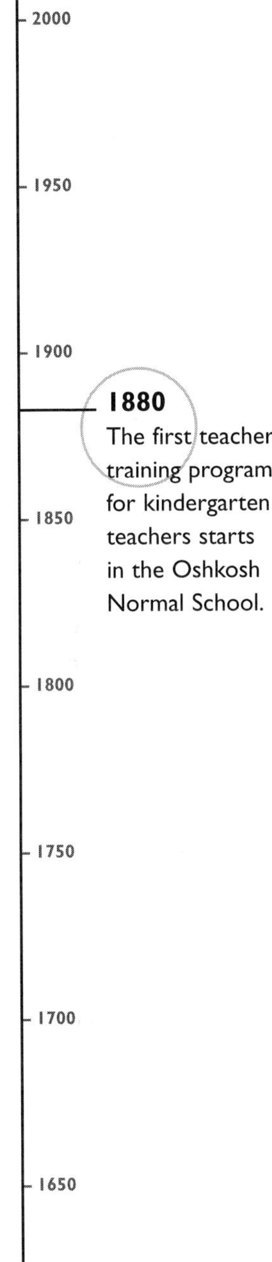

Effective inclusion programs use naturalistic teaching strategies within the context of daily routines. "Activity-based intervention" strategies involve the kinds of teaching we discussed earlier in our considerations of developmentally appropriate practice. When using these strategies, the early childhood educator plans appropriate active learning experiences by taking into account goals for individual children. Thus, a child who is using a variety of fasteners on the dress-up clothes is working on a fine-motor goal, and one who is invited to use the puppets is working on a language goal. Because each child's goals are addressed within the context of daily activities, early childhood educators have the responsibility of targeting goals, planning materials and activities to further those goals, and regularly assessing progress toward those goals. The planning cycle is part of good practice in every ECEC setting, no matter what the ability of each participating child. In integrated settings, early childhood educators, often with the assistance of other experts, plan modifications in the environment or activity to facilitate involvement of children with special needs.

As early childhood educators understand fully the implications of individualizing programs and curricula, they will see that the inclusion of children with special needs in early childhood settings is simply an extension of this developmentally appropriate practice of individualization. They will be supported in their efforts to help the children with special needs by the active, ongoing involvement of parents, special education teachers and interventionists, and administrators. There has been much learning about inclusion in the past ten years. As you enter the profession, your task is to continue learning how to provide education that respects the uniqueness of all children.

Antibias Curriculum

When you first work with young children in programs, you may find yourself working with children and families who look very much like you, having grown up in similar cultural and community settings, and with the same racial heritage,

MAKING IT HAPPEN

SpeciaLink—The National Centre for Child Care Inclusion

SpeciaLink puts researchers, policy makers, parents, early childhood educators and directors in touch with the inclusive practices in child care centres across Canada. Inclusive practices can be applied to all types of early child development programs. SpeciaLink is committed to the expansion of the quality and quantity of opportunities for inclusion in child care, recreation, education, and other community settings, for young children with special needs and their families.

Partnerships for Inclusion—Nova Scotia (Lero, Irwin & Darisi, 2006) reports on a new approach to inclusion *(Partnerships for Inclusion)* that combines assessment, on-site consultation, and the provision of resources and personal support to directors and early childhood educators in preschool rooms in licensed child care centres. The early findings point to improvements in program quality, staff attitudes about inclusion, and children's access to programs.

Source: http://www.specialinkcanada.org/home_en.html

religious beliefs, and historical traditions. However, given the diversity of the Canadian population, it is more probable that your early child development program will include families with varying structures, including two parents of different genders, two of the same gender, single parents of either gender, and families headed by grandparents, adoptive parents, or foster parents. There may be families of varying income and educational levels. There may be homeless families, families in which children are abused or neglected, and others in which children are well cared for. Families may represent one of any number of the religious, racial, and ethnic groups that live in Canada today. You may also work with children who are learning English as a second language. And, as we have just discussed, you may also work with children whose physical or mental abilities are delayed. But differences can make people uncomfortable, particularly when those differences seem threatening, as they do when no one talks about the reason for the differences, and about the similarities that exist along with the differences. This feeling of discomfort is exactly the rationale for discussions in the early education community about the need for an **antibias** curriculum in educating young children.

Very young children are busily constructing their own self-identity, as well as attitudes about that identity, by observing the ways they are different from and similar to other people and by absorbing the others' verbal and nonverbal messages about the differences. Young children construct self-identity and attitudes through the interaction of three factors:

- experience with their bodies. Children are exploring questions about what their bodies look like and how they are different from those of others.
- experience with their social environments. Children need to know about messages they get, either explicitly or implicitly, about the facts and differences they observe. They need to know about society's evaluation of those differences.

- cognitive functioning. Young children's methods of thinking produce some confused or illogical conclusions, such as the assumption that genital identification or colour might be open to change, or disability contagious.

In this process of identity, children need adults to help them explore some of their questions and curiosity about differences. We know that even very young children can perceive and uncritically absorb the negative messages about diversity in the world, and that these messages can be both powerful and harmful in producing bias. Prejudice and bias are destructive forces, and they can hurt all children.

On one hand, struggling against bias that declares a person inferior because of gender, race, ethnicity, or disability sucks energy from and undercuts a child's full development. On the other hand, learning to believe they are superior because they are white, or male, or able-bodied, dehumanizes and distorts reality for growing children (Derman-Sparks, 1989, p. ix).

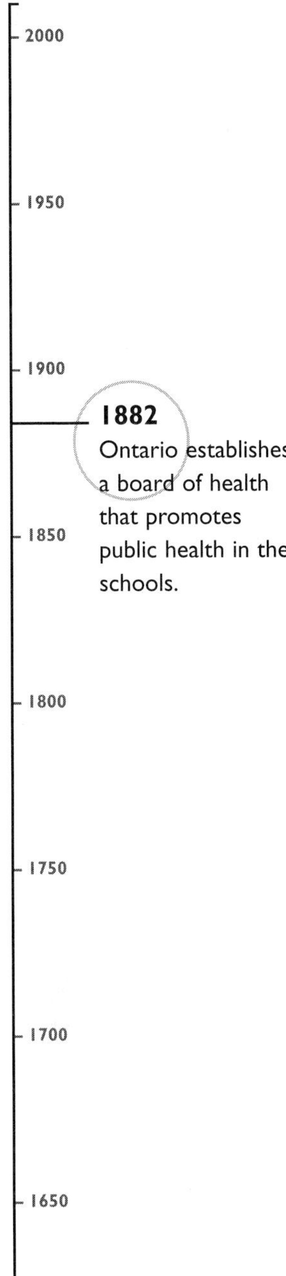

Children need adults who can help them develop positive attitudes about their own identity and that of others. They also need adults who can help them deal with the reality of the world, as well as show them that they can participate in changing ideas from the past to improve their future. The goals of the antibias curriculum are to enable all children "to construct a knowledgeable, confident self-identity; to develop comfortable, empathetic, and just interaction with diversity; and to develop critical thinking and the skills for standing up for oneself and others in the face of injustice" (Derman-Sparks, 1989, p. ix).

Those who see this work as an integral part of what early childhood educators do are quick to explain that the antibias curriculum is an aim and an approach that permeates the existing environment and curriculum, rather than something that is added on. It is looking at everything early childhood educators do and say and at the children's interaction and classroom life "through an antibias lens." The attitude of respect for all people that lies behind the antibias attitude is consistent with the sensitivity to individual children and families. Furthermore, cultural diversity and values are declared principles of early childhood education practice. But the thinking behind the antibias curriculum argues that it is important to go beyond respect and create an environment in which children can actively explore questions about disabilities, gender, and race, in order to understand differences, appreciate similarities, and recognize and confront biased ideas and behaviours.

A collaborative partnership between the School of Child and Youth Care at the University of Victoria and the Meadow Lake Tribal Council in Saskatchewan developed the generative curriculum to early childhood education (Ball, 2005; Pence, 2005). It is an approach that is consistent with contemporary and traditional indigenous values, experiences, and goals while also incorporating a sampling of child development research, theory, and practices. A generative curriculum draws as much as possible on the learner's experiences. It prepares early childhood educators to respect the cultures, wisdom, and values of families and communities. In Aboriginal communities, the Elders' understandings of the needs of children and families is incorporated into the curriculum. Children learn their indigenous language and culture.

MEET THE EARLY CHILDHOOD WORKFORCE

2000

1950

1900

1883

Concerns about preschool-age children being left unsupervised are brought to the Toronto School Board by its chief inspector, James L. Hughes.

G. Stanley Hall publishes "The Content of Children's Minds" in the *Princeton Review.*

The Toronto public school system may establish kindergartens on an optional basis.

1850

1800

1750

1700

1650

Zeenat Janmohamed, ECE Faculty, George Brown College, Toronto

Zeenat graduated from the Early Childhood Education diploma program at Seneca College in 1985. Since 1995, Zeenat has taught ECE students at George Brown College.

"Racism, sexism and class bias is economically, politically, educationally and institutionally produced. Teachers [college faculty] can help [ECE] students overcome these social barriers by engaging them in exploring different ways of resisting oppression. As an educator in a community college environment, I encourage students to challenge their understanding of the norm. In class discussions when I raise various forms of discrimination or prejudice, students often respond by talking about the importance of helping children "get along" and learning to accept all people regardless of difference . . . I challenge their common perceptions of people living on the street, new refugees, or gays and lesbians . . . In order for [ECE] students to articulate and understand systemic barriers, it is the responsibility of educators to create opportunities for transformation . . . .

"When [ECE] students are asked how they integrate anti-bias approaches in field placement, countless numbers have discussed the Spanish music they shared, or how they made fruit salad with 'exotic' fruit. In an effort to be inclusive and to encourage a pluralist approach to education, we have lost the opportunity to challenge the dominant culture ... Clearly a more strategic process in the discourse of anti-racism education needs to develop so that students with early childhood diplomas do not limit their experience to simulated or mock celebrations of Diwali and Hannukah. Instead of focusing on festivals, there needs to be a greater emphasis on the diverse child rearing practices which go beyond the dominant Western understanding of child development."

Source: Janmohamed (2001). Unpublished paper, pp. 20–27.

In other reading, you will likely come across the term "**multicultural** curriculum." This refers to teaching children about other people's cultures, in the hope that they will learn to respect one another and not develop prejudice. This positive intent is obviously similar to the antibias approach, but those who practise the antibias curriculum suggest that the multicultural approach too frequently deteriorates into a "tourist curriculum" (Derman-Sparks, 1989, p. 7). This negative outcome results from presenting other cultures as exotic and foreign, with different food, holiday celebrations, clothing, and so on, rather than dealing with people's real-life experiences. "Children 'visit' non-White cultures, and then 'go home' to the daily classroom, which reflects only the dominant culture" (Derman-Sparks, 1989, p. 7). The danger here is that such experiences fail to communicate real understanding, and stereotypes about differences may actually be reinforced. In addition, the multicultural curriculum usually focuses on other countries—for example, China or Mexico—rather than on the diverse people in our own country whom children actually come in contact with. The antibias approach tries to avoid some of the dangers of this tourist approach. It retains some of the positive ideas from the multicultural curriculum and, at the same time, includes more than just cultural diversity. An antibias curriculum addresses ability, age, and gender differences, as well as the problem of stereotypical or biased behaviour in children's interactions.

There are those who feel that it is beyond the capacity of young children to absorb these concepts. Yet others feel that young children are themselves interested in questions about diversity, and that they may exhibit fearful or prejudiced behaviour when they are not encouraged to understand differences in a positive way.

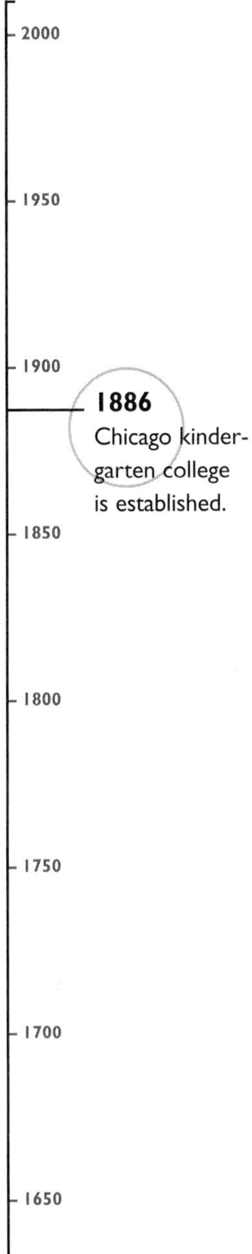

How do early childhood educators prepare themselves to deal with antibias issues with young children? A first and ongoing step is to confront their own attitudes and discomforts, to become aware of how their own identities and attitudes were formed by early experiences. This is a process that may bring pain as well as awareness, but it helps early childhood educators identify their prejudices, which need to be uncovered before they will be able to do antibias work with children.

Early childhood educators then examine their environments, materials, and curriculum activities to find and eliminate stereotypical messages, messages of omission, and to answer the question "What am I currently doing in the curriculum about gender/race/culture/different physical abilities/stereotyping and discriminatory behaviour?" They observe the children and discover the issues in the community that affect their lives, as well as learning the family and community resources for specific antibias activities. Early childhood educators watch for opportunities when children's spoken and unspoken questions show that they need help to understand differences or to be supported in confronting unfair treatment.

Such examinations help early childhood educators discover the steps they will take to slowly make their classrooms into environments where diversity is accepted, and where children know they can explore these important issues with supportive adults. Early childhood educators and parents work together to explore how to handle sensitive and emotional issues, such as how to celebrate holidays, which holidays to celebrate, or whether holidays should be celebrated at all in early education programs. These are deeply felt concerns, and it is through dialogue that adults support one another to help children develop healthy self-identity and attitudes of acceptance of diversity. As Canada's diversity grows, children will be empowered and enriched to interact comfortably with those whose lives, appearance, and experiences are unlike their own. Issues raised in the discussion of multicultural and antibias education free all early childhood educators to find new and positive answers. Involve yourself in these dialogues in later reading, course work, and experiences. We will all benefit.

RESEARCH INTO PRACTICE

Activities to Raise Early Childhood Educator Consciousness of Biases

Sample activities for early childhood educator consciousness-raising:

- Talk about your earliest memories related to your understanding of your ethnic/racial identity, your gender identity, your family's social class, and your physical abilities and limitations. What was good or difficult as you learned about these aspects of your identity?
- Discuss how you agree or disagree with your parents' views on race, gender, social class, ethnicity, and physical abilities. If you disagree, how did your own ideas develop?
- Take a popular European fairy tale (such as *Snow White* or *The Three Bears*) and rewrite it, switching the characters' genders.
- Describe an incidence of racism or sexism that you have encountered in your daily life. What actions did you take? What would you like to do differently?

Sources: Adapted from Derman-Sparks (1989) and Kilbride (1997).

Technology in Early Education

There was a time, not long ago, when there was almost universal horror at the mention of computers and young children in the same sentence. The image of children sitting in front of computer screens suggested a passive learning mode. Most felt that this passive mode conflicted with the idea that children construct their understandings of the world by manipulating objects and actively interacting with others within their environments. It was felt that the computer screen could offer only two-dimensional symbolic representation, instead of the sensory experience and social interaction needed for real early childhood learning.

Today's young children are growing up in a landscape of interactive media. Television and computers have extended their target audience programming down to infancy. Programs such as *Teletubbies* and *Baby Einstein* are designed to appeal to babies and toddlers and a myriad of others are targeted to preschoolers. Although interactive media permeate children's lives, their effects are not well understood (Cleveland et al., 2006).

Empirical research on the effects of interactive media on young children is still thin; at the same time, technology continues to evolve and pervade children's lives.

- Researchers have studied whether media in itself, usually television, was good or bad for children. Its education potential was acknowledged as well as the impact of inappropriate content and its colonization of play and other *real* experience. As the pace of technological change quickens, descriptive studies of young children and technology context are likely to be outdated in a matter of a few years.
- Researchers have also focused on the amount of time children spend watching television, and, to a lesser extent, to the time they spend on the Internet and

playing video games. Higher television viewing has been associated with higher literacy achievement in preschoolers from low SES families but not for children who are advantaged (Searls, Mead & Ward, 1985). Perhaps that is because children from all backgrounds watch more educational programs when they are under six with the highest levels of viewing among two- to three-year-olds (Wright et al., 2000). At this age, children are less likely to be involved in an ELCC program and therefore may watch television more.

- Generally, children six and under spend about two hours a day on screen media—television, computers, and video games. Children as young as two to three years old are reported to spend an average of twenty minutes a day on the computer (Rideout, Vandewater, & Wartella, 2003). Even at this age, boys spend more time on video games than do girls although there are no differences in their engagement with other screen media. As with television, children under six play more educational video and computer games than do older children. Socioeconomic gaps with regard to home access to various media exist, but are narrowing (US Department of Commerce, 2002).
- The effect of technology on learning is inconclusive. From more than fifty years of television research, we know that content is significant. In other words, children learn from high-quality television programs, do not benefit particularly from solely entertainment content, and may be harmed by violent content. (Houston, 2004).
- There has been much concern about the negative impact of violence and other inappropriate content in screen media. The literature shows a positive link between violent interactive media such as video games and aggressive behaviour (Anderson & Bushman, 2001), and also, that there is an increase in effectors over time, that is, the games are becoming more violent and also affecting children more (Anderson & Bushman, 2001; Sherry 2001).
- Research on interactivity and learning is mixed. The nature of interactivity itself is not well understood; nor are the specific aspects of interactivity that support learning. Research on the effects of *talking books* on literacy in young children is mixed. While some aspects of literacy seemed to be supported (phonological awareness), others (word reading) did not (Chera & Wood, 2003). Young children are attracted to the interactive elements in talking books but this can interfere with their interest in decoding text and understanding of the story (deJong & Bus, 2002).

Considering how technology might be used in parenting-support programs, some of the effective parenting programs have used video as a supplement to training. Direct comparisons suggest a combination of video and face-to-face training work best. Broader ways of educating parents through new forms of information communication technology have not yet appeared in the mainstream research literature on early childhood. Given the challenges of Canadian geography, the potential for "virtual face-to-face groups and modeling" could be explored in extending some of the successful group training/centre-based programs developed in urban settings. In looking to the future, it should be noted that the research literature to date does not address how parents might interact with their young children using ICT to foster learning.

1887
The Montreal Day Nursery program opens.

Ontario becomes the first jurisdiction in the world to officially recognize kindergarten as part of the elementary school system.

Should preschool children learn to use computers?

Early childhood educators are currently attempting to come to terms with the idea that **technology** can be an effective and interesting additional choice in the early childhood education and care (ECEC) curriculum. Indeed, sometimes it is their own "technophobia" that causes early childhood educators to dismiss computers so abruptly. In fact, research and observation of children using computers suggests that computers offer children another way to play, enhancing social, emotional, and cognitive development. To ensure that computers in early childhood classrooms support ideas of developmentally appropriate practice and nurture overall child development, it is helpful to keep certain assumptions about computers in mind:

- Computer use is a social activity.
- Computer use is a child-initiated and child-directed activity.
- Computer software is selected so that it allows children to explore, experiment, and solve problems.
- Computers are one of many materials in a classroom (adapted from Davidson & Wright, 1994).

In fact, while adults are struggling to keep up and feel comfortable with technology, young children accept it as a normal part of their environment. Observers note that they are quite comfortable with computers, exhibiting curiosity, rather than fear, when given a new software program. Much recent research indicates that children's learning on computers is generally positive. Children have increased opportunities for social interaction, as many prefer to work with one or two partners, rather than alone, and will more often request help from peers than from the teacher.

There are also high levels of spoken communication and cooperation at the computer. "They interact more frequently and in different ways than they interact when engaged with traditional activities, such as puzzles or blocks. Whereas in sociodramatic play there tends to be a 'leader' of communication, children share leadership roles on the computer" (Clements, 1994, p. 43). Computer use has also been shown to enhance children's belief in their own competency and their enthusiasm for academic subjects such as reading (Orabuchi, in Clements, 1994).

The benefits of computers depend on the kind of software children use and its developmental appropriateness for young children's thinking abilities. Much research has also been done recently on this aspect of technology (see lists and discussion in Wright & Shade, 1994, and Hohmann, Carmody, & McCabe-Branz, 1995). The following criteria for appropriate computer programs suggest overall principles of developmentally appropriate practice:

- Children can use the program independently, without asking for help, no matter what their reading ability.
- Children can control the pace and direction of the program.
- Children have opportunities to explore a number of concepts on different levels.
- Children receive prompt feedback and feel successful.
- There is multisensory capacity for children's natural learning style.
- The program is enjoyable, fun to use, and takes imagination to explore (Bowman & Beyer, 1994).

Another caution regarding the use of technology is that inequities must not be repeated. Girls and boys from all ethnocultural and linguistic backgrounds must be encouraged to use computer software and develop their technological skills. Therefore, the context of the software cannot contain any gender, racial, or cultural biases. All children must feel comfortable and included in the images and actions created by the software. Technology may also be very useful for young children with special needs (Behrmann & Lahn, 1994) by offering alternative communication systems to some children with communication disorders. Children who have difficulty with fine motor coordination (needed for printing and writing) may benefit from using a keyboard instead.

It appears probable that technology will be used increasingly in early childhood programs. You will have opportunities during your program of professional preparation to explore these issues in depth and to discuss how much computers can offer in active learning environments.

SUMMARY

Early childhood education and care programs include a variety of curriculum and pedagogical approaches. Issues currently under discussion—such as academics and the related issues of "readiness" and achievement testing, inclusion, the antibias curriculum, mixed-age groupings, and technology in early childhood settings—directly affect the kinds of programs offered to young children. Other issues will present themselves as you continue your studies and enter the dynamic and developing field of early child development.

REVIEW QUESTIONS

1. Describe different types of approaches to the early child development curriculum.
2. Describe some of the issues related to early academics, readiness, and achievement testing.
3. Discuss what is meant by "inclusion," and list the benefits for the children and adults who are part of integrated early education classrooms.
4. Describe what is meant by an "antibias curriculum" and the rationale for it. How does an antibias approach differ from a multicultural approach?
5. Identify what is meant by "mixed-age groupings" in early education and some of the advantages for children and adults.
6. Describe current thinking about the appropriateness of using technology in the classroom in early education.

STUDY ACTIVITIES

1. Visit an early child development program that is implementing a specific curriculum approach.
2. Go to www.ece.nelson.com and search for information about Reggio Emilia.
3. Visit an early child development setting in your community that includes young children with special learning or developmental needs. Discuss with the early childhood educators the advantages and disadvantages for the children and adults involved. Describe any obvious modifications that have been made in the physical environment to meet the needs of children, and explain why these alterations were made. List any other specialists involved in planning and therapy for the children.
4. Go to the library and find several books that an early childhood educator could use to help raise children's awareness and positive acceptance of diversity in various forms. Share these books with fellow classmates. There is a helpful list in Derman-Sparks's book to get you started.
5. Learn if your community has any early childhood programs or mixed-age groupings in the school system. If so, try to visit a class to observe the children's interactions and the differences in learning environment and curriculum that distinguish the programs.
6. Try to observe young children using computers—maybe in the children's section of your local library or large bookstore. How does the software encourage creativity, problem-solving and logical thinking, social interaction, and independence? What questions about technology does this observation suggest to you for further study?
7. Find out how many languages are spoken by students in your class. Brainstorm with each other about how this resource could be used in your community.

KEY TERMS

absorbent mind: Phrase used by Montessori to describe the active, natural learning style of children in their first years.

antibias curriculum: Philosophical approach developed by Louise Derman-Sparks according to which classroom practices and materials are to be used that foster each child's (1) construction of a knowledgeable, confident self-identity; (2) comfortable, empathetic interactions with diverse people; (3) critical thinking about bias; and (4) ability to stand up for him- or herself and others in the face of bias.

cooperative learning: Learning in which environments and activities are structured so that children can work together.

curriculum: Every learning experience that happens in an early childhood setting, including planned and spontaneous activities and interactions.

developmentally appropriate practice (DAP): NAEYC-defined standards that base teaching practices on age-level standards for children's abilities and on observations for individual differences, including abilities, interests, and cultures.

didactic: Usually refers to materials that teach because they are inherently self-correcting. Montessori developed many didactic materials.

direct instruction: A pedagogical strategy that is initiated by adults and focuses on a specific learning objective to be mastered by the child.

early academics: The introduction of academic content and teaching methods to children before the primary grades.

emergent curriculum: Early childhood educators follow children's leads by observing their interests and needs and then planning the learning environment.

emergent literacy: Awareness of the meaning of print that develops before early reading and writing.

emergent numeracy: Awareness of the meaning of numbers that precedes ability to use numbers in simple computations.

High/Scope: Curriculum based on Piagetian cognitive principles, developed after the Perry study model.

inclusion: Placement of individuals with special needs in classrooms with typically developing individuals, and in which special services are provided within the classroom setting.

key experiences: Eight important cognitive components of the High/Scope curriculum.

mainstreaming: This term is now less frequently used than "inclusion."

mixed-age groupings: Arrangements that group children together across several ages and frequently keep them together for two or more years, rather than separating them by chronological age.

Montessori schools: Schools based on the philosophy of Maria Montessori that, as such, emphasize sensory learning, practical life skills, and didactic materials.

multicultural: Curriculum that teaches awareness of the diversity of cultures and of cultural experience.

National Association for the Education of Young Children (NAEYC): Largest early childhood professional organization in the United States, established in 1926. Current membership over 90 000. Source of position statements on developmentally appropriate practice, code of ethics, etc.

pedagogy: Deliberate process of cultivating development and learning that is closely linked to curriculum.

philosophy: One's beliefs and attitude. Related to early childhood education, one's ideas about how children learn, and how early childhood educators teach.

plan, do, review: Basic methods of the High/Scope cognitive curriculum, in which children make activity choices with teachers' assistance, and then carry out the activity and report on it.

practical life skills: Skills used in daily life, such as washing dishes and sweeping floors. Part of the Montessori curriculum.

readiness: State of being ready. Used in early childhood education, the term indicates a child's ability to learn particular tasks. Readiness tests are frequently used to determine readiness for kindergarten and/or Grade One academic learning.

Reggio Emilia: Early childhood programs in Reggio Emilia, Italy, that are world famous for their child-centred and extensive project approach to learning.

Scaffolding: Process of providing guidance that allows a child to master a concept or skill that he or she could not yet learn alone but can learn with support.

sensitive period: Term used by Montessori to indicate time of readiness for particular learning.

sequential steps: Predictable patterns of development and learning.

special education: Branch of professional study that centres on techniques for working with children with special needs.

standardized tests: Assessment techniques using results accumulated for large groups of children, producing standards or norms for evaluating children's successful learning.

technology: Refers to the knowledge that drives today's machines, particularly computers.

SUGGESTED READINGS

Early Academics, Readiness, and Testing

Bredekamp, Sue, & Rosegrant, Teresa (Eds.). (1992). *Reaching potentials: Appropriate curriculum and assessment for young children.* Washington, DC: NAEYC.

Charlesworth, Rosalind. (1989, March). Behind before they start? Deciding how to deal with the risk of kindergarten failure. *Young Children,* 44 (3), 5–13.

Kamii, C. (1990). *Achievement testing in the early grades: The games grownups play.* Washington, DC: NAEYC.

Meisels, S. (1987, January). Uses and abuses of developmental screening and school readiness testing. *Young Children,* 42 (2), 4–6, 68–73.

Puckett, M., & Black, J. (1994). *Authentic assessment of the young child: Celebrating development and learning.* New York: Merrill.

Inclusion

Canning, M. & Lyon, P. (1990). Young children with special needs. In I. Doxey (Ed.), *Child care and education: Canadian dimensions.* Scarborough, ON: ITP Nelson, 254–68.

Lero, D., Irwin, S. & Darisi, T, K. (2006). *Partnerships for Inclusion—Nova Scotia: An evaluation based on the first cohort of child care centres.* Guelph: Centre for Families, Work and Well-being.

Rose, D. F. & Smith, B. (1993, May). Preschool mainstreaming: Attitude barriers and strategies for addressing them. *Young Children,* 48 (4), 59–62.

The SpeciaLink Newsletters from SpeciaLink: The National Child Care Inclusion Network P.O. Box 775, Sydney, NS B1P 6G9.

Spodek, Bernard & Saracho, Olivia N. (1994). *Dealing with individual differences in the early childhood classroom.* New York: Longman.

Widerstrom, A. H. (1986, December). Educating young handicapped children: What can early childhood education contribute? *Childhood Education,* 63, 78–83.

Wolery, Mark, Holcombe, Ariane, Venn, Martha L., Brookfield, Jeffri, Huffman, Kay, Schroeder, Carol, Martin, Catherine G., & Fleming, Lucy A. (1993, November). Mainstreaming in early childhood programs: Current status and relevant issues. *Young Children*, 49 (1), 78–84.

Antibias Curriculum

Bernhard, J., Lefebvre, M., Chud, G., & Lange, R. (1995). *Path to equity: Cultural, linguistic, and racial diversity in Canadian early childhood education*. Toronto: York Lanes Press, Inc.

Chud, G. (1993, Summer). Anti-bias education: An approach for today and tomorrow. *Interaction*, 18–20.

Clark, Leilani, DeWolf, Sheridan, & Clark, Carl. (1992, July). Teaching teachers to avoid having culturally assaultive classrooms. *Young Children*, 47 (5), 42–49.

Gonzalez-Menza, J. (1993). *Multicultural issues in child care*. Mountainview, CA: Mayfield Publishing Co.

Jones, Elizabeth, & Derman-Sparks, Louise. (1992, January). Meeting the challenge of diversity. *Young Children*, 47 (2), 12–17.

Kilbride, K. (1997). *Include me too! Human diversity in early childhood education*. Toronto: Harcourt Brace.

Pacini-Ketchabaw, & McIvor, O. (2005). Negotiating bilingualism in early childhood—A study of immigrant families and early childhood practitioners. *Research Connection Canada: Supporting Children and Families* 13. 109–126.

Sheldon, Amy. (1990, January). Kings are royaler than queens: Language and socialization. *Young Children*, 45 (2), 4–9. Contact: Early Childhood Multicultural Services, Third Floor, 210 West Broadway, Vancouver, BC V5Y 3W2.

Mixed-Age Grouping

Corson, P. (2005). Multi-age grouping in early childhood education: An alternative discourse. *Research Connections Canada*, 13, p 93–108.

Stone, Sandra. (1994/1995, Winter). Strategies for teaching children in multiage classrooms. *Childhood Education*, 71 (2), 102–05.

Theilheimer, Rachel. (1993, July). Something for everyone: Benefits of mixed-age grouping for children, parents, and teachers. *Young Children*, 48 (5), 82–87.

Technology

Clements, Douglas H., Nastasi, Bonnie K., & Swaminathan, Sudha. (1993, January). Young children and computers: Crossroads and directions from research. *Young Children*, 48 (2), 56–64.

Clements, Douglas H., & Swaminathan, Sudha. (1995). Technology and school change: New lamps for old? *Childhood Education, Annual Theme Issue*, 71 (5), 275–81.

Wartella, E., Caplovitz, A., & Lee, J. (2004) *From Einstein to Leapfrog, from Doom to the Sims, from instant messaging to internet chat rooms.* Social Policy Report, Volume XVIII, Number IV. Society for Research in Child Development.

Wright, June L., & Shade, Daniel D. (Eds.). (1994). *Young children: Active learners in a technological age.* Washington, DC: NAEYC.NEL.

CHAPTER THREE
Quality in Early Child Development Programs

OBJECTIVES

After studying this chapter, students will be able to

- discuss several specific components of quality in early childhood programs;
- describe specific program and policy decisions that exemplify each component;
- identify dynamic, framework, and context components of quality; and
- identify several components that are not found in quality programs.

Quality in early childhood settings takes many forms and has unique faces. Yet there are specific descriptions that can be applied no matter what the age group or population served or the structure of the program. It may seem a daunting task to describe and recognize factors that denote quality in early childhood programs. Indeed, it is a task that researchers, scholars, and commissions have laboured over for years, and their combined efforts still precipitate spirited debate. To some extent, the difficulty is that quality is often defined subjectively. If you have visited sites of early child development programs, you have likely been attracted to (or dismayed by) some space in the room or some activity that resonated with meaning for you, often for subconscious reasons.

But standards for quality must go beyond subjective opinion, to find their basis in concrete and observable phenomena that can be discussed and explained. In this chapter, we will explore some of the specific components of quality in early education and describe how these components may manifest themselves. You will be asked to actively consider each component as we move through the discussion, to help you as you begin to construct your own standards of quality in early education. In later course work, you will learn more about how early childhood educators create the environments that allow excellent education to occur; for now, it is important that you begin to evaluate child care and learning environments.

Thinking about Quality

High-quality early child care and education can be defined from many perspectives, including those of children, parents, early childhood educators, researchers, employers, and the community. When parents are asked to describe what they are looking for in a program for their children, they often list health and safety as their primary concerns. In a recent U.S. study of quality in family child care and relative care, both mothers and caregivers identified health and safety as prime concerns, as well as communication with the family child care provider and the provider's warmth and attention to the child (Galinsky et al., 1994). Early childhood educators, on the other hand, are likely to define a high-quality program as one that

- "supports and assists the child's physical, emotional, social, language, and intellectual development"; and
- "supports and complements the family in its child-rearing role" (CCCF, 1991, in Doherty-Derkowski, 1995, p. 4).

Katz (1993) directs us to consider five different but interrelated perspectives as we consider quality in an early childhood program. The perspectives she describes are those of experts, children participating in early childhood settings, parents who are using early child development services for their children, early childhood educators and other caregivers who work directly with young children to provide early child development programs, and the community or society at large.

- The expert perspective is a *top-down* perspective that examines measurable and quantifiable characteristics, such as adult-child ratios and training of early childhood educators, which set the stage for excellent early childhood education to occur. Many of these things are defined and regulation requirements discussed in this and later chapters. It is important to recognize the correlation between these factors and quality.
- The children's perspective is a *bottom-up* perspective that describes the quality of life experienced by children within the program. This perspective is obtained when adults take children's perspective; propose whether program practices would help children feel individually welcomed and securely accepted within a program; and find engaging, challenging, and absorbing learning experiences. As we think about stories of children in various early child development programs, we draw conclusions about how those settings would affect children's lives.
- The viewpoint of staff members (early childhood educators and others) is the *inside* perspective. Job satisfaction and retention of qualified personnel over time has a major impact on quality. As we consider the components of quality, think about how early childhood educators would perceive their work if these components were either present or absent.
- The parents' perspective, or the *outside-inside* perspective, considers the quality and impact of relationships between early childhood educators and families. The elements crucial from the perspective of parents are mutual respect and relationships that allow early childhood educators to create caring and learning environments that are individually responsive to children.
- The community or society perspective is the *outside* perspective, which describes the relationship between the early childhood program and its community and the larger society beyond. As programs respond to community needs and expectations, and as social decisions and support mesh, good things can happen for children and families.

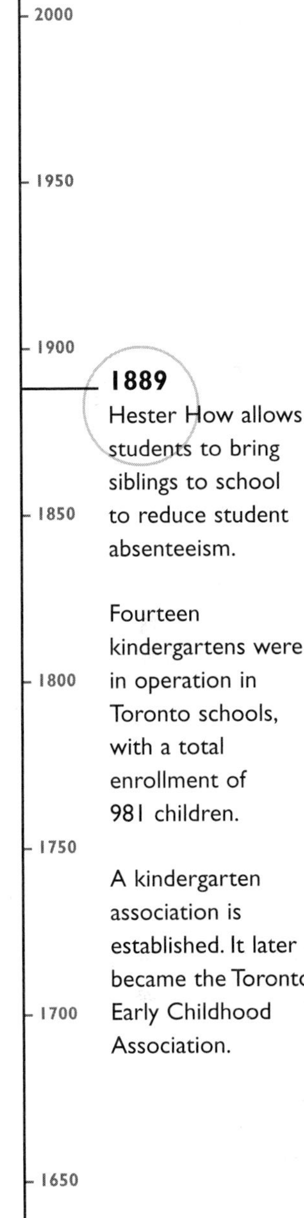

Early childhood educators need to be aware of the complex **interrelationships** of all participants when considering quality. There are differences in what is important in quality early child development programs and questions of when one view should be given more weight than another. The values and beliefs that shape perceptions of quality vary in different cultural contexts.

Gillian Doherty (2000) reviewed the "reality of multiple perspectives" on quality and suggests that the level of quality in a particular early child development program depends on who is making the judgment. Doherty states that it is important to recognize that there are different perspectives and to move away from a judgment of quality that is defined by experts only, without the input of other stakeholders. She does conclude that "there appears to be agreement that there are some values that are so critical to the well-being of children that they should be a core part of any definition of quality" (2000, p. 4). These values are

Sensitivity to children's interests, worries, and passions is central to definition of quality early childhood education and care environments.

- safe care;
- healthful care;
- individualized care that promotes equal opportunity;
- care that provides developmentally appropriate stimulation;
- care that is characterized by positive interaction with adults;
- care that encourages individual emotional growth; and
- care that promotes positive relationships with other children.

Doherty cautions us to keep in mind that there are many ways to carry out these universal values. Our responses can and should vary to reflect our own cultural realities and those of the children and families we work with in early child development settings. "Understanding and ensuring quality involves a continuous process of reconciling the perspectives of different stakeholders within the broader context of universal values. It is not a prescriptive exercise" (Doherty, 2000 p. 5).

Be aware of your own perspective on what is essential in a high-quality early child development program as you consider the research on this subject. Your perspective may be challenged or reinforced. Your ideas about quality will most likely change as your knowledge and skills broaden. Pay attention and be aware of the changes.

A Bird's-Eye View of Quality

Let's look at several ECEC settings to see if our quick glance can yield first clues about quality.

Robin's family child care home. Robin Ferguson, a thirty-two-year-old mother of two school-age children and a three-year-old, cares for her own toddler along with another three-year-old, one two-year-old, and eight-month-old twins in her comfortable home in a small subdivision. She has cared for children at home since her older two were babies.

This morning finds the three-year-olds busy playing in the family room that adjoins the large kitchen. One of them is playing with baby dolls in an area with child-sized kitchen furniture, and one is stringing beads and spools. The child with the beads wanders into the kitchen, where Robin is feeding breakfast to one of the babies, while the other infant sits near her on the floor, fitting cups into each other. Robin helps the bead-stringer tie the beads into a necklace. When he tries to slip the necklace onto the baby on the floor, who protests weakly, Robin redirects him in a conversation admiring the beads, and then changes the topic to the bird feeder on the deck that they filled the day before. The baby on the floor is still unhappy, and Robin gently talks with her as she continues to feed the baby's brother. When this does not soothe her, Robin puts out some Cheerios for the baby she had been feeding in the highchair, rolls the highchair to the doorway, where she can keep an eye on that baby, and scoops up the crying baby. She takes her to the changing table in the family room, commenting to the child playing with the doll that she has to change the baby, and wonders if she has to change her baby, too. She keeps her eyes on the baby's face as she changes the diaper, although her soft conversation includes the older child, as well as the other older child, who has wandered into the room. At Robin's suggestion, he comes over to join her as she sings to the baby, who is now grinning cheerfully.

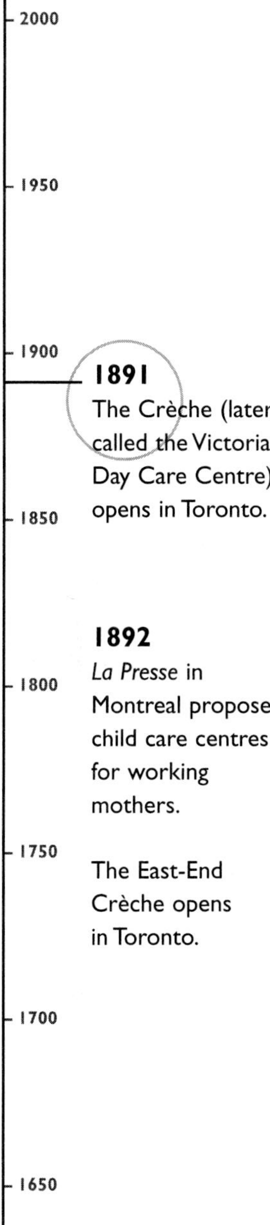

Sam Cooper's K/1 classroom. Sam Cooper teaches in a class that includes five- to seven-year-olds in a public elementary school. During the few minutes that we are in his large, attractive classroom, we see a number of groups, containing three to five children, busy in several areas in the classroom. Three children are talking to one another as they puzzle over a computer game. Four boys are sitting at a round table, busy with notebooks, crayons, pencils, and markers. One boy explains to us that they are writing in their journals. Sam arrives and responds to one child's comment about his work with a specific and enthusiastic response that indicates his familiarity with the child's story. He encourages another child to share his idea with another, and he suggests to a third child that his friend might help him figure out the spelling for the word he asked about.

Sam's glance searches the room, and he moves over to two girls who are in heated discussion about balancing objects on the scale. Sam does not interrupt, listening seriously to each contribution, nodding thoughtfully and supportively, then asking a question. As the girls seem to move into cooperative activity, Sam looks around at other busy children. He notices a child standing by the bookshelf, moves over to discuss his selection, and speaks with him quietly, finally leaving him after giving him a pat and a smile. A child and an adult enter the classroom. Sam moves over to greet them both, and he engages in relaxed conversation with the parent, who seems equally relaxed with Sam. Sam gives the children a prearranged signal to gather at the meeting carpet; the parent has been invited in advance to conduct a mini-lesson about American Sign Language, since the children are interested right now in different methods of communication.

Maia Chen's toddlers. Maia Chen is one of two early childhood educators for a group of ten children aged fourteen months to twenty-four months in a church-sponsored child care centre in a large city. We find them playing outdoors. Maia has added several large, sturdy cartons to their usual playground equipment of climber, low slide, large sand area, and three small swings. Four of the toddlers have climbed into the biggest box; Maia sits near them, commenting on their activity. "You climbed right in the big box, didn't you, Justin? Sarah's in the box with you. Oh my, here comes DuJawn, he's climbing in with you. D.H. thinks there's room too—maybe if you scoot over a bit. Look at that—four children in the box. And jumping, too. It's a jumping box." The children laugh with excitement, and Maia joins in. A shriek from the sandbox gets her immediate attention. "Oh, Derek, that looks uncomfortable. I think Jennifer's trying to tell you that you're crowding her," she says as one toddler attempts to sit where another child already sits. "How about we find a space for you to dig over here? There—now you both can make big holes. Let me see—oh, that hole *is* getting big." Meanwhile, Maia's colleague is pushing three children on the swing, and another child climbs repeatedly up the steps and slides down the slide, never far from Maia's gaze and encouraging smile. Maia reaches into her pocket and pulls out a notebook, in which she jots down two words of a brief observation that she will expand later, and turns to the children who are now pushing the boxes around the playground.

Three early childhood programs, three early childhood educators, and their children, all serving to illustrate some of the components of excellence. Some fundamental concepts lie behind the practice of each of these early childhood educators. Think about it: What has each educator done that seems excellent to you?

Defining Quality for Early Childhood Educators

Standards for quality early child development programs have been defined by several professional organizations. These are important resources with which to become familiar as you learn more about early education.

Later in this chapter we will turn to the national statement on standards for quality early child development programs published by the CCCF in 2000. We will also look at the **position statement** published by the NAEYC in 1987, since this is the most widely acknowledged standard for quality in accrediting early childhood programs in the United States and has influenced Canadian perspectives on quality. But, first, we will examine the components of quality in the vignettes just described. These same components will be found in any excellent early child development program and are supported by considerable research and consensus among early childhood educators.

Dynamic components. These are the child's daily experiences that are based on the relationships children develop with adults and other children. Dynamic components define the nature of the interactions and activities that early childhood educators, children, and their families engage in each day.

Framework components. These are the structural elements that define the social and physical environment in ECEC settings. These elements are important because they also influence the quality of the dynamic components. The actual practice of early childhood educators can benefit or suffer depending on the framework—the number of children, the kind of physical space, the types of play materials and activities available, and the level of knowledge and understanding early childhood educators have of child development.

Context components. These are elements outside the immediate ECEC environment that influence both the framework and the dynamic components of quality. Organizational climate, funding that determines wages and benefits, regulations, sponsorship, and auspice create the structure of the social and physical environment. In turn, they also set the stage for how early childhood educators relate and connect with children and their families.

In quality programs, these components are interrelated and, sometimes, indefinable as separate entities. But we shall try to identify them individually. As we go through this chapter, keep your pencil and notebook handy. You will be asked to think about your own knowledge and experience with the components of quality. Take your time to see what you already know about good early childhood programs.

RESEARCH INTO PRACTICE

Canadian Child Care and Quality

Recent research findings confirm that the quality of children's early environments influences their developmental trajectories. Increased awareness about the importance of the early years places the question of the quality of early childhood programs in general and child care in particular, under a bright spotlight (McCain & Mustard, 1999; Beach & Bertrand, 2000; NICHD, 2000; OECD, 2001). While family environments have a larger impact on child development, experiences in child care and other early childhood experiences do affect developmental outcomes as well as immediate and long-term coping skills and competencies (Cleveland & Krashinsky, 1998; Doherty, 2000; NICHD, 2000; Brooks-Gunn, 2003; Smart Start Evaluation Team, 2003; Beach et al., 2004; Sure Start Research Team, 2005).

Recent findings from Canadian studies are not encouraging. Reports indicate that Canada's child care programs range from programs that support optimal early child development to ones that offer mediocre, custodial services to meet children's basic physical needs.

- The 1998 You Bet I Care! (YBIC) Canadian study of child care staff and quality in child care centres used standardized measures of quality to assess 122 infant toddler rooms and 227 preschool rooms in 234 centres across six provinces and one territory (Goelman, Doherty, Lero, LaGrange, & Tougas, 2000). They assessed curriculum, environment, adult-child interactions, teaching practices, and support improvements to the quality of programs. The findings reveal that the majority of centres provided physically safe environments with caring adults. Only 44.3 percent of preschool rooms and 28.7 percent of toddler and infant rooms offered activities and adult interactions that enhance early learning.
- The You Bet I Care! study of regulated family child care (Doherty, Lero, Goelman, Toguas, & LaGrange, 2000) collected data from 231 regulated family child caregivers across six provinces and one territory. Similar to child care centre staff, family child caregivers typically provided physically safe environments with caring staff, but only 36.8 percent provided stimulating activities. The quality tended to be lower for infants under eighteen months.

(cont'd)

Canadian Child Care and Quality (cont'd)

- An international team of early childhood experts reviewed early childhood education and care programs in six provinces in 2003 (OECD, 2004). They reported that quality in Canada's child care programs was decidedly inadequate. However, the review also pointed to some exemplary quality practices and programs in child care and other early childhood programs.
- A study of Quebec-regulated child care settings in 2003 (home-based and centre-based) reported that overall, 26 percent were good quality; 61 percent were mediocre; and 13 percent were poor quality (Japel et al., 2005).

Dynamics of Quality

The central element in the dynamics of early child development programs is the early childhood educator and what she believes, knows, and is, as a person. This is an important idea to state at the outset, because all of the dimensions in early childhood settings radiate from this basic premise. No matter how good the administration, the education system or philosophy, or the community support, everything of crucial importance in the learning and caring environment comes from the decisions and actions of the early childhood educator. Some of these components are based in attitudes, values, and ideas, and some are based in areas of knowledge. But *all* translate into specific actions the early childhood educator takes that have far-reaching implications for everyone involved. What an astonishing, humbling thought for all of us drawn to consider caring for and educating young children.

The basic components, which we will discuss separately, include the three R's: **respect** for the uniqueness of individuals, **responsiveness** to children's and family's needs, and **reciprocity** of learning interaction.

Respect

To respect someone is to honour and to show consideration and esteem for that person. All of these phrases suggest that respect is a genuine regard for, and sensitivity to, self and others. How does respect manifest itself in an early child development setting?

Respect for children and families. There are several key considerations in respecting children. The principles of developmentally appropriate practice, as stated by the Canadian Child Care Federation (CCCF) (1991), the National Association for the Education of Young Children (NAEYC) (see Bredekamp, 1990), the **Association of Childhood Education International (ACEI)** (Isenberg & Quisenberry, 1988), as well as by other early childhood organizations, emphasize the uniqueness of each child as a crucial determinant in early education and care. The different interests, abilities, talents, and styles of learning, the range of developmental differences within children, as well as the pace with which children move through development, are particular for each child and deserve the early childhood educator's sensitivity and response.

High-quality programs for young children show this respect for individuality in every decision that is made about children's care and curriculum, from considering what to do about naptime for toddlers to choosing materials for the art table so that preschoolers may find something to whet a particular interest or to guarantee certain success. This is a good time for you to note any practices you are aware of in early care and education settings that demonstrate respect for children's individuality or, conversely, any program decisions that fail to demonstrate this component and that treat all children as if they all had the same needs and interests.

The need for respect demands that early childhood educators first acquire knowledge of the children that goes far beyond merely learning characteristics of age-level norms. Such constantly growing knowledge demands that educators continually observe and communicate, as well as avoid the hasty conclusion that they "know the children." Early childhood educators who truly respect children's individuality find themselves always in a suspenseful state of not quite knowing, and always being open to new perceptions and evidence of growth and change.

Respect for children also implies recognizing children as capable and interesting people, who are also filled with the potential and the desire to learn, grow, and develop. Early childhood educators listen carefully to children, recognizing that their insights are valid and their questions are important. They talk with children individually, about things that are of interest and consequence to both child and adult. These are genuine conversations that follow the same rules as those of adult communication; they are not just "pop quizzes" or questions such as "What colour is the ball?" or "How many bears do I have in my hand?" Early childhood educators talk *with* children, not at them.

Children are enjoyed as people, rather than seen as being slightly entertaining because of their less-developed abilities and understanding of the world (*not* as in "Did you hear that? Isn't that cute—he called the lobster a monster.") Early childhood educators accept children's feelings and social interactions with seriousness, but also recognize children's need for guidance and assistance in moving toward greater **self-regulation** (*not* as in, "It's nothing to get upset about. He probably doesn't even understand much about moving to another province.") Early childhood educators see this need for help and guidance not as a defect, but as necessary assistance in the progression of learning (*not* as in "I'm sick and tired of hearing toddlers yell.") Respectful guidance of young children means that educators use techniques and communication that safeguard positive feelings of **self-esteem.** Guidance methods that humiliate or cause feelings of shame and doubt are not seen in excellent programs.

Adults with this kind of respect for childhood are not in a hurry to move children to more advanced learning or behaviours that they are not yet ready for. Instead, they recognize that childhood has an importance of its own, not just as a preparation stage for a later time. This is an important question to consider: How do adults convey to children that their childlike abilities and characteristics are appreciated, enjoyed, and accepted?

Early childhood educators also respect children's individuality when they help children learn to recognize and comfortably acknowledge the **diversity** of race, culture, religion, socioeconomic experiences, gender, and physical ability that

2000

1950

1900

1850

1800

1750

1700

1650

1893
Model day nursery at Chicago World's Fair cares for 10 000 children of sightseeing parents.

1896
John Dewey begins an experimental lab school at the University of Chicago for four- and five-year-olds, called subprimary rather than kindergarten.

In New York, Susan Blow is at Teachers College representing the Froebelian point of view, and Patty Smith Hill represents the newer developmental approach.

Each child has unique interests.

exists within Canadian communities and in early childhood education and care settings. Play materials, visitors, activities, and conversations all help children accept their **self-identity** and that of others. Each child identifies with a specific family and its background. As early childhood educators interact with children's parents, welcoming them into communication and collaboration, children perceive that their own family culture is respected. When parents are drawn into partnership, they are able to help early childhood educators truly understand their children and to guide early childhood educators in creating a curriculum that is responsive to their needs and goals for their children. Without such dialogue, early childhood educators are in constant danger of overstepping the boundaries of appropriateness in the multicultural world in which we live. Respect for individuality includes this acknowledgment of family needs and preferences and the active attempt to work with families. Genuine respect comes when parents and early childhood educators recognize that each has a role in children's lives that is very different, but complementary, rather than cause for antagonism. What are some of the practices in early childhood programs that convey respect for different cultures and that reach out for collaboration with families?

In essence, showing respect means that programs and early childhood educators are **child-sensitive**—that is, they notice that children are unique, acknowledge this as important, and use this knowledge as a significant basis in planning the total program. "Respect" may be a more descriptive term than the frequently used "child-centred," which may seem rather one-sided or totally indulgent toward children. Respect demands responsiveness.

Respect for self. Early childhood educators who have respect for self, recognize the right and personal obligation to be authentic to the values and principles that drive their lives. This begins as early childhood educators consider the philosophy and practices of potential employers, to determine whether these are compatible with their own deeply held personal convictions. Nothing more quickly destroys the joy of personal or professional life than working in a setting that calls for dissonance with self. Sometimes early childhood educators feel they can make compromises that would allow them to keep their job while balancing with their principles. It is true that there are, as yet, few perfect worlds, and that early childhood educators will likely have to live with some situations that are less than ideal. Nevertheless, to be able to maintain congruent feelings of personal and professional integrity, early childhood educators will need to identify those ideals and issues for which there is no room for compromise.

Such insights sometimes come slowly, after experience, as with the early childhood educator who left her first job after several months, saying ruefully, "I didn't realize how strongly I felt about teamwork. I now know that being part of a supportive community of adults and children is necessary for my ability to grow and see myself as a real contributor in the small world of the child care centre. I will never again take a job that doesn't emphasize that feeling of community." Some early childhood educators might want to be able to express their religious beliefs in their daily work; they will need to find programs that permit them to do so. The same is true for early childhood educators who believe so strongly in being able to espouse particular lifestyles that they would be uncomfortable working with other adults who deem them unacceptable. Early childhood educators must identify their defining principles.

Beyond being aware of who they are, early childhood educators also need to value the worth of their ideas and abilities. Humility is an important characteristic for professionals. But this is not a self-effacing humility; rather, it is a confident recognition of one's strengths and capabilities, coupled with an understanding of the need to join with others for maximum effect. In other words, early childhood educators do not have to be all-knowing or all-answering to any question, but can draw on the strengths of others, both adults and children. Early childhood educators who value their worth are confident in knowing that they have a contribution to make in early care and education. They know that their passions and ideas are worth sharing, that their presence is valuable. Such confidence leads toward excellence.

2000
1950
1900
1850
1800
1750
1700
1650

1899
John Dewey publishes *The School and Society*, outlining his philosophy of progressivism—that education is a means of social reform.

Responsiveness

"Good quality child care provides emotional security, frequent communication and encouragement to play and explore. It begins with a nurturing, stimulating relationship between the child and the caregiver, and extends to positive relationships and appropriate activities with other children" (Human Resources Development Canada, 1994, p. 11).

Responsive adults are able to read children's verbal and nonverbal signals, and they react promptly to children's needs and requests. Responsiveness is a sensitivity to a child's emotional state and mood, as well as attention to his physical needs. Children's trust emerges when adults are emotionally and physically available and reliable in meeting their needs. Infants and young children are more likely to form a secure attachment to responsive early childhood educators than they are to less-responsive caregivers.

Research findings in both centre- and home-based programs reveal the benefits of responsive early childhood educators. In studies of children in child care centres, responsive adults are associated with

- children who have more positive social skills with peers (see Rubenstein & Howes, 1979, 1983; Tzelepis et al., 1983; Whitebook et al., 1990, reported in Doherty-Derkowski, 1995); and
- children with higher cognitive and language skills (see Carew, 1980; Rubenstein & Howes, 1983; Melhuish et al., 1990a, 1990b; Whitebook et al., 1990).

Research studies find the same connections in home-based child care settings. Responsive adults bring out better social skills and higher levels of intellectual skills in children (Clarke-Stewart, 1987; Galinsky et al., 1994, reported in Doherty-Derkowski, 1995).

Doherty-Derkowski (1995, p. 26) states that the concept of responsiveness combines

- age-appropriateness;
- appropriateness for this particular child at this time; and
- appropriateness in this particular situation.

Effective early childhood programs recognize that learning takes place in the context of responsive relationships. Much time and effort go into building and sustaining significant relationships. These relationships form complex webs that extend in many directions: from early childhood educator to child; child to child; early childhood educator to parent; early childhood educator to early childhood educator; parent to parent; and, most important, parent to child. The ultimate statement on the importance of relationships in early education comes from the late Loris Malaguzzi (1993, p. 9), of the Reggio Emilia programs in Italy:

1903
In Ontario, legislation is passed allowing municipalities to purchase land for public parks.

> Although (from our experience in Reggio Emilia) we know how strongly children represent the centre of our educational system, we continue to be convinced that without attention to the central importance of children and families, our view of children is incomplete; therefore, our proposition is to consider a triad at the centre of education—children, early childhood educators, and families. To think of a dyad of only an early childhood educator and a child is to create an artificial world that does not reflect reality. . . .
>
> We strive to create an amiable school where children, early childhood educators, and families feel a sense of well-being; therefore, the organization of the school, contents, functions, procedures, motivations, and interests, is designed to bring together the three central protagonists—children, early childhood educators, and parents—and to intensify the interrelationships among them.

"Intensify the interrelationships"—what a strong image. Those who offer good early childhood care and education make procedural and environmental decisions based on their potential for encouraging relationships to flourish. The current practice of assigning **primary caregivers** for the youngest children is based on this concept, as are mixed-age groupings (where children remain together and with the same early childhood educators over two or three years), which many schools and programs are exploring for continuity. How different this is from making decisions based on efficiency; for example, if an early childhood educator had a feeding-table device that allowed her to feed six infants simultaneously, time might be saved, but the quality of personal and physical interaction that promotes emotional attachment would likely suffer. But imagine the benefit to interrelationships if the time-honoured custom of encouraging kindergarten and primary children to "do your own work," by working in silence at separate desks, were changed to having children face one another at tables and encouraging interaction and cooperative learning. Or consider the effects of changing the traditional policy of having the fewest staff members available at the beginning and end of the day so as to permit time for early childhood educators to talk with parents and with one another. What other specific decisions in the procedures, functions, and environment of early childhood settings can you imagine that could enhance the quality of the relationships within the programs?

Reciprocity of Learning

If early childhood educators believe that learning takes place in the context of many complex adult-child relationships and does not result solely from one-way pronouncements and instruction, learning becomes a reciprocal relationship, in which every participant within the system shares responsibility. Most early childhood educators find this concept exciting, as it removes from them the burden of being the sole resource for learning.

Children construct their own increasing understanding of the world by interacting with materials and people in their environments. High-quality programs understand that individuals construct their own reality, with all participants playing both teaching and learning roles. An early childhood educator aptly stated this idea to Margaret Yonemura (1986, p. 50) when she said, "'We all have some learning to do from each other,' expressing her underlying view that we are all resources with practical knowledge . . . the 'all' was inclusive of all children and adults."

The image that conveys the concept of a *nonreciprocal* learning environment is that of the liquid in a pitcher being poured into an empty cup. The early childhood educator is the pitcher, the cup is the child, and the action is all one way, with the child

MAKING IT HAPPEN

Responsiveness in Infant Early Childhood Settings

The early childhood educator enters the room. Sean looks up, eyebrows relaxed, lower eyelids raised, wrinkles in the outer corners of the eyes, cheeks raised, mouth open, and lips up and drawn back. The early childhood educator recognizes this joyful welcome and responds with her own joyful expression and a warm hug. This type of give and take characterizes the "dance" known as the responsive relationship.

Responsive relationships between adults and infants are the foundation upon which infants grow and flourish. Quality infant care provides these relationships. It supports the parent-child relationship, as well as offering security that promotes infant development within the centre. To do this, the early childhood educator must establish security through responsive relationships. She must manage stimulation to reduce stress. Knowledge of the role of temperament is also required to assist the early childhood educator's understanding of individual differences among infants. In addition, the early childhood educator must also be aware of her own needs and how these needs can impact upon her relationship with the infant. When the early childhood educator reads the infant's signals and replies, follows the child's lead and knows the child's rhythms, the child learns that she is understood. The child's security and self-esteem are enhanced.

Responsive relationships are ensured when the early childhood educator obtains information from parents; observes the infant; demonstrates respect for the infant's feelings and behaviour; is emotionally available to the infant and develops creative verbal and nonverbal responses to the infant. Responsive early childhood educators must also manage stimulation, finding the right timing, kind, and amount of stimulation. In order to manage stimulation, an early childhood educator must be sensitive to individual variations in state or level of awareness.

Source: Excerpted from "Building responsive relationships in infant care," Marie Goulet (April 1995) IDEAS, (2) 1 pp 9–13. Reprinted with permission.

This early childhood educator is listening to the child's explanation about the "water pieces falling down."

taking in knowledge from the early childhood educator and giving nothing back, and with no one else involved in the transaction. Instead, the image that could exemplify a reciprocal learning environment, where learning is multidirectional rather than following a single line, is that of a game in which many balls are being thrown at random around a group. A ball leaves one hand, flying across the room to another hand, crossed by the flight of another that goes from a different hand to still another. Another ball suddenly surprises the first thrower, and so on. The possibilities of connections and combinations are limitless. This is the richness of a reciprocal learning environment, in which all participants can teach and learn from one another through interaction.

What would a reciprocal learning environment be like from an early childhood educator's point of view? One of the best descriptions comes from Vivian Paley (1990, p. 136). In her work she continually marvels at how she learns from the children themselves how to present ideas that they can comprehend. Her mistakes with using adult logic are gently changed as she listens carefully to the children and has new insights into the world they have constructed. As Paley also points out, the children learn from one another in ways she cannot teach them. Here she is reflecting on a child's words:

> "Samantha's explanation, 'You're really a helicopter really but you're pretending a baby,' could never be used by an early childhood educator. The statement can only be made by another child, because it must stay within the child's context of reality. . . . In this single exchange between two young children there are important implications for classroom teaching at all levels. Children are able to teach one another best if they are permitted to interact socially and playfully throughout the day."

Read some of Paley's work, such as *Mollie Is Three* (1986), *Bad Guys Don't Have Birthdays* (1988), *The Boy Who Would Be a Helicopter* (1990), and grow into your own understanding of how good early childhood educators learn from children. Janet Gonzalez-Menza also reminds us, in *Multicultural Issues in Child Care* (1993), how early childhood educators can change their limited perspectives as they come to learn reciprocally by listening to parents who have very different views about raising children.

One of the most important, and often undeveloped, reciprocities in early childhood programs is the interaction that should exist between early childhood educators and colleagues. Professional growth and learning does not take place in a vacuum. Opportunities for supportive dialogue and shared reflections, and for joint observation and goal-setting, provide early childhood educators with stimulation and challenges. Excellent programs provide encouragement and environmental supports for forming real collegial systems. Reciprocal learning is possible only when early childhood educators show attitudes of respect for all, and when they recognize the importance of relationships and nurture them.

Think about this concept of reciprocity in good learning environments. What evidence of reciprocity have you encountered in your own learning experiences?

Framework of Quality

The framework of quality is constructed from basic building blocks, including an underlying knowledge of child development and early education practices, the number of children for whom each early childhood educator is responsible, the interrelationship and integration of learning experiences, and environments that are prepared for active learning.

Underlying Developmental Understanding

When early childhood educators make decisions based on facts and **theories** from child development knowledge and research, they are using standards of developmental appropriateness. The question is always this: is our practice supported by what we know to be true about children in general, and these children in particular? The CCCF (1991, p. 4) states that "all practices that take place are based on sound child development theories and current research." While recognizing that the quality of an early childhood program is affected by many factors, the NAEYC states that a major determinant of program quality is the "extent to which knowledge of child development is applied in program practices" (Bredekamp, 1987, p. 1).

Early childhood educators in quality programs work from a base of knowledge of child development that has taught them much about children's abilities and interests at various stages. Therefore, they are able to structure learning experiences in which children can find their own developmental level, guaranteeing success without fear of failure. Recognizing that children, even within a particular chronological grouping, may be far apart in their actual development, they provide materials that children can use with increasing levels of sophistication and skill. Children's freedom to make choices, coupled with support and challenge from the early childhood educator, helps them find the activities they are ready for.

An appropriate curriculum in a good early child development program is created through the interaction of children and all the involved adults, including parents, and through early childhood educators' careful observations of children and knowledge of developmental tasks and goals. That is, early childhood educators are acutely aware of the direction they will help children move toward because they recognize the sequence of development in all domains. Children's interests direct the actual activities, themes, and projects.

Because early childhood educators recognize that young children's learning styles are active and hands-on, the strategies they use to support active learning may look quite different from what many think of as typical teaching behaviours. Early childhood educators in good programs for young children will not be found instructing or lecturing from the front of the room; indeed, you would have a difficult time finding a front to the room! They interact with individuals or small groups busy at work or play. Embedded in their interaction may be challenges or suggestions of new directions to take in exploration, questions that may stimulate more activity or extend thinking, and comments that reinforce or provide information. This is subtle and supportive teaching, adapted to each situation. Occasionally, you will see early childhood educators working with the whole group,

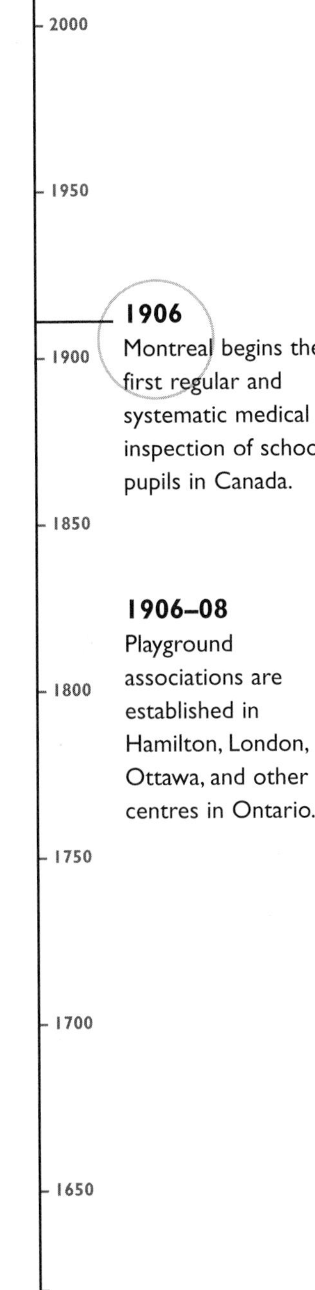

1907 Maria Montessori establishes a school for young children (Casa dei Bambini) in the slums of Rome.

but there is much less direct instruction even in this form, as children and adults interact. As they listen to children's responses and ideas, early childhood educators are continually assessing their progress and seeing what new learning they can facilitate. Teaching styles and strategies are shaped by developmental knowledge of how young children learn. How does this description of early childhood educators' strategies match your image of what you would do as an early childhood educator of young children?

Related postsecondary education increases the likelihood that all caregivers are early childhood educators and have an understanding of development to guide their work with young children. The Canadian Child Care Federation (CCCF) National Statement on Quality in Child Care (1991, p. 3) states that caregivers of young children in centre-based settings should "have experience and formal post-secondary accredited early childhood education and care. Their training minimally includes the study of child development and developmentally appropriate practice for the early years and includes supervised practicum experiences to ensure the transfer of knowledge."

The CCCF National Statement on Quality Child Care (1991, p. 3) considers the training of caregivers who work with young children in home-based early childhood education and care settings. "In terms of learned skills for working with young children, it is important that a provider has an understanding of the developmental needs of children. This information can be acquired through formal child related courses of study and through a variety of life experiences."

The final report of the Child Care Sector Study (Beach et al., 1998, pp. 140–41) recommends that provincial and territorial governments "establish training and education requirements for all caregivers in all regulated settings and an implementation plan with targets and timetables. Requirements should include a two-year postsecondary ECE or equivalent for centre-based caregivers."

Research findings consistently back up these recommendations for postsecondary ECE to prepare early childhood educators. In Canada, staff with postsecondary ECE qualifications are more likely to be associated with high-quality early child development settings and better child development outcomes than those without these qualifications (Goelman & Pence, 1987; Lyon & Canning, 1995; Doherty & Stuart, 1996).

Gillian Doherty (1996, p. 44) tells us that the findings are quite understandable. Education in child development and care,

- assists the adult to understand children's developmental stages and needs. This, in turn, increases the likelihood that the adult will provide activities that are both stimulating and appropriate for the child's developmental level, and will not impose unrealistic expectations;
- helps to compensate for the fact that initially the caregiver cannot know the child's developmental level and needs as well as the parent. An understanding of typical child development enables the caregiver to make "educated guesses" about what is appropriate and desirable for the child; and
- assists the adult to understand and manage the more complex group dynamics and processes among unrelated children who may not have the same history of familiarity and compromise as do brothers and sisters.

Do you think your own studies in a postsecondary early child development program will affect your understanding of young children's development? Take a moment to reflect on what you are learning about children's development and how this may be changing some of your behaviours.

Earlier we discussed the dynamic components of quality in early child development programs—respect, responsiveness, and reciprocity. Your capacity to respect, respond, and reciprocate with young children is clearly the crux of the issue of quality. Of course, your own values, attitudes, and other personal characteristics have an important role in your capacity, but so does your underlying understanding of development. As you become more knowledgeable about the principles of child development and developmentally appropriate practice, your capacity to respect, respond, and reciprocate with all children increases.

College and university early child development programs recognize the importance of both theoretical and practical knowledge in preparing early childhood

RESEARCH INTO PRACTICE

Early Child Development Research in Canada

Early childhood educators can find out about how Canadian scientists are studying early child development. For example:

Better Beginnings Better Futures

Better Beginnings, Better Futures, introduced in Chapter 1, is Canada's most ambitious community-based research project to date on the long-term impacts of early childhood development programming. The model is designed to prevent young children in low-income, high-risk neighbourhoods from experiencing poor developmental outcomes, which then require expensive health, education, and social services. The Better Beginnings model has been implemented in eight socio-economically disadvantaged communities in Ontario since 1991. http://bbbf.queensu.ca

Canadian Institutes of Health Research—Institute of Human Development, Child and Youth Health

The CIHR Institute of Human Development, Child and Youth Health will support research to enhance maternal, child, and youth health and to address causes, prevention, screening, diagnosis, treatment, short- and long-term support systems, and palliation for a wide range of health concerns associated with reproduction, early development, childhood, and adolescence. http://www.cihr-irsc.gc.ca/e/8695.html

Centre for Families, Work and Well-being

The Centre for Families Work and Well-being is an interdisciplinary research and educational centre, responding to dramatic changes in family patterns, paid work, and broader economic and political structures. Research topics include organizational health, family dynamics, social support, and community development. http://www.uoguelph.ca/cfww

Centre of Excellence for Early Child Development

The Centre of Excellence for Early Childhood Development (CEECD) disseminates scientific knowledge on the social and emotional development of young children and the policies and services that influence this development.

(cont'd)

Early Child Development Research in Canada (cont'd)

It also includes formulating recommendations on the services needed to ensure optimum early childhood development.

CEECD has prepared the *Encyclopedia on Early Childhood Development*. This compilation of papers from leading experts covers 33 topics related to the social and emotional development of young children, from conception to age five, and addresses three perspectives: development, services, and policies. http://www.excellence-earlychildhood.ca

Centre for Language and Literacy Research Network

The Canadian Language and Literacy Research Network (CLLRNet) brings leading scientists, clinicians, students, and educators together with public and private partners. It generates, integrates, and disseminates bias-free scientific research and knowledge that is focused on improving and sustaining children's language and literacy development in Canada. http://www.cllrnet.ca

Canadian Council on Social Development

Canadian Council on Social Development (CCSD) is a non-profit social policy and research organization focusing on issues such as poverty, social inclusion, disability, cultural diversity, child well-being, employment, and housing. CCSD produces *The Progress of Canada's Children and Youth*. This publication provides information on different factors that influence the health and well-being of Canadian children and youth, including family life, economic security, physical safety, learning, and more. Because the report tracks this information over time, it helps identify trends, successes, and challenges. http://www.ccsd.ca

Child Care Resource and Research Unit

The Childcare Resource and Research Unit (CRRU) at the University of Toronto is a policy- and research-oriented facility that focuses on early childhood education and care. CRRU provides, synthesizes, analyzes, and disseminates extensive information resources on early childhood education and care policy and research.

CRRU periodically assembles pan-Canadian data to produce the country's most complete snapshot of early childhood care and education. The sixth edition of *Early Childhood Education and Care in Canada* presents 2003 and 2004 data. Together with 1992, 1995, 1998, and 2004 data compiled for earlier editions, these data reveal trends in early child development over more than a decade. http://www.childcarecanada.org

Consortium on Heath, Intervention, Learning, and Development

The Consortium for Health, Intervention, Learning and Development (CHILD) is a multidisciplinary team of academic researchers and community professionals from across British Columbia. They have formed a partnership to conduct research on early childhood development (ECD) within a wide spectrum of community contexts. http://www.earlylearning.ubc.ca/CHILD

Early Childhood Learning Knowledge Centre

The Early Childhood Learning Knowledge Centre brings together the scientific knowledge about the conditions that foster learning in young children up to the age of five years. http://www.ccl-cca.ca/CCL/AboutCCL/KnowledgeCentres/EarlyChildhoodLearning

Experience-based Brain and Biological Development, Canadian Institute of Advanced Studies

CIAR launched the Experience-based Brain and Biological Development program in 2003 to explore the core question of how social experiences "get under the skin" to affect human biology and set early trajectories

(cont'd)

for development and health. The program delves into exactly how, when, and under what circumstances early social experiences change neural, endocrine, and immunological systems. http://www.ciar.ca/web/home.nsf/pages/ebbd

Human Early Learning Partnership

The Human Early Learning Partnership (HELP) is an interdisciplinary research partnership that is directing a world-leading contribution to new understandings and approaches to early child development. HELP facilitates the creation of new knowledge, and helps apply this knowledge in the community by working directly with government and communities.

The Provincial Early Child Development Mapping Unit increases awareness and understanding of healthy child development in neighbourhoods across BC. HELP produces maps that combine Early Development Instrument (EDI) data, socio-demographic factors and community assets and resources. By networking with local coalitions, HELP assists communities in interpreting maps and assessing factors that influence children's development. http://www.earlylearning.ubc.ca

Manitoba Centre for Health Policy

MCHP is a research unit in the University of Manitoba's Faculty of Medicine. MCHP examines patterns of illness in the population, and studies how people use health care services. The primary focus is on the question "What makes people healthy?" and includes consideration of social factors such as income, education, employment, and social circumstances. MCHP sorts out the contribution of each of these factors. Some of their work focuses on the determinants of health in early childhood and the impact of early childhood development on later health and well-being. http://www.umanitoba.ca/centres/mchp/

National Longitudinal Survey of Children and Youth

The National Longitudinal Survey of Children and Youth (NLSCY) is a long-term study of Canadian children that follows their development and well-being from birth to early adulthood. The study is designed to collect information about factors influencing a child's social, emotional, and behavioural development and to monitor the impact of these factors on the child's development over time. The first survey was conducted in 1994/95. http://www.statcan.ca/cgi-bin/imdb/p2SV.pl?Function=getSurvey&SDDS=4450&lang=en&db=IMDB&dbg=f&adm=8&dis=2

Offord Centre for Child Studies

The Offord Centre for Child Studies conducts research on healthy child development in order to improve the life quality and life opportunities of the one in five Canadian children and youth who suffer from serious social and emotional problems. The Centre led the development of the Early Development Instrument to measure children's early social, emotional, cognitive, language, and physical development at a population level. http://www.offordcentre.com

Science of Early Child Development

The Science of Early Child Development (ECD) is an online curriculum resource, presented in a flexible, interactive multimedia format, inspired and informed by the following questions:

- What is the new framework for studying child development?
- Why is it important for early childhood educators to understand science related to young children?
- How can we narrow the gap between research and practice?

http://scienceofecd.com/index.php

educators. Theoretical knowledge encompasses child development principles and learning theory. Practical knowledge focuses on varied strategies and when to use them in guiding children, making decisions that take the immediate situation into account, and following appropriate "rules of thumb" in day-to-day routines (Vander Ven, 1994). We will examine the curricula offered in Canadian college and university programs further in Chapter 5.

1908
London School Clinic is established by the McMillan sisters in response to concern that British children were not reaching school age healthy enough to learn.

Number of Children

It is common sense that the total number of children a caregiver is responsible for will affect the quality of care and education children receive. Can you imagine the quality of care or child development outcomes in situations where one caregiver is responsible for six infants? Basic safety is missing in this situation, let alone an environment of respect, responsiveness, and reciprocity.

Optimal child-adult ratios in early childhood settings allow early childhood educators to interact frequently with each child, respond promptly to children's needs, and observe individual children and the group dynamics. The overall size of the group is another important component. If the group size becomes too large, even when the number of children each early childhood educator is responsible for is small, quality deteriorates. The adults must pay more attention to overall group organization and schedules, taking away from their individualized attention and flexibility in following the lead of children's activity. In large groups, children's play and daily routines must fit into a group schedule and pattern. It becomes much more difficult to respond to individual children without creating chaos in the group.

Research studies help us to understand the optimal child-adult ratios and maximum group sizes for different ages of children. These are the optimal adult-child ratios and maximum group sizes for centre-based early child development programs.

Where a multi-age grouping exists, the adult-child ratio and group size requirements can be based on the age of the majority of children in the group. When infants are included, the ratio and group size for infants should be maintained.

Think about your experiences in early childhood settings during field placements or while working. Can you remember times when you were responsible for more children than is recommended by the research? What was it like? Were you able to engage in conversations? Could you respond to children's nonverbal signals? Did you observe their activity and the dynamics of the group? Or were you mainly focused on "crowd control" and on the safety of children? Was your communication mainly directed at the whole group, rather than at individual children?

Integration of Learning Experiences

High-quality programs consider the **whole child,** meaning there is equal attention paid to needs and growth in all domains of development: **physical, cognitive, emotional, social,** and **moral.** Physical competence, including both **gross motor** and **fine motor** skills, and emotional, social, and intellectual development, are all recognized as important areas of growth that occur simultaneously in young children. "Simultaneously" does not mean at an equal level; rather, it means that all of this learning is occurring in the child at the same time. Furthermore, what is happening in one aspect of development has an effect on what is happening in other aspects. For example, success in learning within the cognitive curriculum of the early elementary years can be predicated on the child's comfort in social situations and ability to respond to the directions and guidance of a new adult. Infants' language development parallels their acquisition of motor abilities to explore the world firsthand. Toddlers' frustration and temper outbursts may be directly related to their limited vocabulary for expression, and so on.

Considering the whole child also means taking into account the child's family. The world at a school or centre makes up only a part, and a small part, of a child's life experiences. Family life is included in the classroom, and the child is recognized at all times as a family member and participant.

Those who sponsor good programs know they cannot expect children to learn in a fragmented way, with learning or subject matter broken up into individual, isolated lessons. Imagine the nonsense of planning an infant's day to include a time to practise the physical skills of crawling on the mat, followed by a short period of language instruction, with an experience in emotional closeness and bonding to come next! Instead, early childhood educators sit near babies crawling on the mat, while smiling, talking, encouraging, and interacting. Development in all domains is being nurtured simultaneously—learning is integrated.

In the same way, a good curriculum for older children consists of an **integrated curriculum** of whole activities, rather than separate subject lessons. Instead of providing a language period, followed by math and then science, teachers have children participate in a cooking activity that allows children to learn all of those concepts in a meaningful activity, as well as develop and use the skills involved.

Integrated learning for children in high-quality programs does not happen by chance. Early childhood educators who observe children continually come to know their abilities, their strengths, and the areas of development that need particular support. They assess individual development in the light of their knowledge of the predictable sequence of developmental abilities, so that they have for each child, a sense of where the child is now and what the next steps will be. These **assessments** are always enhanced by the early childhood educator's dialogues with parents, so that objectives are based on the best available information. In good programs for young children, early childhood educators have a clear sense of direction to guide them in planning the most appropriate learning experiences for each child. The learning may look spontaneous and involve choices and action on the child's part, but it is part of a careful overall plan for each child.

Another factor that contributes to whole rather than fragmented experiences for children and families is the wholeness of the early childhood program itself. Such wholeness is achieved only when a clearly articulated common philosophy connects all participants to an understood framework that is translated into daily actions. Defining common beliefs is crucial to full participation for both staff and families, so that adults knowingly commit themselves to the stated fundamental beliefs that will bind them. Quality programs have clearly stated and understood philosophies to guide their decision-making.

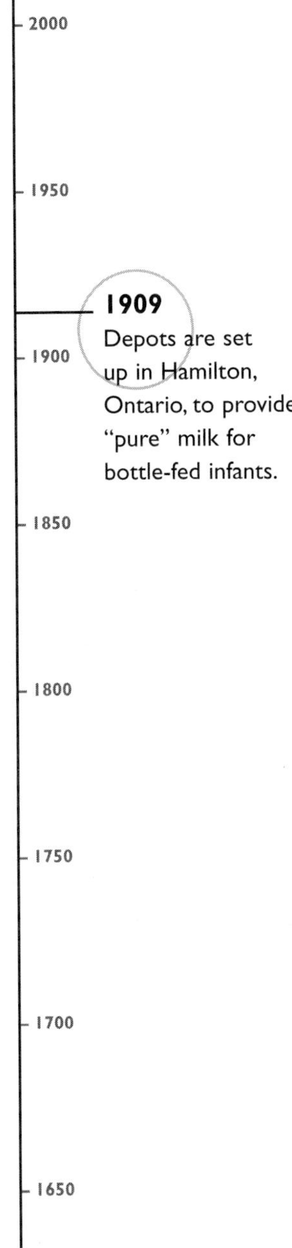

1910

University of Manitoba introduces a child development component to the Faculty of Home Economics.

The Ottawa and Toronto school boards establish "forest schools" to maximize the time "sickly" children spend outdoors.

Physical Environment for Active and Cooperative Learning

The physical **environment** is a powerful influence on our behaviour. Think about how you change your behaviour in different spaces. Large, open spaces encourage big movements. Cozy, small spaces encourage quieter activity. The physical environment gives us messages about what kinds of behaviours are expected.

It follows that excellent programs for young children have environments structured so that early childhood educators are able to continually observe children. Can you think of environmental arrangements, curriculum methods, and early childhood educator functioning that allow early childhood educators to continually observe the children in their care? Specific practices include encouraging individual exploration or small-group interaction, rather than whole-group activities led by early childhood educators; providing **open-ended** materials that do not require adult instruction or assistance; and defining observation and record-keeping as important tasks for early childhood educators come to mind. What else can you add?

Programs designed for children to learn by interacting with materials and people structure the time and space environment for active learning. Classroom environments reflect early childhood educators' beliefs about children and how they learn, about the form and content of the curriculum, and about the importance of social connections. When early childhood educators see environment as an important component of quality, they create physical arrangements for opportunities that encourage "encounter, communication, and relationships" (Gandini, 1993, p. 6).

Because early childhood educators know that children learn through direct manipulation, play, and work with varieties of materials, furniture is used to display the available choices in a logical and organized way, encouraging children's choices and productive use. The environment is organized into logically separated **interest centres,** so that children may decide to work or play alone, with a few other children, or with a larger group. The coherence and unspoken messages of invitation, challenge, and order allow children to feel a measure of control over their learning activities and methods. In quality learning environments, children have opportunities to make choices about which activities they are interested in, about how they will structure their learning activity, and whom they will play and work with, and where.

Environment does convey messages. It can say, "This is a place where you can decide some things that you are going to do today," or "The early childhood educator will always be the one in charge of telling you what to do." It can say, "Work with a friend if you like," or "Stay in your seat and work by yourself." It can say, "Here are some things that will allow you to succeed," or "This stuff is really hard and the early childhood educator thinks you won't be able to learn it without her." It can say, "They care about your work here," or "What you do isn't really very important." It can say, "What you do, think, and communicate with your play is significant," or "After you play then we'll do the important things." It can say, "Your rights to work undisturbed and undistracted will be protected," or "This is not a peaceful place." It can say, "Childhood is valued and appreciated as a separate and distinct time of life," or "Childhood is merely a superficially cute stage." It can say, "You can do as much as possible for yourself here," or "You'll need to depend on grownups to do things for you." It can say, "There are some limits on things that aren't safe or acceptable," or "You'll have to make mistakes and then we'll stop you." It can say, "You belong here as a member of this classroom community," or "Your individuality is not respected." Think about it—in what ways might the design and placement of classroom furniture and materials, the decoration on the walls, or the classroom schedule and routines reflect these messages? What other messages have you been aware of in physical environments? Programs that understand children's active involvement in discovery learning support this involvement with the way they arrange time and space.

High-quality programs for young children emphasize materials and experiences, knowing that children learn through doing, not through simply being told about concepts. Excellent early childhood education and care programs include enticing materials that invite touching. This variety of "loose parts," to use Nicholson's term for open-ended materials (1974), allows children to explore, invent, combine, create, and communicate. Materials are in good repair, are safe, and match the children's manipulative abilities. As well, materials have been carefully selected for the learning environment to correspond with the early childhood educators' goals and children's interests. Think of some of the materials that have been part of any good early childhood program you know. What were some open-ended items that children used in interesting ways?

Daily routines should be an integral part of the daily curriculum. They are learning opportunities that need to respect and to respond to individual children's needs, abilities, and desires.

Large blocks of uninterrupted time are needed for children to become meaningfully involved in their play. The daily schedule will be organized to permit participation, practice, and repetition as children's repertoire of skills and knowledge grows, rather than fragmenting the day into defined times for separate activities, with many confusing **transitions.** When programs recognize that children's self-esteem and confidence as learners result from meaningful, personal involvement in activities, the daily plan permits such involvement.

Quality programs for young children recognize the importance of environmental decisions and create environments that support interaction and activity. The physical environment can greatly enhance early childhood educators' abilities to respect, respond, and reciprocate.

RESEARCH INTO PRACTICE

Quality by Design—Physical Environment

The program setting that includes . . .

- Sufficient well-designed indoor and outdoor space
- First-rate equipment and program resources
- Amenities such as staff room, outside play space, kitchen, windows for natural light
- Connections to the surrounding community

Elements of ELCC environments such as amount of space, access to the outdoors, arrangement of rooms, availability of a variety of materials, air quality, equipment, and lighting play a role not only in safety and health but in children's well-being, happiness and creativity, their learning to live in and with the natural environment, and their cognitive and social development. In addition, elements of the physical environment such as how easy or difficult it is to carry out a program in, whether there are physical amenities that support staff—a staff room and adequate program resources—and whether the nature of the facility conveys that early childhood education is a respected, valued career have an impact on the morale of the people working in the program and, thus, on the quality of the program. In addition—as some commentators have pointed out—as children are the least powerful stakeholders, it is important to find ways to involve them in considering ELCC's physical environments.

Supporting good physical environments means not only high standards or regulations regarding, for example, the number and placement of toilets, windows, exit doors, kitchen and food preparation requirements, placement of sinks for hand washing, height of fencing although these are clearly important and cannot be overlooked. In addition to these basic health and safety considerations, today there is considerable interest in and knowledge concerning design and architecture of children's environments with emphasis on creativity, physical activity, social and cognitive development, aesthetic considerations, and how the physical environment can support rather than hinder implementation of excellent early childhood programs and ensure their visibility as a valued community institution.

Source: M. Friendly, G. Doherty, & J. Beach (2006) *Quality by design*. Toronto: Childcare Resource & Research Institute, University of Toronto.

Context of Quality

The framework of an early child development program sets the stage for the dynamics that occur among children and early childhood educators each day. The context of quality describes the elements outside the immediate early childhood setting that influence both the framework elements and the children's day-to-day experiences. Each early child development program creates a distinctive work environment for early childhood educators, which will influence her ability to provide responsive, respectful, reciprocal, and reliable experiences for children. The work environment, in turn, is influenced by funding, government regulation, nonregulatory measures, and the sponsorship of early child development programs.

Think about your field placements. How did the work environment vary from one setting to another? Did the roles of the director or supervisor differ between settings? What kind of remuneration did early childhood educators receive? Was there a difference in the level of government funding compared to the fees paid by parents? Who was ultimately responsible for the care and education of the children? Did any of these arrangements and practices make a difference to how early childhood educators worked with young children?

The context of quality in early child development programs is a complex and sometimes confusing array of details that seem to have little to do with the work of providing quality nurturing and stimulation to young children. But they are important, and they either contribute or present barriers to your capacity as an early childhood educator. We will consider the various elements of context of quality, including the work environment, funding, regulation, and voluntary standards as well as their impact on quality.

Work Environment

A number of interrelated elements make up the work environment of a child care centre, nursery school, home-based setting, or kindergarten classroom. These elements include the style of administration and supervision, organizational climate, compensation, working conditions, and staff turnover rates, all of which influence early childhood educators' interactions with young children and their ability to organize the physical environment and learning experiences.

Administrative style. In centre-based early childhood education and care programs, the role of the director or supervisor includes program and professional leadership; information, financial, and personnel management; parent and community relationships; and legal compliance. All of these functions underlie the early child development program. Like a building's foundation, the elements are often invisible if they are effective. But ineffective administration and management, like cracks in a building's foundation, have noticeable negative effects.

Program and professional leadership. Child care centre directors, nursery school supervisors, and public school principals share common ground in the influence their leadership has on the early childhood educators and teachers they supervise.

One U.S. study of the director's administrative style in 400 child care centres (Helburn, 1995, reported in Doherty, 2000) found that a director's involvement in both curriculum planning and in the professional community of early childhood

2000
1950
1900
1850
1800
1750
1700
1650

1911

Rachel and Margaret McMillan establish the Deptford School, an open-air nursery school in London, inventing the term "nursery school."

Ottawa Day Nursery opens.

The Vancouver Infants Centre opens at the infants hospital.

First Montessori school in the United States is established.

1913
Caroline Pratt, frustrated with the Froebelian-based teacher preparation at Teachers College, begins an experimental school for five-year-olds in New York City.

education was associated with higher levels of overall quality. A recent study of the child care sector reports that the director in a centre-based early childhood education and care program "is a gatekeeper to program quality who establishes standards of practice and expectations for others to follow" (Beach et al., 1998, p. 99). As well, research identifies school principals who provide academic leadership to teaching staff as a critical component (King & Peart, 1990; Sylva, 1994).

In other words, a competent leader demonstrates and encourages practices that support the dynamics and framework elements of quality, increasing the likelihood that early childhood educators who are working directly with the children will do likewise.

Information, financial, and personnel management. Directors and supervisors in centre-based programs manage information systems, monitor finances, and supervise early childhood educators and other staff members. This role involves a myriad of details and technical skills. It also involves the ability to set clear job expectations, monitor staff performance, and provide constructive feedback. The director's success in carrying out these responsibilities determines the effectiveness of the centre's organization. A well-run centre pays staff members on time and makes accurate deductions; keeps children's records updated and within easy access in case of emergencies; and provides clear, written expectations of job responsibilities.

Parent and community relationships. The director is an important link in establishing partnerships with parents and with other groups in the community.

Legal compliance. All early child development centre-based programs that provide nonparental care are subject to numerous regulations and requirements. The director needs to ensure that these obligations are met and that the necessary records are available for verification. A good information system will go a long way toward fulfilling these obligations.

The administrative style also shapes the work environment in family child care settings. In family child care, an early childhood educator sets his own expectations for program standards, manages information and finances, develops parent and community relationships, and ensures compliance with all legal requirements. His ability to carry out these responsibilities sets the administrative style and influences the quality of the family child care program.

In in-home child care settings, the working relationship between the early childhood educator and the employer is the basis of the administrative style. Both verbal and written communication are key components of the working relationship. The early childhood educator can enhance the administrative style by ensuring that written employment agreements outline both parties' responsibilities and expectations. Because in-home child care takes place in the child's family home, clear communication practices help to maintain personal boundaries. Communication includes the ongoing exchange of information, as well as the discussion of problems and the exploration of solutions. The important exchange of information between family members and an early childhood educator is helped by written daily logs, opportunities for daily verbal reports and transitions, regular parent-nanny conferences, and job performance reviews (Bassett, 1998). Early childhood educators can work with employers to establish these kinds of practices.

If an employment agency is involved, it is likely to provide administrative support in these areas.

Compensation and working conditions. The income, benefits, and working conditions early childhood educators receive in early child development settings are important components of the work environment. These context components do have an impact on job satisfaction and turnover, which influence the dynamics of quality. We will discuss these issues further in Chapters 6 and 9.

Funding

It is fairly simple to determine the cost of a child's participation, whether in a home- or centre-based setting. The biggest expense (usually 80 to 90 percent) is the cost of early childhood educators who provide the services; other expenses include the costs of the physical environment, food, supplies, and play materials. To calculate the cost per child, the total expenses are divided by the number of children enrolled in the program. In Canada, funding for the costs of early child programs comes mostly from two sources: parents who pay the costs or fees and public money from governments, which may fund early child development programs or subsidize the parent's fees.

The impact of funding on the quality of early child development programs is also easy to determine. Quality early child development programs depend on skilled early childhood educators. Reasonable compensation levels help to attract and retain competent early childhood educators in early child development programs. To offer reasonable compensation rates, early child development programs require higher levels of funding, either from higher parent fees or from higher levels of government funding. But higher funding reduces the affordability of child care, both to parents and to governments, making it less accessible to children and their families. We will discuss more about the tensions between quality, compensation, and accessibility in Chapter 9. Now we will look more closely at the costs to parents and to governments, as well as at the types of funding that governments provide in Canada.

The cost of early childhood programs to parents. Parents are responsible for most of the costs of child care centres, nursery schools, regulated and unregulated family child care, and in-home child care. Some parents receive subsidies, which are intended to help low-income families meet the costs of regulated child care. Parents do not pay for the cost of kindergarten programs within the school system, most early intervention services, and early childhood services offered within family resource programs.

The cost of child care centres, nursery schools, and regulated family child care varies from one provincial/territorial jurisdiction to another. Early childhood educators and other caregivers receive different levels of compensation, and there are differences in the types of direct funding to these programs by provincial/territorial governments. Also, there are significant variations in the amount of fee subsidies available to parents.

The cost of early child development programs to government. Governments at all levels contribute to the cost of early child development programs in different ways.

2000
1950
1900
1850
1800
1750
1700
1650

1914
Caroline Pratt designs the first set of unit blocks.

The school nurse is moved into the central position in school medical programs.

Jost Mission Day Nursery opens in Halifax.

Some governments directly fund the programs themselves to cover partial or full operating costs. Public funding to programs also provides fee assistance to low-income families. Other government funding goes to parents to cover the costs of child care, usually as part of employment assistance and training programs. Kindergarten programs operating within the education system are publicly funded as part of the school system and do not charge fees to parents. Finally, governments also fund child care expenses through the income tax system in the form of the Child Care Expense Deduction. Governments' contributions to the funding of early child development programs are complex and subject to frequent change.

The level of public funding influences the compensation levels of early childhood educators across all early childhood settings, which, in turn, affects the education qualification levels and turnover rates of early childhood educators. Consistent, qualified early childhood educators are more likely to provide respectful, responsive, reciprocal, and reliable daily experiences for young children in early childhood settings. Early child development programs that receive higher levels of funding are likely to offer better compensation to early childhood educators.

Regulation

Of the variables that can be regulated (that is, those with set standards), three that affect positive child outcomes in early childhood programs include adult educational qualifications, group size, and adult-child ratios (*Young Children,* 1993, January). These factors determine the quality of relationships within the program.

In Canada, these factors are regulated by provincial/territorial legislation for regulated child care settings. There is considerable variation from one jurisdiction to the next, and no single jurisdiction has regulations for educational qualifications, adult-child ratios, and maximum group size that meet the criteria recommended by the CCCF and the NAEYC.

Kindergarten programs operate within the legislative framework for education in each province and territory. Kindergarten teachers in public school programs are required to meet provincial/territorial qualification requirements for education and certification. In all jurisdictions outside the Northwest Territories, requirements include an undergraduate university degree and specialized teacher preparation education. In many instances, these requirements are combined in a bachelor of education degree, sometimes with specialization in primary education required. In the Northwest Territories, an undergraduate degree is not required, although this is under review, and classroom assistants and Aboriginal-language specialists are qualified to teach kindergarten under the supervision of a certified teacher. Kindergarten teachers are not required to also have ECE credentials or experience, but primary teacher preparation programs and employees often prefer that teachers have this background.

Four provinces and territories stipulate maximum class size for public kindergarten programs. In Yukon, the maximum group size is 23 and the ratio is 1 adult for every 23 children; in New Brunswick the maximum group size is 20 and the ratio is 1 to 20; and in Quebec the ratio for junior kindergarten is 1 to 17 with a maximum of 34 children per group, while senior kindergarten has a maximum group size of 20 and a 1 to 20 ratio. In Ontario the maximum class size is 20 children.

RESEARCH INTO PRACTICE

Public Funding for Early Child Development Programs in Canada

Prenatal/Postnatal	$65 million
Family & Community Support	$400 million
Regulated Early Learning & Child Care	$2.4 billion
Kindergarten (public education system)	$1.57 billion
Research & Information	$80 million
	$4.54 billion

Federal Government

The federal government transfers funds to provinces and territories that are specifically for early child development programs. About $500 000 per year is transferred for a range of early child development programs and additional funds are transferred specifically for early learning and child care (approximately $150 million in 2004).

Provincial/Territorial Government

Each province and territory has established fee subsidies to low-income families with specific criteria for eligibility. The target fee subsidies are usually intended for use only in regulated child care settings. In British Columbia and the Northwest Territories, provincial fee subsidies may be used in unregulated family child care settings.

All provinces and territories offer a number of recurring or operating grants to regulated child care programs. Operating grants are public funding that is paid directly to the child care program to support a portion of its overall operating expenses. Some of these grants are aimed at raising staff salaries or other program expenses, whereas others are applied generally to program budgets.

Sources:

Information in this section is drawn from these sources:

M. Friendly & J. Beach (2005) *Early Childhood Education & Care in Canada in 2004.* Toronto: Childcare Resource & Research Unit at University of Toronto. http://www.childcarecanada.org

Social Development Canada, Public Health Agency of Canada and Indian & Northern Affairs Canada (2005) *Early Childhood Development and Early Learning and Child Care Activities and Expenditures 2003–2004.* Ottawa: Government of Canada. http://www.socialunion.ca

Organization for Economic and Cooperative Development (2004) *Early Childhood Education and Care Policy Note.* Thematic Review of Early Childhood Education and Care. Paris: OECD. http://www.oecd.org/dataoecd/41/36/33852192.pdf

Voluntary Standards

Government regulations really establish minimum standards only to support the framework and dynamic elements of quality. They can influence important structural elements of quality, in particular, requirements for early childhood educators with ECE postsecondary qualifications, maximum group sizes, and the maximum number

TABLE 3.1

Staffing Requirements for Child Care Centres, By Province/Territory, 2004

	Staff-Child Ratios		
Province/Territory	*Age Group*[a]	*Ratio*	*Staff Education/Experience Required*
Newfoundland	0–2 2–3	 1:6	Centre supervisors in preschool and school age need 2-year ECE 2 qualification and 2 years' work experience. Each group or working experience in a licensed centre, or 2-year ECE diploma with no experience required. All staff must complete a 30- to 60-hour orientation course.
Prince Edward Island	0–2 2–3 3–5 5–6 7+	1:3 1:5 1:10 1:12 1:15	Centre supervisors and 1 full-time staff must have 1- or 2-year early childhood development diploma or university child study degree; centre supervisors with 1-year certificates must have at least 3 years' experience; those with 2-year diploma must have at least 2 years' experience. Certification required: 30 hours of in-service training every 3 years for all staff.
Nova Scotia	0–5 17 mo–5 5–12	1:7[b] 1:12 1:15	Centre supervisor and 2/3 of staff must have 1- or 2-year ECE certificate or diploma, or 2 years experience, plus 2 courses and 60-hour workshop on child development and 25 hours on curriculum. All staff must have first-aid training.
New Brunswick	0–2 2–3 3–4 4–5 5–6 6–12	1:3 1:5 1:7 1:10 1:12 1:15	One-quarter of all program staff and the supervisor will be required to have at least an ECE certificate. Staff must be at least 16 years old. Staff 16–19 years old are required to be supervised by a staff member who is at least 19 years old. All staff must have first-aid training.
Quebec	0–18 mo 18 mo–3 4–5 6 –12	1:5 1:8 1:10 1:12	Two-thirds of all staff in CPEs must have ECE college diploma or university degree. One-third of staff in garderies must have a DEC (2-year ECE diploma equivalent) or AEC (1-year ECE certificate equivalent) and 3 years' experience. No staff training requirements for school-age care.
Ontario	0–18 mo 18 mo–2.5 2.5–5 5–6 6–10	3:10 1:5 1:8 1:12 1:15	Centre supervisor must have 2-year ECE diploma plus 2 years' experience. One staff member within each group of children must have 2-year ECE diploma or equivalent.
Manitoba	3–12 mo 1–2 2–3 3–4 5–6 4–5 6–12	1:3 1:4 1:5 1:8 1:10 1:9 1:15	Qualification levels: Child Care Worker (CCW) III: 2-year diploma and advanced certificate, or approved 4-year degree; CCWII: approved 2-year diploma program or a Child Day Care Competency-Based Assessment Program; CCWI: Grade 12 or 1 postsecondary accredited child care course; CCA (child care assistant): less than Grade 12.

(cont'd)

TABLE 3.1

Staffing Requirements for Child Care Centres, By Province/Territory, 2004 (cont'd)

Province/Territory	*Staff-Child Ratios* — *Age Group*[a]	*Ratio*	*Staff Education/Experience Required*
Manitoba (Cont'd)	nursery schools		
	3 mo–2	1:4	Centre supervisors must be qualified as CCWIII, plus 1-year experience, and 2/3 of centre's preschool staff must be CCWII or III. School-age and nursery school directors can be CCWII. All staff must have first-aid training.
	2–6	1:10	
Saskatchewan	6–18 mo	1:3	Centre-based supervisors must have 2-year certificate in child care, or equivalent. All staff must have a minimum of 120 hours of child care orientation course or equivalent. Thirty percent of all staff must have a 1-year certificate equivalent. By January 2007, a further 20% of staff must have a 2-year diploma or equivalent. Staff working with children with special needs must have additional training.
	18–30 mo	1:5	
	30 mo–6	1:10	
	6–12	1:15	
Alberta	0–12 mo	1:3	Three qualification levels: Level 1 (50-hour orientation program); Level 2 (1-year certificate); and Level 3 (2-year diploma). Program directors required to have 2-year diploma in early childhood education. All centre staff must have at least Level 1, and 1 in 4 staff must have Level 2. All other staff required to have at least 50 hours training related to ECE. No training required for school-age care.
	13–18 mo	1:4	
	19–35 mo	1:6	
	3–4.5	1:8	
	4.5–6	1:10	
	nursery schools		
	0–18 mo	1:6	
	19–35 mo	1:10	
	3–5	1:12	
	5–6	1:15	
British Columbia	0–3	1:4	Legislation indicates 3 qualification levels: early childhood educator (1-year basic ECE program and 500 hours of supervised work experience); infant/toddler educator (basic ECE plus post-basic infant/toddler care and education); and special needs educator (basic ECE plus post-basic in special needs). Each preschool group requires 1 early childhood educator plus assistants. Each group (5–8) infants/toddlers requires 1 early childhood educator and 1 infant/toddler educator. In designated special needs child care facilities, one special needs educator is required for each group of children with additional early childhood educators and assistants to maintain a 1:4 ratio. No training requirements for school-age children.
	3–5	1:8	
	5–6	1:10	
	7–12	1:15	
	preschool	1:10	
	specialized	1:4	
Yukon	0–18 mo	1:4	Twenty percent of staff in a centre must have 2 or more ECE training or its equivalent. An additional 30% of staff must have 1-year ECE training. All other staff must complete a 60 hour child care orientation.
	18 mo–2	1:6	
	3–6	1:8	
	6–12	1:12	

(cont'd)

TABLE 3.1

Staffing Requirements for Child Care Centres, By Province/Territory, 2004 (cont'd)

	Staff-Child Ratios		
Province/Territory	*Age Group*[a]	*Ratio*	*Staff Education/Experience Required*
Northwest Territories	0–12 mo	1:3	No early childhood education qualification requirements. First-aid certificate required.
	13–24 mo	1:4	
	25–35 mo	1:6	
	3	1:8	
	4	1:9	
	5–11	1:10	

[a] Age given in years, unless noted otherwise.

[b] There are no specific ratios for children 0–17 months, but the recommended ratio is 1:4.

Sources: Doherty, Friendly & Beach, 2003; Beach et al., 2004; Friendly & Beach, 2005.

of children for every adult. But there are limitations: requirements vary from one jurisdiction to another, monitoring and enforcement cannot ensure full compliance, many of the crucial dynamic elements of quality cannot be regulated, and many early child development settings operate outside the system of regulation.

Voluntary standards offer another mechanism to support and ensure the presence of dynamic, framework, and context elements of quality. The standards are established outside legislation and regulations. In most instances, voluntary standards for early child development programs are established by professional organizations outside the government.

National Standards for Quality Child Care

The CCCF (2000) developed standards for both family- and group-based settings. The statement incorporates major research findings and input from many individuals across Canada. It is meant to be applied in diverse types of services and to be a living document that increases public understanding of and support for quality early child development programs as an essential part of the well-being of Canada's children.

The CCCF statement on program standards identifies what needs to be in place in early childhood education and care settings in ten areas:

- *Conceptual framework.* Program philosophy and a statement of goals and objectives serve as a basis for decision making, daily practice, and program evaluation.
- *Program policies and procedural guidelines.* Program policies and procedural guidelines are in place to enable the conceptual framework to be translated into practice and to support practice consistent with the conceptual framework.
- *Program facility.* The physical facility protects the health and safety of children and adults in the child care program and enables and supports developmentally appropriate programming.
- *Supplies and equipment.* Supplies and equipment of the child care program protect the health and safety of both the children and the adults in the setting

and enable and support developmentally appropriate and culturally sensitive programming.

- *Human resources.* The number and skills of persons working in the program meet program needs.
- *Partnerships with children's families.* Partnerships with children's families are encouraged through policies and procedures that enable and support cooperation and collaboration between program staff and families.
- *Recordkeeping and information system.* A reliable system of record and information storage and retrieval is in place to monitor resources and ensure a purposeful program.
- *Administration.* Administrative policies and procedural guidelines support the program and, consequently, service delivery.
- *Program evaluation.* Mechanisms for program evaluation and monitoring are in place and routinely practised.
- *Governance Standards.* The board of directors or owner sets the overall direction of the centre and is legally responsible for what it does.

The CCCF statement (p. 2) on quality begins with the following advice:

> This is your national statement on quality child care. Take ownership of it. Take it back to your work as a functional support for your efforts to improve quality child care. Take it back to your day care. Discuss it at staff meetings. Incorporate it into your parent policies. Teach it to your students. Do research on quality care. Share the information with parents. Invite governments to study it in the development or revision of standards. Use it as a tool in your lobby efforts. It is really important that you realize that we mean this to be a living document, a document that will continue to change and continue to be integrated into future editions.

Take time now to consider the indicators of quality for home- and centre-based early childhood education and care programs. Identify how you would apply these broad indicators to ensure high-quality early childhood education and care programs, and then check your applications against the statement in the Appendix. Can you find the dynamic, framework, and contextual components of quality in this statement? Are there any contradictions or missing pieces?

Accreditation. All of the components of quality programs that have been discussed in this chapter are discussed in detail in the NAEYC's position statement, *Developmentally Appropriate Practice in Early Childhood Programs Serving Children from Birth through Age 8* (Bredekamp, 1987). That statement represents a consensus of the thinking of many early childhood educators about appropriate and inappropriate practices in programs that span the time from infancy through the early elementary years. In the opening position statement, NAEYC affirms that a "quality early childhood program provides a safe and nurturing environment that promotes the physical, social, emotional, and **cognitive development** of young children while responding to the needs of families" (Bredekamp, 1987, p. 1). Guidelines are presented in the position statement that describes how principles of developmental appropriateness can be applied to four components of early childhood programs: curriculum, adult-child interactions, relations between family and program, and developmental evaluation of children. The statements describe the specifics of integrated components for appropriate and inappropriate practice for

2000

1950

1900

1850

1800

1750

1700

1650

1915
Maria Montessori has an exhibition classroom at the World's Fair in San Francisco.

Prenatal care is introduced through baby clinics in Regina, Saskatchewan.

1916
Women in Manitoba, Alberta, and Saskatchewan gain the right to vote in public elections.

Lucy Sprague Mitchell and Harriet Johnson begin the bureau of Educational Experiments in New York City. The Bureau is later to become the Bank Street School of Education.

infants, toddlers, three-year-olds, four- and five-year-olds, and children from five to eight years.

In 1985, the NAEYC established and administered a national, voluntary **accreditation** system for child care programs in the United States. The accreditation process is based on ten factors: the physical environment, health and safety, nutrition and food service, administration, staff qualifications and development, interactions among staff and children, staff-parent interaction, curriculum, staffing, and evaluation, with specific criteria defined in each factor (Bredekamp, 1990). The process itself involves self-study, guided by the NAEYC publication Accreditation Criteria and Procedures (Bredekamp, 1991).

Administrators, parents, and staff work on constructive improvements to create high-quality programs; excellence is then verified by visits and assessment from representatives of the NAEYC. The position statement on DAP (1987) made some of the desired outcomes regarding self-study and validation visits more explicit. The National Academy of Early Childhood Education Programs is a body within the NAEYC that administers the voluntary accreditation system for child care programs.

In Canada, the province of Alberta introduced the Child Care Accreditation Program in 2002. Funding for programs is tied to meeting the established accreditation standards (Alberta Children's Services, 2004): Child care centres are able to receive two types of funding:

- staff support funding: monthly funding for staff based on certification level; and
- quality funding: based on the licensed capacity and whether the centre generally or consistently is in compliance with licensing requirements.

Family day homes are able to receive two types of funding:

- provider support funding: paid monthly for providers who are in process or have completed mandatory training identified in the Provincial Safety Standards document "Training for Direct Care Providers"; and
- training grant funding: agencies are paid an annual amount per provider to develop training to meet training requirements under Alberta Safety Standards.

Evaluating Quality

Evaluating the quality of early child development programs is important to early childhood educators, to parents, and to policymakers, who might ask the following questions:

- What is the level of quality offered by an individual program?
- What type of early childhood service offers the best experience for my young child?
- What is the most effective use of public funding to promote quality ECEC programs?
- How can the impact of changes in staff qualifications, funding, or daily routines be monitored?

But quality can be looked at from different perspectives, as we saw at the beginning of this chapter. We have also considered the various dynamic, framework, and context elements of quality in early childhood settings. Which of these elements is most critical in evaluating the quality of early child development services?

The first step in answering these questions is to consider which aspect of quality to measure. Policymakers and researchers use three different possibilities:

- program ingredients or characteristics, which are mostly the framework and context quality elements;
- child or parent outcomes, which include the achievements, behaviours, and characteristics of children or parents; and
- program outcomes, which attempt to measure what children actually experience, or the dynamics of quality.

Evaluation Tools

Researchers and early childhood educators have developed tools to evaluate early child development programs. The Early Childhood Environment Rating Scale (ECERS) (Harms & Clifford, 1980) provides a scale with which to review preschool centre-based child care programs. The scale focuses on the physical environment and looks at the use of space, play materials, and learning experiences, as well as at adult-child interactions. There are thirty-seven items on the scale, with a continuum of possible performance. ECERS is the most frequently used measure of quality for research studies and is also useful as a tool to assist individual program development. In addition to the scale for preschool ECERS settings, there are comparable tools for infant and toddler settings, school-age settings, and family child care settings.

Not Found in Quality

Before we finish this discussion about what quality early childhood programs look like, it may be useful to identify what you will *not* see in a developmentally appropriate program.

Institutionalization

When decisions in programs are made to fit adult needs or preconceptions, children are often expected to behave and learn in ways that fit with the requirements of the institution, rather than in ways that nurture their growth and development. What do we mean by this? As you search your memory for early childhood education experiences, you may recall occasions when children have had to do things that were not necessarily good for them, their learning, or their self-esteem, but were deemed necessary for the good of the institution. Examples of this might include keeping exhausted toddlers awake so they can eat their lunch at the time convenient for the kitchen staff; insisting that first graders eat a silent lunch, so they can finish in twenty minutes and allow the next group to use the cafeteria; demanding that three-year-olds all sleep on their tummies at naptime, so they won't look around the room and prolong time for falling asleep; and insisting that two-year-olds give up all pacifiers.

2000

1950

1900

1850

1800

1750

1700

1650

1916–20
Mother's allowances/pensions are introduced in four provinces (British Columbia, Alberta, Manitoba, and Ontario). This provides financial assistance to poor, single mothers and their young children.

1917
Women with property are permitted to hold office in Saskatchewan. Women in British Columbia and Ontario gain the right to vote in provincial elections.

Caroline Pratt's Play School (later to become City and Country School) is growing. Lucy Sprague is one of its teachers.

RESEARCH INTO PRACTICE

What Is Quality Child Care About?

It's about warmth and caring and interesting things to do. It's about high self-esteem and genuine concern about the quality of everyone's day. It's about playing games and singing songs and playing house and holding and laughing and having a nice time. It's about everyone being accepted and respected without reservation—and telling each other this in lots of ways. It's about overlooking transgressions so we can get on with things that really count. It's about children and adults spending the day together and looking forward to spending tomorrow together, too.

What Is Poor Quality Child Care About?

It's about criticism and harsh voices and stern faces and frowns. It's about battles of will between children and adults. It's about threats and time-outs for everything. It's about too many rules and bribery and adults who always stand up and no one can sit in their laps. It's about not much that's interesting going on and waiting for time to go home and wishing you didn't have to come back tomorrow.

Source: Allen (1991), p. 18. Used with permission.

Sometimes inappropriate practices exist because "that's the way we've always done it," and no one is applying the test of developmental appropriateness to it. Sometimes inappropriate practices exist because the adults in charge are thinking about adult convenience, efficiency, time, or budgets. Sometimes they exist because the adults lack child development knowledge or awareness of current thinking about appropriate practices. And sometimes they exist because adults believe that children need to endure negatives to strengthen their character. Whatever the reason, practices that do not nurture development and learning through emphasis on support and acceptance of individuals are bad for us all and dehumanize society.

Failure

If early childhood schools and programs stand ready to adapt to children's individual needs and achievements, there will always be opportunities for children to find a comfortable learning level and style and, thus, to succeed. But when programs apply their own arbitrarily drawn standards for success to children at various ages, there are too many occasions when children will have to fail, since arbitrary standards allow no room for individual timetables. For example, readiness testing before gaining admission to kindergarten is going to exclude some children who have failed to meet the school system's standard for readiness. Proof of having completed toilet training before moving on to the next preschool classroom will negatively characterize those children who are not yet ready. Not yet being ready to move from two to one nap per day may mean that some young toddlers will be denied moving on to the wonderful stimulation of the next class. Standardized testing at the end of Grade Two will find those children deficient who are learning at a less-standardized rate. As long as schools and programs apply firm and arbitrary standards, with no room for individual needs or developmental patterns, children will fail, and they and their parents will be burdened by a negative evaluation that may have a lasting impact on future learning and development (Kamii, 1990).

Indifference

Quality programs for young children depend on adults who have visions of wonderful worlds to support children and families, and who are unwilling to accept mediocre facilities, policies, or curricula as the way it has to be. When early childhood educators and caregivers are not knowledgeable enough to be able to know the mediocre from the excellent, when they become overwhelmed by the discrepancies between what they know should be and what is, or when they become indifferent to lack of quality, too many less-than-wonderful situations for children will exist. Indifference is an enemy to good early childhood education.

This is a good time for you to consider other conditions that you believe you should not find in good early childhood education and care programs for young children. Write them down for later discussion. Recognizing what is opposite to excellence in early childhood education and care will help you define your personal standards.

Partners in Quality

The CCCF and its provincial/affiliate organizations completed a research and development project, called Partners in Quality, on how all the partners or stakeholders in early childhood education and care can work together to improve quality. The project's activities include a questionnaire survey of views on quality, including the views of parents and family members, early childhood educators and other caregivers, early childhood education and care program administrators, child care organizations, governments, training institutions, and communities.

The project distributed copies of surveys across Canada in 1997 and collected thousands of responses from early childhood educators and other stakeholders. The results have been analyzed and used to develop a national framework of resources for enhancing quality including manuals and worksheets to promote community and leadership development. ECE students are partners in quality and have distinctive, if changing, perspectives on quality. The questions in the survey are the basis for a useful tool to consider the similarities and differences between your perspectives and those of your colleagues. The Theory into Practice below provides a questionnaire for ECE students. Compare your responses with your classmates'.

RESEARCH INTO PRACTICE

Partners in Quality Survey for ECE Students

- Complete the following sentence: I consider a child care/early childhood setting as being high quality when it has the following characteristics:
  - The protection of the child's health and safety is a basic requirement for any child care/early childhood setting. List the three other most important requirements that you would seek in such a setting for your own child.
  - What are the two most important ways in which an early childhood educator or an early childhood setting can support families?
  - What kinds of involvement with families do you feel is desirable (e.g., the type and frequency of information sharing)?
  - What do you believe are the main barriers to family involvement?
  - How do you think children should be involved in establishing and implementing daily activities in an early childhood setting? (Identify the age range of the children you have in mind.)
- Here is a list of mechanisms for promoting quality. Rank their importance as very important, important, somewhat important, not too important or not applicable.
  - government regulations
  - government monitoring of its regulations
  - recurring government funding, e.g., an annual grant
  - Early Childhood Education training before starting to provide child care/early childhood education
  - in-service professional development
  - parent/family involvement
  - community involvement
  - staff mutual support groups
  - trade unions
  - professional associations
  - program accreditation
  - program research
  - other (please specify)
- Referring to the mechanisms identified in the question above, please rank the five you believe are the most important for promoting quality.
- Do you believe that any of the mechanisms listed above are barriers to promoting quality? If yes, which mechanisms? How?
- In what ways do you, as a student early childhood educator, try to involve families?
- How do you address situations in which you and the family have different beliefs about or approaches to childrearing?
- Indicate if the programs where you have completed or are currently completing a field placement have regular contact or links with any of the community services listed below. Be specific about the type of link e.g., "information-sharing about specific children"; "joint in-service training programs"; "sit on the same community services planning committee."

(Cont'd)

– elementary school
– family resource program
– public child welfare agency (child and family services)
– public health nurse or unit
– municipal parks and recreation department
– other

- What informal or formal approaches have you found effective in assessing the quality of your daily practice?
- What type of observation notes, program plans, journal and/or record-keeping do you use in your field placement?
- What opportunities to you have for dialogue with colleagues while you are in field placement?
- What changes or additions would you like to make to your field placement program to improve its quality? What is holding you back?
- Have you any additional comments about quality or what is required to provide quality?

Source: Adapted from Canadian Child Care Federation (1997).

SUMMARY

The Canadian Child Care Federation and other organizations have described standards for developmentally appropriate practice. These standards include specific criteria for curriculum, adult-child interaction, relationships with families, and physical early childhood environments for children from birth to twelve years and their families. In this chapter, we examined the dynamic, framework, and context components of quality early childhood settings. These components include respect for the individuals involved, responsiveness to children's needs, reciprocity of learning for all participants, developmental knowledge, optimal numbers of children, integrated learning experiences, physical environments to facilitate active learning, organizational climate, funding, regulation, and non-regulatory mechanisms. Components not found in quality programs include institutionalization, failure, and indifference.

REVIEW QUESTIONS

1. Describe several components to be found in quality early childhood programs. Why are these elements necessary?
2. For each component described above, discuss several practices that might be included in program structure or function.
3. Discuss the CCCF statement on quality child care for both family child care and child care centres.
4. Identify what is meant by the NAEYC position statement on developmentally appropriate practice.
5. Identify several components not found in quality programs. Explain why these practices should be avoided.

STUDY ACTIVITIES

1. Complete the Partners in Quality questionnaire on pages 106–107 and compare your answers with others in your class. Perhaps you can collect students' answers and analyze what elements of quality your class of ECE students rates as the most important.
2. In small groups, discuss with classmates the statements and experiences you reflected on and recorded in your notebook throughout the chapter. Identify experiences that seem to support components discussed in the chapter. Identify experiences that seem at variance with the components. Identify additional ideas discussed by participants.
3. Write a personal statement of your belief or philosophy of quality early childhood care and education, based on your thinking and reading to this point.
4. Prepare a statement to deliver at a school board meeting that discusses whether or not to exclude five-year-olds who fail to achieve a specific score on a readiness test given before admission.
5. Prepare answers to the following questions from parents:
   a. Why do the children spend most of their time playing in your classroom?
   b. Why are some of the two-year-olds beginning toilet training, and some not?
   c. Why doesn't my four-year-old bring home artwork every day, as my neighbour's child does?
   d. Why do you call it teaching when you're not doing reading or math lessons or anything like that?
6. Read the CCCF national statement on quality child care. What key words do you find in the statement?
7. Go to www.ece.nelson.com. What can you find out about different perspectives on quality?

KEY TERMS

accreditation: System of voluntary evaluation of excellence in early childhood centres, administered by the National Academy for Early Childhood Education and established by the NAEYC.

assessment: Evaluation of abilities, skills, and knowledge when referring to persons, or components when referring to environments.

Association of Childhood Education International (ACEI): Oldest early childhood professional organization in the United States. Originally associated with the kindergarten movement.

child-sensitive: (Also called child-centred.) Programs whose practices are responsive to knowledge and observations about children.

cognitive development: Related to mental functions of thinking, perceiving, and learning.

diversity: Variety of differences that exist in a classroom, community, culture, or country. Diversity may refer to ability, gender, age, race, culture, and so on.

emotional development: Related to feelings and expression of them.

environment: Everything that surrounds the children that, therefore, affects their lives. Includes physical arrangements of time and space, materials and activities within the environment, and the people available for interaction.

fine motor: Related to the smaller muscles of the body and limbs, such as those in the fingers, toes, face, sphincters.
gross motor: Related to the whole body and to the larger muscles such as those in the legs, arms, trunk.
integrated curriculum: Centres on activities that address many aspects of development and knowledge, rather than separating curriculum into numerous skill areas.
interest centres: Also called learning centres. Classroom areas arranged for particular activities chosen by children. Examples are art, block, and book centres.
interrelationships: Connections between one aspect of development and another, and between people.
moral development: Related to acquiring a sense of right and wrong behaviour and to the ability to control one's actions according to these internalized standards.
open-ended: Activities, materials, or communications that permit various responses and reactions, rather than one fixed correct response.
physical development: Related to growth and coordination.
position statement: Statement of philosophy of a professional organization, used to guide the practice of professionals.
primary caregiver: Person assigned responsibility for a small subgroup of children within a larger group.
reciprocity: Mutual give-and-take.
respect: Recognition of, and sensitivity to, self and others.
responsiveness: Being sensitive to a child's emotional and physical needs, and taking actions to meet those needs.
self-esteem: Sense of self-worth, or value placed on the image of self.
self-identity: Image of self, constructed by feedback from others and cognitive understanding of gender, race, ability, and the cultural messages about these components.
self-regulation: Ability to regulate one's response to challenges and stresses, related behaviour, attention, and memory.
social development: Steps in learning appropriate social interaction with peers and adults.
staff turnover: Rate at which practitioners leave their place of employment and seek other work.
theory: Set of ideas, principles, or explanations that explain phenomena.
transition: Period of change. Daily classroom schedule contains several, e.g., when children change classrooms.
whole child: Theory that supports recognizing the separate and interrelated aspects of the individual, including the domains of the physical, cognitive, language, emotional, and social development.

SUGGESTED READINGS

Balaban, Nancy. (1990, March). Statement to the Montgomery County Council. *Young Children,* 45 (3), 12–16.

———. (1995, March). Reaffirming a national commitment to children. *Young Children,* 50 (3), 61–63.

Bredekamp, S. & Rosegrant, T. (Eds.). (1991). *Reaching potentials: Appropriate curriculum and assessment for young children.* Washington, DC: NAEYC.

Christie, J. F. & Wardel, F. (1992, March). How much time is needed for play? *Young Children*, 47 (3), 28–32.

Canadian Child Care Federation. (2000). *Partners in quality: Tools for administrators in child care settings*. Ottawa: CCCF.

Doherty, G. (2001). Regulations as a strategy for promoting quality in child care settings. In *Research Connections Canada: Supporting Children and Families*, 6.

Friendly, M., Doherty, G., & Beach, J. (2006). *Quality by design: What do we know about quality in early learning and child care and what do we think? A literature review*. Toronto: Childcare Resource & Research Unit, University of Toronto. Available at http://www.childcarequality.ca, Accessed May 15, 2006.

Greenberg, Polly. (1990, January). Why not academic preschool? (Part 1). *Young Children*, 45 (2), 70–80.

Greenman, Jim. (1994, November). Institutionalized childhoods: Reconsidering our part in the lives of children. *Child Care Information Exchange*, 63–67.

Honig, Alice S. (1989, May). Quality infant/toddler caregiving: Are there magic recipes? *Young Children*, 44 (4), 4–10.

Kamii, Constance. (1985, September). Leading primary education toward excellence. *Young Children*, 40 (6), 3–9.

Katz, Lilian G. (1994, November). What should young children be learning? *Child Care Information Exchange*, 23–25.

Kelman, Anna. (1990, March). Choices for children. *Young Children*, 45 (3), 42–45.

Moss, P. & Pense, A. (Eds.). (1994). *Valuing quality in early childhood services*. New York: Teachers College Press.

NAESP. (1990). *Early childhood education and the elementary school principal: Standards for quality programs for young children*. Alexandria, VA: Author.

NASBE. (1991). *Caring communities: Supporting young children and families*. The Report of the National Task Force on School Readiness. Alexandria, VA: Author.

Sava, Samuel G. (1987, March). Development, not academics. *Young Children*, 42 (3),15.

Section Two

The Early Childhood Workforce

In Section One we examined the organization of early child development programs in Canada. We also discussed quality in early childhood settings. From this framework, it is time to look at the roles of early childhood educators, who make up the early childhood workforce. Chapter 4 will highlight the responsibilities of those who are part of the early childhood workforce. Chapter 5 will examine early childhood educators' motivations for entering the field and paths of early child development. Chapter 6 will look at the work environment and the opportunities and challenges that lie ahead for the early childhood workforce.

Be prepared to think honestly about yourself in relation to the early childhood workforce. Could this be your life?

From *The Good Preschool Teacher*

For these six women, teaching involves a search for meaning in the world. Teaching has become for each a life project, a calling, a vocation that is an organizing center of all other activities. Teaching is past and future as well as present, it is background as well as foreground, it is depth as well as surface. Teaching is pain and humor, joy and anger, dreariness and epiphany. For these six, teaching is world building, it is architecture and design, it is purpose and moral enterprise. Teaching is a way of being in the world that breaks through the boundaries of the traditional job and in the process redefines all life and teaching itself.

"Teaching as identity" is the clearest theme to emerge in this inquiry, and "teaching as identity" is the frame through which each portrait makes sense. In these portraits, there is no clear line delineating the person and the teacher. Teaching is not simply what one does, it is who one is. Teaching is a life, a way of being in the world, an intentional circle for those six outstanding teachers.

There are, of course, teachers who are narrower in their concerns and more clearly bounded in their jobs than those outstanding teachers are. And yet, teaching is the kind of activity that calls out strongly for an investing of oneself. For many, perhaps most teachers, the sense of calling exists. It may be only a flicker of memory or a feeling dulled by years of bureaucratic maneuvering, endless demands, and excruciating complexity; it may exist now only as a shadowy palimpsest, that little erasure that leaves tracks on the page. But somewhere along the way, teaching called out to teachers as a chance to love children, to make a difference in their lives, to remake the world. Teachers somewhere, sometime felt called to teach (William Ayers. [1989]. *The Good Preschool Teacher* [pp. 130–31]).

CHAPTER FOUR

Early Childhood Educators

OBJECTIVES

After studying this chapter, students will be able to

- define the terms "early childhood workforce" and "early childhood educators";
- describe the profiles of early childhood educators who work with young children in early child development programs and in home settings;
- identify several distinct roles played by early childhood educators; and
- discuss how the key roles of early childhood educators support children's optimal development.

Early Childhood Educators

Early childhood educators work with young children and their families.

About 300 000 individuals, mostly women, work with young children in early child development programs and home care settings across Canada. This chapter will focus on those people who are trained and educated as early childhood educators and who may work in child care centres, nursery school programs, home-based child care, family resource programs, and kindergartens.

You are preparing to enter the early childhood workforce. As an early childhood educator, you will have several roles in caring for and educating young children. You will ensure that children are safe and that their basic physical needs are met. You will provide opportunities for learning by creating the framework for good programs and curricula. You will make connections with the larger community that supports children and their families. But your most important role will be getting to know, understanding, and relating to each child and her family.

This image goes far beyond the dictionary definition of the word "teacher." The role of an early childhood educator in any early child development setting is more complex than that of a traditional teacher. The term "caregiver" implies too custodial a function and, to many, overlooks the importance of helping children to develop knowledge and skills. As the search for appropriate terminology continues, the term "early childhood workforce" seems most appropriate to describe the sector of individuals who work with young children and their families in many different settings. "Early childhood educator" describes those within the early childhood workforce who have specific training and education in child development and in early child development practices.

The Early Childhood Workforce Defined

The 300 000 individuals who now work with young children and their families in home-based and group settings have different job titles, earn different salaries and benefits, and spend each day in different kinds of environments. But much of what they do each day is similar. Table 4.1 introduces you to some of the similarities and differences among those who work with young children in Canada. Early childhood educators, as well as those who do not have specific training or education, are included in each group.

Within each of the groups of individuals who work with young children and their families in Table 4.1, there are early childhood educators who have specific postsecondary qualifications in early child development, usually an early childhood education (ECE) credential. In regulated child care centres, 70 percent of all staff working with children have a one-year, two-year, three-year, or higher credential in ECE (Doherty et al, 2000).

Early childhood educators may work in any of the early child development settings described in Chapter 1. In Canada, we find early childhood educators in child care centres, nursery schools, kindergarten classrooms, early intervention services, family literacy programs, family resource programs, family child care, and in-home care. Early childhood educators, working in a variety of early child development settings, make up the early childhood workforce.

TABLE 4.1

Working with Young Children

	Total (N)	*Postsecondary Education*	*Average Income Full-time ($)*
Child Care Centre[a] (including school age child care) & Nursery School Staff	92 480	75%	22 000
Family Child Caregivers	43 695	45%	15 000
In-home Caregivers[b] (including nannies)	92 730	22%	17 450
Family Resource Program Staff[c]	4 000–5 000	n/a	n/a
Early Intervention Staff	26 000+	n/a	n/a
Kindergarten Teachers	30 000	95%	47 000
Kindergarten Educational Assistants	10 000	60%	27 000

[a] Includes school-age child care

[b] Includes nannies

[c] Includes family-child drop-in programs, family literacy programs, toy-lending libraries, etc.

Sources: Adapted from Beach, Bertrand, & Cleveland (1998); Doherty, Lero, Goelman, LeGrange, & Tougas (2000); Beach et al., (2004).

A Diverse Workforce

"Demonstrating diversity in the workforce to children through the visibility of men and women . . . alongside the visibility of people of colour, is an important goal for enhancing the quality of childcare" (Cameron et al., 1999, in Moss, 2000 p. 14).

Is Canada's early childhood workforce a workforce that is representative of the population at large? Look around your class, and consider your field placements.

The first observation that you are likely to make is that the early childhood workforce in Canada is predominantly female—about 97 percent. Early childhood workforces in other countries—Sweden, United States, Australia, Britain, New Zealand, Spain, France, Denmark, Italy, etc.—are also predominantly female (Moss, 2000). In the next section, we will look at some of the challenges facing men in early childhood settings. The care, education, and development of young children remain women's responsibilities. The early childhood workforce is probably the most gendered workforce in North America, Europe, Australia, or New Zealand (Moss, 2000).

However, early childhood educators and ECE classrooms do represent Canada's cultural, linguistic, religious, and ethnic diversity, which is an enormous strength of the early childhood workforce. In urban centres, immigrants, newcomers, and visible minorities make up a large proportion of the population. Approximately 20 percent of early childhood educators and assistants are immigrants, which mirrors the make-up of the Canadian workforce overall (Beach et al., 2004). Immigrants are underrepresented among kindergarten teachers and overrepresented among in-home caregivers (e.g., nannies, babysitters, and parents' helpers).

Few men work in early childhood education and care programs.

Men in the Early Childhood Workforce

If you are a male entering the early childhood field, there are additional issues of respect for you to consider. At this time, men constitute only a small part of all early childhood educators in Canada, probably about 3 percent (Beach et al., 1998). Professional attitudes and practices may have been defined too narrowly as a result of the dominance of females in the field. But it is likely that men avoid the field for specific reasons related to status, economic conditions, and bias.

Most cultures convey to most men the idea that they have to compete in the job field as a measure of their worth. We have already discussed the relatively low status accorded to early childhood teachers, and many men are reluctant to enter a field that is accorded so little recognition. Many men also report that family, friends, and even academic counsellors strongly discourage their working with young children, as they feel it is far beneath their talents. When considering long-term career opportunities, as most men have been socialized to do, the early childhood field appears to have relatively little opportunity for advancement.

2000
1950
1918
The Canadian National Committee for Mental Hygiene is established and transfers ideas on child study from the United States.
1900
1850

Women gain full federal franchise. Women in Nova Scotia gain the right to vote in provincial elections.
1800
1750
1700
1650

The poor salaries in early childhood education and care programs probably encourage more men than women to look for other employment opportunities. Even today, many men still consider careers in the light of being a major contributor to the financial support of a family, and it is difficult to imagine bearing the costs of raising a family on the limited salaries of most early childhood educators. The majority of men who work in the early childhood field are married, with at least one child (Robinson, 1988), and many find they cannot afford to work for long in the field. Men certainly have more options than women do for employment even today, and would more likely opt for those that pay substantially more than early childhood education. And yet this contributes to a vicious cycle: it seems probable that if more men entered the field, the low salaries accorded to a mostly female profession would increase.

Although in the decades since the women's movement, more men play a more active role in parenting, indicating their abilities and interest in nurturing young children, there is still widespread gender bias. This bias translates into both overt action and covert attitudes that prevent males from feeling acceptance in early childhood centres and schools, to say nothing of within ECE postsecondary education programs. Early childhood education is associated with the role of mothering, and men, who obviously cannot be mothers, are seen as less capable of caring for young children. The teaching role is associated with a variety of characteristics that are generally classified as female traits, such as patience, gentle nurturing, and emotional sensitivity, as opposed to aggressiveness and emotional control. Men who are willing to take on these roles are unfairly subjected to conjecture and suspicion about their masculinity.

A few widely publicized cases of sexual abuse in the past decade have added fuel to this discriminatory fire, to the point where men are often subjected to humiliating questions and restrictions. There have been instances when directors have refused to allow male students in rooms where diapers would be changed or have refused employment to well-qualified candidates on the basis that "the parents would be uncomfortable." Men do report bias directed toward them by directors, parents, and even female co-workers. Small wonder that few choose to become uncomfortable minorities within the early childhood field.

And this is a pity. It would appear that men in early childhood programs have much to offer. Seifert (1988) refers to a "compensation hypothesis," meaning that male early childhood educators could perhaps compensate for the lack of male involvement in the lives of many young children, as well as offer children of both sexes a model of a caring, nurturing male. He also speaks of a "social equity hypothesis," meaning that the presence of men in these programs would help society in general, and children in particular, to discover the many options available to men and women. Little research has been done on male early childhood educators; however, it is clear that their presence in the workforce could add a stronger voice for the emergence of a true profession, in which colleagues are not restricted by current stereotypes of "women's work."

As a male, are you willing to recognize the stereotypes and counter them with your own personality and ideals? As a female, are you able to support males as true colleagues, who can work with you for the nurturing and care of young children, as well as for the growth of the profession?

Early Childhood Educator Roles

"We need reflective and well-informed practitioners, who do not assume there is one best practice which suits all, but who are able to recognize, explore, and discuss the arc of human possibilities" (Penn, 1999, p. 4).

When we refer to early childhood educator roles, we are referring to the particular functions and behaviours that early childhood educators are expected to perform and exhibit. If you were to ask experienced early childhood educators what they do on any given day, they might respond with a list of nouns associated with particular actions. That list might include nurse, diplomat, housekeeper, artist, musician, judge, cook, friend, bookkeeper, entertainer, and instructor. They might add some specific skills that have been handy: repairing toys, detecting guilt or sources of strange odours, restoring physical order from chaos, unstopping toilets, and determining fair solutions to playground conflicts.

As we discussed in Chapter 3, early childhood educators are critical to the provision of high-quality early child development. Above all else, early childhood educators must recognize their roles and responsibilities in supporting optimal child development and respecting family relationships. A recent review of research studies in neuroscience, social sciences, education, health, and child development identified four broad determinants of optimal child development: protection, relationships, opportunities, and communities (Guy, 1997). These determinants provide a framework for identifying the early childhood educators' key roles in supporting children's optimal development in early child development settings.

Providing Protection

Early childhood educators meet children's physical needs for safety, nutrition, health care, and hygiene. **Caregiving** means ensuring that children eat healthy foods, get enough rest, and are in safe, secure physical environments.

Early childhood educators working with younger children will find that they spend a great deal of time changing diapers and cleansing, feeding children or helping them learn to feed themselves, serving food and cleaning up afterward, helping with hand-washing and face-wiping, and changing clothes after spills or accidents. Through such commonplace daily acts, adults provide children with gentleness and demonstrate skills that children can eventually acquire themselves. Physical care is a core part of the daily routine and is not something to rush through. Daily routines are opportunities to provide responsive care and learning moments.

Safe and healthy daily routines protect children.

Providing protection also means protecting children from harm. Safety must be a priority for all early childhood educators. You have an obligation to be aware of situations that put children at risk of harm. You also have an obligation to take action if you suspect any form of child maltreatment.

1919

Women in New Brunswick gain the right to vote in provincial elections.

Margaret McMillan publishes *The Nursery School*. (Her sister Rachel died in 1917.)

Harriet Johnson establishes the Nursery School of the Bureau of Educational Experiments.

Establishing Relationships

With the youngest children, the warm physical contact and responsiveness that accompany the providing of physical needs is an interrelated and inseparable part of establishing relationships. The gentle stroking and soft crooning that accompanies the cleansing bath and the warmly enfolding arms that hold the baby being fed the bottle are both **nurturing** to overall development. Young children's healthy social/emotional development (and their cognitive development) depends on their involvement in warm, supportive relationships with caring adults. The most important relationships, of course, are with their parents and other family members. But early childhood educators involved in their care also hold key roles in healthy personality development.

Often, early childhood educators are the first people outside the family with whom children have caring relationships. The need for warm, responsive relationships does not disappear with toddlerhood; preschoolers and school-age children also look for affection and responsiveness from early childhood educators.

Relationships are established through sustained positive interactions between children and early childhood educators. In positive interactions, adults are responsive to children's verbal and nonverbal communication and encourage two-way or turn-taking conversation. Some children enjoy a lot of physical contact, whereas others do not. Early childhood educators can demonstrate warmth and emotional responsiveness to children in many ways: in gentle smiles and eye contact; in a warm tone of voice; in personal attention and shared moments. The exact manner of interaction that builds relationships is individual. Children know when they are genuinely cared for, even though the message may come in different ways.

For babies and toddlers, positive interaction may include being "smoothers of jangled feelings . . . comforters . . . facilitators of parent-child separations" (Balaban, 1992, pp. 69–70), as well as rockers, singers, and tummy-kissers. For preschoolers, care may include touching a child on the arm when passing, offering moments of quiet conversation, and bestowing a special hug to say good morning. For school-age children, it may be offering a joke that the child can appreciate, teasing gently about private secrets, and giving a personal wink or a thumbs-up sign. All of these interactions tell children that early childhood educators know and like them as unique individuals.

Another part of the early childhood educator's role in creating positive relationships is setting limits and guiding behaviour. Young children slowly understand which behaviour is acceptable in their homes and in other environments. Children gradually internalize this understanding to regulate their own behaviour. In the meantime, they need adults who understand how difficult a process this is, and who can guide them positively and effectively as they learn to live within limits.

Young children need to have adults around them who are using their power with warmth, support, encouragement, and good explanations of the limits they must impose. As early childhood educators base their guidance decisions on their developmental understandings of how children think, learn, and develop impulse control, they are more likely to guide as firm and friendly adults. Within the context of caring relationships, children come to trust that adults will help them regulate their behaviour.

Early childhood educators use both direct and indirect guidance as part of their relationships with young children.

- **Indirect guidance** refers to the behind-the-scenes arrangements that early childhood educators make in the environment that not only prevent problems from occurring but also help children learn appropriate behaviour. Indirect guidance actually reduces the number of conflicts or problem situations that arise, making the atmosphere more positive and reducing the need for direct adult intervention.
- **Direct guidance** includes either verbal or nonverbal messages that early childhood educators send to children about appropriate behaviours. These messages include explanations of what the children's limits are, the reasons for them, and what changes in behaviour are necessary. Early childhood educators learn to communicate clearly, in terms that children can understand. They are careful to use words and techniques that teach without shaming or demeaning children. They are less concerned with merely stopping the undesirable behaviour or disciplining the child, and more concerned about what the child can learn about behaviour. Children need to discover that their behaviour affects the way others respond to them and that they cannot hurt other people or ignore their rights. They need to learn that some ways of expressing feelings are unacceptable, especially when they infringe on the rights of others. They need to learn that they can discuss differences and disagreements and do not have to rely on physical force to solve problems. Children need to learn that adults will keep them safe while helping all the children in the group learn to live within limits.

Building positive relationships with children means both directly and indirectly guiding children's behaviour, based on an understanding of children's development. Positive relationships do not include harsh or punitive measures or the withdrawal of warmth and affection. Besides undermining both the adult-child relationship and the child's self-esteem, these actions are ineffective in either changing behaviours or supporting children's abilities to regulate their own behaviour.

Early childhood educators set up the environment to offer learning opportunities for each child.

Designing Learning Opportunities

Children whose physical and emotional needs are met are primed to learn from the world around them. They are active and ready receptors for stimulation from new experiences, which provide them with the learning they need for later competencies.

As resource persons who help children as they construct their own continually shifting knowledge of the world, early childhood educators facilitate children's active learning. They provide time, space, materials, and support for children's active explorations to promote development and learning. They choose to make specific opportunities available based on their knowledge of individual children, child development, and family and ethnocultural goals and needs.

2000
1950
1920
Uniform franchise is established through the *Dominion Election Act*, making permanent the right of women to be elected to Parliament.
1900
1850
1800
1750
1700
1650

In designing learning opportunities that contribute to optimal development, early childhood educators

- are continually learning more about educational theory and practice in general and, in particular, about the children and families with whom they work. They seek out new information and experiences of others, gather information about their own group of children through observations, and set specific goals for supporting children's development and learning.
- organize and create the environment for children's active learning. They decide on the aesthetics of the environment, creating a look that invites children to participate. They set the order and organization of the children's environment, placing objects where they will attract notice and can be used most effectively. They consider what materials, toys, and objects will enhance the environment for particular children.
- match their teaching strategies to what is required to best assist a child's learning. The term "scaffolding" describes the process of helping children reach new levels of understanding (Berk & Winsler, 1995). Russian psychologist Lev Vygotsky used this term to describe the kind of assistance that adults give children in their learning. "If the children have gone from [point] A to B and are getting very close to C, sometimes to reach C, the child needs to borrow assistance from the adult at that very special moment" (Filippini, quoted in Edwards, 1994, p. 153). In helping a child take the next step, the adult functions rather like a scaffold that allows the child to reach further than would be possible unassisted.

Bringing children to learning opportunities is part of the supportive relationship between an early childhood educator and a child; the child learns through active involvement, not through passively receiving information.

Early childhood educators open up learning opportunities for young children when they expect children to become confident and competent. These expectations encourage a young child's hopefulness.

> An amazing quality of the human brain is to create an image of the future. To make an internalization of a better place, a better way, a better life, a better world. This capacity is called hope . . . Some of the most influential people in any person's life may be someone they have never met. They have used that person to create an inner image to aspire to, to idealize, to idolize. Role models, mentors, heroes—all can provide critical formative experiences for children (Perry, 1996, pp. 8–9).

Connecting with Communities

Early childhood educators are part of broader communities—neighbourhood, faith, ethnocultural, school, professional, and workplace communities. They can connect the families they work with to the resources and supports available in various communities. They can connect children to other services to meet their health or developmental needs or to programs that offer specialized opportunities for recreation, sports, and cultural activities.

Across North America, there is a trend in child and family services, including early child development programs, to improve the coordination and integration of a continuum of services at the local level (Benner, 1999; Corter et al., 2006). Early child

Children live in families and families live in communities.

development programs have an important place within this continuum, but early childhood educators will need to be actively involved in planning, delivering, and evaluating these services. Child care centres, nursery schools, and family child care homes cannot best serve children and families if they remain outside this continuum, which includes players from education, health, and social services.

In Canada, there are currently a number of exciting initiatives that provide a holistic view of community. They have incorporated early child development into a continuum of services and programs that are founded on principles of community decision-making and autonomy. These initiatives include South East Grey Community Outreach and the Better Beginnings, Better Futures projects discussed in Chapter 1.

MAKING IT HAPPEN

The Council for Early Child Development

Community Fellows Program

Founded by Dr. Fraser Mustard in 2004, the Council for Early Child Development is based on the recommendations of the *Early Years Study* (McCain & Mustard, 1999). The Board of Directors draws from business, education, health, academia, early child development communities, and private citizens. The Council's operation is supported by foundation and private sector contributions. It is a not-for-profit, non-governmental association of community and scientific networks with a focus on early child development science and community action.

(cont'd)

The Council for Early Child Development (cont'd)

The Council envisions community-based early child development and parenting centres linked to the school system and available to all families and young children. To achieve its vision, the Council will put science into action for children.

The Council developed a Community Leadership Fellows' Program. In February 2006, the inaugural class of Council Fellows' gathered in Toronto for their first networking and planning retreat. These community leaders, several of whom are early childhood educators, were chosen for their community involvement with existing ECD initiatives, their ability to build effective cross-sectoral teams, and their commitment to develop and sustain their community's leadership capacity. The goals of the program are to:

- Leverage existing expertise and knowledge within communities and provinces through cross-fertilization and networking;
- Increase leadership and technical skills necessary for community-based and cross-systems work on early child development; and
- Help build the community's long-term capacity to improve early child development outcomes by enabling community leaders to forge the development of integrated early child development and parenting centres.

The Council's Fellows will be provided with the following supports and resources:

- Strategic retreats
- A peer support system
- Quarterly teleconferences
- Knowledge brokering
- An on-line, multimedia curriculum resource

This first group of Fellows were chosen because of their community involvement with existing early child development and parenting initiatives; ability to build effective cross-sectoral teams; and commitment to develop and sustain their community's leadership capacity.

The Council's ten Community Fellows are taking part in a community leadership program that is designed to work within the parameters of their existing roles and commitments. Each community leader is designing their own goals, objectives, and evaluation outcomes in collaboration with their community team of collaborators and experts. Council Fellows have access to internationally recognized experts, lateral learning and networking opportunities with their peers across Canada, and state-of-the-art training in inter-sectoral collaboration on early child development.

Find out more at http://www.councilecd.ca

MEET THE EARLY CHILDHOOD WORKFORCE

Sheila Murdock

Sheila Murdock, early childhood educator, is one of the Council for Early Child Development's Community Fellows. She lives in the Fisher River Cree Nation that is located between 50 and 350 km from Winnipeg. The Fisher River Cree Nation has an on-reserve population of about 1 600 people, and an off-reserve population of approximately 1 200.

"Why wait for government to tell us how to do it?" says Sheila. The Fisher River Cree Nation began discussing the idea of an early child development hub model in September 2003, when the ECD "single-window" buzz was just starting, and the federal government was beginning to consult with First Nations on this idea. Sheila Murdock took the idea to the band council and their chief. They liked the idea of having a single location where families had access to all the available ECD resources. She got their support when they realized that their reserve could build the hub relatively easily, and the federal government might take years to act. In retrospect, Sheila says the most important step in building support for an integrated hub model linked to the school was getting the chief and council's support.

The hub was possible in part because the band was given funding to set up an Aboriginal Head Start program and needed to build a structure to house the program. Because the band has a flexible funding agreement with Indian and Northern Affairs Canada (it receives funding in 5-year blocks) along with a health transfer agreement, they had some leeway in how they combined and organized these funds.

Once the chief and council agreed to the idea of building an integrated ECD hub model linked to the school, Sheila sought the community's support. Part of the idea of the hub was to have a space connected to the school. To help convince the school to support the idea, the hub building-plan included a gymnasium that was large enough to meet the needs of children up to fourth grade.

Sheila points out that the two biggest challenges to healthy child development for the Fisher River Cree Nation are lack of access to quality ECD programs, and finding the resources to construct a facility in which to implement such programs. Up until now, daycare was only available for parents who worked or were in school, so children who needed care for other reasons (e.g., providing a stimulating environment, respite for parents, etc.) could not access this program. The hub model's outreach program that begins this fall will help to change this—"[A]ll young children in our community will benefit from participating in the ECD hub," says Sheila.

Sheila shares the story of the hub because she is proud of her community's achievement. She often gets calls from other First Nations communities to discuss progress to date on "the hub." "In some ways," notes Sheila, "we are ahead of the mainstream ECD sector in the province, which is now starting to show interest in piloting ECD hub models. We just decided it was what we needed to do, and to stop waiting until governments see what needs to be done."

Source: Sheila Murdoch, Interview 2005

What Early Childhood Educators Do

A number of initiatives have identified the key skills and competencies that early childhood educators working with young children in early childhood settings need. The recent Child Care Sector Study (Beach et al., 1998) describes the skills and competencies early childhood educators need to work with young children, whether in centre or home-based environments.

1921
The first Canadian maternity protection legislation is introduced in British Columbia.

Patty Smith Hill begins a lab nursery school at Columbia Teachers College.

An early childhood educator will

- ensure that the physical environment and daily practices of caregiving promote the health, safety, and well-being of children in care;
- establish a working partnership with parents that supports their responsibilities to their children;
- develop and maintain a responsive relationship with each child and with the children as a group;
- plan and provide daily learning opportunities, routines, and activities that promote positive child development;
- observe and think about children's activity and behaviour;
- act in a manner consistent with principles of fairness, equity, and diversity to support the development and learning of individual children within the context of family, culture, and society; and
- work in partnership with other community members to support the well-being of families (Beach et al., 1998, p. 4).

What Is This Early Childhood Educator Doing?

Before we leave this discussion of roles, it will be useful for you to read the following story of a family child care provider and identify the various roles she is playing in her morning of interaction with her group of children. Although not all of the roles just discussed are represented in this account, it will be useful to see the integration of the roles in a typical scenario of good practice, and, not incidentally, representations of the excellent practice we discussed in the preceding chapter.

A Puzzle, a Picnic, and a Vision: Family Day Care at Its Best

Not long ago I was fortunate enough to be present during an extraordinary drama between a family day care provider and the children in her care.

It was late morning. A three-year-old and a four-year-old were racing small, cast-iron cars along a homemade highway running from the arm of a comfortable chair to the living-room wall. A willing toddler retrieved the cars that had met their demise on the moulding. A mobile eight-month-old infant followed in his wake.

In the kitchen, oblivious to the noise and excitement, Joel, a four-year-old boy, sat at the table, intently working on a hundred-piece puzzle.

After some sixty cars had wrecked themselves on the wall, the older children tired of the game. Hungry and ready for lunch, they advanced toward the kitchen table.

Absorbed in the puzzle, Joel was unaware of the danger headed his way; but the caregiver could see what was about to happen. Scooping up the infant, she placed herself between the group and the kitchen. "Joel is working at the table," she said. "I'll go and see how he's doing. You wait here."

She stood over the boy a moment before she said, "The other children are hungry. Are you ready to stop for lunch?"

Joel looked up, but only for an instant. "I'm not," he said.

Passing me on her way to the children, the provider explained, "He worked on a different puzzle for over an hour yesterday. When he was finished, he picked out this one to do today."

To the children she said, "Joel is still working on the puzzle." She gave out the information evenly, the way someone might read a telephone number from the phone book.

"So?" asked the four-year-old.

"Let's take a minute and think about what we should do." The caregiver released the infant and sat down on the floor with the children. "Let's see. We could wait and give Joel time to finish what he's doing."

"We're hungry now!"

"Well, then that won't work. What else could we do?"

The infant shrieked, but no one else said anything.

"I can think of things," the caregiver said in the kind of voice that lets children know something special is about to happen.

"Like what?"

"Well, we could fast. We could skip lunch for today and see how we felt." The provider dangled this as bait, but the preschoolers knew enough not to bite.

"All right, we could make Joel stop. We could tell him it isn't fair for him to keep working when we're hungry. We could mess up his puzzle because he's kept us waiting."

Unaware of the momentousness of this suggestion, the infant and the toddler were making their way back to the cars. Transfixed, the older children held their breath.

"We shouldn't do that," the four-year-old finally said.

"I agree, Sara. I'm glad you said that." The caregiver smiled at Sara and then, with a flourish, pulled the rabbit out of the hat: "We could have a picnic, instead, in the living room."

"A picnic! A picnic! We want the picnic!"

Looking down from his observation post in his highchair, the infant watched as the caregiver, the toddler, and the two preschool children spread a blanket, a plastic tablecloth, sandwiches, milk, and fruit on the rug.

When everyone was seated, Joel left the table and joined the group.

"How come he gets to have a picnic with us?" the three-year-old asked.

"Why?" the caregiver returned the question.

"Because he wasn't finished with the puzzle."

"Is it finished now?" she asked Joel. She couldn't see the tabletop from the floor, where she was kneeling.

"Not yet."

"You'll be able to work on it again later, after the picnic, if you want to," she said.

"Yeah. Because we're having a picnic and you didn't have to move it!" the three-year-old exclaimed.

This whole drama took no more than five minutes, and yet, so inspired was this caregiver's nurturing, the moment lives with me still. She had a vision of what a child—a person—could become. She nurtured the children's highest qualities—the ability to listen to their own conscience, the ability to talk about their feelings,

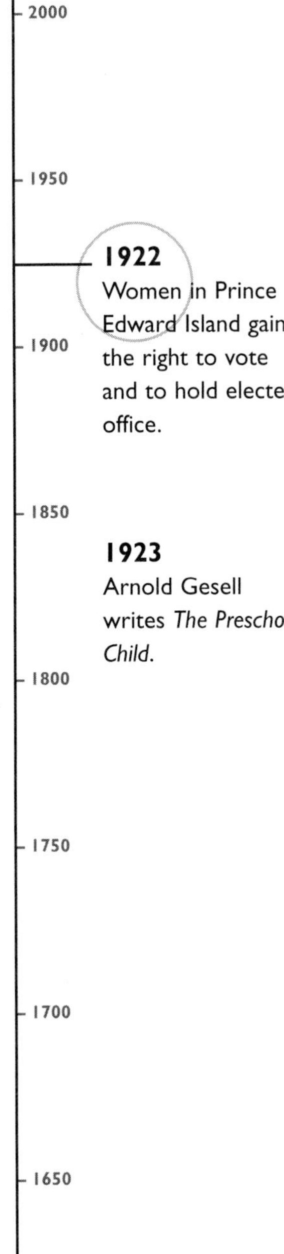

the ability to correct their mistakes and go on. She was looking for more than good behaviour from them; she had a commitment to the human spirit.

She knew intuitively how to guide them. "We could mess up Joel's puzzle," she said in a voice so beguiling it caused my heart to skip a beat. Only a moment before, the children had been on their way to do just that. But the caregiver knew what she was doing. The children didn't take off for the kitchen; they paused and considered. "We shouldn't do that," Sara said. And this time Sara knew that she was right.

The same skill is evident in the provider's conversation with Joel. She could easily have decided whether or not to let him continue with the puzzle. But more is at issue here than lunch. It is important for Joel to learn to recognize his feelings and speak on his own behalf. And so the caregiver invites him to consider the problem. His answer reveals her nurturing—he knows that he matters.

As I left this home, I thought of how fortunate these children were to have this adult for their caregiver. Her vision was profound, her instincts were true, and her touch was light. Child care can't get much better than that (Baker, Amy C. [1992]. A puzzle, a picnic and a vision: Family day care at its best. *Young Children,* 47 (5), 36–38).

Consider the effectiveness of the various roles this teacher played. These are the roles you too will play as you become an early childhood professional.

SUMMARY

Early childhood educators take on numerous roles and responsibilities in various early child development settings. Motivations to enter the early childhood workforce include enjoying children, wanting to make a difference to families, desiring variety and challenges, and seeing a demand for early childhood educators in the workforce. Competent early childhood educators bring together personal characteristics and dispositions with knowledge and experience.

REVIEW QUESTIONS

1. Identify several of the roles of early childhood educators discussed in this chapter.
2. Discuss briefly your understanding of the rationale for each role, including specifics about what that role might look like in particular settings.
3. Discuss the interrelationships among the various roles.

STUDY ACTIVITIES

1. Identify the early childhood educator roles that you find in the following examples. Remember that the various roles are interrelated, so you may find more than one role.
   a. A family child care provider writes a newsletter describing some of the children's recent learning activities. In the letter, she includes a copy of her philosophy of discipline, and invites parents to comment on it. She also solicits donations of old kitchen utensils.

b. An early childhood educator of infants displays family photos, under clear plastic paper, above the baseboards in the room.
c. A preschool early childhood educator prepares for her fall conferences with families by organizing the anecdotal observations the two teachers in the room made on each child and noting questions that she wants to ask each parent.
d. A kindergarten teacher clips newspaper articles on pending local legislation that will affect adult-child ratios in child care centres, and posts them on her parent bulletin board, along with the addresses of local representatives.
e. A Head Start early childhood educator arranges for her director to observe a child in her group who frequently hurts other children.
f. An early childhood educator of toddlers creates a cozy area in her room with piles of soft pillows and stuffed animals. She frequently sits here with children.
g. A kindergarten teacher adds several new containers of objects to his counting centre.
h. An early childhood educator of infants rocks a fussy baby, then places him on a mat with some colourful objects just out of his reach. He's been crawling for a week now.

2. Go back to the scenarios that began this chapter. Now what roles do you find?
3. Complete the following statements:
   When I first thought about becoming an early childhood educator, I thought that educating meant . . .
   Now I'm beginning to think that educating also means . . .
   One early childhood educator role that appeals to me a great deal is . . .
   One early childhood educator role that concerns me at this point is . . .
4. Observe in an early childhood education and care setting for a morning. Take detailed objective notes on one scenario. Later, label each early childhood educator role and define its purpose.

KEY TERMS

caregiving: Physical nurturing and protection of young children.
direct guidance: Teaching children appropriate behaviour through direct methods, including verbal and nonverbal messages. An alternative term, discipline, is used infrequently because of its negative connotations.
indirect guidance: Arrangements teachers make in the time and space environment that influence children's behaviour by both preventing problems and creating a positive learning environment.
nurturing: Providing care and fulfilling needs to promote development.

SUGGESTED READINGS

Beach, J. & Costigliola, B. (2005). *A snapshot of the child care workforce.* Ottawa: Child Care Human Resource Sector Council.

Benjamin, Ann C. (1994). Observations in early childhood classrooms: Advice from the field. *Young Children,* 49 (6), 14–20.

Bergen, Doris. (1994, Summer). Developing the art and science of team teaching. *Childhood Education*, 70 (4), 242–243.

Bredekamp, Sue. (1993, November). Reflections on Reggio Emilia. *Young Children*, 49 (1), 3–16.

Cameron, C. (2004) Building an integrated workforce for a long-term vision of universal early education and care. Leading the Vision Policy Papers: No 3. London: Daycare Trust.

Duckworth, Eleanor. (1987). *The having of wonderful ideas and other essays on teaching and learning*. New York: Teachers College Press.

Feeney, Stephanie & Chun, Robyn. (1985, November). Effective teachers of young children. *Young Children*, 41 (1), 47–52.

Ferguson, E. E. (1995). *Child care . . . becoming visible*. Halifax: Child Care Connection, NS.

Klass, Carol S. (1987, March). Childrearing interactions within developmental home- or center-based early education. *Young Children*, 42 (3), 9–13, 67–70.

Nelson, Bryan G. & Sheppard, Bruce (Eds.). (1992). *Men in child care and early education: A handbook for administrators and educators*. Minneapolis MN: Men in Child Care Project.

Powell, Douglas R. (1986, September). Effects of program models and teaching practices. *Young Children*, 41 (6), 60–66.

Rogers, Dwight L., Waller, Cathleen Boggs, & Perrin, Marilyn Sheerer. (1987, May). Learning more about what makes a good teacher good through collaborative research in the classroom. *Young Children*, 42 (4), 34–39.

Saracho, Olivia N. (1988). Cognitive style and early childhood practice. In Bernard Spodek, Olivia N. Saracho, & Donald L. Peters (Eds.), *Professionalism and the early childhood educator*. New York: Teachers College Press.

Spodek, Bernard, Saracho, Olivia N., & Peters, Donald L. (1988). Professionalism, semi-professionalism, and craftsmanship. In Bernard Spodek, Olivia N. Saracho, & Donald L. Peters (Eds.), *Professionalism and the early childhood educator*. New York: Teachers College Press.

Stephens, Karen. (1994, January). Bringing light to the darkness: A tribute to teachers. *Young Children*, 49 (2), 44–46.

Toronto First Duty (2005) *A Guide to Early Childhood Service Integration*. Available at http://www.toronto.ca/firstduty, October 2006.

CHAPTER FIVE
Becoming an Early Childhood Educator

OBJECTIVES

After studying this chapter, students will be able to

- identify and discuss some motivations for entering the early childhood workforce;
- discuss the importance of self-knowledge in becoming an early childhood educator;
- identify stages of development as a student and as a practising early childhood educator;
- discuss why different types of educational preparation for early childhood educators exist; and
- identify and describe the Canadian Child Care Federation's Training Guidelines.

Why do individuals choose to be early childhood educators and make a career in early child development? We will look at the motivations of several people who decided to work with young children. We will also explore the personal characteristics and attitudes that are important for members of the early childhood workforce.

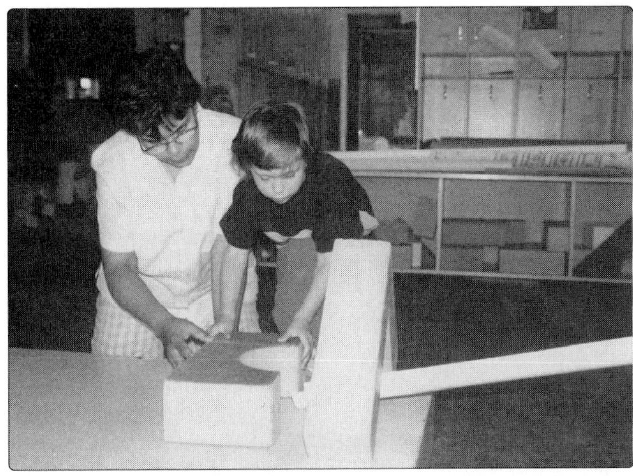

The enjoyment of being with children and guiding their development of new skills and abilities is strong motivation for many early childhood educators.

Why Become an Early Childhood Educator?

In Canada each year a few thousand women and men enter the field of early child development through college ECE programs. But, the truth is, many do not end up working in early childhood settings, and many others who begin a career in child care centres, kindergartens, or family child care programs leave their work for other employment. Why do they come or decide to leave? Clearly, educating and caring for young children demands much of those who accept the task. So the education and care of young children is not an endeavour that can be entered into casually or accidentally—at least, not if the early childhood educator is to remain satisfied and productive and stay in the field.

Your participation in an ECE postsecondary education program represents your own intention to examine issues of early child development with some seriousness. As you read about early childhood educators who decided to work with young children, think about your own motivations and expectations of what working with young children as a career can offer you.

Motivators toward a given profession are both large and small. Some are related to human characteristics, including the emotions and meaning for the individual, and others are related to structural aspects, meaning the way the profession itself is organized. We will consider the human motivators first—enjoyment of children and making a difference to children and their families—and then look at the motivators related to the structure of the sector.

1924

Lawrence Frank, administering the Rockefeller Foundation grant, is the first to begin using a multidisciplinary approach to studying children at Columbia University.

St. George's School for Child Study (later the Institute of Child Study) at the University of Toronto and McGill Day Nursery are founded through a grant from the Laura Spellman Rockefeller Foundation.

Enjoyment of Children

For most early childhood educators, the fact that they genuinely enjoy being with young children is the main reason they consider a career in early child education care, and it is definitely the reason they stay.

> "What other job can you have that lets you play with kids, and watch them playing? They're great—I mean really fun. Amazing things come out of their mouths. They know so much, and they're learning so much. And never, I mean never, boring. Kids are so real."—Connie
>
> "I'd never really paid much attention to children until I had my own. Then I was blown away. There's these little people, and every single day they find something new. And the world is really brand new for them, and their eyes are so wide, taking it all in. And I get to look at it all again too, because I'm with them. It's like getting a second chance at the world."—David
>
> "I just like being with kids. They're honest and funny and smart, and they love your singing, even if nobody else does. I can just let myself go and be silly right along with them. Nothing else is so much fun."—Laura
>
> "Hutch was a year old and my first day with him I was hooked ... Hutch was just a joy to be with . . . I remember one time early on, it just happened that I had Hutch and Eric on the same day because their mothers asked me, and I was fascinated by the interaction between them. It wasn't some kind of underdeveloped, superficial play that you might read about. I was amazed at how full and engaged it was."—JoAnne

A deep and genuine enjoyment of children and a desire to be with them is a primary motivator for early childhood educators. They recognize that children are interesting and valuable in their own right, and they don't approach children primarily as persons in need of change or instruction. This enjoyment goes beyond the sentimental view that is frequently phrased as "I just love children, they're so sweet." Early childhood educators can enjoy young children while still being quite realistic about their developmental characteristics. These characteristics may include stubbornness, illogical thinking, uncontrolled outbursts, and a tendency not to care about other people's needs or rights. They recognize that children are not always sweet—they can scream, whine, and kick, and are frequently smelly and sticky!

Making a Difference to Children and Families

Another primary motivation for most early childhood educators is the tangible evidence that they are making a difference in the lives of children and their families.

Every early childhood educator knows of some specific impact she has had on children, and that impact has a lasting effect on these children's lives. Research proves it. **Longitudinal studies** of children show that participating in early education contributed to their later school success and social adjustment.

One review of the impact of early child development programs on later development shows that the results of thirteen longitudinal studies point in the same direction (Tremblay & Craig, 1995). Children who participated in early childhood programs tended to complete higher levels of education, have fewer social problems, and more easily find employment than their counterparts who did not to participate in early education programs.

A particularly well-known longitudinal study in the United States shows that early education programs have a dramatic impact in the lives of children who are at risk. Lazer and Darlington (1982) demonstrate that early education programs enable children to progress satisfactorily through later grades without failure or the need for special assistance. The Perry Preschool Project of Ypsilanti, Michigan, has followed participants of a compensatory preschool program for twenty-seven years (Schweinhart and Weikart, 1993), as well as contemporaries who did not have the benefit of an early education program. There were noteworthy differences not only in school success, but, also, in social factors such as involvement with crime, marriage, and job and salary levels. The researchers found specific positive correlations between participation in early childhood learning experiences and later positive accomplishments. *"It was the development of specific personal and social dispositions that enabled a high-quality early childhood program to significantly influence participants' adult performance"* [emphasis added] (Schweinhart and Weikart, 1993, pp. 11–12).

In France, all children may attend preschool programs, which are part of the public school system, and most children attend at least two years of full-time preschool education before entering formal schooling in Grade One. Researchers and educators have found that children from all socioeconomic and family backgrounds are likely to be more successful in elementary school if they have at least two years' preschool experience (Bergmann, 1996).

A Canadian survey (Canadian Child Care Advocacy Association and Canadian Child Day Care Federation, 1992) identifies enjoyment in working with children as the primary source of satisfaction for staff working in child care centres. Family child care providers echoed this sentiment in the Child Care Sector Study (Beach et al., 1998), in a survey of regulated family child care (Goss Gilroy, 1998) and in a labour market update (Beach et al., 2004).

As a child, how did a particular adult make a difference in your life? As an adult, have you been able to touch a child's life with lasting impact? How was that important to you?

Of course, children do not come as independent beings to early child care and education settings—they are part of families. Early childhood educators reach beyond the confines of their settings to support the lives of families, acknowledging that strong and stable families mean healthy communities. Parents of the youngest children need information and emotional support to best nurture their children's development. They need the security of knowing they can leave their children in the hands of trusted and competent early childhood educators while

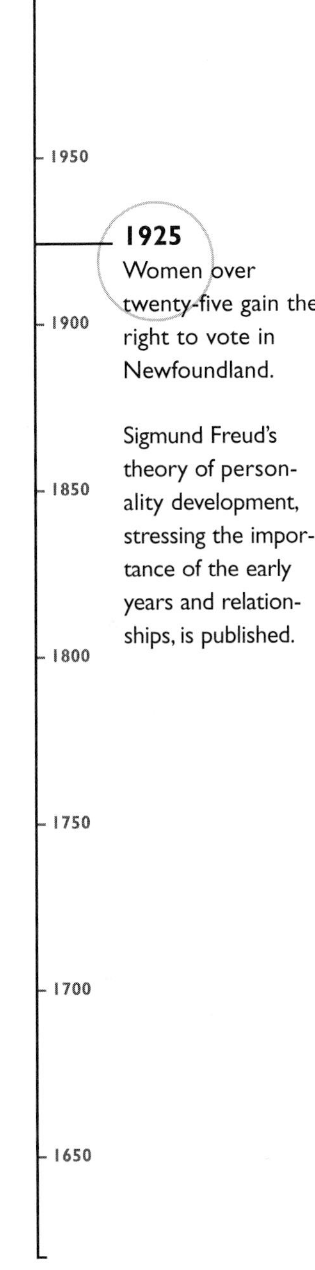

1926
Jean Piaget publishes *The Language and Thought of the Child*, outlining the four periods of the growth of intelligence.

Canada's first nursery schools open at the St. George School for Child Study in Toronto and at McGill University in Montreal.

The Canadian Council on Child Welfare sponsors prenatal and preschool letters to mothers eager to find out the most up-to-date child-rearing advice.

they go to work. They need connections with community resources that will help them perform all the tasks of parenting. They need to trust early childhood educators to help their children become interested in learning and in school. They need to be welcomed into the centre, school, or home to contribute to their children's lives away from the family home. They need to feel respected by other adults and by society for their primary importance in their children's growth and development.

Early childhood educators are on the frontlines, between parents and the society at large. They are often the first people outside the family who have prolonged contact with children and parents. Their support and relationships may be crucial determinants in families' optimum functioning. They have the power to help parents understand and accept their children and to support parent-child relationships.

Variety and Challenge

Some people are attracted to work that is never predictable, in which challenges and questions arise continually, and each day is likely to be different from the day before. Life in early child care and education settings with children from birth through elementary school is just that—and then some.

As you read the descriptions of quality programs in Chapter 3, you probably realized that the active, hands-on learning that is required means that early childhood educators live in a world of movement, noise, choice, and activity. In such an environment, there are an infinite number of tasks that call for attention simultaneously. A typical scenario may be four children splashing at the water table, while another needs assistance in the bathroom, and yet another is crying quietly in the book area, when the phone rings and a parent walks in the door. Working with young children demands energy, knowledge, patience, and creativity, as well as the capacity to be flexible in the face of diverse demands.

Much of the variety in an early childhood educator's day comes from the children and their families. With rapidly developing children, change is the operative word. Today's crawlers are tomorrow's walkers; abilities to use a spoon, catch a ball, or climb stairs are acquired in quick spurts; and the use of language often seems to explode overnight. The diversity of **inherited** potential and environmental experience offered by each family means that a roomful of three-year-old children will have stunningly different interests, needs, and ideas.

Early childhood educators have to develop the skills and intuition to adapt to a great many unknowns in the course of a day. Sometimes the small events indicate larger happenings: the six-month-old baby seems unusually fussy, until you find a new tooth about to pop through; the six-year-old cries when he's forgotten his library book, then reveals that he left it in his Dad's car when Dad picked him up from Mom's house after the weekend visit.

You learn to make adjustments to children's individual styles and idiosyncrasies, as well as to new skills and abilities. The variety and challenges of working with unique children and families should motivate, rather than frustrate, you. Early childhood educators who are stimulated and excited by this part of the work environment are continually challenged to learn new things and develop new skills.

Early childhood educators encounter beings who are constantly changing and becoming, and they themselves are challenged to continue to grow. The sector is not clearly defined; rather, it is dynamic and offers a number of paths to follow.

Demand for Early Childhood Educators

One motivator for people considering a particular occupation or field is the availability of job opportunities; that is, the need for employees in the sector. The good news about early child care and education is that there appears to be no end to the demand for competent early childhood educators. Whether you are drawn to work with school-age children or with younger ones, there are many opportunities in every community across Canada.

Growing as an Early Childhood Educator

"A good teacher is first and foremost a person, and this fact is the most important and determining thing about him" (Combs, Blume, Newman, & Wass, 1974, p. 6). If you think back on the good educators you have known, you will likely confirm this statement. No doubt each educator stands out in your mind as a unique person, with a particular personality, values, beliefs, methods, and techniques.

The demand for early childhood educators to work with young children and their families is growing.

Self-Knowledge

A good early childhood educator is the sum of the experiences, thoughts, and learning that have occurred in her life, all of which interact with the environment in which she works with young children. Since the self is the tool with which early childhood educators fulfill their caring and educating roles, both new and experienced members of the early childhood workforce benefit from an understanding of themselves—both a self-awareness and a self-acceptance.

Early childhood educators who examine their personal lives, including the experiences that have helped shape their values and the ways they live and relate with others, take part in an ongoing, important process. A word that is frequently used to describe educators who take the time and effort to analyze their actions and evaluate their experiences is *reflective* (Kochendorfer, 1994). An effective early childhood educator extends this concept to reflect on her whole life.

Take a moment to reflect on your own life. What early influences made you the person you are today? Who were the important people in your life? What picture comes to mind as a place you liked to be? What were you like when you were ten? Who gave you your name, and why?

What strong childhood memories do you have? How do these memories influence you as you think about working with children? Do you see an influence from

1928
John Watson publishes *Psychological Care of Infant and Child*, which suggests that parents not hug or kiss their children, or let them sit on laps.

1929
Women are deemed "persons" and can therefore be appointed to the Senate.

your family on your decision to care for and educate young children? How have you been influenced by colleagues or mentors? What outstanding early childhood educators or caregivers do you remember? What were their central teaching and caring ideas and styles?

When did you decide to work with young children? What was it about early childhood education that attracted you? Were there any chance factors that led you to consider early education? How did you feel after you had made the decision? What are your goals for children?

What is important to you beyond early education? What do you do about it? What concerns you most about the state of the world and about the state of children and families? What have you read recently that was important to you? What do you see yourself doing five or ten years from now?

Disposition, Knowledge, and Experiences

It is impossible to list all the criteria and characteristics of the perfect early childhood educator. But we do know that good early childhood educators are a combination of particular dispositions, knowledge, and experiences that contribute to their abilities to care for and educate young children.

A disposition is an attitude or a tendency to behave in a certain way (Carter & Curtis, 1994; Katz, 1995). It is closely linked to personal characteristics that typify how an individual thinks, relates to others, and deals with daily life. Some characteristics that we expect from adults who will spend their days working with young children include patience, energy, enthusiasm, and a sense of humour.

The recent Canadian Child Care Sector Study on quality (Beach et al., 1998) asked early childhood educators and other caregivers working in child care settings what they thought were the most important characteristics for those who work with children. Patience topped the list, followed by respect for children and the ability to communicate.

There are several other dispositions that are important qualities for early childhood educators:

Commitment to self-discovery. Good early childhood educators recognize that the preparation for their work is an ongoing, never-ending process. Just as they recognize that their work with children is a process of facilitating development over time, rather than achieving specific, easily observable and quick goals, so, too, early childhood educators acknowledge that they continue to create their teaching, their understanding of what they do and how they do it, and their personal perspective. They continue to question, to puzzle, to set goals, to remain open to new learning. In so doing, they model for children the active process of becoming human beings. "The good early childhood educator is not a finished product, but a human process" (Combs et al., 1974, p. 144).

Being committed to self-discovery allows early childhood educators to grow. Early childhood educators must recognize and welcome their constant state of growth and change, and realize that they do not yet know what lies ahead, and what directions they will take. This uncertainty should not be regarded as daunting, but intriguing with its wealth of possibilities and unknowns. Good early childhood educators are curious about themselves, as well as about much else in their worlds.

In addition to curiosity, early childhood educators need an ability to engage in self-criticism, to uncover the new challenges and demands that call for growth.

Feelings of adequacy. Competent early childhood educators accept themselves and feel comfortable with who they are. Basic feelings of adequacy allow early childhood educators to perform their daily tasks with the confidence and maturity to focus on the job at hand, rather than constantly evaluating their ability to perform or others' responses to them. Early childhood educators need to be able to transcend their own needs and pay attention to those of others. Working with young children is not about meeting the early childhood educator's needs for attention and affection. This is not to say that there are no emotional rewards for early childhood educators from their interaction with children and their families; rather, these emotional rewards are not sought to adjust early childhood educators' feelings of inadequacy. The early childhood educator must be focused on the needs of others, not self-indulgent of personal needs.

Flexible thinking. Each day, early childhood educators are required to make hundreds of decisions, both large and small. They have to select responses and methods that are appropriate to complex and unique circumstances. Often they are faced with situations that they have not encountered before and with behaviours that require them to adapt existing ideas and techniques to fit complicated circumstances. They must create their own answers to immediate questions and move beyond the theories to find appropriate answers to concrete conditions and feelings for children and adults.

The child care environment demands that early childhood educators depend on their own problem-solving abilities, rather than resorting to a "cook" approach that predetermines what the solutions are. Early childhood educators work from a solid knowledge base but are able to fit the knowledge of children, philosophy, and goals to the immediate conditions and discover the best course of action.

Autonomy. Early childhood educators who have developed autonomy are able to function in the flexible manner described above. They do not heavily depend on others' opinions to guide their actions or decisions. They understand their own goals and motivations and feel comfortable functioning independently. To be able to make choices, early childhood educators must have a healthy sense of autonomy, which allows them to accept ultimate responsibility for their work and their decisions. Being autonomous does not necessarily mean being solitary, however. Early childhood educators can assume responsibility and leadership, while still being able to work as a member of a team.

Empathy. Early childhood educators require the ability to identify with others, including the children with whom they work, their parents, and the other team members. Empathy is based on understanding the complexity of human development, and on respect and concern for others' personalities and feelings. Empathy grows as early childhood educators are able to focus on others' needs and feelings, an ability that arises from the early childhood educator's maturity and willingness to transcend issues of self. This allows early childhood educators to be really tuned in to children and adults, to recognize and accept their differences. Early childhood educators gain this knowledge of others by observing and making connections to allow others to reveal themselves.

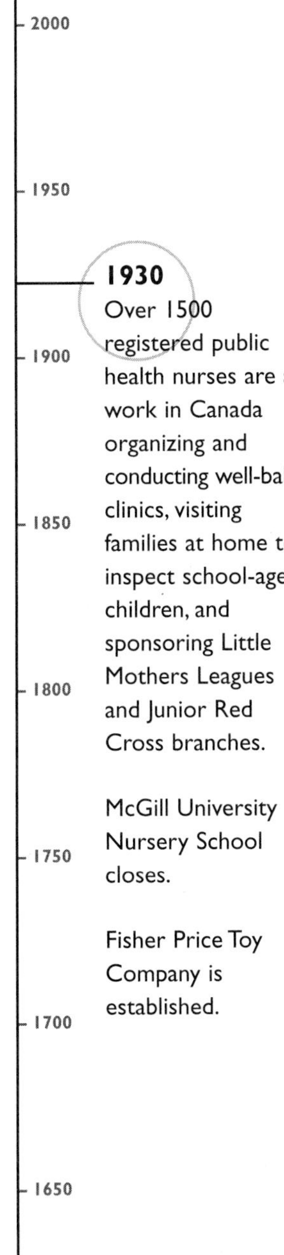

1931 Mother Craft Society is introduced to Canada-trained well-baby nurses.

Empathy prevents early childhood educators from exhibiting biases or prejudices; they are able to get past narrow thinking, as they take another's perspective, rather than shying away from others who are different.

A sense of the "big picture." Early childhood educators need to have a philosophy that connects their work with young children to the important issues in their lives, so as not to get bogged down in the minutiae of early care. This larger philosophy is likely what Almy (1975) referred to in her list of important personal characteristics of early childhood teachers as "world-mindedness," an interest and a view that extend beyond the family child care or group care setting and connect the early childhood educator to webs of deeper meaning and social relevance. When early childhood educators understand the values and themes that are important in their lives, they find ways of embodying these ideas in their early childhood settings and practices.

Knowledge of child development and early education practices and experience are essential to competent early childhood educators. Research findings are clear that early childhood educators are more likely to be competent when they have postsecondary education, particularly in child development and early childhood education (Goelman & Pence, 1987; Helburn et al., 1995; Lyon & Canning, 1995; Doherty & Stuart, 1996). As noted in Chapter 3, educational qualifications are a key factor of quality. Experience also builds practical knowledge and helps early childhood educators refine their skills and their practice. "Teaching is an eminently practical activity, best learned in the exercise of it and in the thoughtful reflection that must accompany that" (Ayers, 1993, p. 12).

Stages of Early Childhood Educator Development

As you are beginning your training and career in early child development, it may be interesting for you to learn that some study has been done on the various sequences of professional development and growth of early childhood educators. Recognizing the common emotions and experiences and their needed supports at the various stages may be helpful. Katz (1995) discusses four distinct phases, with unique developmental tasks and training needs. The stages are generally linked to experience acquired over time.

Stage I: Survival. During this period, which may last at least a year, early childhood educators are mainly concerned with surviving—getting through the day or week in one piece, doing the work, and being accepted without doing something dreadful. Many early childhood educators feel inadequate and unprepared as they face the realities of a classroom of energetic, developing children. Early childhood educators at this stage need direct help with specific skills, as well as encouragement, reassurance, comfort, support, and understanding, as they develop basic concepts of what young children are like and what to expect of them.

Stage II: Consolidation. After some time, early childhood educators believe they will survive the immediate crises and stay in the profession. They are now ready to consolidate their overall achievements and to concentrate on learning specific new skills. They begin to focus on individual children and situations that are troublesome and to look for answers to questions for children whose behaviour departs from the norm. Early childhood educators at this stage benefit from discussion with more experienced colleagues about possible alternatives for action and resources.

RESEARCH INTO PRACTICE

Another View of Dispositions

Seven dispositions characterize master early childhood educators and are the desired outcomes of training and education:

- delighting in and being curious about children;
- valuing children's play;
- expecting continuous change and challenge;
- being willing to take risks and make mistakes;
- providing time for regular personal reflection and self-examination;
- seeking collaboration and peer support; and
- acting as an advocate for children and families (Carter & Curtis, 1994).

Source: Adapted from Front Line Profile, IDEAS, Volume 4, Number 2, December 1997, p. 19.

Stage III: Renewal. Frequently, after several years of teaching, early childhood educators get tired of doing the same old things and the same activities for successive groups of children. They become interested in learning about new developments in the field. It is often useful for early childhood educators at this stage to meet colleagues from other programs, to attend local and regional conferences, to read more widely, and to set new learning goals for themselves. Supports for all of these educational endeavours are helpful.

Stage IV: Maturity. After several years of teaching, many early childhood educators have reached a comfortable level of confidence in their own abilities. The questions they ask are deeper, more philosophical, and more abstract. Early childhood educators at this stage search for insight, perspective, and realism. These early childhood educators are ready to interact with other educators as they work on problem areas on many different levels. (See more about these stages in Katz, 1995.)

Stages of Student Early Childhood Educator Development

You may also be interested to know that someone has organized some typical patterns that student early childhood educators often experience. It might be comforting to know that you are not alone when some of these feelings and situations occur during your first practicum and teaching experiences. If you read through them all, you will see that there *is* light at the end of the tunnel, even though on some days, that seems doubtful.

Phase I: Anxiety/euphoria

- Easily identifies with children—because it is important to be liked by them.
- Starts making friends—an important early step in developing the authority relationship necessary in teaching.

1932
Subsidies begin to decrease and costs to provide services increase; parent fees rise to twenty-five cents a day.

Phase II: Confusion/clarity

- Thinks, "I don't know anything about planning curriculum."
- Asks, "What are rules?"
- Asks, "How should routines proceed?"
- Wonders, "When should I intercede between children?"
- Sometimes avoids situations out of fear or not knowing whether it is the early childhood educator's role.

Phase III: Competence/adequacy

- Feels triumph in guiding children.
- Comes up with a good idea during planning.
- Gets a hug.
- Needs strong reinforcement from supervisor. Focuses on the positive.
- Even though progress has been made, still feels everyone else seems to "know it all."
- Feels there's so much to learn.
- Wonders, "Will I ever be that good?"
- Still finds it difficult to be a controlling figure or disciplinarian.

Phase IV: Criticism/new awareness

- Says, "If it were my classroom, I would do it differently."
- Begins to notice imperfections.
- Starts to find fault with practicum of early childhood educator.
- Starts to question as part of the growth process.

Phase V: More confidence/greater inadequacy

- No longer questions—has acquired a sense of stability.
- Knows she'll make it.
- Experiences success more frequently.
- Wants more responsibility.

Phase VI: Loss/relief

- Has to depart from children with whom she's become close.
- Puts standards of performance in proper perspective.
- Finds returning to classes somewhat difficult (Caruso, 1977).

You will notice that individual variations during the phases may range from experiencing success and confidence to discovering this may not be the field that best matches student capabilities. Many student early childhood educators find that keeping a **journal** during their experiences helps them express their feelings and keep track of their learning experiences (Surbeck, 1994).

> Growing early childhood educators is different from training them. Oddly, we more often think about growing plants than about growing people. People, especially the young, are to be domesticated—trained as dogs and horses are—to make them reliable, responsible members of society. . . . An alternative to domestication is liberation (Freire, 1970). Early childhood educators, like other people need some of both. (Jones, 1993, p. xi)

ECE Postsecondary Education

As you prepare to join the early childhood workforce, you will want to know what educational training and professional experience you need to work with young children in early childhood education settings. As you can imagine from what you have already learned about early education, the answers to this question are not simple. Quite different educational requirements are necessary for the various kinds of settings.

Diversity in Early Childhood Educator Preparation

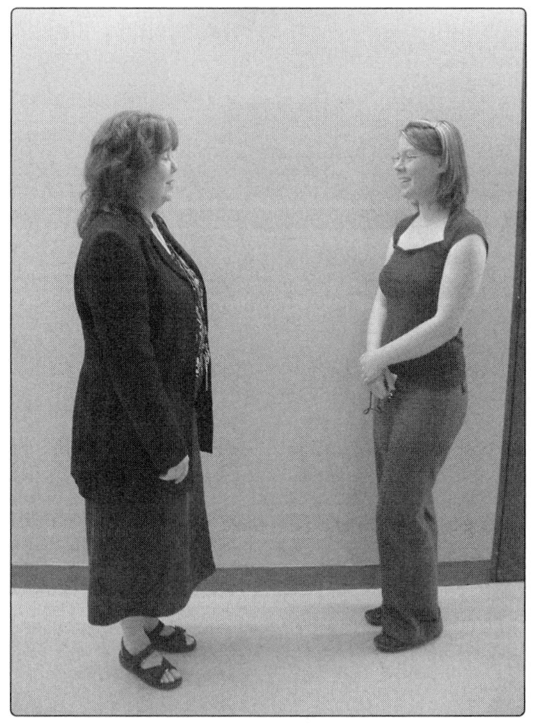

ECE students are guided by early childhood educators in their field placements.

Cheryl W. is currently a student at a community college, where she will earn a diploma in ECE. She plans to work in a child care program with preschool children. The centre where she hopes to teach has two early childhood educators with four-year degrees in ECE and teacher certification credentials; one who has a bachelor's degree with a major in abnormal psychology; two who have earned a certificate in ECE offered through continuing education at a community college; and four who have no related training.

Christy S. is a university student, completing a bachelor of education degree, with a major in primary education. When she graduates, she will be eligible to apply for certification as a school teacher. She hopes to be a kindergarten teacher. After high school, Christy took a year off school and worked in a YMCA kindergarten child care program as an assistant. During that year, she participated in professional development activities, such as a recreation leadership course, creative movement workshops, and conflict resolution sessions, which were offered by her employer.

Charmaine is a family child care provider and a student in a family child care certificate program offered through continuing education at the local community college. She has five children under six years attending her family child care program and looks forward to using some of the new ideas she is learning about in her classes. Charmaine has been providing family child care for seven years.

Why are there such differences in the educational paths these women took, when many of them have similar career goals? What do these differences in education and training mean to their performance in ECE programs and, ultimately, to the question of quality in programs for young children? Today you will find such differences in every program for children, in every province or territory and location you visit. What do you already know about the provincial/territorial requirements where you hope to work?

One reason for the multiplicity of educational paths is that there are also several typical routes by which people become early childhood professionals: the traditional route, the parent route, and the "serendipitous" route (Bredekamp, 1992). When early childhood educators come into the profession via different routes, the profession must respond with different kinds of training and education.

- *Preservice training* and education refers to professional education acquired before entering the early childhood workforce.
- *In-service training* and education refers to professional education and development acquired, while employed in an early childhood setting.

RESEARCH INTO PRACTICE

This was written in 1920 by Jessie Van Stanton, who would later become director of the Bank Street Nursery School, after one year of teaching at the City and Country School. It was an assignment to write an exposition about the ideal teacher. She says she wrote it while "oppressed by a sense of dreadful inadequacy, convinced that I could never learn to be a teacher." This summary recognizes that there is no ideal for an early childhood educator.

The Ideal Teacher and How She Grows

The teacher of young children should have a strong physique and a strong well-balanced nervous system. She should be plump and round and have curly short hair. Her cheeks should be rosy and her teeth pearly white. She should have a pleasing personality and a quiet firm manner. She should be poised and of a high moral character. She should have sentiment but not sentimentality. She should be gentle but not sloppy, strong but not impetuous when bitten or scratched.

She should have a fair education. By this I mean she should take a doctor's degree in psychology and medicine. Sociology as a background is advisable.

She should be an experienced carpenter, mason, and plumber and a thoroughly trained musician and poet. At least five years' practical experience in each of these branches is essential.

She should be a close observer and a judge of character and should be able to deal with young and old. She should be able to hypnotize the parents of her young pupils and to cause them to change life-long habits of thinking in two mothers' meetings.

Tested at birth and found to have an I.Q. of 150, she was taken from her parents and brought up in totally disinfected surroundings. She was given a cold bath and a globule of gland each morning and her health was carefully watched.

From early childhood she was given every sort of tool and taught to practise close observation. She spent every morning seeing and sawing. In the afternoons, her time was spent on music, hearing, howling, and handling. She spent her evenings practising manners, masonry, mechanics, mesmerism, and musing on metamorphosis. Thus she acquired early in life the inestimably useful habit of using every second to its highest capacity. *Now, at 63 she is ready!*

But, added to all the virtues and attainments for a teacher, the ideal director should have a spine of steel—to stand the long hours and the tremendous demands made upon her. Her spine must bend easily, however, so that she can crawl under radiators with the cleaning man to dig out the dirt—or put away blocks for two-year-olds on shelves close to the floor. She should have feet of iron so that she can go up and downstairs tirelessly all day long from kitchen to roof to classroom to office.

Now she has studied. Now she has taught. *Now, at 83—she is ready to direct!*

Source: Stanton (1990). Used with permission of New York State AEYC. Originally published in *New York Nursery Education News* (Winter 1954).

Regulation and Certification

Why do early childhood educators take different educational paths to achieve similar goals? One reason is found in the differences among the provincial/territorial licensing requirements in regulated child care and nursery school settings. (Look back at Chapter 3 to review the various qualification requirements.)

- Preservice professional education is not required for all positions in licensed child care or nursery school programs in any province or territory.
- There are few educational requirements for regulated family child care in any jurisdiction, although there are some requirements for early childhood educators in these settings to participate in professional development activities.
- In some jurisdictions there are no educational qualifications for staff in regulated child care programs.

There are also variations in the requirements for government approval of educational qualifications. As we discussed in Chapter 3, in some provincial jurisdictions, governments issue licenses or certificates or authorize specific classifications to early childhood educators.

- In British Columbia, the government issues a license to practice to early childhood educators who have the necessary educational qualifications and hours of work experience.
- In Alberta, Prince Edward Island, and Manitoba, early childhood educators must submit their education qualifications to the provincial government, which will then assign the appropriate classification for regulated centre-based programs.
- In Newfoundland, all qualified ECE staff in regulated child care centres are required (by the provincial child care legislation) to have their certification from the provincial organization, the Association of Early Childhood Educators, Newfoundland and Labrador.
- The government of Ontario is establishing a new College of Early Childhood Educators which will set the qualifications and standards for professionals who work in early learning and child care.

Each province and territory also has different requirements for early childhood educators who are kindergarten and primary or early elementary teachers within the school system, and those who are working in other types of early child development programs. In all provinces and territories, teachers in the school system are required to have a university degree and teacher education qualifications. There are a few professional education programs in Canada that offer joint ECE and teacher education programs. Early childhood educators who complete these programs are qualified for either system.

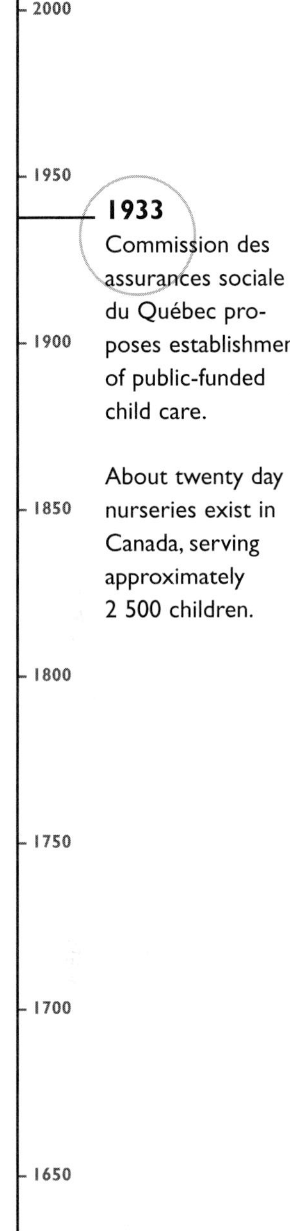

Equivalency

The recognition of out-of-province educational qualifications to meet requirements for credentials is another aspect of regulation and certification. Each jurisdiction (with the exception of New Brunswick, the Northwest Territories, and Newfoundland, where there are no educational qualification requirements) sets up its own process for determining if educational qualifications from outside that province/territory are comparable or equivalent to those recognized within its boundaries.

It is important for you to be familiar with the requirements in your province or territory. If you think you may wish to move to a different part of Canada, you will want to know how your credentials will apply. You may also want to know how the credits you are now earning could be applied to further education.

1934
The Dionne quintuplets are born in Callander, Ontario.

College and University ECE Programs

In Canada, postsecondary education, like regulated child care, is the responsibility of the provinces and territories. The federal government does transfer funding to provincial and territorial governments for postsecondary education, and to support research, and participates in initiatives to coordinate education across Canada. But it is the provincial and territorial governments that establish postsecondary institutions and policies for their governance. So, like the delivery of regulated child care and other early childhood education and care programs, each jurisdiction sets up its own system. This adds to the diversity of early childhood workforce across Canada.

Most of the preparatory training and education of early childhood educators is offered through two types of postsecondary institutions—colleges and universities. There are more than 120 postsecondary institutions offering ECEC certificate, diploma, and degree programs across Canada (ACCC, 1997; Beach et al., 2004).

The length of programs varies from two-semester certificate programs to three- or four-year degree programs. Degree programs are usually offered in universities, although there are a few colleges that now have degree-granting status. Some programs are full-time, and others are available part-time through continuing education or distance education programs.

Provinces and territories establish broad guidelines and procedures for both college and university programs. Universities are autonomous institutions, with their own boards of governors, which establish their own curriculum content and methods of teaching and assessment within the broad provincial/territorial policy framework. Colleges may be autonomous, or they may be directly operated by the provincial/territorial government. College programs usually receive more direction from provincial/territorial governments than do university programs.

Universities provide degree programs leading to certification for teaching kindergarten and elementary grades in the school system. Teacher education programs are driven by provincial/territorial policies and curriculum guidelines with little consideration of the ECEC sector. This is similar to the situation in the United States (Spodek, 1994).

RESEARCH INTO PRACTICE

Early Childhood Education Training (ECE) Programs in Canada

The Child Care Human Resource Sector Council (CCHRSC) is a Canadian, non-profit organization that addresses pressing human resources issues in the child care sector. Projects develop research, strategies, and tools to meet the needs of the child care workforce and achieve related goals. The volunteer board includes representation from:

- National and provincial child care or labour organizations
- Child care centers, nursery and preschools, or their own homes as early childhood educators or employers
- Post-secondary training institutions
- Government

CCHRSC has developed an extensive database of the many professional education programs to choose from in colleges, institutes, and universities across Canada.

The courses vary in length from one to four years, most being one or two years. They range in commitment from full-time to part-time. On-line and distance-learning courses are available, offering access if there is no training institution in your community or if your schedule requires more flexibility.

To learn about on-line learning opportunities or the programs in your province or territory, go to http://www.ccsc-cssge.ca.

ECE Certificate and Diploma Programs

Canadian colleges and Quebec's CEGEP programs offer 135 ECE certificate and ECE diploma programs (Beach et al., 2004) and graduate approximately 4000 early childhood educators each year. The programs prepare early childhood educators to work with young children in early child development settings, particularly child care centres and nursery schools. Specific curriculum content in ECE certificate and diploma programs is shaped by the particular institution, by provincial/territorial postsecondary education requirements, by provincial/territorial requirements for regulated child care, and by the early childhood workforce and its organizations in that jurisdiction.

MAKING IT HAPPEN

Red River College, Winnipeg, Manitoba

Red River College is a postsecondary institution located in Winnipeg, Manitoba, which offers a two-year ECE diploma program. Graduates from this program are eligible for classification as Early Childhood Educator II by the Manitoba government, and are thus qualified staff members in Manitoba's licensed child care centres and nursery schools.

The ECE diploma program was first offered at Red River College in 1971. Since that time, the program has continuously evolved to remain current and to meet the needs of its community. For example, when the provincial government increased its requirements for educational qualifications for program staff in regulated child care centres, Red River College moved management courses to a post-diploma program and increased the focus on child development, curriculum, and professionalism in the ECE diploma program. When the federal government established the Aboriginal Child Care initiative, Red River College developed many partnerships with First Nations communities for community-based training in rural and remote communities.

Since 1986, the ECE program at Red River College has delivered the program following a competency-based model. The curriculum is organized around core competencies for entry-level early childhood educators

(cont'd)

Red River College, Winnipeg, Manitoba (cont'd)

as defined by experts in the field. Each of the courses or modules has a learning package or "Com Pac," which faculty members review regularly and update to include current research and best practices. The individual learning packages are clear about what the student needs to learn and how she can demonstrate the learning. Faculty members produce an instructor's guide, accompanying readings, and assignments for each module. In addition to course work, ECE students complete four field placements, the equivalent of about seventeen weeks.

The detailed, thoroughly developed curriculum has made the program very portable, providing flexibility for various delivery modes and communities. As well, with the course content organized in learning packages, there is considerable flexibility for students to switch from part-time or distance education to the full-time program with full recognition of their course credits. It has also allowed for a consistent recognition of credits through Prior Learning Assessment.

Currently, the ECE program is offered on-site on a full-time basis as well as through continuing education, distance education, and Prior Learning Assessment. The program is also delivering an ECE Workplace model in an attempt to relieve the shortage of trained ECEs in Manitoba. In this program, students are experienced employees who continue to work three days a week and attend classes two days a week. Prior Learning Assessment, workplace practicum, Gap training, and regular classes are all components of this accelerated program.

The program has also been delivered full-time in ten locations in First Nations communities outside Winnipeg, including several remote fly-in communities. These projects enabled many students to graduate who would never have been able to attend classes in Winnipeg. The competency-based approach, with learning objectives clearly defined, allows for considerable community and cultural relevance. There are many paths to competency, and under the supervision of an experienced off-site coordinator, instructors and students can adapt learning tasks and assignments to be relevant to their communities. Inspired by both the shortage of culturally relevant resources and the fine work being done by aboriginal ECE students at Red River College, the program was successful in obtaining funding to develop a video series *Our Children, Our Ways: Early Childhood Education in First Nations and Inuit Communities*. This series is now used across Canada and internationally with diverse groups.

The program has also collaborated with other agencies to develop and deliver full-time programs that include some ECE content as well as other curriculum content, tailored to meet the needs of a specific group.

In partnership with community agencies the program has developed and delivered a Family Daycare Training Project, a Child Care Assistant Training Project, a Family Support Worker Training project, and a Childminders program, which combines part-time ECE and English and a Second Language content for immigrant women.

With a shortage of trained ECEs in Manitoba, graduates from Red River College enjoy a healthy employment record. In 2003/2004, 92 percent reported employment in areas related to their studies and the remaining 8 percent are continuing their education. Also, Red River College graduates may transfer their ECE diploma credits to university studies. The college has several articulation agreements with universities enabling graduates to obtain credits toward degrees in the areas of developmental studies, family studies, and human services.

Most ECE graduates go on to join the early childhood workforce and find employment in a child care centre or nursery school. Many return to Red River College to participate in one of its continuing education post-diploma programs (Studies in Aboriginal Child Care, Studies in Special Needs Child Care, or Infant Care). With experience and this additional professional education, a number of graduates achieve an ECEIII classification and move on to positions as directors of child care centres or in early childhood intervention services. The ECE graduates from Red River College meet the requirements for staff qualifications in most jurisdictions across Canada.

In Canada, Red River College is an acknowledged leader in several areas, including,

- implementation of a competency-based approach to ECE programs;
- articulation agreements with universities, allowing ECE grads to articulate to degree programs;
- very high student accessibility through alternative but equivalent delivery of ECE programs;
- community-based training programs in partnership with urban aboriginal and First Nations communities; and
- the production of multimedia resources for ECE training.

In 1999 the program embarked on a substantial program review process that included the input of community, graduates, and faculty. The main outcomes of this review were the reorganization of content into forty-hour packages, delivering all practicum as block placements and more emphasis on emergent curriculum and creating high-quality play environments for young children. The program will participate in another program review process in 2006.

Other innovative initiatives include the proposed development of a core curriculum resource that would translate the most recent research findings related to neurological development in young children to a flexible, learner-friendly, core multimedia resource. As well, the program has recently produced a video series and documentary for broadcast profiling best practices in Family Resource Programs across Canada.

The program has also recently participated in two international projects, in Vietnam and the Philippines, which involved staff from Red River College going to those countries, and Vietnamese and Philippine staff spending time at Red River College.

The ECE program at Red River College continues to evolve to maintain currency and quality and to meet the needs of its community.

Since 2002, the program has partnered with the Atkinson Centre for Society and Child Development at the University of Toronto and Founders' Network to develop an on-line media-rich curriculum resource called "The Science of Early Child Development." The resource is like an interactive multimedia textbook that presents new research related to early child development, much of it from the fields of neurobiology and genetics, and links it to early childhood practice. The Science of Early Child Development consists of five modules: Developmental Health, Brain Development, Genetics and Experience, Coping and Competence, and Communication and Learning—each comprised of interviews with researchers, video of children parents and caregivers, links, readings, and games.

Source: Based on interview with Joan Kunderman, Chair, Community Services, Red River College (2001).

In spite of differing institutional and provincial/territorial requirements, the recent Child Care Sector Study (Beach et al., 1998) found remarkable similarities across all Canadian ECE certificate and diploma programs.

- All programs include course content related to child development, teaching/caregiving practices, and behaviour guidance.
- Most (about 90 percent) include course content in health, safety and nutrition, observation skills, interpersonal communication, and the foundations or history of early education theory.
- Ninety percent focus their program's course content on centre-based settings, whereas only 10 percent include specific curriculum content related to other ECEC settings, such as family child care.

ECE students at Red River College in Winnipeg, Manitoba.

- All certificate and diploma ECE programs include field placement requirements.
- ECE certificate and diploma programs contain general education content, in addition to the professional education related to ECEC.

The study also identified a number of gaps in ECE certificate and diploma programs, including the need for a more family-centred approach, for more content related to infant/toddler and school-age care, for the inclusion of children with special needs, and for greater attention to cultural, linguistic, and racial diversity.

Guidelines for ECE Programs

To prepare early childhood educators, postsecondary education programs must expose students to general knowledge and specific competencies associated with all groups within the early childhood span—infants, toddlers, preschoolers, and primary-aged children. Students must learn about children with needs beyond those of the typically developing child. They must also have course work and practica that particularize their knowledge about some of these age groups.

In addition to this general knowledge, some professionals in particular roles, such as a director of an early childhood program or a family child care provider, require specialized knowledge. Some roles also will require greater depth of knowledge for teachers to be effective, such as learning more about special education or language delays. And because of the complexity of their roles, early childhood educators must reach beyond child development and early childhood education and learn the communication skills that will allow them to work effectively with colleagues on the teaching team and on more extended professional teams, with parents and others in families, and with the community beyond. At each successive level of preparation, from the introductory courses and certificate programs through to graduate degree levels, professionals become increasingly able to apply, analyze, and refine the core knowledge to improve practices. It is recognized that higher levels of general education are linked to quality in programs for children, as professionals are able to apply their specialized knowledge. General knowledge also helps early childhood teachers create learning experiences for children that draw on the broad content of general studies in the arts and sciences.

The Canadian Child Care Federation (CCCF) has responded to the need to improve the preparation of early childhood educators and to ensure greater consistency of ECE postsecondary education programs. In 1989, the CCCF established a national training committee to study educational issues and concerns. Over the next several years, the committee facilitated a series of national discussions about ECE postsecondary programs. These discussions led to the 1993 CCCF conference, where there was clear support to move forward to develop national guidelines. After considerable consultation with interested individuals, organizations, educational institutions, and government departments across the country, the com-

RESEARCH INTO PRACTICE

National Guidelines in ECE Training

Program Content

- Studies in self-awareness and communication are essential for the learning and application of knowledge, skills, and attitudes.
- Knowledge of human development and an appreciation of the role of the family serve as the foundation for promoting each child's optimal development.
- Specialized studies in early child development form the framework for supporting professional theory and practice.

Learning Environment

- Faculty in ECE programs play a key role in facilitating a student-centred learning process.
- Administrators have a responsibility to support an optimal learning environment.
- Students have a responsibility to contribute to an optimal learning environment.
- Advisory bodies, as representatives of the early childhood community, ensure the link between training programs and the broader early childhood education and care field.
- Governments and policymakers have responsibility to provide the financial support and the regulatory framework.
- All stakeholders share responsibility for ensuring the delivery of quality program content in a quality learning environment.

Source: Canadian Childcare Federation (1997). Used with permission.

mittee prepared *National Guidelines for Training in Child Development.* The guidelines are built on common values and beliefs and identify the essential components of the ECE postsecondary education necessary to prepare entry-level early childhood educators. The guidelines include items related to curriculum content and the learning environment. They can be applied to full-time, part-time, and distance education programs. In addition to the guidelines, the committee developed a companion document, *Towards Excellence in ECCE Training Programs: A Self-Assessment Guide,* which provides a tool for educational institutions to review their ECEC programs.

To date, several community colleges have reviewed their ECE programs using the guidelines and assessment guide. The guidelines provide a common reference point for ECE postsecondary programs offered by institutions in various provinces and territories and could be the basis to develop closer coordination of programs, which would enable early childhood educators to more easily transfer their ECE credits.

NAEYC revised and expanded its guidelines for associate and baccalaureate professional preparation programs (1995). Those changes reflect a clear emphasis on preparing practitioners for working in environments that fully include children with disabilities and special learning and developmental needs with typically developing children. In addition, the revised guidelines include a greater depth of preparation for working with families and a more family-centred approach, as well as more in-depth preparation for working collaboratively with other adults. A final area of change in the guidelines is increased emphasis on individualizing curriculum and assessment to reflect cultural and linguistic diversity (Bredekamp, 1995).

1940
Women in Quebec gain the right to vote in the provincial elections, completing the enfranchisement of women in Canada.

1941
4.5 percent of married women in Canada work outside the home.

Other Professional ECE Preparation Programs

ECE university degree programs. There are about a dozen ECE degree programs offered at Canadian universities, which can extend early childhood educators' career opportunities. Some of these university programs are offered as bachelor of arts programs; others are bachelor of child studies or child and youth studies. The ECE degree credentials extend early childhood educators' careers. A few programs have developed in collaboration with ECE college-level programs or offer concurrent ECE degree/diploma programs.

Admission requirements to ECE degree programs vary. A few require an ECE diploma or other postsecondary education, and others may give advanced standing for college-level ECE credentials.

The curriculum of ECE degree programs often focuses on working with children with special needs and on early intervention strategies in specialized and regular early childhood education and care settings. Many programs offer students specialization options. Some ECE degree programs emphasize preparation for further graduate study.

Family child care certificate programs. Many early childhood educators who have completed ECE certificate or diploma programs operate family child care programs in their own homes. Other family child caregivers enroll in ECE certificate or diploma programs through continuing education or distance education. Only British Columbia and Ontario provide certificate programs specifically designed for family child care.

Specialized post-certificate and post-diploma programs. A number of postsecondary education institutions in British Columbia, Manitoba, and Ontario offer post-certificate or post-diploma programs specializing in child care management and administration, children with special needs, infants and toddlers, and school-age children.

Teacher education programs. Teachers in the school system in Canada complete a university degree and specific teacher education programs to be eligible for provincial/territorial teaching credentials. Teacher education programs usually lead to a Bachelor of Education degree. B.Ed. degrees may be earned as a first university degree or as a second degree (Canadian Education Association, 1999).

A first degree B.Ed. program takes four to five years to complete and is open to students with a secondary school diploma. It is often offered as a conjoint, concurrent, or integrated program and includes study both in professional training for elementary or secondary education and in an academic discipline area. Students then graduate with both a B.Ed. and another degree such as a B.A. or a B.Sc.

RESEARCH INTO PRACTICE

Perspectives of Early Childhood Education Students

Working for a Change was a research study of the child care workforce. It included surveys and focus groups with ECE students from across Canada. The researchers found that:

- Most students wanted their training to be longer and thought that all child care staff should have a post secondary education qualification.
- The cost of college and university programs and the distance from programs were cited as barriers to access.
- Most students were very positive about the education they were receiving—75 percent rated all components of their programs as good or excellent.
- Almost one-third of students surveyed did not think that their programs prepared them to work with children with special needs.
- Only half of the students in focus groups intend to work in child care upon graduation.

Source: Beach et al. (2004) *Working for a change.* Ottawa: Child Care Human Resource Sector Council.

Students with ECE certificates or diplomas are usually eligible for admission to these programs, even if they do not have the required secondary school diploma. In a few instances, there are articulation agreements between a B.Ed. program in a university and an ECE program in a college that allow for advanced standing into the second year of the teacher education program.

Other teacher education programs are organized as a second degree (a B.Ed.), after the completion of another university degree program, including a degree in early childhood education or child studies.

Mentoring

During the past several years, a new pattern has been added to opportunities for professional growth and learning in many early childhood communities. It is possible that you will have an opportunity to benefit from a mentoring program, either as a student or as a professional. In mentoring programs, experienced and effective early childhood educators are given specialized training, to help beginning early childhood educators gain skills and become more effective practitioners. Students or beginning early childhood educators, called protégés, mentees, or apprentices, are paired with the **mentor** early childhood educator, generally in the mentor's early child development program. Here, during experiential learning, mentors act as backup support, offering feedback that allows the beginner to move to a higher level of skilled performance.

Obviously, both participants gain from such arrangements. Experienced early childhood educators receive recognition, advanced education, and increased salaries when they act as mentors. They can remain in their early child development settings

MAKING IT HAPPEN

Mentoring Programs in Canada

Recent initiatives in Canada studied the effectiveness of a mentoring approach in ECE field placements:

- Pollard (1996) examines both mentor and supervisory roles involved in the relationship between an early childhood education student and the child care centre staff member who is a cooperating teacher in field placement situations. The study concludes that early childhood education students in field placement benefit from a mentor-mentee relationship with the sponsoring/cooperating teacher.
- Singleton (1997) tried out a mentoring model with ECE students completing field placement at the lab centres at the College of the North Atlantic in St. John's, Newfoundland. The mentors planned scheduled conferences and journal writing for students to reflect on their practice experiences. The study reports benefits for both the mentors and the students because the mentoring process led both to examine, reflect on, and improve their childhood care practices.
- Child Care Connections—NS developed the Child Care Substitute Youth Internship program (Ferguson, 1998) for fifteen youth in Halifax and Sydney. The interns spent two weeks in a child care centre and then had two weeks of course work, combined with sessions between the intern, mentor, and practice coordinator during the practice period to reflect on and evaluate their performance. The four-week cycle continued over six months. Each intern was matched with a mentor who was a skilled child care practitioner working in one of the child care settings. Mentors received training in communication, problem-solving, and teamwork to support their work with the interns. The mentors and interns both reported valuable learning and insights from their participation in the mentoring process.

with children, using their developed skills and expertise, and yet feel that they have advanced in their own professional careers, taking on new positions of leadership in their centres and communities. They are more likely to remain in the field, with the new status and enhanced salaries, as well as with the new interest in leadership and professional development. Their own practice is likely to improve, as the mentors increase their reflection on their teaching to share with the protégé. Protégés are also more likely to remain in the field over time, having been given the opportunity to develop the skills needed to prevent the overwhelming frustration of the unskilled. Having formed a relationship with an experienced early childhood educator, they see that early childhood is a viable profession over time. They have received the coaching, guidance, and counselling that help during the initial adjustments to any new experience. In lessening the probability of staff turnover and in developing more educated and skilled practitioners, mentoring programs are making important contributions to communities and early childhood programs. Therefore, the quality of services to children and families is directly affected by the development of such opportunities.

There are diverse ways to structure mentoring programs, according to community resources and needs. For examples of successful programs, see Whitebook, Hnatiuk, & Bellm, 1994.

SUMMARY

This chapter suggests that good early childhood educators are people who have certain dispositions and characteristics that allow them to grow as early childhood educators and as individuals. These attributes include having feelings of adequacy, the ability to think flexibly, a sense of autonomy, an ability to empathize, values and philosophy that enable teachers to take in the big picture, the ability to disclose oneself to others, and the acceptance of being a growing person. Knowledge and skill development will enhance teacher effectiveness. Growing early childhood educators—and student early childhood educators—experience common problems and feelings at different stages. This chapter has discussed the varying methods of preparing for professional roles in the early childhood field. There is little uniformity in current requirements, owing to the nature of provincial/territorial regulatory requirements for licensed early child development programs, the provision of postsecondary education in Canada, and the autonomy of most educational institutions. Currently, organizations in Canada and the United States are attempting to create a comprehensive framework for the preparation of early childhood educators. This framework includes consistent guidelines for postsecondary education programs, flexibility of entry point and preparation options, and an increase in the level of postsecondary education that is required for all early childhood educators.

After reading this chapter, you likely have a clearer perspective of where your own goals and training fit into the larger picture. It is important that you understand the options open to you and comprehend the purposes behind the design of your current program. A well-prepared early childhood professional can con-

REVIEW QUESTIONS

1. Identify and discuss the motivators described in this chapter.
2. Which motivators have personal meaning for you?
3. Discuss your understanding of why self-knowledge is important to the development of an early childhood educator.
4. Describe several attributes that are important for early childhood educator growth and optimum functioning.
5. Describe several characteristics of the various stages of early childhood educator and student early childhood educator development.
6. Discuss the differences between licensing and certification.
7. Identify reasons for diversity in early childhood preparation requirements.
8. Discuss the concept of mentoring as it is currently being used in early education professional development.

STUDY ACTIVITIES

1. Interview early childhood educators about why they chose this field and their motivations for staying. Also ask them about the characteristics they feel workers in this field need, and about things they dislike about the field or their job.

2. Many of the following questions are for your consideration in your private notebook or journal. Some are appropriate to share with a partner.
   a. List ten words that you would use to describe yourself, to yourself only. List ten words that someone who knows you well would use to describe you. List ten words that an acquaintance would use to describe you. List ten words with which you would *like* to be described. Reflect on these lists. What do the similarities and differences mean?
   b. How have you changed in the last three years? What would you like to accomplish in the next three years? What thing that you don't know how to do right now would you like to learn in the future?
   c. What is your favourite thing to do alone? With others? What is something that is special to you that you would like to share with a child?
   d. Complete these sentences:
      I want to be an early childhood educator who . . .
      I want to be an early childhood educator who believes . . .
      I want to be an early childhood educator who feels . . .
      I don't want to be an early childhood educator who . . .
      I don't want to be an early childhood educator who believes . . .
      I don't want to be an early childhood educator who feels . . .
      I feel most competent when . . .
      I feel most unsure of myself when . . .
      It really bothers me when children . . .
      I love it when children . . .
   e. Ask your ECE faculty to describe their educational background.
   f. In what stage of early childhood educator or student early childhood educator development do you think you are at this time? What makes you think so? What would be most helpful to your growth as an early childhood educator right now?
   g. Analyze your early childhood program to see how the various courses provide the kinds of knowledge recommended by the CCCF statement on core knowledge for early childhood professionals, practical experience, and general knowledge.
   h. Check if there are any other ECE-related programs offered at your college. Is your ECE program eligible for advanced standing or special consideration for admission into an ECE degree program?

KEY TERMS

inherited: Characteristics directly transmitted to children from parents' genetic combinations.

journal: In early childhood education, notes made by student early childhood educator to document progress of children and teacher.

longitudinal studies: Research that follows the same individuals over a long time.

mentor: Experienced individual who supports someone with less experience.

SUGGESTED READINGS

Ball, J. (2005). Supporting First Nations' constructions of early childhood care and development through community-university partnerships. *Research connections Canada: Supporting children and families,* 13. Ottawa: Canadian Child Care Federation. P. 21–40.

Beach, J. & Costigliola, B. (2005). *The future child care workforce: Perspectives of early childhood education students.* Ottawa: Child Care Human Resources Sector Council.

National Research Council (2001) *Eager to learn: Educating our preschoolers.* Washington DC: National Academic Press.

CHAPTER SIX

The Work Environment

OBJECTIVES

After studying this chapter, students will be able to

- discuss the characteristics of the work environment in early childhood settings;
- identify and describe what is meant by the term "career lattice," and discuss various career options in the early childhood field;
- identify and describe working conditions in early child development centres;
- describe several helpful supports for early childhood educators facing challenges; and
- prepare to apply for employment in an early child development setting.

In this chapter, we will juxtapose the positive aspects of a career in the early childhood workforce with the challenges faced by the early childhood workforce in Canada today. The early childhood workforce offers opportunities for a variety of career directions, and options for skilled early childhood educators in Canada are expanding. The words and stories of early childhood educators who find fulfillment and satisfaction in their work suggest that the early childhood workforce can allow you to achieve your personal and professional goals. The recognition of our value in working with young children and supporting families is growing.

Nevertheless, there are challenges, and early childhood educators are often overworked, underpaid, and undervalued. But the field is expanding and becoming more visible, which expands the horizons for early childhood educators.

Some of the challenges must be accepted as things that cannot be changed. Others you can remedy through your own efforts and commitment as you become increasingly competent in the role of early childhood educator.

Career Directions

As you look ahead to your career, you may be looking toward thirty or more years. During that period, you may be involved in different kinds of work in the early education field. Today, as the field continues to grow and expand, there are numerous possibilities for those who choose to focus their life's work on early childhood.

As larger numbers of children live in families where both parents work, more early childhood professionals are needed to care for and teach these children. Families also need people to help them find care, and they need assistance paying for this care. In addition, our society has become more concerned with how this care affects young children and what quality child care really means. These concerns have led to more jobs: we need more family and early intervention specialists to help families find the kind of care they need; more researchers to find out what produces quality child care programs; more trainers and consultants to ensure child care programs are meeting the quality requirements; and more administrators to help organize all these people and projects.

Many early childhood educators work directly with children in a centre-based program.

Careers in the early childhood field include those that serve children directly; those that serve families directly; those that organize services for children and families; those that provide information about children and families; and those that provide goods and services to businesses and governments and affect children and families. We will explore some of these careers here. Remember that within each type of position, there are many different job positions, and the particular responsibilities and requirements, as well as salary ranges, will vary with specific organizations.

Careers That Serve Children Directly

Working in centre-based programs. Child care centres or nursery schools will likely be a starting point for many of you. Almost every other related career requires that professionals have some direct experience with young children. Many of you may decide this is where you want to stay for many years; others may consider the experience an important foundation for other goals. From your reading of earlier chapters, you will know that there are many different kinds of centre-based programs to choose from, depending on your educational preparation. These may include public programs, such as kindergartens or primary grades in the school system; before- and after-school care programs; Head Start programs; child care centres that may be operated by churches, not-for-profit corporations, or for-profit organizations or owners; employer- or government-sponsored agencies; and part-day preschools. Some early childhood educators may operate out of a centre-based program but work as home visitors either in family child care or an early intervention service.

Early childhood educators in home-based programs. Early childhood educators may work with young children in their own home or in the child's home. In-home early childhood educators, sometimes referred to as nannies, may be hired by individual families. Family child care programs may be regulated or may operate outside provincial/territorial child care requirements beyond adhering to the maximum number of children. Many early childhood educators choose to work with young children in their own homes for reasons of convenience for their own families and preference for the types of relationships fostered in the home-like setting.

Resource teachers. Early childhood educators may decide to work with children with special needs and their families to ensure that they are able to fully participate in early childhood education and care programs. As the special needs of each child and the concerns of the family are identified, resource teachers and other service providers work with the family to create a plan to meet those needs. This plan is called an Individualized Program Plan (IPP) or Individualized Family Services Plan (IFSP), depending on the age of the child. (You will learn much more

1942
The *Dominion-Provincial Wartime Day Nurseries Agreement* is established. The federal government passes an Order-in-Council authorizing the Ministry of Labour to enter into cost-sharing agreements with any provincial government willing to establish day care services.

1942–45
Six community-based preschool child care centres are established in Montreal to support the war effort. Ontario establishes twenty-eight preschool and forty-two school-age day nursery programs.

about this terminology and this process in your later coursework on children with special needs.) Resource teachers work with other early childhood educators to implement the plan and include the child in the daily program. Resource teachers often help families access other support and remedial services as needed.

Child development specialist on health team. Professionals with a background in child development are often included on the assessment and education teams that provide services to children with special needs. Education specialists may interact with children during screening or assessment sessions, may help provide appropriate stimulation for children in small group therapy sessions, or may provide appropriate knowledge and guidance for family members. Some health departments include child development specialists on their teams to provide information about typical development of young children for parents. Other child development specialists may be part of the staff facilitating children's play in the play therapy room of hospital pediatric units. Some health agencies, such as the Red Cross, employ early childhood educators in their community education programs.

Recreation leaders. Some recreation facilities, such as city park and recreation programs and residential camps, employ early childhood educators to staff and administer their recreation programs for children. There are companies who sponsor exercise, dance, and fitness programs for children, and others that provide child care for parents who participate. Some library systems employ individuals with early childhood backgrounds to be storytellers and provide other services in children's rooms.

Careers That Serve Families Directly

Family support program staff. Family resource programs, parenting centres, and family literacy programs usually have a multidisciplinary team that includes early childhood educators. In these programs, early childhood educators will work directly with young children and their family members and other caregivers. They plan and carry out curriculum that is both adult- and child-focused and strives to actively involve parents and other caregivers in their children's early development and learning.

Family specialists. Family specialists include a broad spectrum of early childhood professionals who help families gain access to the services they need to care for their children. Many community agencies support families in the complex tasks of parenting and help find them the resources they need. A family specialist may provide information and education, refer families to services, help them gain access to funds to pay for services, or give direct support services. Family specialists may deliver services in agency offices, in child care programs, or in the family's home. Some have specialized expertise, such as child care referral counsellors, social workers, or family counsellors. Examples of programs that employ family specialists are child care resource and referral agencies, Head Start programs, community mental health and child abuse prevention agencies, and health departments.

Early intervention specialists. Early intervention is an interdisciplinary field that includes health, human services, and educational services for young children with special needs and their families. These specialists work directly with children and their families, in both homes and child care programs. They also work with other specialists who provide direct services to children and their families, such as child care providers, speech and language diagnosticians and therapists, physical and occupational therapists, medical personnel, and social workers. Early intervention specialists often develop and use Individual Program Plans or Individual Family Plans that are used by resource teachers (described in the previous section).

Early intervention specialists coordinate activities between the family and the other professionals working with the child, and they help plan and deliver services. These duties require specialists to use their knowledge of child development, assessment, and family needs. They must also be skillful in working with other professionals, in communicating with parents, and in applying techniques for working successfully with children.

Early intervention specialists design individualized programs to support the development of children with special needs.

Careers That Organize Services

Early childhood education and care program administrators. Program administrators usually have several years of early childhood education and care work experience, as well as specialized studies in administration and business matters. Administrators have responsibility for ensuring that programs offer developmentally appropriate experiences for children and meet all legal standards; helping teachers to grow and develop professionally; supporting the needs of families and involving them in their children's lives at the centre; and supervising the daily flow of all centre operations, including maintaining staff, collecting fees, meeting nutritional needs, and ordering equipment, materials, and supplies. Fiscal management is an additional challenge, and some may also have responsibilities for fundraising. Because the director is usually the one who handles crises, the job may include plumbing, first aid in emergencies, social work, and counselling on any given day. The differences in centre-based programs help determine what is expected of directors. Some very large centres also have an assistant director to help meet these responsibilities.

In large early childhood settings, program administrators may have much greater responsibility for arranging wider goals and priorities than for dealing with the day-to-day minute details of operating a program. For example, an upper-level manager may be the executive director of a child care resource and referral agency or a director of a multisite Head Start program. Program or project coordinators often manage a single specialty area, such as the education coordinator of a program, or a child care coordinator in a local department of social services.

Regulators. Regulators, or licensing specialists, ensure that early childhood programs comply with government requirements by visiting programs. In addition, many regulators provide directors and teachers with technical assistance and training to help them meet the standards. The knowledge required by regulators is comprehensive: they must know child development, appropriate programming and curriculum, effective guidance, and health and safety precautions. In addition, communication skills for working in the often difficult situation of monitoring others' practice are required. Most regulators are employed by provincial or local government agencies. Some monitor child care centres or homes; others monitor food programs or complaints of abuse or neglect.

1943

British Columbia becomes the first province to license child care centres under welfare legislation.

Representatives from the government, the Children's Welfare Council, and the Institute of Child Studies attend a conference to establish guidelines for the wartime day nurseries in Ontario and Quebec.

Ontario establishes The Day Nurseries Branch, Canada's first provincial child care authority.

Junior kindergartens are introduced into Toronto Public Schools.

Marsh Report on Social Security in Canada recommends that maternity leave and benefits be extended to Canadian women.

Consultants. Early childhood consultants provide assistance and information to businesses, communities, and other organizations to help them develop child care programs or meet various standards. Usually, consultants work on-site to help the organization assess its current program, resources, and future plans. There is a growing need for consultants to help employers work out methods of providing for their employees' child care needs. In addition to knowledge of child development and child care program administration, consultants who work with the corporate community need specialized knowledge about market research and employee benefits.

Careers That Provide Information

Resource librarian/information officer. The expanding knowledge base about the science and practice of early child development creates new opportunities for early childhood educators. Resource centres, research institutes, early childhood organizations and governments are exploring ways to translate new knowledge and information to the early childhood workforce, parents, and communities. Early childhood educators understand the daily lives of front-line staff and families in early childhood settings and can translate what new policies and research findings may be relevant.

Researchers. As programs and policies regarding children continue to expand, there is an ever-increasing need to understand all aspects of children's development and programming. Researchers generally focus attention on specific service aspects, such as child care, health services, early intervention programs, and nutrition. Much research focuses on children at various stages of development and on family variables and needs. Possible employers include colleges and universities, research institutes that may be affiliated with universities, government agencies, foundations, professional associations, and advocacy organizations. In addition to having a wide background in child and family development knowledge, many researchers need knowledge of observation and other data collection methods, as well as data analysis techniques. Many researchers begin their careers as part-time research assistants or interns.

Trainers and instructors. Those who work with practitioners have the important responsibility of helping those adults gain the knowledge and skills they need to work effectively with young children and their families. In addition to having a depth of knowledge in child development and all aspects of effective early childhood education and programming, they must understand adult development and learning as well as useful teaching strategies. Effective trainers and instructors have generally had considerable firsthand experience in early childhood settings with children. Many experienced early childhood professionals train others part-time in addition to working in the classroom with young children, by participating in workshops, taking part in local conferences, or teaching part-time at a local college. This is a satisfying way of making a larger contribution to the field, while still maintaining the connection to early childhood education and care programs.

You will recall from the discussion of mentoring that many early childhood educators work in their own programs with children while supporting students and other new practitioners in learning effective practice through mentoring. Others, such as regulators, family specialists, and early intervention specialists, also occasionally provide training as part of their jobs. Still others, such as college and university ECE faculty or high school child development teachers, teach other

MEET THE EARLY CHILDHOOD WORKFORCE

Michelle Turiano

Michelle is a resource librarian at the Childcare Resource and Research Unit at the University of Toronto. (Many of the references and information boxes in this book have been supplied by the Childcare Resource and Resource Unit.) Michelle graduated from Ryerson University in 1995 with a B.A.A. in ECE.

While in high school, Michelle worked in an after-school program. She was drawn to the close, responsive relationships that the early childhood staff in the program established with young children and their families. Michelle recalls how one early childhood educator (who was her supervisor) made a huge difference in the lives of children who participated in the program. "I decided that I would like to do that," says Michelle. "The selling point of entering the field is the gratification that comes from relationships with children and their parents. At story time the children would cuddle up. They valued my presence and I valued their milestones. During my first field placement, I pushed myself hard to make room for small talk with parents in the morning and at the end of the day. I found it rewarding to share the day with parents."

Michelle's experiences as a front-line practitioner are put to good use at the Childcare Resource and Research Unit. Michelle is responsible for maintaining the documents in the Unit's vast library, preparing new content for the Web site and gathering new information, reports, and documents from across Canada and from international sources. Michelle is able to sort through a vast amount of material and pull out what is really relevant to early child development policies and practices. Because she understands the day-to-day realities of early childhood education and care programs, Michelle is able to guide ECE students and practitioners to new research findings and policies. She also provides assistance to the Unit's various research projects, and finds that her practical experience brings a valuable perspective to the research work.

Michelle may work directly in an early childhood education and care program in the future. But for now, "The work here is challenging and another way to view the field. It is exciting to know about current policy developments, different reports, and cutting-edge research. I am able to bring this information to the field and to students entering the field."

practitioners full-time. Some large child care programs with multiple centres employ their own educational specialists to work with their staff.

Authors and editors. There are a number of local and national publications devoted entirely to children's and family issues. These vary from the large, glossy magazines sold nationally on newsstands and by subscription, to local publications sometimes distributed free of charge in doctors' offices and schools. All of these publications offer professionals opportunities to share their knowledge about children and families, in print.

1945

Attachment theory is discussed by Rene Spitz in *Hospitalism: An Inquiry into the Genesis of Psychiatric Conditions in Early Childhood.*

The federal Family Allowance program is introduced.

Quebec closes wartime centres. Ontario tries to but is stopped by the effective public campaign mounted by the Day Nursery and Day Care Parents Association.

Careers That Provide Goods and Services

Merchandisers. There is a large consumer market for developmentally appropriate toys and materials, books, teaching materials, clothing, and other items used in the care and teaching of young children. Merchandisers may sell their products in stores or at local or national conferences. Many corporations prefer to have their items marketed by individuals with knowledge of child development.

Politicians and advocates. Although a background or experience in child development is not a prerequisite, gaining a voice in elected local, provincial/territorial, or federal government is one way individuals who care about children's and family issues can be effective. Legislators have a direct impact on creating the laws and policy that influence the lives of families and of childhood education programs. In our modern world of increasingly larger organizations set up to deal with the complexities of the legislative process, some people with early childhood interests may find there are opportunities to influence others by working as advocates with advocacy groups. Here, again, child development and other professional knowledge can make legislators and advocates far more effective.

Career Pathways

A conceptual framework of ECE postsecondary education and development must achieve a balance between inclusivity and exclusivity. It must fully embrace the diversity of roles and levels of preparation required for early childhood educators working with young children to provide high-quality services. It must also recognize that individuals enter the profession with diverse educational qualifications and experience, and promote a system that encourages ongoing professional development for individuals at all levels and in all roles. The framework must also set high standards for professional performance and distinguish the specialized skills and knowledge of the early childhood profession from those of other professions. (See Johnson & McCracken, 1994, p. 11.)

The symbol of a **career lattice** conveys the needed combination of diversity and development. The career lattice includes the idea of the multiple roles and levels (horizontal strands) and settings (vertical strands) within early childhood education, as well as diverse entry points and bridges between roles and settings in terms of professional preparation and responsibility (diagonals). It allows for the possibility of upward movement with increasing responsibility and compensation within that role, as well as intersecting movement across the various roles. This seems a better image for a field as diverse as early childhood education than the more traditional ladder, which implies that there is just one clearly defined path to professional development and that one must step over others to advance.

The lattice, on the other hand, allows for the scenario of someone who is employed as a child care assistant without any preservice training. After two years of experience, she is given a promotion to lead early childhood educator and encouraged to enter a program at a community college, where she completes a two-year degree in early childhood education. Some time later, she seeks employment as a lead early childhood educator in a Head Start program, where she is encouraged to continue her education in a degree program. A number of years later, she applies for the assistant director position at her original child care centre.

The career lattice concept also allows for the scenario of a parent in a Head Start program who is hired as a bus driver/aide. He takes an introductory course in ECE at a local community college, then completes an ECE certificate through continuing education and, after a number of years, becomes a lead teacher in a Head Start program. While teaching in the program, he continues his education to obtain his teacher's certification, and he later becomes a kindergarten teacher in a local elementary school.

Early childhood educators work in many different types of settings and under many different working conditions.

The lattice allows for the entry of people like these into the profession, and allows them to continue their professional growth and move into various roles. It allows entry, as well, for those who followed the more traditional routes of enrolling in a teacher certification program or degree program immediately after high school graduation, obtaining preservice credentials before gaining employment in the field, and then, perhaps, making several changes in the early childhood settings chosen for employment.

The lattice distinguishes the early childhood field from the early childhood profession; the field includes anyone engaged in providing early childhood services, whereas the profession includes those who have acquired some professional training and are on a professional path. It defines distinct categories on a continuum of professional development.

RESEARCH INTO PRACTICE

Quality by Design—Human Resources

Qualified personnel and support that includes ...

- Leadership at all levels (policy, supervisory, educational and program)
- A critical mass of knowledgeable policymakers, post-secondary early childhood instructors and researchers
- Post-secondary level training in early childhood with lead staff at degree levels
- Human services management training for program supervisory staff
- Pre-service and in-service training
- Good wages
- Working conditions that encourage good morale and low turnover
- System support for program level staff
- Support, respect and recognition for the value of the work

The human resources—the people—who make up an ELCC system include frontline early childhood educators, family child care providers, centre directors, program managers, local, provincial/territorial and federal policymakers, post secondary early childhood instructors, researchers and experts. In all of these categories, leadership, innovation, creativity, and a strong knowledge base are foundational. As ELCC programs in Canada expand and expectations for their achievements grow, the complexities of providing high quality programs will require highly skilled people at all levels.

(cont'd)

Quality by Design—Human Resources (cont'd)

It is fundamental that high quality ELCC programs have staff that are well educated in early childhood education, skilled, competent, well respected and well remunerated. The considerable body of research supporting this comes from Canada, the United States and other countries. There is evidence of strong associations between high quality child care and the wages and working conditions, post secondary education in early childhood education, and job satisfaction of staff. Strong pedagogical leadership and competent human resources management at the centre level is important for supporting, nurturing and developing the staff team and implementing the reflective practices known to improve quality.

The interactions between staff and children and the environment created by staff contribute to positive early child development and children's well-being. In turn, high quality programs for children contribute to good working environments for staff, which help attract and retain a qualified workforce.

In Starting Strong [sic] the OECD notes that:

Quality ECEC depends on strong staff training and fair working conditions across the sector. Initial and in-service training might be broadened to take into account the growing educational and social responsibilities of the profession. There is a critical need to develop strategies to recruit and retain a qualified and diverse, mixed-gender workforce and to ensure that a career in ECEC is satisfying, respected and financially viable.

As provincial/territorial governments in Canada develop plans to increase the supply of regulated child care, a coordinated human resources plan will be essential to ensure the skilled workforce necessary to support the development of quality programs.

Human resources plans will need to address the high turnover of ELCC staff through a recruitment and retention strategy, changes to the low wages and poor benefits in much of the sector, the need for additional pre-service and ongoing education and training for both front-line staff and supervisors, a body of knowledgeable early childhood instructors at the post secondary level, educating at the post graduate level a body of researchers and policy experts working in the various disciplines associated with ELCC (child development, education, sociology, economics, political science), and public education to increase public awareness of the value of the work of caring for young children.

At the provincial/territorial, federal and local levels there will be a need for a critical mass of experienced policy makers knowledgeable in ELCC to design, implement and monitor strategic plans.

Source: Excerpt from M. Friendly & J. Beach (2005) *Quality by design.* Toronto: Childcare Resource and Research Unit, University of Toronto.

Working Conditions

Working conditions are the income, benefits, workloads, and characteristics of the social and physical environment. Provincial regulations and legislation about employment standards set the basic requirements for a minimum wage, mandatory vacations, and maximum numbers of hours of work per week.

Early childhood educators may be employed by parents, nonprofit organizations, local or provincial governments, businesses, or school boards, or they may be self-employed. The type of early child development setting affects the employment status of early childhood educators and the related working conditions.

The working conditions in each early child development setting create a climate for adults and children. If the salary and benefits are reasonable, job responsibilities and obligations are clear, health and safety are protected, and early childhood educators are valued, the working climate is positive. A positive work climate helps create a quality setting for young children and their families. (See Chapter 3 for further discussion about quality.)

Compensation

The good news is that income levels of early childhood educators are improving. For example, the average annual wage of an early childhood educator (who has primary responsibility for a group of children) in a regulated child care centre rose to an average annual salary of $22 717 in 1998, up from $18 000 in 1991 (Doherty et al., 2000).

But the still too-low income levels of early childhood educators are a major issue for the sector. Recent studies report that low remuneration remains a significant problem for those working in centre-based, family child care, and in-home settings, as well as for government officials, representatives from provincial/territorial and national sector organizations, and faculty members from colleges and universities (Beach et al., 1998; Doherty et al., 2000).

It is difficult to compare income levels for early childhood educators in different settings. Early childhood educators who work with children in centre-based programs or care for young children in the child's own home are usually employees. But early childhood educators in regulated or unregulated family child care settings are self-employed. Wages earned as an employee are subject to different deductions and taxation than is income earned through self-employment. Nevertheless, it is quite clear that both groups receive remuneration that fails to reflect the responsibilities and skills involved in working with young children.

Centre-based early childhood educators. A recent Child Care Sector Study reports that early childhood educators "with a college diploma or certificate working full-time and for the full year [in licensed child care programs] received less than 75 percent of the annual income of the average full-time, full-year female worker with the same education" (Beach et al., 1998, p. 77).

You Bet I Care! (2000) is a major study of the wages and working conditions of staff employed in licensed child care centres across Canada in 1998. Higher education, more experience, unionization, and nonprofit status were factors found to be related to higher income levels, even within the same province or territory. *You Bet I Care!* also reported on benefits that staff in child care centres received. Only 25 percent of full-time staff reported pension benefits, and 26 percent did not have sick leave benefits. About half of the staff members in the survey reported that they did not have long-term disability benefits.

Early childhood educators in regulated family child care. A 1996 survey of caregivers in regulated family child care reported on the wages and working conditions for this group (Goss Gilroy, 1998). Most are self-employed, and their child care programs are set up as small businesses. They are able to deduct reasonable expenses from the child care fees they receive, either directly from parents or through government fee subsidy programs. In 1996, the average gross income (before eligible deductions) was $15 600; the average net income (after deductions) was $8 400.

The income of early childhood educators in family child care is affected by the number of children in the settings. The maximum number of children is determined by the provincial/territorial regulations and varies from one region to

1946

The Common Sense Book of Baby and Child Care is published by Dr. Benjamin Spock.

Arnold Gesell, doing child development research at Yale, establishes the first descriptions of children at different chronological ages, using normative data.

The withdrawal of federal government funding leads to the closure of all forty-two school-age programs in Ontario.

2000
1950
1946
The American baby boom begins.

Ontario legislature passes the *Day Nurseries Act*. Federal funding for day nurseries ends.

1900
1850

1947
The Canadian baby boom begins and continues until 1964.

1800

1950
Eric Erikson publishes *Childhood and Society*, outlining his theory of psychosocial development.

1750

Nursery Education Association of Ontario (later AECEO) is started.

1700
1650

another, but many providers care for fewer children than is allowed by government regulations.

The 1996 survey of regulated family child care found that providers have access to few employment benefits—only 7 percent had paid vacation time and only 2 percent had access to pension plans or sick leave (Goss Gilroy, 1998). Early childhood educators working in family child care are self-employed and, therefore, would have to purchase benefits on their own.

In the United States, some of the highest-paid early childhood educators employed in child care centres earn less than $16 000 annually (Whitebook, Howes, & Phillips, 1993), and the average foregone annual wage—the additional money the worker could have earned in other female-dominated occupations—was $5 238 for early childhood educators and $3 582 for assistants (NAEYC, 1995).

Employment Contracts

A contract of employment outlines the terms or "rules" of an employment arrangement. It is an agreement between the employer (e.g., the early child development setting) and the employees (i.e., early childhood educators). In a unionized setting it is called a collective agreement and is negotiated by a process of collective bargaining.

A contract of employment usually includes

- job title;
- employment status;
- salary;
- benefits;
- work requirements; and
- employment procedures (hiring, termination).

Health and Safety

Your early childhood education studies emphasize the issues of health and safety of children in various early child development settings. Policies and practices ensure the physical environment is safe. There are also significant issues related to early childhood educators' health and safety in their work environments; early childhood educators are particularly vulnerable to infectious diseases, musculoskeletal disorders, and stress.

Getting sick is an occupational hazard in early childhood settings. Young children get colds, with runny noses and crusty eyes. They get gastrointestinal viruses and may vomit or have diarrhea. Early childhood educators who are exposed to these germs, and other common childhood diseases, risk becoming sick. Personal health care and preventive measures, as well as excellent hygiene practices in the early childhood setting, help to reduce the likelihood of illness. But, compared to most work environments, there is increased exposure to infectious diseases in work with young children.

Working with young children is physically demanding. Babies, children, furnishings, and equipment are carried or moved throughout the day's activities. Backs, knees, and joints can suffer.

Health and safety challenges are reduced by good working conditions that minimize the risks. As well, when illness or injury happens, sick leave and extended health care benefits can make a big difference.

Stress and Isolation

Early childhood educators are exposed to several sources of stress in their daily work environments, including the need for constant attention to keep children safe; frustrations connected to a lack of resources and too many demands from too many people; children's unpredictable interests, emotions, and behaviours; and emotional involvement with children and their families. Although the variety of situations and constant interactions with people are what attract and motivate many early childhood educators to work with young children, these same characteristics can be overwhelming.

Often in early child development settings, resources—human and physical—are in short supply. There may be too many children and too few adults to provide optimal experiences for young children. The quality of materials that the early childhood educator can provide for children is constrained by the program's budget. Early childhood educators know what they should do with children and what they would like to do, but they are often unable to do so because of situational constraints.

Beach et al. (p. 129) report that "the demands for, and expectations of child care are changing and often the caregiver bears the brunt of the inability of the sector to respond adequately to these changes. The sector is having difficulty responding to the needs of parents and offering high-quality care. Yet parents are becoming more aware of the importance of quality care and early experiences to their child's development, and are expecting more of caregivers." As resources become tighter and family expectations grow, early childhood educators feel the squeeze in trying to meet increased expectations with fewer materials, and with cutbacks in public health, social services, and public school programs.

Working with young children can be isolating.

The fact is that most of your time as an early childhood educator will be spent in the company of young children from infancy through to twelve years of age. Early childhood educators often work with other colleagues and assistants, but most of their conversations and contacts will be with the children. Even when parents and other family members are invited to spend time in the early childhood setting, the amount of time they spend there will be a small fraction of the workday. Though working with young children is rewarding and satisfying, it is also demanding.

The 1996 survey of providers in regulated family child care settings (Goss Gilroy, 1998) identified isolation and lack of contact with other adults as a work challenge. Almost half of the providers in the survey report dissatisfaction with the long and irregular hours, which interfered with their personal and family lives.

1951
11.2 percent of married women in Canada work outside the home.

We will examine some of the characteristics of the work environment that often contribute to stress and isolation.

Variety and unpredictability. There is constant change in work with young children; no two days are the same. Although a moderate amount of variety is stimulating and exciting to most people, a constant barrage of unpredictable events may result in psychological overload. The need to adapt continually may be exhausting, both physically and emotionally, even while it is exhilarating.

Imagine the adjustments an early childhood educator needs to make when she discovers that her co-worker has had a car break down and is running late; that two of the children in her class have just been diagnosed as having chicken pox, and the other ten families need to be informed; that there is no red paint for the planned art activity this morning and the child who is painting at the easel is demanding a substitute for the blue paint provided; that the puzzle table that is usually quite attractive to her group of children draws only uninterested glances this morning; that the birthday party scheduled for lunchtime will have to be moved to morning snack time to accommodate working parents' schedules; and that the child who usually separates from her grandmother easily has chosen today to run after her with heartbroken screams. After order is restored, the early childhood educator may feel a boost in self-confidence as she realizes that she has coped with these and other impromptu decisions and situations, but, at the time she has undoubtedly experienced a good deal of the stress that comes with having to adapt quickly.

Let's analyze the reasons behind the stress in such a scenario. One reason is that early childhood educators are inextricably bound to a variety of other adults, both co-workers and the parents of the children. Their schedules, needs, and wishes, to say nothing of values, all have to be acknowledged and do have an effect on the early childhood educator's actions and schedule. A second reason is that early childhood educators have so many roles to play, and to play simultaneously. Concurrently, this early childhood educator is concerned with ensuring the health and safety of children, communicating with parents, planning and providing appropriate learning resources and a daily schedule, and providing emotional support. Small wonder that there is room for stress. Another reason is that young children are "predictably unpredictable" (Hyson, 1982, p. 26).

Fast-changing interests, emotions, and behaviour mean that teachers are never quite sure how children will react to activities or situations, as in the case of the unexpected **separation** distress. With emphasis in the early childhood curriculum on children's choice and independent exploratory play, early childhood educators regularly have to adapt to children's preferences in the use of materials. The unpredictable process of responding to children's choices means that early childhood educators face stress in trying to provide appropriate curriculum activities and materials, often without advance planning.

For many early childhood educators, this spectacular lack of limits—the variety, freedom, open-ended, and unpredictable nature of the early childhood setting—is attractive. For others, this same variety and freedom may create anxiety and stress. What about you? Are you the kind of person who enjoys seeing your capacities challenged, who feels energized when stretched into new territory and decisions? Or are you continually anxious when you move into unfamiliar territory?

Frustrations. Early childhood educators often have chosen their profession because of their high ideals and their desire to influence children's development in important ways. "They impose upon themselves the responsibility for unlocking each child's potential" (Hyson, 1982, p. 27). Each child comes with a particular background and cultural context and with unique abilities, interests, and needs. There are enormous differences in what each child needs from the teacher and in the teacher's ability to respond to each child and family. Good early childhood educators try their best to rise to each specific challenge and to find the resources to help when they are unable to do the job themselves. They spread themselves around as much as they can, often painfully aware that although there are one or perhaps two adults in a setting, there may be three, five, or even ten times as many children, all demanding and deserving of help. There is never enough time to do all that early childhood educators feel should be done, and it is frustrating to feel unable to meet that need.

Frustration also comes from the complexities of the early childhood educator's tasks. The children are the main focus, of course, but every early childhood educator would like to have more time to talk with parents, to share ideas with colleagues, to prepare new play materials, and to reach out to educate the community about young children's needs. The multiplicity of aims and goals may be daunting. Time just does not permit a sense of completion in all these activities, and early childhood educators can feel frustrated in knowing that they could do their jobs better, "if only . . ."

Frustration comes from not only being unable to accomplish everything one would like with children or families, but also the fact that resources are often inadequate to support the work of early child development. In times of tight budgets, it is extremely rare to work in settings that provide all the materials and equipment that early childhood educators feel are essential to their task. Indeed, the programs that serve the needs of children and families often seem to be the first to feel the sting of budget cuts. On a day-to-day basis, limited resources mean constant efforts to stretch inadequate staff, materials, and supplies, in ways that are frustrating and sometimes downright humiliating. "I'm sorry," apologizes the infant early childhood educator, "We've run out of diapers so I'll have to ask you to bring some in for your child." "Only one cup of juice; we'll get seconds of water." "Just one dot of glue."

Frustration is a part of many occupations today that are stretched to do complex jobs with inadequate supports or resources. If early childhood educators are to avoid the **burnout** that comes with ever-mounting frustration, they will need to find the satisfaction that outweighs the frustrations in their work. What about your own response to frustration? Can you learn to live with the idea that your best efforts may never be quite enough to meet all needs? Understanding that there will be inevitable frustrations is important to your future well-being as a teacher. Your ability to focus on accomplishments instead of on uncompleted tasks is a factor of a positive outlook, related to the old question: Is this glass half-full or half-empty? What is your answer?

Changing times. One challenge for early childhood educators is that their roles, which are always somewhat loosely defined, are even more nebulous as society's demands and needs for the care and education of young children continue to grow and multiply. They sometimes feel they are asked to become counsellors, psychologists, and social workers, as they tend to the stresses of both children and parents.

2000 — 1950 — 1900 — 1850 — 1800 — 1750 — 1700 — 1650

1952
John Bowlby publishes *Maternal Care and Mental Health.*

1953
Arnold Gesell publishes *Infant Development.*

1954
B.F. Skinner publishes *Science and Human Behaviour,* applying behaviourist theory to parenting and education.

2000
1950
1900
1850
1800
1750
1700
1650

1957
Sputnik is launched by the Soviet Union (U.S.S.R.), precipitating much discussion about the effectiveness of American and Canadian education.

What about you? How do you feel about the idea that the changes in contemporary society expand general perceptions about what early childhood educators should be doing? Can you be realistic about your contribution to society without placing impossible demands upon yourself, or allowing others to impose them on you?

Attachment and loss. In many early childhood settings, children leave and move on to new relationships with other teachers at least once a year. Early childhood educators work by creating warm and nurturing relationships with the children in their care and with their families. Especially in child care situations with very young children, they are intimately involved with the daily care that leads to closeness and with the momentous events that bring satisfaction to both child and adult. Those mutual relationships often lead to strong attachments, which also fulfill some of the early childhood educators' emotional needs. Early childhood educators often discover that the severing of ties with children and families on a regular, cyclical basis is difficult.

Some early childhood educators protect themselves from the pain of loss by not forming meaningful attachments to the children under their care; however, they are then unable to be truly effective with children, as they have not created reciprocal relationships. Early childhood educators have to learn, instead, to recognize the temporary, though important, nature of their work with children. The inevitable sense of loss will be tempered by the knowledge of what they have accomplished through the relationship. Early childhood educators also must learn to have most of their emotional needs met outside classroom relationships, lest they become too dependent on those relationships.

> It was all connected, I realized, to a feeling of loss. Cathy and I were not only leaving the children, we were losing the ability to influence their lives. Who would these children talk to when they left us? Would their parents continue our work? Would their next caregivers love them as much as we did? There were no answers to these questions. In the end, we told ourselves that it didn't really matter. We had done our best: we had given the kids a good beginning. No one could take that away from them—or from us, either. (Wollman, 1994, p. 269)

What about you? Are you able to fulfill most of your emotional needs through the relationships in your personal life, so that you will not become too dependent on the relationships with the children you teach? Can you balance the sadness of leaving relationships with children with the realization of your indelible effect on their lives?

Adult isolation. Many administrators complain that their staff congregates together on the playground. Rather than being a sign of indifference to the need for supervising children, this congregating probably speaks of early childhood educators' needs for adult communication. Infrequent staff meetings or quick breaks are often the only chance early childhood educators have to speak with other adults for any period. And the isolation of adults who work alone means not only that they are often hungry to talk and share ideas with other adults, but also that the total responsibility for the care of the children rests on them. It is not unusual to hear caregivers in home child care settings comment that they never even have anyone to leave the children with so they can use the bathroom or make a telephone call. Such continuous on-duty time and lack of privacy can be exhausting, both physically and emotionally.

What about you? How would you respond to spending most of your time in the company of young children, rather than with other adults? Would the feeling of complete responsibility for a group during the day regularly result in severe stress? If so, you will need to find ways to renew yourself. Has this been something you've been able to do in the past when you have borne a lot of responsibility? If not, you may want to consider how you will cope with isolation.

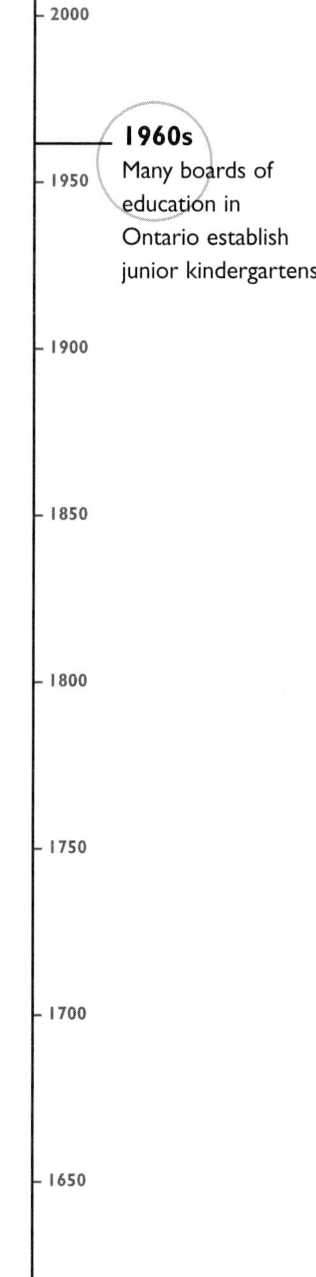

Process rather than product. Perhaps one of the most difficult parts of being an early childhood educator is that there is not necessarily a finished product to show for all the effort. What results there are may be intangible and virtually unobservable. Human development is a process of becoming. Parents get the rewards, as well as the headaches, of being able to watch the unfolding results of their efforts over long periods of time. Their child eventually becomes a responsible, caring adult in the best scenario, and parents are able to see the payoff of their efforts and worries. Early childhood educators, on the other hand, function for a relatively brief period in children's lives. Although they may see progress during the time they work with children, they usually have no way of knowing what the final outcomes will be. The doctor knows when the medicine that was prescribed cures the symptoms; the TV repairperson knows when the correct wire has been connected to fix the problem; the painter sees the appearance of the house improve with a new coat of paint. Much of what early childhood educators do is based on hope and belief in the future benefits of their present efforts.

What about you? Are you the kind of person who needs immediate feedback and evidence that your work is productive? If so, teaching may be difficult for you, since so much of it is based on a concept of promise of future results. Can you happily live with the concept that your efforts may bear fruit long after you are around to see it?

There is a resurgence of interest in Montessori schools in Canada and the USA, following the post-Sputnik discussions about the need for more structured programs for early education.

Ideals versus realities. Few early childhood educators enter the profession without some images of what it will be like and without ideals that drive their efforts. Though you may have imagined working with always delightfully smiling and responsive children, your studies and practical experience will likely replace this image with a more realistic one before you have finished your program. But this is not to suggest that your ideals also need replacing. One of the most disillusioning things that early childhood educators often encounter early on is people and institutions that try to strip them of their ideals. Although it is certainly true that beginning early childhood educators have to adapt to the real situations in which they find themselves, this by no means implies that they must discard the ideals and goals that drive them. In fact, those ideals allow early childhood educators to continue to grow, develop, and demand the best of themselves, their colleagues, and their schools. "It is important to be both a dreamer and a doer, to hold onto ideals but also to struggle continually to enact those ideals in concrete situations" (Ayers, 1993, p. 131).

What about you? Can you maintain your ideals even when people try to convince you that the real world demands giving them up? Can you be realistic enough to accept the things that cannot be changed and to work with others to change things that can and should be changed?

2000
1960
20.8 percent of married women work outside the home.
1950
1900
1850
1800
1750
1700
1650

Respect and Recognition

In Canada, the early childhood workforce struggles to be recognized as a valued occupation and to be adequately compensated. Unfortunately, there is a societal lack of respect for those who educate and care for young children. It is widely viewed as work that is an extension of women's traditional roles as mothers and homemakers. "Caring—the looking after, responding to and supporting of others—has traditionally been carried out by women and is often viewed as women's natural role" (Beach et al., 1998, p. 123).

Surveys and consultations with early childhood educators working in child care centres, nursery schools, family child care, and in-home child care identify lack of respect as a significant problem and a barrier to recognition of the value of their work (Canadian Child Care Advocacy Association and Canadian Child Care Federation, 1992; Beach et al., 1998; Goss Gilroy, 1998). The lack of respect is related to low compensation levels throughout the sector. If Canadians valued early child development, public investment and pay levels would be higher, and early childhood educators would have more incentives to stay in the field and to continue expanding their knowledge and skills related to child development and early childhood education practices.

Some related terminology implies that the work is not very important. Who wants to be called a "baby sitter" when, to most of us, the term implies a temporary, and purely custodial, function? The provincial/territorial legislative bodies that set training requirements for regulated child care programs suggest that not everyone requires special preparation. Part of this attitude is no doubt a side effect of the sexist assumption in society that work that is primarily carried out by mothers and other women is not very valuable. It is an interesting paradox that our North American culture pays vehement verbal respect to the importance of children and the power of mothering, yet finds few concrete ways to translate this rhetorical tribute into real support (Modligiani, 1988). In Canada and the United States, teaching of the youngest children, even in the early grades in elementary schools, has always been primarily women's work and, thus, is linked with a sense that it is somehow inferior and requires little skill or knowledge.

Facing Challenges

As you prepare to enter the early childhood workforce, it is important that you face the less attractive aspects of the sector. There is no question that the work is important and necessary and the field needs many new early childhood educators every year. But those who are entering the early childhood workforce will also face some challenges.

Think about how the people close to you responded when you told them you were considering early child development as a career. Write these responses in your journal.

When Christie S. announced to her friends and family that she would major in early childhood education and planned to be an early childhood educator, she was dismayed by their responses. Rather than congratulating her on her choice of doing meaningful, important work, as she saw it, her parents kept asking "Why?" To Christie, their question seemed to imply "Why do this work, when you obviously have a good deal of intelligence and could do something more important?" And "Why be a teacher of young children, when other work could be far more profitable for you?" Her father put it rather bluntly: "I'm afraid I'll still have to support you after you are finished with college." And one friend said, "You call that educating—what can you possibly teach those little kids?" Perhaps you have also encountered these responses; they are indeed discouraging, since they imply an absence of respect for the work that you have decided is meaningful and important to you. And, even more discouraging, these questions reflect some of the issues and attitudes that trouble the early childhood profession today.

When Christie turned to early childhood educators who were already employed in early childhood centres and schools for reassurance and support, she was dismayed to discover that here, too, were numerous rumbles of discontent. One spoke to her of his frustration with the gender bias he encountered; another complained of the stress of dealing with too many conflicting needs and unmet goals. Several stated that they would be moving on to work that allowed them to earn salaries that would reflect their education. It took a number of conversations with an early childhood educator who had also experienced frustration and stress, but who still felt that the satisfactions of the work were strong enough to outweigh the negatives, before Christie was reassured that her decision was a good one. She continued with her plans to become an early childhood educator, knowing that there would be financial, physical, emotional, and social hurdles ahead. It is interesting to note that some of the advantages that were discussed in earlier chapters also contribute to the stress and frustration that early childhood educators experience. Almy suggests that those working with young children would need a tolerance for ambiguity (1975). This implies that the same characteristic of the work that makes it attractive also makes it difficult. Ambiguity suggests, as well, that tolerance for stress is a highly individual and subjective response; what is intolerable to one person may provide interest and excitement to another.

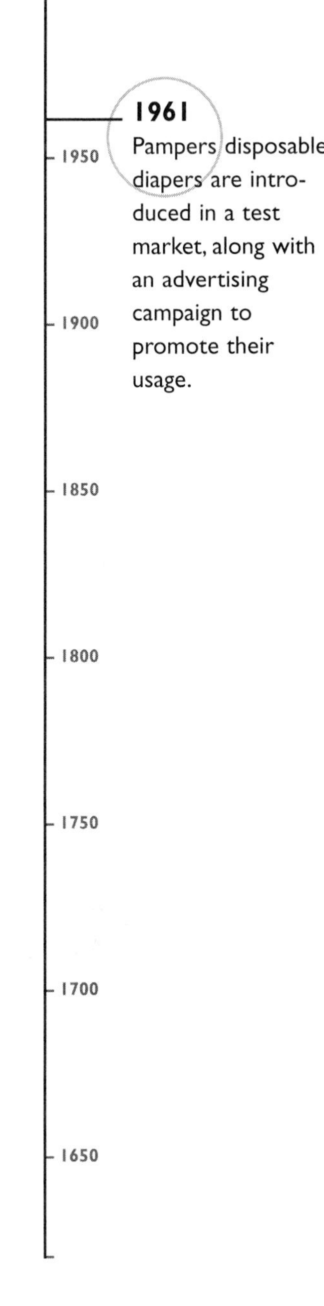

1961
Pampers disposable diapers are introduced in a test market, along with an advertising campaign to promote their usage.

J. McVicker Hunt, in *Intelligence and Experience* (1961), states that deficits in early stimulation can be corrected by early education.

Solutions to many of the challenges are intricately connected with the challenges of quality, affordability, and accessibility in early child development programs. We will consider these challenges and how we can take action in Chapter 9.

Now, let's examine the central challenges that early childhood educators face today:

1. Early childhood educators are subject to many sources of stress and often work in isolated settings.
2. Financial compensation is low compared with other occupations, and benefits are scarce.
3. Early childhood educators face health and safety risks in their work environments.
4. Early childhood educators are often confronted by those who do not recognize their skills and the value of their work with young children.
5. Men who choose to work with young children face gender-bias challenges.

The first challenge listed is inevitable for those who choose to work in early childhood settings. This challenge is an unchangeable reality, which early childhood educators must come to terms with as part of the nature of the occupation. The next four areas of challenge can be changed and, indeed, are slowly changing, through the efforts of early childhood educators, families, communities, and

Canadian society as a whole. In the final chapters of this book, we will examine those efforts, but here we will simply consider the challenges themselves.

There will be subtle and not-so-subtle pressures on you to give up the idea of caring for and educating young children, and to leave it to someone else to change the world, while you are urged to grow up and recognize harsh realities as unchangeable facts. You, and you alone, know how you feel as you contemplate these challenges and how you think about them as they will affect your future teaching. Think long and hard about the difficulties involved in early childhood education. There is a long line of early childhood educators, past and present, who hope that you, too, will decide this is worthy work and that you will take the challenge.

You are encouraged to take every opportunity to discuss these ideas with experienced early childhood educators, to hear about their real experiences and how they have made their choices to stay, and taken action to face the challenges. Let us consider some of the support available.

Knowledge

Opportunities to learn and develop skills will help early childhood educators deal with the pressure of decision-making and adaptation. The more you learn about current research and knowledge in early education, the more confident you will feel in the face of challenges and opposition. It is less frustrating when early childhood educators can focus on what they can do with children, rather than on what they cannot. Learning about current social conditions helps teachers see their positions within community efforts to support families. Understanding lifelong development will help teachers focus on the process of which they are a part. Continuing to learn and grow as a teacher allows teachers to face challenges with increasing confidence.

You are now embarking on a program of preservice education. But you also will continue to acquire knowledge after you have completed that initial degree. The challenges will keep coming; it is important that your knowledge continues also.

Support

Challenges seem less overwhelming when early childhood educators are not attempting to face them alone. Forming connections with colleagues allows early childhood educators to release feelings and get emotional support, to generate more ideas for solutions to problems both large and small, and to decrease feelings of isolation. Early childhood educators can obtain this collegial support from several sources. It is important to choose employment in a setting where collegiality is encouraged and facilitated by administrative support for teamwork and opportunities for collaboration. Membership in local professional organizations also can provide a sense of collective purpose and strength. A source of support often overlooked by many teachers is parents. Taking the time to form relationships and communicate with parents not only decreases many challenges but also increases insights and strength for meeting existing challenges.

Alliances

The challenges that can be changed—those that are primarily related to social attitudes and social policy decisions—require the work and effort of all early childhood professionals. The energy and sense of optimism that result from joining alliances and working together contribute to early childhood educators' sense of professional well-being, as well as producing concrete results. The progress that has been made in the past decade in gaining political support for children's issues proves the efficacy of joint efforts when trying to educate the public or garner legislative or corporate support. Meeting challenges requires memberships in alliances; it is virtually impossible to go it alone. We will come back to the question of alliances in Chapter 8.

Early childhood educators often find support from their colleagues.

Supervisor Support

In early childhood settings, supervisors can either add to or ease caregiver stress and frustration. It is important that early childhood educators open communication with their supervisors, who can be a positive source of support for individuals and for developing team opportunities. Early childhood educators need to avoid distancing themselves from their supervisors and to recognize that their supervisors have the same interests.

As one early childhood educator stated, "All of my good feelings [about the early childhood educator role] are to a large extent due to the fact that my supervisor is a person who goes out of her way for all of us. She trusts her staff in making decisions, is always searching for new ways of improving the program, and is open to ideas for these changes. Most important she listens . . . Our parents respect her, because they know they can depend on her honesty and integrity. As a result, the atmosphere is friendly and warm and it's a good place to work" (Carson, 1978).

SUMMARY

An increasing number of career opportunities exist for the early childhood workforce. Those entering the workforce should investigate the possibilities in both education and employment that match their personal and professional goals.

Working conditions for early childhood educators are improving, but those who enter the early childhood workforce face some challenges including stress and isolation, compensation, and health and safety risks. Early childhood educators who expect to meet these challenges will benefit from knowledge, support systems, and supervisor support.

REVIEW QUESTIONS

1. Identify six of the challenges discussed in this chapter, including at least one that is being slowly changed by the efforts of early childhood professionals.

2. Describe at least three of the conditions that help early childhood educators face challenges.
3. Discuss what is meant by a "career lattice" and its significance for the early childhood workforce.
4. Discuss various career options within the early childhood field, under the following headings: working directly with children, working directly with families, organizing services for children and families, providing information about children and families, and providing goods and services affecting children and families.

STUDY ACTIVITIES

1. Go to www.ece.nelson.com. Look in the associations' Web sites to find information about employment opportunities for early childhood educators.
2. Think about any negative responses others had about your decision to become an early childhood educator (which you recorded in your journal). How do you now feel about these responses?
3. Reflect on the challenges of the field. Are there any that may seriously influence your wish to become an early childhood educator? Are there any that you feel will not be a particular problem for you?
4. Work with classmates to identify people in as many of the careers listed in this chapter as you can. Choose three careers that you would like to investigate further. If possible, make an appointment to discuss the work with someone currently involved in it.

KEY TERMS

burnout: Physical and emotional weariness caused by stress related to work.
career lattice: Diversity of educational backgrounds, entry points, and employment opportunities within the early childhood field.
separation: Process of learning to be apart from someone the child feels attached to. A developmental task of toddlerhood.
stress: Physical and emotional responses associated with coping with situations beyond one's control.

SUGGESTED READINGS

Beach, J., Bertrand, J., Michal, D., & Tougas, J. (2004). Profiles and case studies: *Working for change: Canada's child care workforce.* Ottawa: Child Care Human Resources Sector Council

Carter, Gloria J. (1992, September). How can the teaching intern deal with the disparity between how she is taught to teach and how she is expected to teach in "real world" primary grades? *Young Children,* 47 (6), 68–72.

Doherty, G., Lero, D., Goelman, H., LaGrange, A., & Tougas, J. (2000). *You bet I care! A Canada-wide study on: Wages, working conditions and practices in child care centres.* Guelph: Centre for Families, Work, and Well-being, University of Guelph, Ontario.

Jorde-Bloom, P. (1988, September). Teachers need "TLC" too. *Young Children,* 43 (6), 4–8.

Lay-Dopyera, M. & Dopyera, J. (1990). *Becoming a teacher of young children* (4th ed.). New York: McGraw-Hill.

Section Three

The Early Childhood Workforce Comes of Age

Having considered personal motivations and challenges in becoming an early childhood educator, we now will consider the workforce at large. In this section we will consider the early childhood workforce: what it has been, what it is now, and the directions for the future. Chapter 7 looks back at the historical roots of work with young children. Chapter 8 discusses the early childhood workforce as a modern profession that creates philosophical bases for discussion of common ideals, practices, and ethics. Chapter 9 describes the role of advocacy in addressing the challenging issues facing the workforce and leaves students to embark on their personal journeys as early childhood educators and passionate early child development advocates. Again, you are challenged to see yourself taking a place within the ranks of this workforce.

Why Ontario Should Act Now

We know that the development of the brain in the early years of life, particularly the first three years, sets the base of competence and coping skills for the later stages of life. Improving the prospects for the next generation of Ontarians—with respect to school performance, health and quality of life, and success in the labour market—will improve the future for all of us.

The entrants to the workforce of 2025 will be born next year [2000]. From this generation will come a key factor in determining the wealth base of Ontario in 25 years. They will be Ontario's community leaders and innovators in the next century. Brain development in the period from conception to six years sets a base for learning, behaviour, and health over the life cycle. Ensuring that all our future citizens are able to develop their full potential has to be a high priority for everyone. It is crucial if we are to reverse "the real brain drain."

Investment by all sectors of society in the early years is as important as our investment in education to ensure Ontario has a highly competent and well-educated population, all necessary for a strong economy and a thriving democracy. Ontario has an opportunity to create a better future for our children and grandchildren—by building a strong base that exists today and engaging all sectors of society in establishing a new "system" for early child development and parenting. That system will provide the base for children's learning and development in the school system and postsecondary education system. Action now will put our children and our society on a firmer foundation for the future. This action is necessary, not only to keep a reasonable standard of living, but also because it is the right thing to do for our young children . . .

We can take a major leap into the future, just as we did when we had the chance to provide safe water and immunize all children against diseases that had taken a terrible toll in infancy for centuries. When science provided us with the tools—inoculation against polio, smallpox, diphtheria, and other scourges of childhood—we used them. We used them to protect individual children and society as a whole. We have new knowledge today. We must seize the opportunity to use that knowledge to benefit all children.

We believe the priorities and choices are clear. (Reprinted with permission from M. McCain & J. F. Mustard. [1999]. *The Early Years,* pp. 2–3.)

CHAPTER SEVEN

The Roots of Early Child Development Programs in Canada

OBJECTIVES

After studying this chapter, students will be able to

- discuss several reasons for examining the history of early child development programs;
- identify contributors to beliefs about early education and childrearing;
- recognize the role of psychology in current early childhood care and education practices;
- discuss social context in the history of early child development;
- differentiate between beginnings of child care systems, education systems, and recreation systems; and
- identify contributors to the field of early childhood care and education.

Many eyes glaze over with a section on history. Those who are beginning in a profession today may feel there is little relevance about learning in what people did in past centuries or decades. But the roots of early education beliefs and practices have clear connections to conditions, patterns, and beliefs that you will encounter in your immediate experience. George Santayana, an author of the late nineteenth and early twentieth centuries once commented that "those who forget the past are condemned to repeat it." In the case of early education, we study history to understand how it has created our present and to better comprehend the work to be done in the future.

As you have been reading through the text, you have encountered the Timeline in the margin of some pages, documenting events, sociological trends, and contributions of people who have been of some importance in creating our present. This Timeline symbolizes the idea that our current concerns and immediate issues are played against the backdrop of ideas and events from earlier times. As we examine contemporary conditions in early care and education, some of the reasons these conditions exist may become clear when seen in the light of past history.

In this chapter, you will look at the historical roots of work with young children in centre-based settings and the patterns that have developed into the present. You will find out how our understanding of early childhood has evolved over the past few hundred years. We begin by examining two divergent philosophical approaches to how children develop and learn. We then move to an overview of this century's study of psychology and its influence on early childhood education and child-rearing practices.

We will also consider how cultural, technological, political, and economic contexts have shaped how we view children's growth and development during their early years.

You will then learn the story of Canada's earliest child care, kindergarten, and recreation programs, trace the development of nursery schools and related teacher preparation from the 1920s on, follow the development of day nurseries during World War II, and note the explosion of child care centres during the 1980s.

Reasons for Understanding the History of Early Education

There are important reasons to understand the roots of the multiple traditions that have created the complex world of early education. First, it is worthwhile to recognize that the ideas and passionate efforts of many people live on today in the daily practice of contemporary early educators. The significance of play in children's active learning, for example, is an idea that was formed before the defining of developmentally appropriate practice in the late twentieth century. The concept of uniqueness in learning styles and the need for early childhood programs to include families also have earlier roots, as we shall see. "The lack of historical perspective leads us to interpret too much of what passes for reform as new when, in fact, much of the reform had an earlier history" (Perrone, 1991, p. 120). There is a sense of continuity, of being in a long line of persons who have cared about young children, that is somewhat humbling, as well as uplifting, for today's professionals. So, on the Timeline and in this and the next two chapters, you will learn about people who have contributed to the theory and practice of what we do.

Second, it is crucial in appreciating the importance of early education to understand that real events in history and sociological trends shape a profession and its practitioners, in response to particular events and needs in society. So, as you have read the Timeline, you have noted statistics that suggest changes in family structure and resulting needs, as well as events that have focused national attention on children's education. These events, which comprise the social context of early child development in Canada, will be discussed in this chapter as well.

A baby having a bath before the days of running water.

Third, it is important for developing professionals to be able to articulate the theoretical basis for their practice—the *why* that undergirds the *what* of what they do. The contributions of the various thinkers and researchers in the field of early education have been noted on the Timeline and will be discussed in this chapter in connection with the educational trends they influenced.

Fourth, and last, is the reason that understanding of our diversity in structure, professional preparation, social status, and attitudes comes with recognizing the separate forms of early childhood education that developed in North America in the last decades of the nineteenth century and into the twentieth century. These forms are only recently coming together, and not without difficulty; each form has developed its own approach, practices, and culture. In fact, this last idea may be the most compelling reason to examine our historical roots—to help us see that the difficulties in getting professional consensus and public support result from differences within the structure of the profession, rather than from a lack of will or ability to work together. Once we understand the original separations, it may be easier to remove them. It is this last idea that will focus our discussion in this chapter, as we identify questions and trends that divided early education professionals and separated professionals from policymakers.

Philosophical Views of Early Childhood

The establishment of the first early child development programs extends back through the lines of philosophical thinking about children and education.

The English philosopher, John Locke (1632–1704), wrote of the importance of early experiences and was one of the first to point out the individuality of children. He noted the importance of children's learning through play and emphasized natural education, rather than the harsh discipline more common in his time.

Another who wrote of the importance of natural methods of childrearing was the French philosopher Jean Jacques Rousseau (1712–78). In *Emile*, his fictional account of raising a child, he discussed the need to protect children from the evils of society and the importance of planning educational experiences that were directly related to children's interests.

Both Locke and Rousseau influenced the thinking of Johann Pestalozzi (1746–1827), who is known as the first early childhood educator, since he opened a school for young children in Yverdon, Switzerland, in 1801. He believed that children are capable of making their own discoveries, and he encouraged his teachers to respect each child's individuality. His school was influential in allowing others to observe his theories in practice; Robert Owen, who opened the first infant school, visited his school, and Friedrich Froebel taught there.

The Study and Science of Psychology

In the middle of the twentieth century, the study of child development grew into a respected academic field in North America, Europe, Britain, Australia, and New Zealand. In North America three theoretical approaches dominated:

- *Psychoanalytic theories* emphasize the role of the unconscious, or that which is beyond our awareness, in human development.
- *Learning theories* are based on the assumption that development is a result of learning, which is a long-lasting change in behaviour based on experience or adaptation to the environment.
- *Cognitive theories* of child development emphasize children's conscious thoughts. They focus primarily on the structure and development of an individual's thought processes and how thinking affects an individual's understanding of the world.

Moving into the twenty-first century, the focus has shifted to more systemic approaches that recognize the interactions between individuals and their environments. The following section describes the major theories that have shaped early childhood education.

2000

1950

1900

1850

1800

1750

1700

1650

1962

Jean Piaget publishes *Play, Dreams, and Imitation in Children* in English.

Dr. Susan Gray establishes Early Training Project in Tennessee, which includes centre-based programs and home visitors.

David Weikart and associates establish the Perry Preschool Project in Ypsilanti, Michigan. This is the most famous of the early preschool programs established for early intervention because of the extensive longitudinal follow-up on the children in the program.

Behaviourism was a new perspective on human development that emerged during the early part of the twentieth century. This approach to development is concerned with behaviours that can be directly observed and objectively measured. It continues to influence researchers and practitioners working with children and youth. Behaviourism views human development as continuous, rather than occurring in stages.

Behaviourist researchers and psychologists considered that children were shaped by external forces in the environment and that all behaviour, including cognitive activities, can be learned through experience. *Social learning theory* evolved from behaviourism as an explanation of children's social behaviour.

- Russian physiologist Ivan Pavlov (1849–1936) carried out a number of studies of animal learning (Cleverly & Phillips, 1986). Pavlov realized that the dogs would salivate before they actually tasted food. In fact, Pavlov observed that the dogs would start to salivate when the trainer came into the laboratory and headed toward the food storage cupboard. Pavlov decided that the dogs had learned to associate a neutral stimulus (the trainer) with another stimulus (food) that produces a reflexive response (salivation). Because they had learned this association, the neutral stimulus (the trainer) could bring about the response by itself. Pavlov went on to design experiments in which dogs learned to salivate at the sound of a bell that rang when they were fed.
- The American behaviourist John B. Watson (1849–1958) applied the classical theories of learning to young children. He argued that a child is shaped completely by his or her experiences. Watson described a newborn as a "lively squirming bit of flesh, capable of making a few simple responses. . . . Parents take this raw material and begin to fashion it"(Watson, 1928, 9. 46).
- B.F. Skinner (1904–1990) was the most prominent theorist of **behavioural theory.** Behaviourists believe that children are shaped by external forces in the environment and that almost all behaviour can be learned through experience. Specific behaviours can be strengthened or weakened by the responses children are given following the behaviour. Skinner became interested in the effects of reinforcements of particular types of behaviours.
- American psychologist Albert Bandura (1925) is recognized as the main architect of social learning theory. Bandura believes that cognitive processes are important mediators of environment-behaviour connections. His research focuses on *observational learning,* or learning that occurs through watching what others do. Observational learning is sometimes referred to as imitation or modeling. Bandura proposes that people cognitively represent the behaviour of others and then try to adopt this behaviour for themselves.

Sigmund Freud. Sigmund Freud (1856–1939) was the founder of **psychoanalytic theory.** His work with adults with psychological problems led him to believe that childhood is the source of difficulties in personality formation. His work describing the stages of emotional development in childhood forever changed our thinking about the nature of the child. Freud's ideas were more readily adopted by the nursery school movement than by those in kindergarten education, partly because of the work of Susan Isaacs (1885–1948). In 1929, her book, *The Nursery Years,* interpreted Freudian theory for teachers and suggested how early education schools should apply this new insight about the unconscious to their work with children.

Freud believed that we form our basic personality in the first few years of life. He identified five stages of personality development from infancy to adolescence during which the individual must deal with conflicts between their biological and sexual urges for pleasure and the demands of society. During the stages, the urge for pleasure shifts from the mouth to the anus and then to the genitals. Freud proposed that adult personality is formed by the way conflicts between the early sources of pleasure and the reality of social demands are resolved.

Erik Erikson. Erik Erikson (1902–94) further developed Freud's thought into a **psycho-social** theory of personality development, extending through the life span. He theorized that each stage of life offers a specific psychological struggle that contributes to a major aspect of personality. Erikson was one of the first to suggest that children develop in the context of their societies' expectations and prohibitions. His theory continues to influence our understanding of the environmental responses and supports that help children achieve healthy development.

Erik Erikson worked as a Freudian psychoanalyst in Vienna, before fleeing Nazism and coming to United States in 1933. His professional and personal experiences influenced his views and extended and expanded Freud's theories. He became the most important neo-Freudian in the field of child development.

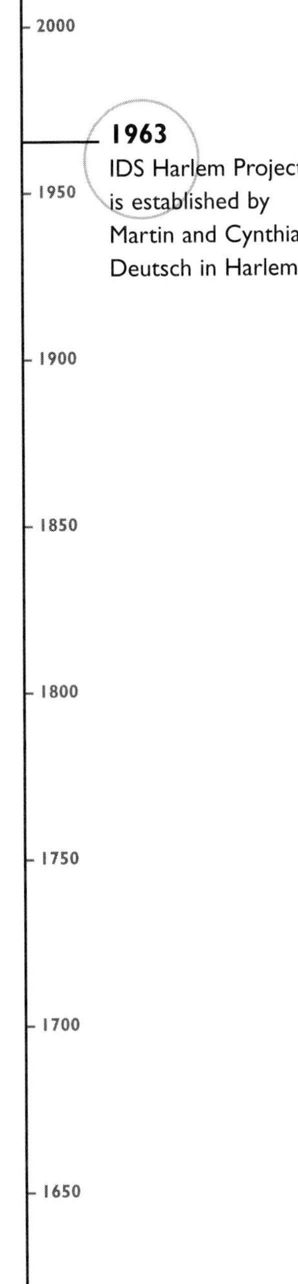

Jean Piaget. Swiss psychologist Jean Piaget's (1896–1980) substantial body of work has greatly influenced early childhood education today, with his focus on the cognitive development of children. His theory explained how children's understanding of the world continues to grow through adaptations made as a result of interaction between the individual and the physical and social environment. Piaget has influenced the way we believe children think and learn, with implications for our educational settings that allow children to explore, experiment, and manipulate materials.

Piaget stressed that children actively construct their own knowledge as they manipulate and explore their world, and their cognitive development takes place in stages. He believed that children adapt their thinking to include new ideas and that the additional information furthers understanding. Perhaps his greatest insight was that studying the development of human children was one way to integrate philosophical speculation with the scientific approach (Gopnik et al., 1999).

Since the 1960s Piaget's theories dominated both developmental child psychology research and educational practices for the second half of the 20th century. They provide a framework of understanding that matched North American's attention to improving environments and intellectual achievement of all children.

Lawrence Kohlberg. Lawrence Kohlberg (1927–87), influenced by the work of Piaget, developed his own theory of moral reasoning based on cognitive development. Both Piaget and Kohlberg believed that children form their own moral views based on their development of reasoning. Unlike Piaget, Kohlberg differentiated between the moral reasoning of children and adults. Kohlberg believed that children's moral development occurs in three fixed and invariable developmental levels of moral thinking through which all children pass, though perhaps at different rates.

Lev Vygotsky. Russian psychologist Lev Vygotsky (1896–1934), one of Piaget's contemporaries whose work has been translated into English more recently, also believed that children construct their own understandings of the world. He differed from Piaget by emphasizing that social interaction and experience with others is the major learning process for children. For Vygotsky, the development of language is a primary task of learning. Vygotsky's theory has important implications for early educators because it stresses the adult's role in assisting children with collaborative learning.

Vygotsky recognized that children's cognitive and language development do not happen in isolation. However, his ideas and theories did not gain much prominence in North America until toward the end of the century. Vygotsky's sociocultural theory of human development focuses on how culture (the values, beliefs, customs, skills, and tools of a social group) is transmitted or passed on to the next generation. Vygotsky's short life (he died when he was 38 years old), and his isolation within the young Communist world in Russia, both contributed to the passage of time before his theories became of interest to North American researchers and practitioners. The current attention to cross-cultural studies brings Vygotsky's theories and ideas into focus for many early childhood educators.

Information Processing

Influenced by modern technology, *information processing theory* studies how individuals process information about their world compared to the way computers analyze and process data. Of course, a human baby is capable of synthesizing new information in ways that are beyond the capability of the most advanced computers. However, information processing theorists propose that we can study and understand step-by-step mechanics of human thinking just as we learn to program computers for various tasks. They suggest that if we learn to understand the mechanics of thinking, we will be better able to understand cognitive development (Siegler, 1994).

Information theory is interested in mental activities that involve noticing, mentally manipulating, storing, combining, retrieving or acting on information. Like computers, humans must store large amounts of information, get access to that information when it is needed, and analyze problems to get correct solutions. Information processing theorists believe that human cognitive development is a continuous process of learning to take in and understand information.

Urie Bronfenbrenner. Ecology is the study of the relationship between organisms and their environment. One of the most influential theories of human development emphasizes how the environment influences a child's development and how the developing child influences his or her environment. Urie Bronfenbrenner's (1917–) ecological theory of human development has received considerable attention over the past three decades (Bronfenbrenner, 1979).

Bronfenbrenner proposed a framework for organizing sets of environmental systems. He conceived that the child's world is organized "as a set of nested structures, each inside the next, like a set of Russian dolls" (1979, p. 22). These systems range from the most immediate setting, such as family, to more remote contexts that do not directly involve the child, such as society's legal system or beliefs.

Howard Gardner. A theorist who has received attention related to educational issues is Howard Gardner (1943–), with his theory of **multiple intelligences.** He identifies seven intelligences: linguistic, musical, logical-mathematical, spatial, bodily kinesthetic, interpersonal, and intrapersonal, rather than measuring intelligence from one perspective. This theory has interesting implications for the individualizing of learning experiences and expectations.

Developmental Health

Developmental health is a twenty first-century conceptual framework for understanding human development. It integrates knowledge from the biological sciences with knowledge from developmental psychology and other sciences. Developmental health explains how our earliest social and physical experiences shape the brain's development and set the foundation for learning, behaviour, and health. Dan Keating and Clyde Hertzman (1999), both Canadian scientists, and their colleagues at the Canadian Institute for Advanced Research, have marshalled evidence to support the developmental health theory.

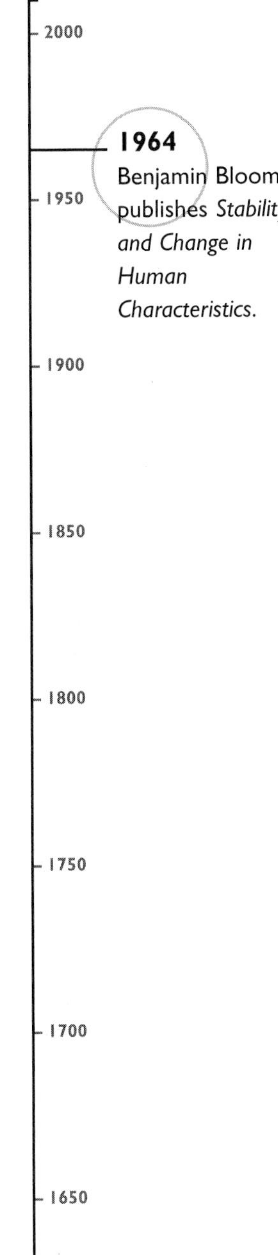

Social Context

Ideas about early childhood and psychological theories of child development and early learning do not occur in a vacuum; they are always products of the larger social context, which includes the structure of families, work, governments, and communities; the dominant political and economic systems; and the values and beliefs of a particular society.

Early Beginnings: Education and Social Welfare

Today's early childhood settings find their beginnings in the nineteenth century. In the early part of that century, Canada as a nation did not exist. Instead, a British colony struggled to bring together the worlds of French- and English-speaking people, or Upper and Lower Canada. The birth of Canada as a nation within the British Empire was a practical solution.

From the mid-nineteenth into the twentieth century, industrialization grew in Canada. Commercial and manufacturing development brought rapid growth in urban centres, such as Montreal and Toronto. In the early part of the nineteenth century, women and children, as well as men, were sought by employers to work outside the home in factories. However, by the middle of the 1800s, the supply of workers exceeded the jobs available. Children from working-class and poor families were now often idle, without supervision or direction. Immigration had increased to meet the demands of populating the new nation and filling its workforce. The resulting pressures of rapid population growth and industrialization brought problems for children and their families. Child advocates and charitable organization solutions looked for ways to organize and structure young children's time and activity.

Infant Schools

In the early nineteenth century, Robert Owen, a factory owner in Scotland, wanted to increase the number of workers available in the local community to work in his factory. His strong commitment to the education of young children led him to establish infant schools to educate very young children and to provide supplemental care while parents worked (Pence, 1990).

The infant schools were popular, and the early experiment in early childhood education and care tied to labour participation spread to North America (Pence, 1990; Prochner, 2000). Infant schools were introduced to Canada in the 1830s by factory

1965
Project Head Start is established in the United States on May 18 by President Lyndon B. Johnson, as part of the War on Poverty, and administered under the Office of Economic Opportunity.

A summer program of Head Start is held in the United States, serving 536 108 children in programs that ran two to six weeks.

owners in Halifax who wanted to attract women and older children to work in their factories (Pence, 1990). These infant schools and others located in Canadian urban centres were based on the models developed in Scotland. Particularly in North America, the philosophy of infant schools promoted the notion that these early education settings were beneficial to all children (Pence, 1990). But by the middle of the nineteenth century, Victorian attitudes and beliefs about the sanctity of motherhood brought about the demise of infant schools in Britain and the United States (Pence, 1990), although in Canada, some infant schools continued to operate into the 1870s (Prochner, 2000).

Crèches, Day Nurseries, and Salles d'Asile

In the 1800s, work was the only alternative to starvation for many mothers who were poor, widowed, or deserted. Many women who had young children were employed as domestic servants or wet nurses.

Beginning in the mid-nineteenth century and continuing into the twentieth century in Montreal and Toronto, and then other Canadian urban centres, **philanthropic organizations,** churches, and settlement houses founded institutions to care for the children of poor working mothers. These institutions were established to encourage the poor to help themselves through their own labour (Prochner, 2000). The early child care centres were called salles d'asile, crèches, nurseries, or day nurseries. Crèches, first established in France, were **custodial settings** in which the children of poor, working women were looked after. In Britain, these programs were called day nurseries. Salles d'asile in Quebec were primarily educational programs for young children from working poor and wealthier families.

Roman Catholic nuns opened Canada's first crèche in Montreal in 1850 (Schulz, 1978). In 1857, a group of wealthy Toronto women started the Public Nursery, which was the first English crèche (Prochner, 1996). Its initial focus was to provide infant day care but later became an orphanage for girls. Roman Catholic nuns in Montreal established numerous salles d'asile in the 1850s (Schultz, 1978).

Around the turn of the century, crèches or day nursery programs expanded across English-speaking Canada (Schultz, 1978). They provided care, sometimes into the school years, to young children of poor, working mothers or of mothers who were physically unable to care for their children. In 1887, the English-speaking Montreal Day Nursery programs opened, and were followed in the next twenty years by crèches in Toronto, Ottawa, and Halifax.

Canada's early crèche and day nursery programs were typically funded by private charities and sponsored by well-to-do women volunteers or by churches, missions, or settlement houses (organizations that provided services to new immigrants to Canada). Mothers were usually asked to pay a small fee for the care of their children. Government involvement in either funding or monitoring these early programs was minimal.

In Vancouver, the development of early centres to care for children of working mothers was the one instance that did involve government participation (Schulz, 1978). In 1910, the Infants Hospital in Vancouver opened a crèche for infants and preschool children of working mothers, and the Associated Charities and the City of Vancouver jointly organized another crèche. In 1916, both programs were placed under the jurisdiction of the Health Department of British Columbia

(Schulz, 1978). The salles d'asile received provincial grants from the Quebec government, as well as charitable donations and parent fees.

Children experienced custodial care at most crèches and day nurseries at the turn of the century. Physical space was often limited to a couple of rooms. The staff included untrained nannies and housekeepers, usually supervised by a matron. In one report, a matron, a nanny, and a cook were responsible for forty-five infants and children (Schultz, 1978). For school-age children, care usually included a hot lunch and loose supervision by a housekeeper after school (Young, 1994). Hygienic practices and routines to encourage obedience and moral development

MAKING IT HAPPEN

The Crèche, Toronto

Hester How taught Grade Four in downtown Toronto in the 1880s at Elizabeth Street Public School. She became concerned that many of her students, particularly the girls, were frequently staying home to look after younger siblings. She allowed them to bring the young brothers and sisters to class. Once the problem became more visible and unmanageable, How convinced the school trustees to support the establishment of The Crèche in 1891. The Crèche was operated by a group of volunteer women as a charitable service. It cared for preschool children and for school-age children outside school hours.

Hester How in her Grade Four classroom with her students' young siblings in attendance.

2000

1950

1900

1850

1800

1750

1700

1650

1966

A direct instruction program is developed by Bereiter and Engelmann, marketed under the trademark DISTAR.

Canada Assistance Plan makes federal funds available for subsidized day care.

The *Ontario Day Nurseries Act* is amended to allow school-age children to participate in licensed group child care.

kept children physically safe, clean, and behaved. This kind of care was often thought to address the dangerous side effects of poverty and neglect faced by many of the children living in urban poverty (Schultz, 1978).

The crèches and day nurseries did provide other types of services to children and their families, including health care; the distribution of free milk, food, and clothing; and social events. But perhaps the most notable service apart from the care of young children was their employment assistance.

The primary stated purpose of many crèches was "to enable struggling and deserving women to help themselves, by taking care of their children by the day, or the week, and by so doing make it easier for the parent to earn the necessary means of support for her family" (ref. 16 in Schulz, 1978, p. 140).

In addition to the provision of care for the children of working mothers, many of the early crèches operated as employment agencies for the mothers themselves. The crèches that operated to provide employment for destitute young mothers were usually provided by charitable organizations, efforts of upper-class women, and private donations. Young women who found themselves alone with a child to support in urban settings used these services to care for their children while they worked, often as domestic servants.

> The majority of the women using the centres were domestic servants, and a chronic shortage of domestic help throughout the early part of the twentieth century made these agencies very useful to the same class of women who were members and managers of the centres. Annual reports consistently outline the number of days of care provided for children, and the number of days of employment provided for parents in the same paragraph. (Schulz, 1978, p. 141)

The institutional records of the early crèches reveal examples of job training for young mothers. For instance, during World War I, the West End Crèche in Toronto set up a laundry so that the women could do soldiers' washing and offered night classes in how to do laundry. By the end of the Depression, mothers with young children could usually find regular employment, so the employment agency aspect of these centres was discontinued (Schulz, 1978).

Public Schools

During the early nineteenth century, a variety of schools flourished in local communities throughout Upper and Lower Canada. They were supported by families, churches, and concerned public benefactors. Wealthy parents sent their children to private schools, and "ragged schools" were set up by individuals or charities to provide education and clothing for poor children.

Universal education was proposed as the answer to the ills facing a changing society. In order to be available to all children, it had to be free. School reformers proposed that common or parish schools, which had emerged in communities during the first half of the nineteenth century, and had been partially subsidized by government grants in most provinces, be entirely sustained by a combination of provincial grants and assessment on local property. Egerton Ryerson, in his *Report on a System of Elementary Public Instruction for Upper Canada*, published in 1847, stated that "a system of general education amongst the people is the most effectual preventative of pauperism, and its natural companions, misery and crime."

The campaign for universal education was based on

- the realization that an educated population would stimulate economic growth and ensure social stability;
- the recognition of education as a means of achieving desired social and political attitudes in support of the status quo, that is, loyalty to Britain and British institutions;
- the promotion of education as an equalizer that could break down barriers between classes, and increased social harmony; and
- the view of schools as agents of social control, which could influence the development of loyal citizens.

The mid-century shift of education as a responsibility of families, churches, and communities to that of being public institutions free and distinct from social and denominational interests was dramatic. Schools were becoming part of an educational system, instead of programs created by communities. (Of course, the accommodation of both Protestant and Roman Catholic interests did result in two public systems of education in most parts of Canada.) Egerton Ryerson was the

MAKING IT HAPPEN

The Nineteenth Century: The Century of Schooling

1816 — *Introduction of local boards of school trustees*
- Loose governmental involvement in administration of local schools (schools are private and voluntary; some are aided by government grants or church assistance; and all are supported by student fees)

1841 — Common School Act
- First legislation to provide a uniform school system for United Province of Canada

1843 — Second Common School Act
- Increased centralization

1844–76 — *Egerton Ryerson*
- Appointed superintendent for schools in Canada West

1846 — Common School Act *(Canada West)*
- Standardization of curriculum, textbooks, and teachers

1850 — *Great Charter of Common School Education*
- Recognition of principle of universal property assessment

1867 — British North America Act
- Confederation of Canada
- Provisions made for Roman Catholic separate schools

1871 — School Act
- Ontario government compels communities to provide free common schools; attendance is compulsory for children aged seven to twelve for at least four months each year. Other provinces follow this direction.

Sources: Adapted from Corbett, B. (1989); Young (1994) Mathien (2001).

superintendent of education for Upper Canada (later Ontario) from 1844 to 1876. He, along with Alexander Forrester in Nova Scotia and John Jessop in British Columbia, worked to establish universal, publicly funded elementary education (Gaffield, 1991). The School Acts from 1841 to 1871 in what is now Ontario set out the foundation for that province's school system and for more education acts in most other parts of the country.

The new educational system responded to industry's growing demand for skilled labour and for scientific and technological advances. During the second half of the nineteenth century, the curricula introduced manual training, as a means to prepare students to enter the workforce, and an emphasis on rote learning. School inspectors ensured standardization of curriculum, textbooks, and teachers.

Kindergarten

Friedrich Froebel (1782–1852) is known as the originator of the kindergarten, a German word meaning "children's garden." He believed that children could grow and flourish like plants in the right environment, developing internal impulses that would unfold naturally. Kindergarten was designed for children between the ages of three and six, and Froebel's curriculum emphasized language, numbers, forms, and eye-hand coordination to train children in ways that would establish courtesy, punctuality, neatness, and cleanliness, as well as respect for others.

The most notable elements of his tradition were the curriculum materials that he called gifts and occupations. The gifts were a series of ten concrete, manipulative materials, such as woollen balls, wooden shapes and cubes of various sizes, tablets, wooden sticks, and a variety of natural objects, all presented to children at defined intervals with specific skills and symbolic concepts to learn. The occupations included sewing, perforating paper, weaving, working with clay, and cutting paper. As Froebel said, "What the child tries to represent, he begins to understand" (Olmsted, 1992, p. 4). Although this idea seems very familiar to us, it was considered quite revolutionary to educate children in a group outside the home and use play materials.

During the 1870s, Froebel kindergartens first appeared in Canada as private institutions supported by parent fees or charitable donations. Egerton Ryerson's work in establishing the school system in Ontario did much to lay the groundwork for acceptance of kindergartens in schools in Ontario and other provinces (Corbett, 1989). He added Pestalozzi's object lessons to the curriculum and accepted Christianity (but not specific formal religions) as central to the school curriculum. By 1871, school attendance was compulsory for children from seven to twelve years for at least four months a year, but children often attended for considerably more time. Particularly in urban areas, children younger than six years were often in attendance.

The first Canadian public school kindergarten program opened in 1883 at Louisa Street School, in Toronto. James L. Hughes, the chief school inspector for the Toronto School Board at the time, had studied the writings of Pestalozzi and Froebel and was convinced of the value of education to support the whole child. Faced with concerns about growing numbers of preschool children left unattended while their mothers worked, Hughes (who supported Hester How's efforts to initiate The Crèche to care for young children left on their own) introduced Froebel kindergartens. The program, which responded to concerns about young children's environments, was also a vehicle for promoting curriculum innovation (Mathien, 1990, 2001).

The Froebel kindergarten at the Toronto Normal School, circa 1890.

Ada Maream (who later married James Hughes) was the first teacher, or **kindergartener** (the term used for a Froebel kindergarten teacher), in the Toronto public school kindergarten. She had studied Froebel education in the United States and opened private kindergartens, first in New Brunswick and then in Toronto, in 1878 (Corbett, 1989). Her first public school kindergarten was a class of eighty children. Seven kindergarteners-in-training assisted her. Maream's professional education and her strong connections with American kindergarten activities provided the basis for her leadership in Ontario's and Canada's kindergarten programs as part of school systems.

In 1885, Ontario officially recognized kindergartens as part of the public school system. In 1887, the province began to provide grants to school boards to establish kindergarten programs for children three to seven years old. Kindergarten was introduced in several schools in Toronto and in towns and cities across the province. By 1900, there were 120 public school kindergartens across Ontario (Mathien, 1990). Quebec established kindergartens within its school system in 1892.

In 1885, a kindergarten course was introduced at the Toronto Normal School (a teacher-training facility), and in 1889, the Toronto Kindergarten Association for kindergarten teachers was established.

RESEARCH INTO PRACTICE

Kindergartens in the United States

Froebel's ideas and model of the kindergarten were imported to the United States primarily by German immigrants who had been trained in Froebelian principles in Germany. In 1856, Margarethe Schurz opened the first German-language kindergarten in her home in Wisconsin and was the person who explained the Froebelian principles to Elizabeth Peabody. Elizabeth Peabody (1804–1894) opened the first English-language kindergarten in Boston in 1860, and is generally credited with gaining acceptance for the kindergarten movement in the United States. It was Peabody who influenced the superintendent of the St. Louis schools to sponsor the first public kindergarten in the United States in 1873. At one of her lectures, Milton Bradley, the toy manufacturer, first learned of Froebelian methods, and he later began to manufacture the gifts and materials for the occupations (such as stitching and threading). Kindergarten normal schools followed, including the Oshkosh Normal School in 1880, the Chicago Kindergarten College in 1886, and the Wheelock School in Boston in 1888. In 1978, Peabody founded the American Froebel Association for interested kindergartners.

(cont'd)

Kindergartens in the United States (cont'd)

The first public school kindergarten opened in St. Louis, Missouri, in 1873. But public school sponsorship of kindergartens came slowly, and, for a time during the late nineteenth and early twentieth centuries, many were sponsored by churches, charitable organizations, and settlement houses. Patty Smith Hill, writing in 1926, said, "When the kindergarten was introduced into this country more than a century ago, it survived as a philanthropy long before it was accepted as an organic member of the educational system" (Hill, 1987, p. 12). This was the time of heavy immigration, when slums were developing in major cities, accompanied by the social problems of crime, delinquency, and other difficulties associated with rapid increases in foreign population. Settlement houses were created in major cities to combat the problems and to help new citizens assimilate. The philanthropists adopted kindergartens in the hope that improving the lot of young children could improve society. The first president of the New York Kindergarten Association stated, "The kindergarten age marks our earliest opportunities to catch the little Russian, the little Italian ... and begin to make good American citizens of them. The children are brought into a new social order" (Youcha, 1995, p. 148).

The standard kindergarten schedule of morning classroom programs left the kindergarten teachers free to visit in the afternoons, essentially functioning as social welfare workers, "seeking work for the unemployed; space in hospitals for ill mothers, sisters, and brothers; physicians who would remove adenoids and tonsils; or dentists who would extract diseased teeth" (Hill, 1987, p. 13). Gradually, according to Hill's account, the philanthropists turned to the schools to ask them to accept the kindergarten "as a member in good and regular standing." They usually asked to be able to use an empty room in the school, and the philanthropic agencies still paid for the teacher's salary and the program expenses. Gradually, the boards of education were persuaded to take full responsibility for the kindergartens, and, so, the kindergartens became part of the public school systems.

But there were problems in their acceptance within the school systems. Kindergarten teachers had been trained in normal schools, which were separate from other teacher-training schools, and that used curricula, materials and methods—encouraging children to "talk, sing, dance, dramatize, model, paint, draw, build, and construct" that seemed quite foreign to teachers who used a curriculum "based upon the acquirement of the three Rs in their baldest and most barren form" (Hill, 1987, p. 14). The kindergarten method of handling behavioural problems was considered soft and sentimental, and it certainly did not prepare the children to enter Grade One. Hill comments that kindergarten children were not welcomed by Grade One teachers, through no fault of either the kindergarten or Grade One teachers. "It was due to the fact that children were supposed to pass on from one teacher to another with continuity of work when the two teachers were trained in diametrically opposed philosophies, curricula, and methods" (Hill, 1987, p. 14). (This comment certainly sounds like it was written today, instead of eighty years ago!)

Moving into the Twentieth Century

The first two decades of the twentieth century witnessed the ongoing evolution of early child care and education. The early crèches and day nurseries continued with a few additions, but the majority of working women relied on family and neighbourhood arrangements, rather than on organized child care programs. In urban settings across Canada, organized playgrounds responded to the needs of school-age children for out-of-school hours, and kindergarten programs continued to expand. Interest in child study heightened attention to different approaches to early education, including Montessori and nursery schools. Early educators looked to progressive education and psychological theory for answers on how best to educate young children. Some crèches and day nursery programs began to employ teachers with kindergartener training or those who were knowledgeable about child development.

World War I reminded Canadians of human vulnerabilities and the destruction that comes from hate and violence. After the war, people wanted to get on with the business of raising children and earning a living in a safe, secure world. They wanted to benefit from growing modern conveniences and health advances, including new understandings of mental hygiene (the term used for mental health) from Freud and others.

The suffrage movement, led by middle-class women, never took issue with the notion that a woman's place was in the home. The right of women to work and the right of children to high-quality child care were not demands of the movement. Their campaign for support to single, widowed, and deserted women did result in the introduction of Mother's Allowance (social assistance or welfare) in the 1920s. Once women had gained some support for their children without having to enter the workforce, the need for crèches and day nurseries actually decreased.

Across Canada, the 1930s were difficult economic times for children and families. The Depression dragged on, with high levels of unemployment and little in the way of social support networks. There were drops in both women's participation in the labour market and in the birth rate. Many of the crèches and their related employment agencies for women were forced to close.

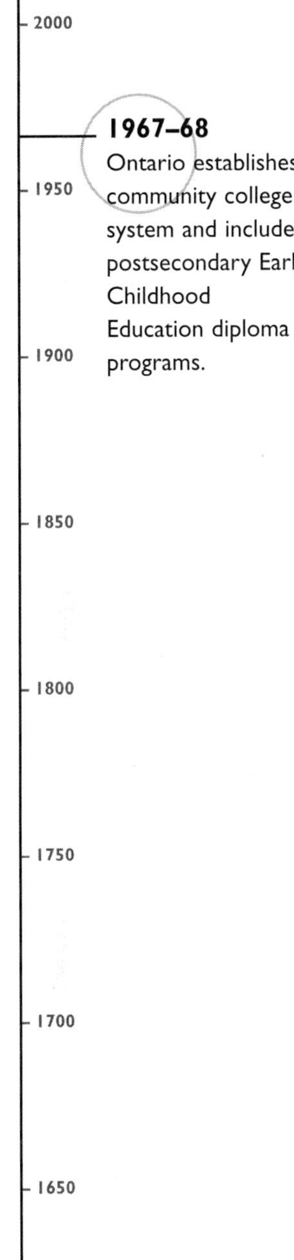

Children's Playgrounds

At the beginning of the nineteenth century, there was considerable interest in camping and fresh air experiences. Settlement houses acquired properties for family camping outside urban centres and made this a specific service available to supported children and their parents. The value of organized play programs for children in kindergarten was extended to older children. As well, concerns about unsupervised children on city streets and their enticement into criminal activity gave rise to the development of children's playgrounds, which offered supervised, outdoor play spaces for children outside school hours. Their development became connected to local governments and community organizations (Young, 1994). For example,

- in 1900, inner-city settlement houses in Toronto operated summer playgrounds and provided noon-hour meals;
- in 1903, Ontario allowed municipalities to purchase land for public parks;
- in the 1900s, playground associations were established in Toronto, Hamilton, London, Ottawa, and in other urban centres.

James Hughes viewed playgrounds as an extension of kindergartens and led the Toronto School Board's establishment of supervised playgrounds in eighteen of its schools; the Toronto municipal government took responsibility for programs in municipal parks (Young, 1994).

Public Health

In the eighteenth century, public health outreach programs played a role in helping to support mothers and their infants and young children. Immigration, urbanization, and industrialization brought larger numbers of people together, increasing the

Children playing in a supervised Toronto playground circa 1910.

risk of infectious disease and mortality. Diseases that thrived in crowded, dirty living conditions could not be contained, and their transmission to upper-middle class environments was inevitable. Therefore, prevention of diseases attracted attention and interest from all socioeconomic groups.

Research evidence identified health prevention measures that could greatly reduce the spread of infectious disease and reduce mortality, particularly amongst infants and children (Sutherland, 1976). Canadian historian Neil Sutherland identifies three events in 1882 that shaped the direction of public health: "Louis Pasteur proved the effectiveness of immunization for anthrax in sheep, Robert Koch discovered the tuberculosis germ, and Ontario established a board of health" (1976, p. 40). The establishment of public health boards in other provinces followed. The emerging public health movement in Canada built upon the achievements of nineteenth century improvements in sanitation and on the dramatic bacteriological discoveries of the 1880s and 1890s.

Public health initiatives brought prenatal and well-baby clinics, milk depots, and home visiting to communities throughout the province (Sutherland, 1976; Arnup, 1994). These measures reduced infant deaths and improved maternal health (Sutherland, 1976).

The public health nurse's responsibilities for well-baby clinics and home visits encompassed a parent education role. In many instances she became a friendly adviser who was able to suggest changes in caregiving practices and promote healthy habits (Sutherland, 1976). The approach to parent education was often patronizing and didactic (Kellerman & Kyle, 1999) but was typically directed at all families with young children, not just those living in poverty, consistent with the notion that everyone was vulnerable, and it was in everybody's best interest to avoid or prevent disease.

By 1914, the public health nurse's role in the schools was becoming central in school health programs (Sutherland, 1976). In addition to preventative health (such as routine inspections, maintenance of medical records, and teaching healthy habits, including nose-blowing and tooth-brushing drills), school nurses often led health clubs after school such as the Little Nurses League in Winnipeg or Little Mothers in Vancouver, Regina, Victoria, and Stratford (Sutherland, 1976). Such clubs provided after-school activities for school-age children while promoting health prevention.

Public health initiatives in the early part of the twentieth century are the historical roots of many early child development programs for children and their families.

First Nursery Schools

Nursery schools evolved from British and European experiments at giving children from disadvantaged backgrounds an early head start (Prochner, 2000). Maria Montessori, and Margaret and Rachel MacMillan, established programs specifically designed to intervene in children's early lives and ameliorate the effects of poverty and poor housing conditions.

Maria Montessori. Maria Montessori (1870–1952) was the first Italian woman to earn a medical degree. From her observations of children, Montessori recognized the uniqueness of each child. Her phrase, "the absorbent mind," captures her philosophy of children educating themselves, actively, in a prepared environment, using carefully selected didactic materials. From the opening of her *Casa dei Bambini* (Children's House) in the tenements of Rome in 1907 until the present, Montessori's philosophy has had an impact on early childhood education, although not universal acceptance. Her book, *The Montessori Method*, was translated into English and became available in North America. There were Montessori schools in Canada and the United States within the next decade, but the real popularity of Montessori education in North America did not happen until the resurgence of interest in early childhood education in the 1960s. Nevertheless, kindergartners and others working with young children were, in the meantime, exposed to her approach and did absorb some of her ideas and practises.

The lasting contributions of the Montessori philosophy include:

- an attitude of respect for children;
- the idea that young children are essentially self-didactic, or learn through their own activities and adaptations;
- the concept that teachers learn through their interaction with children;
- the emphasis on a prepared, attractive environment, with child-sized furniture; and
- the focus on the quality of manipulative materials (Elkind, 1983).

Some contemporary educators suggest that much Montessori practice may not fall within the guidelines for developmentally appropriate practice due to

- its emphasis on work and the absence of fantasy;
- children's lack of freedom to experiment with materials, once they have been introduced to their appropriate use;
- the discouragement of cooperative and collegial planning and conversation;
- the strictly sequenced series of activities; and
- tight teacher control of how space, time, and materials are used (Greenberg, 1990).

Because Montessori philosophy and training have been maintained so separately from other institutions within early education, Montessori and her schools maintain a unique place in our history.

McMillan Sisters. Meanwhile, in England, another form of early education was evolving for even younger children. A British government report in 1908 had pointed out that although most children were born healthy, about 80 percent arrived at school age in poor health. In response, that same year, Rachel and Margaret McMillan established the London School Clinic for children under five years. Then in 1911, in Deptford, they established the Deptford School (later renamed the Rachel McMillan School) as an open-air **nursery school.** This was the first time that the term "nursery school" was used. The Deptford school emphasized healthy living for children, as well as nurturing for the whole child.

Throughout the early twentieth century, the McMillan sisters operated fresh air camps in Britain with a strong emphasis on hygiene, health, and physical activities to strengthen children's bodies (Prochner, 2000).

2000
1950
1900
1850
1800
1750
1700
1650

1968

The University of Illinois establishes the ERIC clearinghouse on early childhood education.

Living and Learning, the Hall and Dennison report on the public school system, is released in Ontario and recommends child-centred learning environments.

1969

The Report of the Royal Commission on the Status of Women recommends universal child care.

Sesame Street begins on public television on November 19.

1970

White House Conference on Children identifies child care as one of the major problems facing the American public.

Toy libraries are introduced in Canada through community programs such as public libraries and community centres.

High/Scope Educational Research Foundation is incorporated.

Other tenets of the nursery school philosophy were that schools should develop close links with children's families and communities and that teachers of young children should be well trained. Therefore the nursery school also functioned for many years as a teacher training-laboratory. Although Rachel McMillan died in 1917, Margaret continued her influential work in nursery education. She published *The Nursery School* in 1919, and her advocacy of government support for nursery schools led to the establishment of public nursery schools in England as part of the national education system.

Progressive Education and the Child Study Movement

The original Froebelian methods found in the early kindergarten programs began to be perceived as too rigid and abstract, centred as they were on prescribed methods and symbols with precisely ordered activities. During the 1920s, new learning about children was emerging from university-based scientific research on child development, known as the **child study movement.** The "progressives" felt the kindergarten curriculum should be based on scientific knowledge, rather than the mystic religious tenets of Froebelian philosophy.

The child study movement was brought about by two Americans, John Dewey and G. Stanley Hall, whose ideas about appropriate education for young children were influencing educators in both the United States and Canada. With his progressive philosophy, John Dewey (1859–1952) believed that education was a method of social reform, that information and knowledge would enable individuals to improve the quality of their lives, and that schools must represent life. He opposed the idealistic, religious philosophy of Froebel and his concept of "unfolding" and wanted to base the education of young children on scientific knowledge about their abilities. He was opposed to the traditional method of teaching children by **rote learning,** which is a form of learning by repetition, memory, and habit, rather than firsthand understanding. Dewey wanted the active involvement of the whole child and interaction, as described in *My Pedagogic Creed*, published in 1897. In 1896, he and his wife opened a laboratory at the University of Chicago for four- and five-year-olds, which he called "subprimary," rather than a kindergarten, possibly to distinguish it from the Froebelian model. Dewey's influence on the growing early childhood education movement was profound, as was his influence on the whole scope of **progressive education** in North America, which promotes active involvement of the child in learning.

G. Stanley Hall (1844–1924) is credited with beginning the scientific study of children. His *Content of Children's Minds* (1883) focused on descriptions of children's concepts, and the educational implications of these findings for teachers. "Hall criticized Froebelian kindergarten theory as being superficial and fantastic—he considered that young children needed large, bold movements rather than the sedentary activities of gifts and occupations and asserted that free play could serve their developmental needs" (Spodek & Saracho in Osborn, 1991, p. 76). Hall's influence on the movement away from the Froebelian kindergarten was eventually profound, although at a seminar in 1895, most of the kindergartners assembled to hear his child development research left infuriated.

At the same time, the mental hygiene movement was launched in the United States (Prochner, 2000). The movement shifted from treatment and prevention of mental illness to the promotion of mental health. Researchers and practitioners in mental health disciplines agreed that the roots of mental health were found in early childhood. Attention turned to the need to understand how children develop and what conditions are necessary to promote mental health.

The theories and practices of progressive education, the child study movement, and the mental hygiene movement converged to influence emerging kindergarten and nursery school programs in both Canada and the United States.

The Child Study Movement in Canada

In Canada, establishment of child study and nursery school programs was stimulated by the progressive education, child study, and mental hygiene movements in the United States and by the new social science—psychology. The experiments of the McMillan sisters in Britain and Maria Montessori in Italy did not find a direct translation in Canadian nursery schools that first appeared in the 1920s. However, they did offer powerful examples of how early child development programs could be targeted to disadvantaged children.

Because of the widespread interest in the development of young children generated by the child study movement, nursery schools were established in laboratory settings as part of child study programs. Funds were provided by the will of Laura Spelman Rockefeller in 1923 to establish child study centres in major research universities, such as Yale, the University of California, the University of Minnesota, the University of Iowa, and Columbia University.

The impetus to start a nursery school in Toronto came from this interest and from concerns about mental hygiene. Clare Hincks, a Toronto physician and a leader of the mental hygiene movement, worked closely with E. A. Bott, who headed the psychiatry department at the University of Toronto. They were successful in securing a grant from the Laura Spelman Rockerfeller Fund to establish the St. George's School for Child Study at the University of Toronto in 1925. It later became the Institute of Child Studies, a site of extensive child studies, as well as a working model of early childhood care and education practice.

McGill University also secured funding from the same source to establish the McGill University Day Care in Montreal, which operated from 1925 to 1930. In other university settings, child development studies were introduced as part of psychology and home economic departments.

William Blatz, a physician who graduated from the University of Toronto and then pursued a Ph.D. in psychology at the University of Chicago, is recognized as the founder of Canada's child study movement. In 1926, he opened a nursery school at St. George's School for Child Study. The nursery school was a laboratory where Blatz experimented with precise organization of children's time and daily routines. He believed this approach helped to develop regular habits and a strong sense of security for the young child. Blatz created a program of guidance and education for children from two to five years of age that influenced practices and regulations in early childhood care and education across Canada for decades. From the beginning, parent education, early educator training, and child development research were also major components of the St. George's School for Child Study, in addition to the nursery school.

1970–73
Federal funding through Local Initiatives Projects for child care centres and advocacy groups encourages expansion of community-based child care as well as day care advocacy activities across Canada.

1970s
The introduction of legislated standards and limited funding for each province signals the beginning of the modern era of child care.

In the first year of operation, four adults developed the program for eighteen children at the school. Blatz's recent studies in psychology had introduced him to the work of Watson's behaviourism, Dewey's progressive education, and psychoanalytical ideas about mental hygiene. Because he did not have direct experience with either kindergarten or nursery school settings, he worked with the school staff to develop the program. Della Dingle, who had studied at the College of Home Economics at Cornell University in New York, was the first nursery school director.

Blatz and his team did not have a cohesive understanding of young children or a theoretical framework to guide their practice. Instead, they were eager to explore new ideas about child development and took a "let's watch the children and find out" approach (Raymond, 1991). Blatz did encourage a smooth-running routine that promoted the habit of regularity in the lives of young children. The nursery school established such practices as staggered enrollment and a staff timetable that covered every situation in a nursery school day. Within the parameters of daily routines (such as eating, washing hands, using the toilet, and napping), children were encouraged to explore environments designed for open-ended play activity. Over the years, the research of Blatz and others explored environmental influences on child development and the importance of adult-child relationships in developing emotional security.

The focus of the St. George's School for Child Study was not just child-oriented; parent education was championed from the beginning. Blatz began an infant-mother drop-in program and promoted parent training in his frequent lectures broadcast on CBC radio (Raymond 1991). Parents whose children attended the nursery school program at St. George's School for Child Study participated in parent education classes (Wright, 2000) and were encouraged to read Blatz's publications for parents.

Children follow lunch routine at St. George's Nursery School, circa 1930.

A dramatic event in the 1930s propelled William Blatz and his approach to child studies and parent education into a very public international spotlight. In 1934, the Dionne quintuplets were born to a French-Canadian couple living in rural northern Ontario. The babies were made wards of the province and cared for in a controlled environment (Wright, 2000). Blatz and his colleagues were given the opportunity to study the children for over two years. In retrospect, it was a horrific situation for the young children (Berton, 1977), but it did offer a unique opportunity to study environmental influences and development among five children who were thought to have identical genetic inheritance (Wright, 2000).

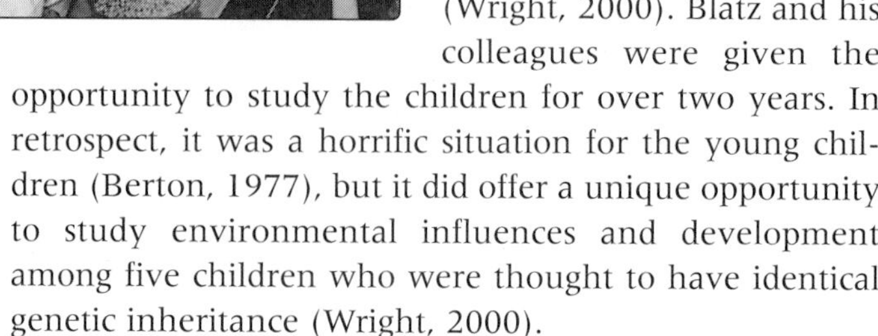

RESEARCH INTO PRACTICE

The Dionne Quintuplets and Scientific Child Rearing

The Dionne quintuplets, Yvonne, Annette, Cecile, Emilie, and Marie, were the first group of identical quintuplets to live beyond a few days after birth. Their Franco-Ontarian parents found themselves at the centre of public interest and media attention. They struggled to care for the vulnerable infants in a northern Ontario farmhouse without central heating or running water. The parents signed over guardianship of the infant girls to the provincial government. A specially designed hospital/laboratory, complete with observation rooms open to the public, was built in Callendar.

In 1936, William Blatz was put in charge of how the babies were raised. Nurses and teachers implemented his model program with instructions for minute-by-minute routines. Habit reinforcement through repetition and praise were blended with a structured play program following the model that Blatz had developed at St. George Nursery School. Blatz was conducting a scientific experiment in a controlled laboratory with more precision than could ever be possible in the St. George Nursery School.

Blatz had good intentions. He wanted the girls to be treated in a rational and scientific manner that was considered to be progressive at the time. Blatz hoped to send the girls to school along with other children their age. However, the fame of the quintuplets and the provincial government's unwillingness to disappoint fans (or lose out on the funds raised by this lucrative attraction) interfered. Blatz's involvement and the high profile modern psychology experiment ended in 1938.

Eventually the girls were returned to their parents' authority. Catholic family values, francophone culture, and religious order replaced the psychologists' approaches. Their future was generally unhappy. Probably the well-intentioned but intrusive early interventions disrupted the family relationships. Blatz and his colleagues' failure to establish a working relationship with the parents seems astonishing now.

Their birthplace in Ontario illustrates many of the controversies that surrounded the upbringing of the girls. The Dionne farmhouse was in a rural area between two towns, Corbeil and Callendar in northern Ontario. The parents registered the birth in Corbeil which was predominately home to Franco-Ontarians. Callender, a larger and mostly English town, and the location of Blatz's laboratory, reaped most of the commercial benefits and some sources say they were born there.

Source: Strong-Boag, 1985; Wright 2000; Bertrand, 2001.

In 1938, the St. George's School for Child Study became the Institute of Child Study, and within a year began to offer courses to kindergarten teachers. During the next two decades, it remained a leader in the development of early childhood care and education programs.

Other nursery schools followed the lead of the St. George's Nursery School and began to open in the late 1920s. They joined private kindergarten programs (operated outside the public school system) in offering educational programs to young children. For example, by 1928, there were several private nursery school/kindergarten programs operating in Calgary. Most were half-day programs for middle-class children from age two to five years, which relied on parent fees. Many were unable to survive the economic depression of the 1930s.

Working Women: Day Nurseries to Early Childhood Education and Care

2000
1950
1900
1850
1800
1750
1700
1650

1971

Unemployment Insurance Act provides fifteen weeks of maternity benefits after twenty or more weeks of full employment.

The Mothercraft infant caregiver training program begins in Canada.

Health and Welfare Canada begins to collect statistical information on Canadian day cares.

There are 17 391 regulated day care spaces in Canada.

The past sixty years have repeatedly brought early childhood care and education to the forefront of social policy, education, and employment initiatives. The types of programs vary, but their relationship to women's employment in the labour force has remained constant. Periods of strong demand for the participation of women in the workforce resulted in government support of full-time early childhood care and education. However, during periods of women's decreased participation in the labour force, the emphasis shifted to part-time early childhood programs that focused on children's development and education needs.

World War II brought an acute labour shortage in Canada, and the government began to recruit women to work in industry. The government first recruited single women, then married women, and finally married women with children. After the war, attention turned to maintaining a prosperous economy in peaceful times, and social policies were introduced to ensure basic protection for families from the economic devastation of the Depression era. The consumption of goods and services, combined with a boom in babies, created the conditions for economic expansion and the expansion of government social programs. By the 1960s and 1970s, women were receiving higher levels of education and had greater employment opportunities. At the same time, lone-parent families, the need for more than one income to sustain family standards of living, and the consciousness-raising efforts of the women's movement led many women with young children into the workforce.

War-Time Day Nurseries

As women were recruited for work in war-related industries, the image of the perfect Canadian woman changed from being the foundation of hearth and home to the industrious beauty on the assembly line. The recruitment drive made it necessary to consider alternative care for children. In 1942, the federal government passed the *Dominion-Provincial Wartime Day Nurseries Agreement,* authorizing the Ministry of Labour to enter into cost-sharing agreements with any provincial government willing to establish day nursery services.

Quebec and Ontario were the only provinces to take advantage of the scheme—the other provinces maintained that the need did not exist. The federal government stipulated that at least 75 percent of day nursery spaces had to be given to children whose mothers worked in essential war industries. In both provinces, day nursery operating standards were established. In Ontario, the St. George's School of Child Study provided a model for a rapidly expanding system and established short training courses for staff.

By the end of the war, there were twenty-eight nurseries for preschoolers and forty-two programs for school-age children in Ontario; in Quebec there were five community-based centres. The Ontario centres were located in Toronto, Ottawa, Hamilton, and Windsor. The cost was $1.05 per day, shared roughly equally between parents and the federal and provincial governments. There was no provision for infant care.

After the war, governments undertook a campaign to get women back to hearth and home and introduced Family Allowance ("baby bonus") benefits. In Quebec, the government closed all five centres, despite enrollment to capacity and long waiting lists. In Ontario, all three governments (federal, provincial, and municipal) tried to close the centres but were met with strong resistance through the Day Nursery and Day Care Parents Association. Federal funding ceased, but the Ontario government then passed the *Day Nurseries Act,* which included provisions for licensing day nursery and nursery school programs and 50 percent provincial cost-sharing of fee subsidies to municipalities. The regulations were based on routines and practices in place at the Institute of Child Study (formerly called St. George's) nursery school. Sixteen of the twenty-eight preschool centres survived, but all forty-two school-age programs closed due to lack of funding and political support (Schulz, 1978).

Baby Boom Time

The campaign for women to remain with *kuchen* and *kinder* continued throughout the 1950s and early 1960s. To the extent that day nurseries existed in Canada, they continued to operate mostly as charitable institutions for women in need. However, with increased births and growing numbers of young children, nursery schools offering part-time enrichment programs for children (and breaks for full-time mothers) were popular throughout Canada.

MAKING IT HAPPEN

Establishing a Day Care Centre

Procedure in establishing and operating day care centres is gradually becoming crystallized. The School Board investigates the need by a prepared questionnaire sent to the parents. Upon receipt of twenty or more applications, a plan and budget are set out to meet the specific requirements of each school setup. These are submitted by the board to the Provincial Advisory Committee, and from thence to the Department of Labour, Dominion Government. Upon approval, they are returned to the Board for administration. Officers of the Wartime Day Nursery Branch of the Department of Public Welfare act to advise and assist in establishing each centre.

Fitting day care into a school organization is a challenge in ingenuity. Even its most obvious aspects of time, place and personnel have required considerable forethought. Adequate care necessitates a programme from 7:00 in the morning until 6:00 or 6:30 in the evening. Space in crowded school buildings is difficult to spare. Assembly halls, gymnasiums, music rooms, and even classrooms, are variously used. In a few cases the ideal has been reached—namely, provision of a room of their own. Here, surroundings can be made attractive and conducive to easy, enjoyable but busy living. A sense of belonging and possessing can be achieved, and thus, more basic objectives of the programme approached. A demonstration has been attempted in one Toronto school. The room—an empty classroom—is decorated in soft green; gay curtains relieve its classroom severity; coloured tables and chairs built to suit recreational needs break the monotony; a reading corner furnished with comfortable chairs is conducive to relaxation.

(cont'd)

Establishing a Day Care Centre (cont'd)

Serving lunch at school has presented, on first glance, insurmountable difficulties. In a majority of centres, it has been possible through community cooperation to arrange meal service in a nearby church or other community building. The Board remains in charge of this service, providing adequate facilities where these are lacking. The child's well-being is built up and maintained by a nutrition programme planned through the Provincial Department. Staff from the Nutrition Department of the University of Toronto give directions to this programme.

For staff to carry out the day care programme, authorities have turned, in the first instance, to those whose work they know and value—namely, the teachers. These have given their services regularly and unstintingly in overtime hours. It is recognized, however, by those participating, that time is required for planning a day care programme, time not possible to the busy teacher. In a few centres, a regular staff has been provided whose one responsibility it is to plan for the needs of a particular group of children.

Source: Millichamp (1944, November), p. 248.

Parent cooperative preschool programs, which had surfaced in Canada as part of the nursery school movement, expanded during this period. In 1950, Vaughan Road Nursery School was established in Toronto. Daisy Dotsch was the teacher in charge, and she became a leader in the development of preschool philosophy in Canada (Stevenson, 1990).

The Nursery Education Association of Ontario (which later became the Association for Early Childhood Education, Ontario) started up in 1950. An organization for nursery school and day care teachers, it offered extension courses and began a voluntary system of certification for early childhood education staff.

The preschool curriculum during the 1950s reflected an emphasis on the personality development of young children. Blatz's theory of security guided the focus on the interaction between adults and children in preschool settings. The development of children's emotionally healthy relationships dominated preschool programs, and skill development was a less dominant goal (Millichamp, 1974).

Times A' Changing

The 1960s and 1970s saw enormous changes in Canadian society. A growing awareness of poverty and the importance of the early years led to increased attention to early childhood education research and curriculum methodology. Education reform became an important issue throughout school systems and universities. Federal legislation was introduced to provide assistance to low-income Canadians, including provision for day care fee subsidies. The booming economy created thousands of new jobs in the service sector, and the participation of women began to increase rapidly. In 1967, fewer than 20 percent of women with children younger than six years were in the labour force; by the end of the 1970s almost half of all women with children under six were in the labour force.

To meet the need for affordable child care, the federal government made day care a cost-shareable welfare service under the terms of the Canada Assistance Plan in 1966. By 1977, all provinces had passed legislation enabling their governments to take advantage of the federal funding.

Several provincial/territorial governments introduced legislation to regulate day care and nursery school programs and improve quality. As a result of funding and demand, the number of licensed day care centres began to rise.

During the 1960s and into the 1970s, preschool education began to emphasize cognitive development from the cognitive development theory of Jean Piaget and the direct instruction theories, which come from a behaviourist orientation. The makeup of childhood care and education in Canada at this time was influenced by campus programs, government employment programs, and compensatory education initiatives. University campuses across Canada established day care centres for infants and toddlers, often as outgrowths of students' or women's organizations. Typically, these programs involved parents as participants, set up collective decision-making structures, and attempted to provide an environment free of gender stereotypes. They often operated at odds with the prevailing licensing and professional standards and guidelines. Many of the campus child care centres are still in existence. More importantly, they changed ECE postsecondary education programs and government regulations by illustrating support for full-day child care for very young children as a viable choice for families, not just for those in social need.

The federal government launched a number of employment programs such as the Local Initiatives Programs (LIP) during the late 1960s and early 1970s. In the winter of 1972–73, 215 children's programs, mostly day care centres, were created. LIP provided these programs with funds for workers to organize day care centres for neighbourhood children. Many LIP-initiated child care programs set up community/parent boards of directors and sought fee subsidies from provincial governments to continue operation after the LIP grants ran out.

Throughout the 1970s, day care activists across the country continued to campaign for more day care and higher-quality day care, pointing to the enormous gap between demand and supply. In 1973, there were only 28 000 regulated day care spaces in Canada. Although this rose to over 125 000 spaces by 1982, it in no way kept pace with need.

Compensatory Preschool Programs

During the 1960s and 1970s, child development research on the importance of early experiences on later abilities and the growing movements to end racial segregation and poverty in the United States pointed to early childhood care and education solutions.

Child advocates, policymakers, and researchers pursued early child development initiatives with high hopes that enriched early childhood experiences could change the life course of disadvantaged children, especially African-American children. Head Start, the Perry Preschool Project, and *Sesame Street* are three initiatives that attempted to improve disadvantaged children's developmental outcomes and ameliorate the effects of poverty, social marginalization, and racism.

1. Head Start was established in 1965 as part of President Lyndon Johnson's War on Poverty to expose young children (ages three to five years) living in disadvantaged environments to experiences that would minimize the effects of poverty and racial discrimination. The purpose of the program was to improve children's health and well-being; develop physical skills, social opportunities, and cognitive functioning; and involve parents in their children's educational

2000
1950
1900
1850
1800
1750
1700
1650

1971 (cont'd)
The Child Care Expense Deduction is introduced through the income tax system in Canada.

French immersion kindergartens are introduced into Toronto public schools.

The First National Day Care Conference is organized by the Canadian Council on Social Development and helps to focus on child care as a national issue.

1972
Home Start programs are established in the United States to provide Head Start's comprehensive services to children and families at home.

First National Canadian Conference on day care.

1973
West Side Family Place, a parent-child resource program, opens in Vancouver.

In the United States, the Children's Defense Fund of the Washington Research Project is established by Marian Wright Edelman, later to become the Children's Defense Fund.

There are only 28 000 regulated day care spaces in Canada.

experiences. In addition, the program offered medical, dental, and nutritional screening and services for children and social services for their families.

2. The Perry Preschool Project was a carefully designed experimental longitudinal study on the effects of compensatory preschool education programs for children three and four years old in the 1960s. Preschool teachers worked closely with child development and educational experts to develop a cognitive-developmental program based on Piagetian theory of cognitive development. The findings dramatically endorsed the financial and social benefits of compensatory preschool education as an intervention for disadvantaged, marginalized children (Schweinhart & Weikart, 1993). The follow-up studies found that children who attended the half-day program were more successful in school, less likely to be involved in the criminal justice system, and less likely to be on social assistance. The cost-benefit analysis of the results illustrated a seven-dollar savings for every dollar spent on the targeted program delivered to at-risk children and their families.
3. *Sesame Street,* the best-known children's educational show in North America, began in 1969. The Children's Television Workshop produced the daily program to foster intellectual and social development. The initial program proposal stated that *Sesame Street* would respond to "the national demand that we give the disadvantaged a fair chance in the beginning" (Liebart & Sprafkin, 1988, p. 219). The creators drew on both ideology and research to design a show that would bring stimulation and opportunities for learning into disadvantaged children's homes through the television to compensate for resources presumed to be available to affluent families. Both earlier assessments (Liebert & Sprafkin, 1988) and more recent studies (Wright & Huston, 1995) report positive benefits for low-income children who regularly view the show. *Sesame Street* as a curriculum model is discussed in Chapter 2.

A number of smaller-scale programs based on Head Start and the Perry Preschool Project emerged in Canada during the 1970s. Several of the programs funded by the federal government's youth employment program (Local Initiatives Program) launched preschool compensatory programs for poor children. These programs often adapted the cognitively oriented curriculum of the Perry Preschool Program and a Head Start approach that combined enriched early childhood education experiences with additional family supports.

In 1974, Moncton Headstart Inc. (described in Chapter 1) began as a free day care for a few children whose parents could not afford outside care and were having difficulties in their parenting role (Bradshaw, 1997). It quickly adapted the Perry Preschool Program's curriculum and included programs to support families. Parent participation in the children's program and in parent sessions was required. Adjunct programs that meet families' basic physical needs (food, shelter, and safety) and adult education activities were also offered.

The University of Western Ontario Preschool Project began in 1973 as an experiment to assess the impact of compensatory preschool education on low-income children (Howe, Jacobs, & Fiorentino, 2000). Mary J. Wright, who headed the project, developed a constructivist type of curriculum with an emphasis on cognitive development (similar to the High Scope curriculum) as well as a focus on the development of social competence and emotional control (derived from her work with William Blatz at the Institute for Child Studies). Children from economically disadvantaged families attended the University of Western Ontario Preschool for one or two years alongside children from middle-class families. Low-income children who attended the program for two years demonstrated greater cognitive and self-management skills than low-income children who attended for only one year. Follow-up assessments after Grade Three found that 82 percent of the low-income children who attended for either one or two years were at grade level compared to only 58 percent of a low-income control group of children who had not attended any preschool program. "Overall, the findings of the UWO Preschool Project supported the idea that compensatory education can have long-term beneficial outcomes for low–socioeconomic status children, particularly if the preschool experience is two years in length. A word of caution is in order: the study was based on a very small number of subjects, and it is difficult to generalize the findings" (Howe, Jacobs, & Fiorentino, 2000, p. 226).

The Child Care Decade

Action Day Care was established in Toronto in 1979 to advocate for free, high-quality, nonprofit child care for all families, with demands for a universal child care system. It grew out of a decade of rapid expansion of both regulated child care programs and the labour force participation of women with young children. Action Day Care developed the neighbourhood hub model to deliver comprehensive child care programs and, together with other day care and early childhood advocates, labour groups, women's organizations, parents, and other concerned citizens, the new agenda for child care spread across the country. During the 1980s, provincial organizations with similar demands sprang up.

The 1980s saw rapid growth in other early child development programs. Several provinces introduced regulations for family care, and kindergarten within the school system expanded. Family support programs, such as family resource programs, toy-lending libraries, and parent-child drop-in programs expanded in many parts of the country (Beach & Bertrand, 2000). Some were aimed at high-risk families and focused on enhancing parenting skills. Others offered informal child care providers with opportunities to get together with each other, perhaps take part in some training activities and group play activities for the children. And some were provided to more advantaged at-home parents.

The 1980s also witnessed the initiation of two national child care organizations. The second Canadian Conference on Day Care brought advocates, early childhood experts, and policymakers from across Canada together, for the first time in ten years. The tumultuous conference grabbed media attention and had several concrete outcomes. It passed resolutions calling for the enactment of national legislation to create a universally accessible, high-quality, nonprofit child care system and a mandate to form a broad-based national child care advocacy organization.

In 1983, the Canadian Day Care Advocacy Association (later called the Child Care Advocacy Association of Canada - CCAAC) was established by some of the child care activists who attended the 1982 conference. Each province and territory elected representatives to advocate for the development of a universal, publicly-funded child care system. A couple of years later, other organizers from Winnipeg established the

Canadian Child Care Federation (CCCF) as a professional organization that promotes quality child care. The need for two national organizations reflected the split among child care advocates (including early childhood educators). The CCAAC adopted a strong position on the auspice issue and was (and is) not in favour of directing public dollars to commercial programs. The CCCF does not make a distinction between commercial and non-profit programs (Friendly 2000; Prentice, 2001). Both organizations continue to exist and often collaborate to promote public investment in child care.

The Federal Government and Child Care in the 1980s and 1990s

Throughout the 1980s and 1990s, an increasingly organized and wide-spread advocacy for a child care system demanded that the federal government adopt a new policy role. The federal governments of the day attempted to establish a national approach to child care while recognizing the primacy of the provincial role in education and social services (Friendly & Beach, 2005). However, their efforts were not successful.

- In 1983, the federal Liberal government led by Prime Minister Trudeau, established the Task Force on Child Care to report to the federal government on the development of a system of quality child care in Canada. In 1985, the Task Force on Child Care released its report, which was widely reported in the media (Cooke et al., 1986). The report called for the development of publicly funded child care and paid parental leave to be implemented over a fifteen-year period. The background study and research conducted for the report provided a comprehensive look at child care issues to date.
- In 1986, the new federal Conservative government responded to the Task Force on Child Care report and established the Special Committee on Child Care. The Committee held public hearings across the country in over thirty locations in Canada, from Newfoundland to Vancouver. The Special Committee on Child Care recommended increased tax credits for families, continuation of subsidies to low-income families through the Canada Assistance Plan, small operating grants for profit and nonprofit programs, enhancement of maternity leave to six months, and small capital grants to child care programs. The report did not recommend the establishment of a coherent national child care system (Friendly & Beach, 2005; Prentice, 2001).
- At the end of 1987, the federal Conservative government did announce a proposal for a National Child Care strategy (including new child care tax deductions and funding for projects and research) and in 1988, it introduced the *Canada Child Care Act.* The act would have allowed $3.2 billion to be matched by the provinces over seven years; provinces would make decisions about how the funds would be spent. It was met with widespread, persistent opposition from child care advocates who wanted to ensure public dollars were not allocated to commercial programs. The act was left to die on the Order table—it was not passed into legislation before the next federal election. After the election, the Federal government did not pursue a national strategy for child care.

Looking back, it is clear that the events of the late 1980s contributed to today's child care policy environment. The commitment to research and projects has sustained a number of initiatives, including the regular publication of the status of early childhood education and care in each province and territory (Friendly & Beach, 2005), academic research on child care environments (for example, Doherty et al., 2000), and created a plethora of resources for professional development and education. The inability to pass the *Canada Child Care Act* has made it difficult to create a national child care system and left developments up to the provinces and territories.

In 1993, the federal government changed and the Liberals, led by Prime Minister Jean Chretien, made an election commitment to once again pursue a national child care strategy. However, federal-provincial arrangements in Canada shifted and because there was no pre-existing federal child care legislation, federal government involvement in shaping a national child care program became more problematic (Beach & Bertrand, 2000; Friendly 2000). In 1996, the Canada Assistance Plan that provided matching federal funding for provincial dollars spent on child care subsidies, was abolished along with ability for the federal government to impose any conditions on child care spending. Federal dollars for provincial health, education, and welfare programs were consolidated into a block fund, the Canada Health and Social Transfer. This means provinces and territories can decide how to allocate funds and are not obligated to spend any of these dollars on child care. Nor can they receive matching new federal dollars if they increase spending on child care.

By the end of the 1990s, the federal government was working with provincial and territorial governments to establish a National Child Care Agenda (Social Development Canada, Public Health Agency of Canada, and Indian & Northern Affairs Canada (2005). The framework for this discussion positioned child care within the broader context of early child development programs. The tensions between child care as a distinct program apart from other early child development programs and child care as an integral part of an early child development approach to programs continues.

SUMMARY

It is important to understand the heritage of early childhood education and care, to recognize the continuity with earlier practitioners and theorists, to realize how real events and trends influence the response of the profession, and to answer questions that separate early child development programs today. These questions include: Who cares for and educates the children? Who supports parents and other caregivers? What role will the federal and provincial/territorial governments play in early childhood education and care? Why are care and education seen as separate activities?

Kindergarten, nursery school, child care programs, and family support programs in both Canada and the United States came from very different traditions. Understanding the traditions, and the reasons behind the different professional preparation patterns and organizations, may help today's early childhood educators find new ways to find common ground with other professionals who are working in early child development programs.

REVIEW QUESTIONS

1. List several reasons for studying the history of early education.
2. Identify the different occasions when the federal government has taken a role in supporting early care and education.
3. Explain why early care and education are thought of as two separate entities.
4. Discuss the separate developments of kindergartens and nursery schools in Europe and in North America, identifying key names in each tradition.
5. Order the following names chronologically, stating for each his or her importance in early childhood education and care: William Blatz; Erik Erikson; Sigmund Freud; Howard Gardner; Harriet Johnson; Lawrence Kohlberg; Ada Maream Hughes; Maria Montessori; Jean Piaget; Caroline Pratt; B. F. Skinner; Daniel Keating.

STUDY ACTIVITIES

1. Read one of the articles or books listed in the Suggested Readings or References section to learn more about one of the individuals in this chapter.
2. Write up the history of a nursery school or child care centre in your community.
3. Look for some older ECE texts in your college's library. What differences and similarities about early childhood education and care programs and practices do you see in comparison to today's texts?

KEY TERMS

behavioural theory: Also called "learning theory." A psychological theory developed in the United States, according to which behaviour is learned and can be modified by changing the environmental responses of reward and punishment.

child study movement: University-based scientific research on child development that began to be widespread in the 1920s and that facilitated the development of early childhood education.

custodial care: Looking after the basic (primarily physical) needs of children and protecting them from danger.

developmental health: Explains how our earliest social and physical experiences shape the brain's development and set the foundation for learning, behaviour, and health.

kindergarteners: Term used for the first Froebelian-trained kindergarten teachers in the nineteenth and early twentieth centuries.

multiple intelligences: Theory, originated by Howard Gardner, that suggests intelligence may be organized into seven different kinds of abilities.

nursery schools: Programs modelled after the MacMillan philosophy of physical, emotional, and social development, usually for three- and four-year-olds and usually operated on a part-day basis.

parent cooperative: Nursery schools that involve parents in the classroom and in the administration of the school.

philanthropic organization: Organization established for the provision of social services to better the lives of its clients.

progressive education: Educational philosophy that, based on the tenets of John Dewey, promotes active involvement of the individual in learning.
psychosocial theory: Erik Erikson's theory of personality development, in which the individual must resolve conflict with the environment, including other persons.
rote learning: Learning by repetition, memory, and habit, rather than from first-hand understanding.

SUGGESTED READINGS

Baylor, R. (1965). *Elizabeth Peabody: Kindergarten pioneer.* Philadelphia: University of Pennsylvania Press.

Bradburn, E. (1989). *Margaret MacMillan: Portrait of a pioneer.* London: Routledge.

Froebel, Friedrich. (1896). *The education of man.* New York: Appleton.

Gardner, Howard. (1985). *Frames of mind: The theory of multiple intelligence.* New York: Basic Books.

Gesell, Arnold. (1940). The significance of the nursery school. *Childhood Education,* 1(1), 11–20.

Greenberg, Polly. (1990, September). Head Start—Part of a multi-pronged anti-poverty effort for children and their families . . . Before the beginning: A participant's view. *Young Children,* 45 (6), 41–52.

Isaacs, Susan. (1968). *The nursery years.* New York: Schocken Books.

Johnson, Harriet. (1928). *Children in the nursery school.* New York: John Day.

Kohlberg, Lawrence & Lickona, Thomas. (1986). *The stages of ethical development: From childhood through old age.* New York: Harper Books.

MacMillan, Margaret. (1919). *The nursery school.* New York: E. P. Dutton.

Montessori, Maria. (1967). *The Montessori method.* (Anne E. George, Trans.) Cambridge, MA.

Paciorek, Karen & Munro, Joyce. (Eds.). (1996). *Sources: Notable selections in early childhood education.* Guilford, CT: Dushkin Publishing Group. (Selections from writings by many of the early theorists and practitioners, such as Abigail Eliot, Katherine Read, Elizabeth Peabody, Patty Smith Hill, Friedrich Froebel, Lucy Sprague Mitchell, Maria Montessori, Harriet Johnson, John Dewey, Susan Blow, Margaret MacMillan, Arnold Gesell, Robert Owen, and G. Stanley Hall.)

Prentice, S. (2001). *Changing child care: Five decades of child care advocacy and policy in Canada.* Halifax: Fernwood Publishing.

Prochner, L. & Howe, N. (2000). *Early childhood care and education in Canada.* Vancouver: UBC Press.

Reeves, Carolyn, Howard, Esther, & Grace, Cathy. (1990, Fall). A model preschool: London's Rachel MacMillan Nursery School. *Dimensions,* 19 (1), 10–13.

Strong-Boag, V. (1982). "Intruders in the nursery: Childcare professionals reshape the years one to five, 1920–1940." In J. Parr (ed.), *Childhood and family in Canadian history*. Toronto: McClelland & Stewart.

Weber, E. (1984) *Ideas influencing early childhood education: A theoretical analysis.* New York: Teachers College Press.

Zinsser, C. (1988). The best day care there ever was. In *Early Childhood Education 88/89.* Guilford, CT: Dushkin Publishing Group.

CHAPTER EIGHT
The Modern Profession

OBJECTIVES

After studying this chapter, students will be able to

- identify eight characteristics of a profession and discuss how the early childhood workforce compares to each of the eight;
- identify Canadian and U.S. professional and advocacy organizations and some of their contributions to the field;
- explain the process and importance of the Canadian Child Care Federation's National Standards of Practice and identify major components of the statement; and
- describe the importance of a code of ethics for early childhood educators and identify Canadian examples.

As we consider the modern emergence of the early childhood workforce, it is both surprising and exciting to realize that you are entering this field only about forty years into the modern era. As Chapter 7 explained, that era began with the rapid growth of day care centres in Canada and the establishment of Head Start programs and other compensatory programs in both Canada and the United States, which signalled a new period of interest in the importance of early childhood education. These early childhood education and care programs were also a reflection of the social currents that demanded equality for racial minorities and women and that emphasized the need to expand the field.

Forty years is a relatively brief period when the development of a profession is considered. As we shall see, it took some time before early childhood leaders in Canada and the United States questioned how caring for and educating young children and supporting their families compared with other professions and how unity could strengthen the efforts of the field. This chapter will describe the discussions that guided some of the developments. Only in the past couple of decades have dialogues, position statements, and other pronouncements by professional groups given early childhood educators substantive evidence that there are indeed unifying ideas and issues that help the profession continue to evolve.

The concept of a profession suggests that there is already unity and consensus. However, as you have already realized, early childhood educators have likely come to their work via different entry points and varied training, traditions, and preparation. And the work they do is itself very different. This diversity is atypical of many other professions. This chapter will continue to illustrate this diversity, as it traces the various steps that have been taken to define cohesive knowledge and practices in an evolving profession.

Is the Early Childhood Workforce a Profession?

Sarah C. works as an assistant in a classroom for toddlers. She took the job because it was advertised in her local newspaper, and she thought it might be fun for a while. She has no training beyond the orientation given by her director for new staff, and she has no plans to get anything beyond the sixteen hours of workshops she is required to attend each year by child care licensing requirements. Eventually, she'd like to study interior design.

Tom B. is a Head Start teacher. He took the job of assistant several years ago, after volunteering when his daughter attended a Head Start program. He liked the teaching and decided to stay and to take advantage of the continuing education ECE certificate program training offered. He has recently earned the ECE credential and is considering beginning work on a four-year degree, so that he will be certified to teach in elementary schools. This would offer him a better salary and benefits.

Mary A. is the lead teacher in a mixed-age preschool classroom. She completed an ECE degree at her local college, which she attended immediately after graduating from high school.

Rachel F. is a family child care provider. Originally trained as a data entry operator, she began her centre so that she could be at home while her own children were young. Although she is currently active in her local family child care provider organization and has completed a short training program for home care providers, she plans eventually to return to data entry.

Martha H. has almost completed a master's degree in early childhood education. After five years in preschool classrooms, she has just accepted a promotion that includes doing some administration as well as staff training at her centre.

Towanya B. is a teacher's aide in a Grade Two classroom. Her major duties include individual tutoring in reading and checking the children's work. She is a high school graduate with one semester of college general education courses.

Susanne S. teaches a K–2 mixed-age grouping in a private school.

Are these early childhood educators all early childhood **professionals**? What criteria did you use to decide whether they were professionals? Keep these criteria in mind as we continue our discussion of professionalism.

These individuals demonstrate the complexity of discussing early childhood education as a profession. Working in different strands of the field, with varying educational and training backgrounds and quite separate goals, they illustrate the breadth that must be included in any discussion about early childhood education as a profession. Throughout this book, we have been using the term "profession" to refer to those who are involved in teaching and caring in the early years. This is, in fact, the terminology being used by leaders in the field during the current discussions. For example, Sue Bredekamp, Director of Professional Development for NAEYC, clarifies her use of the term "early childhood professional": "The term early childhood professional or early childhood educator is used here to refer to individuals who are responsible for the care and education of children, birth through age eight, in centres, homes, and schools, and others who support that delivery of service" (Bredekamp, 1992, p. 52).

The origin of the word "professional" takes us back to "medieval times when an individual took *vows* in order to be received in a religious community. It was the act of openly declaring or publicly *professing* a belief or faith" (Giles & Proudfoot, 1994, p. 333).

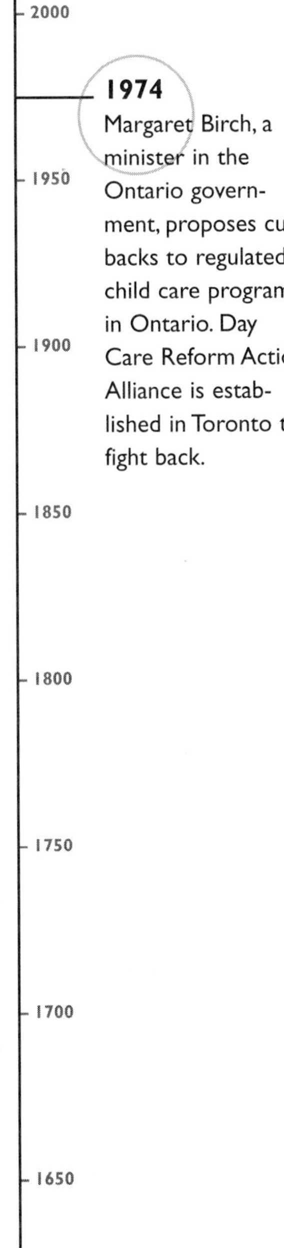

1974
Margaret Birch, a minister in the Ontario government, proposes cutbacks to regulated child care programs in Ontario. Day Care Reform Action Alliance is established in Toronto to fight back.

1975
Two parent-child resource programs—the Parent Preschool Resource Centre in Ottawa and the Children's Storefront in Toronto—are established.

The National Association of Toy Libraries is established.

Over time, "professional" came to mean a particular occupation that required specific knowledge and high standards of practice (Giles & Proudfoot, 1994).

Whether or not early childhood education is truly a profession is something that has been debated in recent years. Sandra Griffin (1994), a Canadian early childhood educator, academic, and researcher, points out that if there is to be a child care system in Canada, the early childhood workforce must build a profession as the infrastructure to develop and maintain the quality of that system.

However, Milly Almy (1988) has stated flatly that although the early childhood educator role requires professional attitudes and behaviours, it does not meet the standards for a profession. "With its shaky knowledge base, its ambiguous clientele, and its lack of a code of ethics, early childhood education qualifies only as an occupation or, at best, a semiprofession" (Almy, 1988, p. 50). (*Note:* We shall see that the lack of a code of ethics has been remedied since her statement.) Almy describes early childhood educators as double specialists; these double specialties include teaching young children, assessing their development, and working with children and with adults; and thinking concretely in practice, and formally, in theory. This certainly sounds like demanding work for something she claims is not a profession.

Ade (1982) agreed that the unique characteristics associated with professional status, including "specialized knowledge, a desirable service, and an assurance of quality, dependability, and effectiveness" (p. 25), were lacking in early childhood care, but that certain changes in the field could help move it closer to professionalization. The changes he identified are:

- to require a greater familiarity with the field's knowledge base, thus increasing the specialized knowledge needed to practice and extending the length of the training period;
- to identify and establish uniform criteria for admitting new members, including entry criteria for training and content of training;
- to develop the kind of practitioner licensing system that would ensure meeting of criteria and exclusion of those who do not meet the criteria;
- to gain internal control of the licensing system to allow members to have input for requirements and thus greater self-regulation; and
- to obtain stronger voices by joining with parents and other decision-makers to determine needs and the provision of appropriate services to meet those needs.

Spodek, Saracho, and Peters (1988) suggest that "professional" is used in a variety of ways, including individuals who are paid to do certain work, without implication of level of skill and those "with a high degree of skill and competence" (p. 7), but more often implying one of the learned professions, which require a high degree of training and usually involve mental rather than physical work. The fields that require less preparation, and therefore, often have lower levels of status, including teaching, social work, and counselling, might be called semiprofessions, having some but not all of the attributes of true professions.

Criteria of a Profession

Lilian Katz (1995) suggests that eight criteria must be met before an occupation can be classified as a profession, and that those in the early childhood community must work to gain consensus and take needed steps in the following areas.

Today's early childhood educators are creating a new kind of profession.

MEET THE EARLY CHILDHOOD WORKFORCE

Joanne Murrell, Early Childhood Educator, Toronto

"I'm a keener who jumps on things," says Joanne Murrell. About a year and a half ago, this keener jumped right into one of the most interesting and innovative projects on early learning and care. Joanne coordinated one of the Toronto First Duty (TFD) sites—Corvette Early Years (CEY) project from April 2002–2005. CEY set out to create a community where child care, kindergarten, school, health and community programs and services work together to create a seamless program for all young children and their families. Joanne's job was to coordinate the partners and seek opportunities to enhance existing capacity through increased collaboration and integration.

Kindergarten teachers, ECEs, and family resource staff met regularly to plan program activities, and look at early intervention strategies. Joanne says that integrating staff in multiple areas provides support for the team, for parents and children, and opportunities to exchange ideas on curriculum. Everyone benefits in the end, but it requires leadership and commitment to get there.

Joanne says that Toronto First Duty was, and is, an exciting, innovative initiative—you can never be sure where it will go next. In addition to its strong ECE focus, TFD involves parenting and health promotion. Joanne says that family resource programs sometimes lack the child development focus, and child care often misses parenting opportunities. TFD has the flexibility to develop new programming that knits the various perspectives together.

(cont'd)

Joanne is now working for the City of Toronto in using her knowledge and experience of Toronto First Duty to inform the implementation of the new provincial program, Best Start in Toronto.

For Joanne, working at CEY was like going back to her career roots in Great Britain, where her first early childhood care experience was working with others in a team. Born in England in the 1960s, Joanne attended college and received her NNEB in 1986. (This is a British early childhood education qualification received after completing a three-and-a-half-year postsecondary education program.) Joanne has worked as a nanny, in child care programs, community health centres, and family resource programs.

Joanne is now enrolled part-time in the ECE degree program at the University of Toronto (through continuing education). Her work with TFD rekindled interest in early childhood education. Previous child care experiences had turned her off because of the custodial nature of the work, and the lack of emphasis on programming, child development, and curriculum. But Toronto First Duty has demonstrated a program delivery model that allows early childhood educators to practice a profession rather than focus on caretaking tasks.

Social necessity. The work of a profession is essential to the well-being of a society, and society would be weakened if the profession did not function. There are few in the early childhood field who do not believe in the absolute importance of the nurturance and development of children in the first eight years of life. Increasingly, public attention and support have been drawn to this truth by the advocacy efforts of practitioners. The longitudinal studies on effects of early childhood education offer empirical evidence about these previously more subjective ideas. But the lack of public respect and fiscal support for early childhood programs suggests that society does not fully understand the absolute necessity of these supports for children and families.

Altruism. A profession is said to be altruistic when it is directed toward service instead of profits and is performed unselfishly, with an emphasis on social goals. From the beginning, early childhood education has been grounded in principles of social improvement of the lives of children and families. Early childhood educators certainly rank highly in this characteristic of professionalism, since their salaries could be said to be truly sacrificial, and their concerns are with children and families.

Autonomy. Professionals are said to be autonomous when clients do not dictate what services are to be delivered, or how they are to be delivered. Early childhood educators are in the somewhat complicated position of defining children, parents, and society as clients and are challenged by trying to respond to various opposing ideas about goals and methods for practice. For example, what does the teacher do when parental demands suggest a curriculum that teachers feel is not in children's developmental interests? Or when the community defines family support systems that seem to usurp parental roles? Early childhood educators are often caught in the middle and are forced to respond to ideas that limit their autonomy. As they are often under the direction of school boards that argue for standards that teachers feel may not be in children's best interests, or of licensing requirements dictated by laypeople in the legislature, early childhood teachers are a long way from having the autonomy that would allow them to decide independently on optimal educational directions.

Distance from client. Since the practice of a profession requires applying knowledge to particular situations involving individuals, the relationship between professionals and those served is expected to be distinguished by emotional distance that would prevent clouded judgment. In this tradition, for example, doctors are not expected to treat members of their own families. Many practitioners in early education question this aspect of professionalism, noting that it is more important to meet children's needs for closeness and affection than to create professional distance. Early childhood teachers struggle with the idea of creating caring relationships with children and families while maintaining some distance that is helpful to all parties. Katz notes that maintaining an "optimum distance" allows teachers to be compassionate and caring and to exercise professional judgment, while protecting teachers from the dangers of emotional over-involvement and burnout.

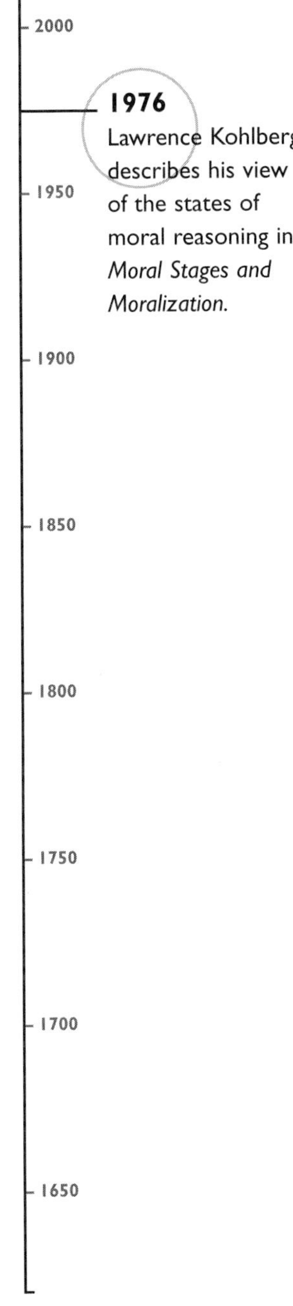

Code of ethics. A profession requires conformity to standards that are defined by a **code of ethics.** This code is adopted by all members of a profession to ensure there will be uniformly high standards of acceptable conduct. In addition, there is a professional body that institutes procedures for ensuring members do not violate this code. The NAEYC, after working through various stages to gain consensus, adopted and published a code of ethics in 1989. However, many practitioners are likely unaware of the code's existence, and there are no means of enforcing or disciplining those who violate its precepts. Nevertheless, the discussions that have ensued among professionals during the development of the code, and since, are a part of the process of defining the issues that unite the profession. A little later in this chapter, we will examine the code and its meaning for early childhood educators.

Standards of practice. Professions adopt standards of practice to ensure that professionals apply uniform procedures and principles in response to typical situations using their best professional judgment, and that no professional's behaviour will fall below the standards. One area still lacking in professionalization of the early childhood field is the identification of typical situations, as Lilian Katz points out in her classic discussion of how a professional early childhood teacher would teach in the situation where children are in a conflict over a tricycle (Katz, 1984). But a step toward standards of practice was taken when the NAEYC adopted the position statements on developmentally appropriate practice in 1987, and on curriculum and assessment in 1992. The discussions, debate, and the refining of these position statements will continue to move practitioners toward a profession with clear standards, as well as toward a fuller understanding of the nature of their work.

Prolonged training. A major characteristic of a profession is that entrants are required to undergo extensive training, with requirements for entry that screen out individuals. The training is specialized and contains a common core of knowledge. The training is also expected to be difficult. By stretching cognitive abilities, it is more extensive than daily practice requires, and it is offered by accredited training institutions. In addition, regular continuing education is systematically required of the profession's practitioners.

As you will recall from our examples at the beginning of this chapter, there are enormous variations in the amounts and types of preservice and in-service training required of early childhood educators, ranging from almost nothing at all to advanced degrees. Further, because of the shortages of caregivers, trained or otherwise, there are virtually no entry requirements for practitioners, other than

Early childhood educators are guided by standards of practice.

age and minimal literacy, in many settings. In too many cases, quality of programs is compromised by the lack of training and the acceptance of unprepared and unqualified workers. This is a complex dilemma that relates to some of the challenges regarding wages and status of the work that we discussed in Chapter 6. Yet, as we saw in that chapter, the career lattice plan attempts to respond to the varying entry points and training options that currently exist in the field, while facilitating professionalization for all who are employed in programs for young children.

Specialized knowledge. There is fairly universal agreement that a profession is work that involves specialized knowledge and skills that are based on a systematic body of principles. The knowledge is abstract, relevant to practice, and expressed in technical terminology; it is also exclusive, known only to those who have been trained in the profession. In as much as developmentally appropriate practice is an attempt to base decisions about best practices for young children on child development research and current knowledge of learning, this offers a body of specialized knowledge to trained early childhood teachers. When, however, untrained teachers base their actions on goodwill and what comes naturally, they are likely using the best intuitions about childrearing, which parents and laypeople have used for generations.

"The problem for childcare workers is that the care of normal preschoolers is very familiar to everyone," and especially to their parent-clients. Thus for early childhood education, the main struggle with clients is to be acknowledged as "professional . . . to make the status leap from babysitter to educator" (Joffe, 1977, p. 22).

It is not surprising, therefore, that when these teachers base their actions on intuition, they do not garner the professional respect they deserve.

In considering these eight characteristics of being a professional, you can see that the idea of a semiprofession, or of not quite achieving full professional status, has some validity. Yet the impressive progress that has been made in the past decade or so, provides hope, and this progress has brought early childhood education closer to becoming a true profession.

However, saying that you are a professional doesn't make it so; others have to perceive you as professional. Vander Ven (1988) suggests that professionalization refers to the public recognition of, and demand for, a specialized service that can be provided only by people prepared to do it. It will require the joint efforts of us all to make this kind of professionalism a reality. It is this movement toward professionalism that will overcome some of the challenges discussed in Chapter 6 and in Chapter 9.

Spodek et al. (1988) define seven questions that need to be the focus of efforts toward professionalism.

- How do we establish standards of quality for practitioners in the field?
- What standards of early childhood professionalism are reasonable in our field?
- How should entry to the field be determined?
- Should the field of early childhood education become more inclusive or more exclusive?
- How should standards be applied, and by whom?
- How should gender and economic issues be dealt with?
- How do we define professional knowledge and values?

Silin (1985) injects a cautionary note into these discussions about professionalism, noting that "early childhood education has a unique history that needs to be taken into account when exploring these issues" (p. 42). He suggests that our authority as professionals is not only based on knowledge of child development but also on moral, ethical, and aesthetic notions of what is right and true, knowledge that is not highly valued in our society. Therefore, too much emphasis on a search for professional status through "pedagogic reforms or technical knowledge" (p. 45) might deflect attention from relevant questions about the need for socio-economic and philosophical changes in society at large.

While the discussion of professionalism is ongoing, it is worth noting that even some leaders in the field recognize these kinds of concerns, as well as the benefits inherent in the idea of professionalizing. Specific concerns include

- the possibility that professionals will become separated from contact with children, as happens when increased qualifications and status are associated with positions that remove professionals from the classroom;
- parents' concern that increasing training and professionalism of early childhood teachers will mean increasing institutionalization and uncaring environments for children;
- a wish to avoid the hierarchical systems that result when distinctions are made between nonprofessionals, paraprofessionals, and more highly trained professionals;
- the increased cost of services that comes with improved compensation that is necessary for raising the level of professionalism; and

2000
1950
1900
1850
1800
1750
1700
1650

1977
All provinces passed legislation enabling their governments to take advantage of the federal funding.

1978
The world's first test-tube baby, "Baby Louise," is born in England.

1979

Longitudinal study done by Lazar et al. reports that there are significant, lasting effects of the Head Start programs.

Action Day Care is established in Toronto. It is an organization of child care activists—parents, caregivers, and other supporters—who are calling for universal child care.

The United Nations officially names the "Year of the Child."

- the possibility of excluding individuals who typically are denied access to higher education because of economic factors, yet who are needed in early childhood education to represent the cultural diversity of our society.

But the advantages of enhancing professionalism are unmistakable. The benefits include

- better care and education for children, resulting from a shared knowledge base;
- consistency across the settings and developmental continuity between programs;
- ethical behaviour;
- shared meanings and expanded knowledge; and
- improved compensation (Willer and Bredekamp, 1993).

Willer and Bredekamp (1993) express the problem of professionalism in a field that includes a wide variety of configurations of experience, training, and entry into the field. Drawing particular lines to show acceptable criteria for entry into the field will "always be too high for some and too low for others, and as the field changes over time, it will likely become obsolete" (p. 64).

It may be more useful to focus on the process of *professionalizing* and on the concept of *professionalism*, rather than on the *professional*. Defining early childhood educators as professional assumes that everyone who works with young children is involved in a process of professional development. *Professionalism* is the belief in the vision and ideals of a profession that guide daily practice. *Professionalization* describes the kinds of activities and actions that an early childhood educator or the early childhood workforce as a whole use to achieve the goal of a profession.

As a beginning early childhood educator, it is important that you recognize there is work to be done in the profession as a whole but also begin to think of yourself as a member of a profession that has made—and continues to make—major contributions to Canadian families and society. This recognition will allow you to begin with a sense of self-respect and will enable you to represent the educated and articulate practitioners who work to gain public recognition of the value of early childhood education. Your program of training will help you see how your own competence and knowledge are developing as you progress through courses and practicums. You will see your own movement on the continuum toward increasingly professional behaviour and attitudes. As time goes by, you can work more effectively with children and families, truly representing the best of professional practice, and also contribute to this growing profession.

Professionalization of the Early Childhood Workforce in Canada

The professionalization of the Canadian early childhood workforce includes the following components:

- core knowledge;
- codes of ethics;
- standards of practice;
- credentialing;

- self-governance; and
- professional development.

In this chapter we will look at the six components and their current status in the Canadian context.

Core Knowledge

One of the prerequisites to the recognition of early childhood education and care as a profession is identifying the **core knowledge** that defines the early childhood profession. A characteristic of any profession is a specialized body of knowledge and skills shared by all its members. This core of common knowledge is defined by answering these two questions (Willer, 1994):

1. "Is this knowledge or skill required of every early childhood professional, regardless of level or setting or professional role?" (p. 13). That is, does every early childhood teacher have to know and be able to do this in order to be effective?
2. "Does the sum of this body of knowledge and competencies uniquely distinguish the early childhood professional from all other professionals?" (p. 13). That is, although other professionals may share some of this knowledge, is most of it different from that required by other professionals?

Core knowledge in early childhood education and care, or what an early childhood educator needs to be able to do, was described in Chapter 4. This description was compiled from a number of initiatives that have identified the key skills and competencies—or core knowledge—for early childhood educators working in early childhood development settings. It is adapted to reflect the core knowledge needed to fulfill the occupational requirements in the Research into Practice box on page 232.

The core knowledge of the early childhood workforce combines both theoretical and practical knowledge. Elaine Ferguson from Child Care Connections in Nova Scotia has written extensively on the need to recognize and value both theory and practice elements of core knowledge. She recognizes the "importance of a [theoretical] foundation in early childhood education and care and the practice skills necessary to integrate the theory into developmentally appropriate practice" (Ferguson, 1997, p. 2). Ferguson (1995) cautions us to remember this balance and to not devalue or forget the less-visible skills of practical caring as we move forward with more precise definitions of our core knowledge.

In the United States, a similar body of core knowledge has been identified by comparing common elements in the guidelines for professional teacher preparation programs at the associate and baccalaureate levels (NAEYC, 1991; 1995). These common components suggest that all early childhood educators should be able to do the following:

- demonstrate an understanding of *child development* and apply this knowledge in practice;
- *observe and assess children's behaviour* in planning and individualizing teaching practices and curriculum;
- establish and maintain a *safe and healthy environment* for children;

2000

1980
United States has the highest percentage of children living in poverty of all western nations, a figure that continues to rise throughout the 1980s and 90s.

1950

1900

Toronto Board of Education releases its *Comprehensive Child Care Report.*

1850

1980s
Nobody's Perfect, a parenting program, is developed through public health groups in Atlantic Canada and is widely adopted across Canada.

1800

1750

1700

1650

- *plan and implement a developmentally appropriate curriculum* that advances all areas of children's learning and development, including social, emotional, intellectual, and physical competence;
- establish supportive relationships with children and implement developmentally appropriate techniques of *guidance and group management;*
- establish and maintain positive and productive *relationships with families;*
- support the development and learning of individual children, recognizing that children are best understood in the context of *family, culture, and society;* and
- demonstrate an understanding of the early childhood profession and make a commitment to *professionalism.* (Willer, 1994, p. 13).

Phillips (1994) identifies five themes that address content that every professional in the field should know:

1. children develop in context;
2. strategies for working with children are constructed each day;
3. effective practice requires a comprehensive set of skills;
4. early childhood professionals know they belong to a profession; and
5. even skilled professionals have limitations.

In recent years the shift from a focus on centre-based preschool to one that is inclusive of all children from infancy through age twelve in home- and centre-based programs and related early childhood services has changed the core of knowledge that early childhood educators need. Early childhood educators gain core knowledge from professional preparation programs, experiences in early childhood education and care settings, and ongoing professional development.

Everything that is learned is used, as professionals increasingly refine their skills and broaden their knowledge. This ongoing discussion about what early

MAKING IT HAPPEN

The Theory and Practice of Early Childhood Education and Care

An early childhood educator will

- ensure that the physical environment and daily practices of caregiving promote the *health, safety, and well-being* of children in their care;
- establish a *working partnership with families* that supports their responsibilities to their children;
- develop and maintain a responsive relationship with each child and the group of children to *guide children's behaviour and manage group dynamics;*
- plan and provide daily learning opportunities, routines, and activities that promote *positive child development;*
- *observe and assess* children's activity and behaviour;
- act in a manner consistent with the *principles of fairness, equity, and diversity* to support the development and learning of individual children within the context of family, culture, and society; and
- work in *partnership with other community members* to support the well-being of families.

Source: Adapted from Beach et al. (1998), p. 4.

childhood professionals need to know will enrich and include, rather than stagnate and exclude.

Codes of Ethics

We noted earlier in the chapter that a profession has a code of ethics, which is a "statement of principle that governs moral behaviour and ethical decisions" (Beach et al., 1998, p. 129). In Canada several professional organizations have developed code of ethics statements for early childhood educators, to be used as a guide in making day-to-day decisions.

Early childhood educators are frequently faced with ethical dilemmas in their work with young children and their families.

- What would you do when a parent demanded to know who bit her child?
- What would you do when a co-worker complained to you about another co-worker's treatment of a child?
- What would you do if a neighbour told you she heard bad things about the last centre you worked in?
- What would your responsibility be when another teacher told you that symptoms made her suspect child abuse, but that she was afraid to report it?

Often, early childhood educators have to take action in situations in which all the facts are not known, or there is no single course of action that is clearly right or wrong. It is sometimes difficult to decide what an ethical response might be. Making ethical decisions and taking ethical actions in early childhood education and care may require being able to see beyond short-term consequences to consider long-range consequences.

When you work in early childhood education and care settings, you will be asked to make many decisions about appropriate behaviour. Some of these decisions will require more than your accumulated knowledge of child development or educational practice. Some will pose genuine moral dilemmas, where you have to weigh your actions carefully in considering the parties involved.

The issues raised above, and others like them, are answered only by considering professional ethics, or the system of morals that defines a profession's proper work practices. A code of ethics is "a set of statements that helps us to deal with the temptations inherent in our occupations . . . helps us to act in terms of that which we believe to be right rather than what is expedient—especially when doing what we believe is right carries risks" (Katz, 1991, p. 3). Such risks could be losing a job or alienating others with whom one must work. A code expresses the profession's belief about correct, rather than expedient, behaviour; about good, rather than merely practical, actions; and about what professionals must never do or condone, for the good and protection of those they serve.

The value in having an explicit code is that members have a document that helps them go past their intuition and individual beliefs to focus on core professional values; "it is not so much what I care about but rather what the good early childhood educator should care about" (Kipnis, 1987, p. 28). The code can remind early childhood educators of their priorities and responsibilities, and it can provide solid guidance and professional support for the decisions and behaviour of an individual early childhood educator.

Early childhood educators face ethical decisions each day.

The Early Childhood Educators of British Columbia (ECEBC) developed a code of ethics statement in 1992, which guides early childhood educators in their daily professional practice. Early childhood educators in that organization adopted the ECEBC Code of Ethics after a considerable period of discussion and consultation with members, government representatives, and college and university faculty. It has been a model for the development of code of ethics statements in other provincial organizations. In 2004, the Canadian Child Care federation adopted a Code of Ethics that was adapted from the ECEBC Code of Ethics as part of its occupational standards for child care practitioners (Doherty, 2003). This is becoming the pan-Canadian early childhood educator Code of Ethics.

In the United States, the NAEYC developed its code of ethical conduct gradually, after gaining insights from many professionals and practitioners. The NAEYC board appointed an ethics commission to explore and clarify the early childhood profession's understanding of its ethics. The commission surveyed members to learn concerns, held workshops to identify and explore issues, and followed up with another survey of members to help formulate principles of ethical action. After further refining a draft code, the NAEYC's governing board approved the final document in July 1989. (The National Education Association has had a code of ethics since 1929 for teachers in school systems; however, there is nothing in the current code about parent-teacher relationships, so the NAEYC code is likely more relevant to your practice in early education.) The preamble states that the focus of the guidelines is on daily practice with children and their families in programs and classrooms, although many of the provisions also apply to specialists who do not work directly with children.

Standards of Practice

Standards of practice indicate the skills and abilities needed to perform tasks effectively. Included are standards of performance; input standards, or the skills and knowledge an individual brings to an occupation; and process standards, or the tasks required by an occupation (Employment & Immigration Canada, 1993).

> In child care, supporting and fostering child well-being and development (performance standards) requires the provision of certain experiences (process standards). The extent to which experiences are appropriate and effective depends, in part, on the skills, knowledge, and abilities of the child care provider (input standards) (Doherty, 1998, p. 1).

MAKING IT HAPPEN

Code of Ethics, Canadian Child Care Federation

Child care practitioners

- promote the health and well-being of all children
- enable all children to participate to their full potential in environments that are carefully planned to serve individual needs and to facilitate the child's progress
- demonstrate caring for children in all aspects of their practice
- work in partnership with parents, recognizing that parents have primary responsibility for the care of their children, valuing their commitment to their children and supporting them in meeting their responsibilities to their children
- work in partnership with colleagues and other service providers to support the well-being of children and their families
- work in ways to enhance human dignity in trusting, caring and co-operative relationships that respect the worth and uniqueness of the individual
- pursue, on an ongoing basis, the knowledge, skills and self-awareness needed to be professionally competent
- demonstrate integrity in all of their professional relationships

Source: Canadian Child Care Federation, 2003.

Standards of practice are useful to a profession in establishing its own benchmarks of quality beyond the basics of regulatory requirements and contributing to the overall quality of early childhood education and care settings (Griffin, 1994). Teaching and nursing professional organizations establish and monitor standards of practice for their practitioners (Beach et al., 1998). Standards of practice can be used along with the body of core knowledge to guide professional preparation and development, to establish criteria for certifying early childhood educators, and to provide a basis for job descriptions and performance evaluation procedures. A coherent standard of practice statement that has broad support and endorsement can be a useful tool in informational advocacy activities aimed at raising public understanding of value of early childhood educators' work.

The Canadian Child Care Federation and the Association of Canadian Community Colleges have prepared occupational standards for practitioners in child care settings (Doherty, 2003). Occupational standards are written descriptions of the knowledge, skills, and abilities required to do a specific job in a competent fashion and the behaviours that are acceptable with recipients of the service and with colleagues. The standards are applicable to early childhood educators working in regulated child care, preschool and nursery school programs, family child care, and family support programs. The standards are designed to identify specific skills and abilities necessary to perform required tasks in a competent manner.

The occupational standards include (Doherty, 2003, p. 1):

1. Protect and promote the psychological and physical safety, health, and well-being of each child.
2. Develop and maintain a warm, caring, and responsive relationship with each child and with the group of children.
3. Plan and provide daily experiences that support and promote each child's physical, emotional, social, communication, cognitive, ethical, and creative development.
4. Use observations to assess children's skills, abilities, interests, and needs.
5. Recognize signs and symptoms of emotional or developmental delays or challenges and take appropriate action.
6. Establish and maintain an open, cooperative relationship with each child's family.
7. Establish and maintain supportive, collaborative relationships with other community service providers working in the child care setting.
8. Establish and maintain collaborative relationships with other community service providers working with the child.
9. Reflect on one's own knowledge, attitudes, and skills, and take appropriate action.

The Canadian Child Care Federation and its provincial/territorial affiliates have developed and adopted the Occupational Standards for child care practitioners (Doherty, 2003). The standards include input and process standards, which are drawn from previous efforts to identify the elements of competent knowledge, skills, and abilities.

Credentialing

Credentials are the evidence that an individual has both the knowledge and skills needed to practice in a specific occupation. **Credentialing** is the process of evaluating knowledge and skills. Doherty (1997) defines three methods of credentialing in the North American early childhood education and care: equivalency validation, certification or licensing of early childhood education graduates, and competency-based assessment. We will define each of these processes and consider their application in Canada.

- Equivalency validation credentials verify that an early childhood educator who does not meet a particular jurisdiction's qualification requirements has comparable or equivalent education and experience. All provinces and territories that have educational qualification requirements for early childhood educators in early childhood education and care settings have some established procedures for assessing qualifications and credentials from other jurisdictions.
- Credentials of graduates from ECE certificate, diploma, and degree programs may be issued by the government, as a license or classification, or they may be

issued by a professional organization, as voluntary recognition or certification. For example, in British Columbia, early childhood educators are required to have a government license to practice to be recognized as qualified staff in a regulated child care centre or preschool. To be eligible for the license to practice, early childhood educators must have an ECE academic qualification and documented work experience. Volunteer certification is provided by a few professional organizations and is discussed in more detail later in this chapter.

- Competency-based assessment "testifies that a person whose formal educational qualifications related to child care are less than those required for entry into the field has the practical competencies required to provide competent child care" (Doherty, 2003, p. 5). The only competency-based assessment process (outside of prior-learning assessment in colleges and universities) is in Manitoba and is conducted by the provincial government.

Voluntary Certification

Voluntary certification recognizes and endorses the educational qualifications and, sometimes, the performance levels of early childhood educators, regardless of their work setting. It is a mechanism to monitor standards of practice and to promote both the quality of early childhood education and care services and the professionalism of the early childhood workforce.

Three provincial professional organizations offer voluntary certification to their members: the Association of Early Childhood Educators of Ontario (AECEO), the Early Childhood Professional Association of Alberta (ECPAA), and the Certification Council of Early Childhood Education of Nova Scotia (CCECENS).

- The AECEO requires eligible applicants to have an ECE diploma or equivalent, to be members of the organization, and to be working in an early childhood education and care setting for at least twenty hours a week. Applicants submit a written personal profile of their philosophy of early childhood education and take an examination within a year of their original application. The examination is based on the expected learning outcomes for students graduating from Ontario's community college ECE diploma programs. Once certification is granted to an early childhood educator, she is a professional member of the organization and maintains her certification credentials as long as she remains a member of the AECEO (Trainer, 1998).
- The ECPAA certification process requires that applicants have educational qualifications, experience, and a letter from their current employer describing their work performance. Neither observation nor examinations are required.
- The CCECENS certification process stipulates that eligible applicants must have an ECE education qualification and at least two years' experience working in an early childhood education and care setting with young children. Applicants are observed at their workplace by a facilitator (who is an early childhood educator with CCECENS certification) to assess their performance against fifteen standards of practice, which have been developed by the CCECENS. The process can be repeated several times until the applicant meets the criteria. At this point a validator reviews written evaluations, observes the applicant, and makes a recommendation to the CCECENS, where the final decision is made. A certified

2000
1950
1900
1850
1800
1750
1700
1650

1981
Laurier Lapierre and Ada Scherman write *To Herald a Young Child.*

The Ontario Coalition for Better Day Care (later renamed the Ontario Coalition for Better Child Care) is established.

1982

Mary Ainsworth continues the discussion of attachment in infancy, in *Early Caregiving and Later Patterns of Attachment.*

There are 125 000 day care spaces in Canada.

The Toronto Board of Education decides to facilitate the development of parent-operated centres in vacant classroom space.

The second National Child Care Conference is held in Winnipeg. Child care activists and early educators pass resolutions calling for a national day care act, national standards, and support the goal of universally accessible day care for all Canadians.

early childhood educator maintains her certification by paying an annual fee and by providing proof of her participation in professional development.

The voluntary certification processes in Canada aim to improve quality and increase professionalism. However, there are some limitations. Only a small proportion of early childhood educators in each of these provinces is certified. Although in some early childhood education and care programs, certification is recognized and valued, there is little overall recognition or motivation to become certified, as it is not required. In both Alberta and Ontario the ECE educational qualification establishes eligibility and, therefore, provides the standards of practice to be assessed. In Nova Scotia the process has introduced an assessment of an early childhood educator's practice based on criteria established by other practitioners. Unfortunately, the automatic renewal in certification in the three provinces fails to provide a mechanism to ensure that early childhood educators' knowledge remains current (Doherty, 1997).

Self-Governance

The self-governance of a profession refers to its authority to establish bodies to regulate its members and their practice through certification, standards of practice, discipline, and requirements for professional education. Self-governance recognizes bodies outside government or organizations that represent the economic or professional development interest of practitioners. The recognition is usually embedded in legislation.

Provincial/territorial professional organizations have taken on tasks—such as voluntary certification, development of codes of ethics, consultation with governments on issues related to equivalency validation, and appropriate course content for professional education programs—which are often associated with self-governance. There is only one self-governing body in Canada, the Association of Early Childhood Educators, Newfoundland.

The Certification Council of Early Childhood Education, Nova Scotia, the Association of Early Childhood Educators Ontario, and the Early Childhood Educators of British Columbia have proposed legislated or mandated self-regulatory bodies, which would regulate early childhood educators within each of the provincial jurisdictions. To date, the proposals have not been adapted.

The Ontario government is working with the child care sector and early childhood educators to establish a College of Early Childhood Educators, a self-regulating professional body. Members of the College will be required to meet entry standards and continuing competence in order to be licensed with the College. It is anticipated that certification and licensing with the College will be required in regulated early childhood settings (AECEO, 2005).

Professional Development

Not all early childhood professional education and development is part of postsecondary education programs or part of professional preparation (Beach, 1999). In fact, most of the professional preparation we have considered in this chapter will equip you only with the entry-level skills and knowledge of an early childhood educator. Most early childhood educators take part in other activities, often offered by professional organizations, which promote ongoing learning, professional development, and professional practice in working with young children and their families.

The range of development opportunities that promote skills and knowledge includes workshops, seminars, conferences, publications, and networking. These resources are offered by early childhood education and care organizations, government departments, community groups, family resource programs, family child care agencies, and child care organizations.

Publications

Most national and provincial/territorial organizations produce a regular newsletter for members. There are also a number of journals prepared for the early childhood workforce that report on research studies, policy developments, and innovations in early childhood education and care programs.

- *Interaction* is a bilingual journal published bimonthly by the Canadian Child Care Federation. It includes articles on current research and public policy in early childhood education and care and related fields. It also profiles individuals and organizations from across the country and provides a comprehensive listing of upcoming events.
- *Young Child* is a peer-reviewed journal from the Canadian Association of Young Children that reports on applied research findings and innovative models of practice from early childhood education and care programs.
- *Canadian Journal of Research in Early Childhood Education* is a bilingual journal that features Canadian research projects related to early childhood education and care. Published twice yearly by Concordia University in Montreal, its mandate is to inform early childhood educators of findings from past and current Canadian research. It also includes reviews of early childhood education texts and notes upcoming conferences and seminars.

Professionalization Dilemmas

As the early childhood workforce becomes more like a profession in Canada, it is faced with a number of dilemmas:

- As the workforce becomes more professionalized, a hierarchy develops, and the direct work with young children is the least valued and rewarded.
- The drive for increased professionalization is often isolated and separate from other challenges facing early childhood educators.
- Currently, only a small percentage of qualified early childhood educators and an even smaller percentage of all caregivers are members of professional organizations.
- The numbers of early childhood educators who have educational or equivalent qualifications are increasing in early childhood education and care settings, but most individuals working with young children do not have them. The professionalization of this workforce may exclude those many experienced caregivers and limit the participation of caregivers from particular ethnocultural backgrounds.
- The diversity of work environments in early childhood education and care programs makes it difficult to find common ground to build professional practices for early childhood educators.

2000
1950
1900
1850
1800
1750
1700
1650

1983
The Canadian Day Care Advocacy Association (later the Canadian Child Care Advocacy Association) is established.

Howard Gardner publishes *Frames of Mind*, describing his theory of multiple intelligences.

- Many of these issues are raised and discussed in the course of the child care sector study. The final report notes that the early childhood workforce "has the opportunity to define a new form of professionalism which includes all caregivers who want to provide quality experiences for young children and their families, and recognizes various levels of credentials, experience and employment setting" (Beach et al., 1998, p. 128).

RESEARCH INTO PRACTICE

Coming of Age

Within the last couple of generations in Canada, providing child care services for pay began to emerge as a legitimate occupation, with recognized standards, training, and public recognition. This process is still incomplete and most of the shared concerns and future tasks articulated in this report [Child Care Sector Study] are related to the intense desire and need by child care workers to define themselves as a legitimate, respected, and reasonably compensated occupation and to get the public acceptance and legislative recognition they deserve.

Child care as an occupation (or series of related occupations) is marked by its origins. For most of this century, in North America at least, the task of raising children has been one that women were expected to do by staying at home when children were young. As women moved into the labour force, they typically made arrangements through the family and extended family, or with neighbours, to provide child care, generally in exchange for non-monetary types of rewards (as part of intra-family obligations, or mutual help arrangements with neighbours, etc.).

Then, it would have seemed foolish to suggest that those providing child care needed special training; women were assumed to learn these talents at their mothers' knees. Child care as a distinct occupation requiring formal education and ongoing training, regulations, and standards, has taken a long time to emerge from this history. The attitudes of many toward child care and its workers is rooted here. Current lack of self-organization and divisions between different types of caregivers have much to do with this history.

There are many types of child care and of caregivers. This report [Child Care Sector Study] and the general set of occupations with which it deals, include early childhood educators in licensed centre care, in nursery schools, and in licensed family day care homes. It includes nannies and informal caregivers who organize themselves into associations and who provide care as a continuing business or occupation. It does not include the very heterogeneous group of caregivers who provide care informally within their own neighbourhoods and may provide care for only a short period.

For all of the caregivers with whom this Report is concerned, a central objective is to convince parents, the general public, and governments that there are, at least on average, dramatic differences in reliability and positive child development effects of the care they provide, and that are provided in a more ad-hoc way by this part of the informal sector. Care in this less organized part of the informal sector (partly because of its favourable tax treatment, partly because of its poorer facilities, partly because its workers do not have good labour market alternatives) is typically cheaper than for other child care services. One way of interpreting the central shared objective of child care workers as we have described it, comes down to convincing parents, the general public, and governments that the service they provide is well worth its extra cost.

Workers across the child care sector have a strong interest in convincing parents, the public and governments that better quality child care matters—that it has very important differential effects on child development, socially, intellectually, emotionally, etc. Similarly, child care workers have a collective interest in anything that educates parents about child care quality and that helps them to know how to judge the different aspects of quality. Unless parents appreciate the distinctive contribution of good child care, there will be no basis to resolve issues of lack of respect, appreciation, poor remuneration, etc. that plague the sector. There are many ways to contribute to this: supporting studies of the effects of quality child care on children's development by add-ons to the National Longitudinal Survey of Children and Youth, accreditation of centres and homes (seal of quality), public awards and honours drawing attention to good quality child care, etc. This list is only suggestive; there are lots of other ways of studying, evaluating, and generally raising the profile of quality issues in child care.

Child care is leaving its adolescence and coming of age; there are difficult issues of direction to resolve at this crucial time. It is the end of a rather long period of growth in all parts of the sector as the demand for non-parental paid child care has grown largely for mothers' labour force reasons. Although there may be continuing growth, it will not be so rapid and will depend very much on government initiatives, like the ones recently announced in Quebec (of course, it is unclear whether they will have the budget to fulfill this commitment).

The predominant governmental trends are still in the opposite direction: move to the CHST from CAP, failure to live up to the Red Book commitments, reduction of support for the licensed sector, encouragement of use of informal care, opening subsidies to all segments of the informal sector, etc. What government does matters a great deal to the future of child care and child care workers.

The child care sector is beset with a series of environmental issues such as: perception of a lack of recognition of the value of the work done, concern about low pay and poor benefits, public perception that child care is, generally, not a lifelong occupation but a temporary way station, concern that there is no career ladder or reward for improving your skills in the sector. These issues appear to be linked to the lack of clarity in the sector and amongst parents and the public about what the main purpose of child care is.

From the point of view of many parents and many child care providers, it appears that facilitating labour force participation is the key objective of child care. The implication is that child development occurs at home, or later, in the child's life at school, and that a warm, caring, custodial child care arrangement is quite satisfactory. The further implication is that good child care is cheap child care, that the convenience of the parents is the paramount concern, and that the caregiver need only be someone with whom the parent feels comfortable (similar background, education level, etc.).

The alternative perspective is that the key purpose of child care is child development. In this view, trained child care workers should be seen as distinctly different from untrained ones: there should be pressure to increase the length and intensity of child care training; there should be tools which facilitate the choice by parents of good, rather than not-so-good child care centres; and centres should be competing to hire the best quality staff.

The point of the above discussion is that it makes sense for child care workers of different types to join in working to clarify in the public mind how child care should be seen. This choice determines one's attitude to most issues of public policy toward the sector and toward the compensation and regulation of the workers in it.

The dilemma facing child care workers is a difficult one. Child care workers work in an industry/sector which is extremely labour-intensive, and in which, compared to other labour-intensive sectors, there is no obvious way that computerization, or intelligent rethinking of the service provided can lower the amount of labour required. This means that every dollar of wages or benefits received by workers, translates directly into higher cost child care. And, every improvement of the staff-child ratio, or the ratio of trained to untrained staff, directly increases the cost of child care. This is not a cheap service either. Child care is a big-ticket item.

In a country like Canada, in which the price of labour is relatively high, good child care is seen by many as a luxury item. Many parents settle for not-very-good child care (you can see this by looking at the average expenditures of families on child care; some spend a lot, but many spend not very much).

(cont'd)

Coming of Age (cont'd)

Child care has, then, a choice (a difficult choice) of self-definition: either it goes for what parents are able and willing to pay for, which is not-very-good child care (in this case, the downward pressure on wages and benefits is inevitable, but the private demand for the service will be strong), or, it goes for a strong child development, quality-enhancement, self-definition. This may be the right choice in the long run, but it requires both increased private and public dollars.

This means convincing parents and opinion leaders of the key importance of good child care in early years. It means continual public education programs and encouragement of research into what a difference quality child care makes. It might (or might not) mean accreditation programs to publicly distinguish good quality child care. It might (or might not) mean moves toward professionalization of the occupation (not in a narrow, craft unionist sense). It might (or might not) mean increased contact with kindergarten teachers to emphasize the similarity of the child development roles that these workers play. It might (or might not) mean encouraging investigation of how much difference a B.A. (E.C.E.) versus a two year diploma, versus a one-year certificate makes, and so on.

Consultation with the sector suggests that the second route is the one that child care workers should take and that various structures and processes should be established which could facilitate this.

It is within the above perspectives that we have to judge the current type of training that ECEs receive across the country. Is the level and type of education adequate and more than adequate? Are ECEs well prepared to provide a level and type of care that will be recognized as distinct and developmental? Do ECE schools do a good enough job trying to raise standards in the occupation (all parts)? Do they provide home care training? Do they effectively restrict entry into the occupation in a desirable way (improving quality, enhancing standards)? Do colleges require some level of academic performance in high school as a minimum condition for entry? Are workers well enough trained in communication skills to represent the occupation well to parents and others? Should there be room on the career ladder for university educated child care workers with in-depth knowledge about child development, education, child care programming, etc.?

We will need to reach conclusions on ways that child care workers can organize themselves to work collectively to get recognition for the skills and importance of their occupation. Is there a need for a sector council to work over time on common projects and interests related to quality promotion, encouragement of explicit standards of performance and training in different parts of the sector, of lobbying government to recognize the centrality of quality issues in relation to child development? Would moves toward professionalization hurt or help the occupation to come of age? What role should various child care associations/organizations play? What positive role do unions have in standardizing the pay and benefits of child care workers and encouraging a longer term view on the part of employers in the child care field? What do current and potential relationships with kindergarten teachers have to do with this?

Source: Gordon Cleveland (unpublished) prepared for the Child Care Sector Study (Beach, Bertrand & Cleveland, 1998), reprinted with permission.

Early Childhood Education and Care Organizations

There are early childhood education and care organizations and associations at the national, provincial/territorial, and local levels that support the early childhood workforce and advocate for its recognition. In addition to their involvement in advocacy and activities related to professionalism, these groups carry out a range of professional education and development activities.

The early childhood workforce is coming of age.

The Child Care Sector Study (Beach et al., 1998) found that organizations face several challenges in their ability to meet the needs of the early childhood workforce:

- Most organizations operate with little or no public funding and rely on considerable volunteer labour to carry out their activities.
- The ability of early childhood educators and early childhood education and care programs to sustain organizations through membership fees is limited, reflecting, in part, the low compensation that early childhood educators receive.
- Membership in early childhood education and care organizations is voluntary, and most early childhood educators do not belong to any organization.

Canadian Child Care Federation (CCCF)

The CCCF is a national organization committed to improving the quality of early childhood care and education services across Canada. Its membership includes thirteen affiliated provincial/territorial organizations, with a total of more than 9 000 members across Canada. The CCCF provides leadership to the early childhood workforce on a number of fronts, including development of national principles for quality early childhood education and care programs and guidelines for professional education programs. It also provides research, publications, conferences and workshops, and information services. The CCCF sponsors projects to develop a national framework for quality assurance and guidelines for family child care training, and is also working with the Association of Canadian Community Colleges to consider an accreditation process for ECE certificate and diploma programs in Canada.

Provincial/Territorial Early Childhood Education and Care Organizations

There is at least one organization in every province and territory (except for the Northwest Territories and Nunavut) that represents the early childhood workforce. These groups have grown from the needs of early childhood educators and do not have government-defined mandates.

MAKING IT HAPPEN

Early Learning and Child Care Organizations in Canada

Early childhood educators have access to professional, advocacy, and resource organizations across Canada. The following list is an overview of the organizations and resource groups and their primary purpose. You can find links to their Web sites at www.ece.nelson.com. There are also local groups that provide support to early childhood educators.

National

Canadian Child Care Federation
Works to improve quality of child care services across Canada, build an infrastructure for the early childhood education and care community, and provide extensive information and resource services. Includes thirteen provincial and territorial affiliate members. Provides a complete listing of all organizations, professional education and development programs, and related resource groups.

Child Care Advocacy Association of Canada

Advocates for comprehensive, universally accessible, high-quality, and nonprofit child care programs. The CCAAC works for:

- Child care as a cornerstone of progressive family policies.
- The right of all children to access a child care system supported by public funds.
- A child care system that is comprehensive, inclusive, accessible, affordable, high quality and non-profit.
- A range of child care services for children birth to twelve years.

Canadian Association for Young Children

Promotes professional development and communication among early childhood educators in child care programs and school settings.

Family Resource Programs Canada

Provides consultation and support for program development, publications, and professional development to a national network of family resource programs.

SpeciaLink

Promotes inclusion of children with special needs in child care and other community programs and provides research, resources and information, networking, and training to early childhood educators and related services.

Childcare Resource and Research Unit

Provides public education, consultation, and publications; organizes and disseminates information and resources; conducts child care-related research projects; and provides a circulating library and database of resources.

Child and Family Canada

On-line network of organizations related to child and family issues in Canada.

Newfoundland

Association of Early Childhood Educators, Newfoundland and Labrador
Provides awareness of quality child care and advocates for early childhood educators.

Prince Edward Island

Early Childhood Development Association, P.E.I.
Promotes knowledge of early childhood education, promotes professionalism, and provides support to membership.

Nova Scotia

Child Care Advocacy Association of Nova Scotia
Represents caregivers in nonprofit child care centres and family child care.

Nova Scotia Family Day Care Association

Provides networking opportunities for caregivers in regulated child care.

Certification Council of Early Childhood Education of Nova Scotia

Offers voluntary certification process for early childhood educators since 1988.

Child Care Professional Development Association of Nova Scotia

Provides licensure of child care practitioners.

Child Care Connection—Nova Scotia

Connects child care professionals to resources, promotes certification and administration, operates a resource centre library, and sponsors professional development events.

New Brunswick

Early Childhood Care and Education New Brunswick/Soin et Education to la Petite Enfance du Nouveau-Brunswick (ECCENB/SEPENB)
Represents child care workers and those who have an interest in quality child care.

(cont'd)

Early Learning and Child Care Organizations in Canada (cont'd)

Quebec

Quebec Association for Preschool Development
Promotes and supports child care administration.

Concentration Inter-régionale des garderies du Québec
Advocates for quality, nonprofit child care.

Association of Early Childhood Educators, Québec
Represents early childhood educators and promotes professionalism. Provides voluntary certification process for early childhood educators.

Association des services de garde en milieu scolaire du Québec
Promotes increased access to school-age child care.

Ontario

Association of Day Care Operators of Ontario
Represents and promotes private operators.

Association of Early Childhood Educators, Ontario (affiliate member of CCCF)
Represents early childhood educators and promotes professionalism. Provides voluntary certification process for early childhood educators.

Home Child Care Association of Ontario
Promotes and supports quality home child care, with primary focus on regulated home child care.

Ontario Network of Home Child Care Provider Groups
Promotes and advocates for family child care providers.

Ontario Coalition for Better Child Care
Advocates and promotes quality nonprofit child care and represents nonprofit child care programs.

Ontario Association of Family Resource Programs
Represents and provides support to provincial family resource programs.

Manitoba

Manitoba Child Care Association (CCCF affiliate)
Advocates for a quality child care system, represents nonprofit child care programs and regulated family child care, provides services to membership, and advances child care as a profession.

Saskatchewan

Saskatchewan Child Care Association (CCCF affiliate)
Supports caregivers in centre-based care and family child care.

Alberta

Alberta Child Care Network Association
A coalition of several recognized child care organizations within Alberta with representation from various stakeholders within government who have a vested interest in child care issues.

Alberta Family Day Care Association

Provides support to regulated family child care.

ECE Professional Association of Alberta (CCCF affiliate)

Supports ECE staff and promotes professional development. Provides voluntary certification process for early childhood educators.

B.C. Aboriginal Child Care Society

Supports Aboriginal communities in developing high quality, integrated child care services within Aboriginal culture and building an Aboriginal child care network in B.C.

Early Childhood Educators of British Columbia (CCCF affiliate)

Promotes and supports early childhood educators.

Western Canadian Family Child Care Association

Promotes, supports, and advocates for quality family child care.

British Columbia School Age Association

Promotes and supports school-age child care and represents school-age child care staff.

B.C. Coalition of Child Care Advocates

Promotes and advocates for quality child care.

Westcoast Child Care Resource Centre

Provides child care resources, information and referral services, and professional development with and through affiliate early childhood education and care organizations.

Yukon

Yukon Child Care Association
Promotes centre-based and family child care.

MAKING IT HAPPEN

Provincial Early Childhood Education and Care Organizations

The Association of Early Childhood Educators, Ontario (AECEO)

The AECEO is a professional organization concerned with the quality of care and education for young children. It provides leadership and vision as the unified voice of early education in Ontario. Its mission is to be the leader in promoting the professional development and recognition of early childhood educators, on behalf of children in Ontario.

The AECEO was established in 1950 as the Nursery Education Association of Ontario (NEAO). It evolved from the increasing demand for child care and nursery schools after World War II, the absence of government regulations, and the lack of formal training in child care studies.

In the early years, the AECEO worked tirelessly to foster the development of training programs. Cooperating with the Institute of Child Studies at the University of Toronto, Ryerson Polytechnical Institute (now Ryerson Polytechnical University), and the Ontario Agricultural College (now University of Guelph), the AECEO began some of the first courses in child studies. Later, under AECEO sponsorship, the extension departments of six Ontario universities began offering evening and summer training programs for those already working in the field. Parent resource centres were also set up in some localities.

In the 1960s, AECEO was a major help in the development of the two-year diploma program for the new community colleges. The diploma course is now the standard for qualification as a professional early childhood educator in Ontario. In 1964, the AECEO established a certification process to encourage individual achievement in formal early childhood education studies and practical experience.

In 1969, the organization changed its name to the Association for Early Childhood Education, Ontario (AECEO). In 1980, the AECEO held its first annual Week of the Child promotion, following the UN International Year of the Child in 1979. Every October a broad series of public events and professional development activities are sponsored across Ontario during the Week of the Child.

In 1993, the Association changed its name to the Association of Early Childhood Educators Ontario to better reflect its current mission, which is "to be the leader in promoting the professional development and recognition of early childhood educators, on behalf of the children of Ontario."

The AECEO has more than 2 500 members distributed across twenty-four branches that represent the entire province. It is governed by a board of directors with representation from the membership. Its strategic goals are

- to continue to strengthen the organization and base of the operations;
- to pursue legislative recognition for ECEs; and
- to enhance public education and awareness of the importance of quality early childhood education.

In 2005, the AECEO joined with the Ontario Coalition for Better Child Care and other provincial organizations to establish the Common Table for Childhood Development and Care to promote collaboration in advocacy and delivery of services to children and families in Ontario. The Common Table signals a new era of cooperation among early childhood educators in Ontario. The two organizations co-hosted a conference in 2006 and continue to work together to influence the provincial government's establishment of a College of Early Childhood Educators.

Sources: AECEO (2005), Beach et al. (2004), Thomas (2000),

Early childhood educators often seek out opportunities to share experiences and learn from their colleagues.

SUMMARY

As you have read about the work of professional organizations, it should be obvious that there are many resources and vehicles for early childhood educators to achieve professionalization, both as individuals and with colleagues.

Joining a professional organization as a student or new teacher is critical for professional awareness and growth.

REVIEW QUESTIONS

1. Describe several of the characteristics of a profession, and discuss how early childhood care and education matches the standard.
2. Name two major early childhood professional organizations, discussing the services of each.
3. Discuss the ECEBC code of ethics, its component parts, and its uses for early childhood educators.
4. Discuss the importance of the position statement on developmentally appropriate practice.

STUDY ACTIVITIES

1. Visit your school library to learn what journals from professional early childhood organizations are available. Read several articles from a representative issue, and write brief reports that indicate the kinds of knowledge you obtain. Examine the issues for regular features that would be helpful to early childhood teachers in their practice and in their learning about policy and wider issues of the profession.
2. Using your community resource guide and contacts with early childhood teachers, learn what professional organizations are available and used by teachers in your area. If possible, attend a local meeting. Talk with local teachers who are members of the organization to learn how they have benefited from their membership. If there are no local groups, call or write the nearest affiliate to get a listing of their current activities and to get on their mailing list, if possible.
3. Find out if there is a Week of the Young Child activity held in your community. If there is, find out how you and other students can become involved. If there is not, what could you do to initiate one?
4. With classmates, use the ECEBC code of ethics to discuss the following issues that could occur in a classroom.
   a. A parent asks an infant caregiver to please not feed the baby in the late afternoon, so that she can feed her at home and put her to sleep. The baby cries each day until her mother comes.
   b. A co-worker has discussed a family at your child care centre with her boyfriend's family, who ask you about the situation.
   c. A four-year-old is angry when his mother leaves him each morning, and he treats other children aggressively. The assistant teacher is bothered by the lead teacher's response, which is to put him in time-out for long periods.
   d. An early childhood educator is told by her supervisor that a child who is absent has contagious diarrhea, so teachers should wash hands carefully. The early childhood educator is surprised that a notice is not posted to inform parents.
   e. An early childhood educator working with three-year-olds is unaware when she is first employed, that the number of children in her room exceeds the adult-child ratio standards of the provincial/territorial day care regulations. When the licensing officer comes to inspect, the director tells him that the cook also works regularly in the program.
   f. A mother asks you not to let her four-year-old son nap in the afternoon, since he then wants to stay up late at night and she has to get up early to go to work. The child seems to need his nap to play happily in the afternoon.
5. Check out early childhood organizations in your province or territory at www.ece.nelson.com. Are there any student membership rates? What services are available?

KEY TERMS

code of ethics: Statements of a profession that govern moral behaviour and ethical decisions. The NAEYC adopted and published its early childhood code of ethics in 1989.

core knowledge: Basic knowledge a professional group acknowledges to be needed by all its members.

credentialing: Evaluating professional qualifications from recognized educational institutions or professional organizations.

professional: Practitioner who has met the standards of knowledge and performance required by a profession.

SUGGESTED READINGS

Buck, Linda. (1987, January). Directors: How to sell accreditation to staff, board, and parents. *Young Children,* 42 (2), 46–49.

Canadian Child Care Federation. (2000). *Tools for practitioners in child care settings: Standards of practice, code of ethics, guide to self-reflection.* Ottawa.

Doherty, G. (2003) *Occupational Standards.* Ottawa: Canadian Child Care Federation. http://www.cccf-fcsge.ca/subsites/training/pdf/occupational-final-e.pdf

Ferguson, E.E. (1995). *Child care . . . Becoming visible.* Halifax: Child Care Connection-Nova Scotia.

Ferguson, L. (1991). The child care crises: Realities of women's caring. In C. Baines, P. Evans, & S. Newysmith (Eds.), *Women's caring, feminist perspectives on social welfare.* Toronto: McClelland & Stewart, 21–36.

Radomski, Mary Ann. (1986, July). Professionalization of early childhood educators: How far have we progressed? *Young Children,* 41 (5), 20–23.

CHAPTER NINE
Advocacy

OBJECTIVES

After studying this chapter, students will be able to

- discuss the relationship between quality experiences for children, compensation, and economic conditions for the early childhood workforce, and accessibility to programs for families;
- identify personal and collective approaches to advocating for early child development programs and its workforce;
- recognize the role of advocacy organizations and other organizations in addressing the issues of quality, compensation, and accessibility; and
- discuss several personal actions that will contribute to successful growth as an early childhood educator and advocate.

Advocacy is the act of defending o0r stating a cause for yourself or another. The role of advocacy is played out within early childhood education and care settings and in the world at large. Personal advocacy involves our day-to-day actions that promote children's healthy development, support families, and recognize our own value. Public policy advocacy is the collective effort to address three interconnected issues within early childhood education and care programs and the early childhood workforce in Canada: quality, compensation, and accessibility. Informational advocacy seeks to raise public awareness of the importance of children's early years and the potential of early childhood education and care programs to contribute to healthy children, strong families, and cohesive communities.

In this expanding early childhood workforce, responses to the needs of children, families, and early childhood educators are propelling changes that affect us all. Some of these trends will strengthen the workforce itself, making it more likely that you will see enormous changes during your career. As you enter the early childhood workforce, it is important that you consider the complexity of these issues and decide how you can advocate for yourself and for the children and families with whom you work.

Before you read any further, note in your journal the ideas that you believe might be included in this discussion of advocacy issues. Think about the ideas you have encountered already in your own work experiences and in the course of your early childhood education studies. Reflect on the challenges raised in the first and second sections of this book, where you examined early child development programs and the early childhood workforce, and in Chapter 7, where you considered their historical development.

As you continue your ECE studies and embark on your journey as an early childhood educator, there are guidelines for personal daily practice. The most effective advocate for early childhood education and care programs is a dedicated, reflective practitioner. Your knowledge, skills, and abilities shape the daily lives of young children and families. You also influence the public (local and global) perceptions about how we should move the early child development agenda forward in the twenty-first century.

Early childhood educators are advocates for young children.

Personal Advocacy

Every early childhood educator can be a personal advocate for herself and for the children and families with whom she works, as well as for other early childhood educators, children, and families. Personal advocacy is based on the way in which you carry out your daily practice and communication with others. It can be as simple as gently correcting a friend or neighbour who suggests that what you do is "just babysitting—something anyone could do" or taking the initiative to ensure a child you are working with has access to needed specialized services. It may mean going out into your community to find out what types of early child development programs are really needed and wanted by families and then trying to match them with local resources.

Personal advocacy includes being a watchdog and a whistle-blower. As you learn about child development and appropriate practices, you are more likely to resist pressure to accept less-than-optimal conditions in early childhood settings. You will advocate for conditions that support the delivery of high-quality care and education. This means being aware of situations in your local communities that may have an adverse effect on children's health, safety, or well-being. For instance, there may be physical dangers in playgrounds or schoolyards or a need for safer crossing points on busy streets. Keeping yourself informed and becoming involved in making changes to improve children's environments are part of personal advocacy.

Children cannot vote on issues that affect them, but you can. You should be registered to vote where you live and exercise your right to vote during elections. To influence how you vote, you'll need to know which politicians represent you and keep an eye on how they vote on issues that affect children and early childhood education and care programs.

Public Policy Advocacy

In early education, public policy advocacy is the act of defending or stating the cause of early childhood education and care programs and the workforce. Kagan suggests public advocacy in child care and early education has three main rationales:

1. to safeguard what has been achieved;
2. to increase the capacity to provide services; and
3. to make important changes (Kagan, 1988).

In the current climate of deregulation, decentralization, and deficit-cutting, these will continue to be powerful motivations for early childhood educators to be involved in public policy advocacy.

MEET THE EARLY CHILDHOOD WORKFORCE

Jamie Kass

Jamie Kass is the National Child Care Co-ordinator for the Canadian Union of Postal Workers. She coordinates a $2 million fund that creates flexible, quality child care spaces for postal workers.

Jamie became interested in working with young children while she was studying at university and taking child development courses. In the summer of 1975, she worked in a school-age program and found the work so meaningful that she was hooked. In 1976, Jamie started to work full-time in a community-based child care centre. During her three years at the centre she was a preschool teacher, a cook, and a coordinator. At the same time, Jamie pursued studies in the ECE diploma program at Algonquin College.

In 1978, child care staff faced provincial cutbacks that threatened both their salaries and the survival of child care programs. Jamie was a leader in bringing child care workers together to discuss how to fight for better wages and working conditions. The next step was looking at the feasibility of joining a union. After much debate and consideration of the options, Jamie and others opted to join the Canadian Union of Public Employees (CUPE). It was a national union with research and communication resources. The new local was CUPE 2204, and child care workers from five centres joined.

Jamie continued to work within the union movement to advance the wages and working conditions of the child care workforce and the quality of child care programs. In her role today at Canadian Union of Postal Workers (CUPW), Jamie is enthusiastic about how the fund is able to extend child care options for shift workers and workers with children with special needs. She is able to work directly with local child care communities to create more flexible child care services. Jamie plays a key role in bridging the understanding of the child care sector and the union movement.

Jamie sees the challenges and opportunities for people entering the early childhood workforce. It is difficult to find the balance of enjoying the work with young children and their families and making a commitment to make it better. In order to improve the quality of child care for young children, the conditions of work must be improved. She calls on new members of the workforce to become advocates for themselves and more child care. Jamie points out that political or public advocacy are important to improving quality of today's child care in Canada. By raising these kinds of issues within local neighbourhoods and communities, there are real opportunities to make a difference for the children, families, and the child care workforce.

"There are rich opportunities and potential when you work in this field. Part of the potential is in the direct work with children and part is in joining the child care advocacy movement."

Public policy advocacy for early child development programs and the early childhood workforce is based on the view that children and families should have access to quality services and that early childhood educators should be recognized as a critical component of these services.

Understanding the Child Care Links: Quality, Compensation, and Accessibility

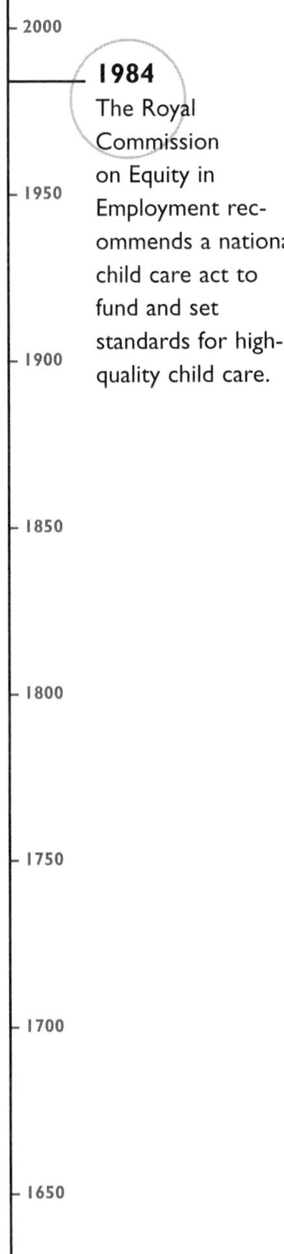

This section examines the links between **quality, compensation, and accessibility.** The future of the early childhood workforce and programs depends on these three intertwined issues. There is a clear relationship between the quality of care and education children receive in child care programs and the compensation and working conditions of early childhood educators. There is also a clear relationship between children's and families' access to quality programs and the costs, which mainly go toward covering early childhood educators' wages.

> "Quality child care depends on significant investments of public dollars to maintain stable programs, make them affordable to parents and to provide reasonable wages, benefits and working conditions for staff and caregivers." (Beach et al., 2004, p. 124)

This section considers various strategies to address these issues and to advocate for quality programs for children, equitable compensation for early childhood educators, and accessibility for families. These issues are important to all early childhood professionals. You will learn about how early childhood educators personally advocate for public policies, work together on campaigns, and participate in raising public awareness and understanding of the underlying issues. As you continue with your professional development, you will be involved in some of the processes that work toward solutions, resolutions, and further actions. There are many exciting developments in our immediate and distant futures.

Quality and compensation. To explore the first link between quality of early childhood education and programs and compensation, we will rely on Canadian and U.S. research. There is only one Canadian large-scale, on-site study of the quality of centre-based and home-based early childhood education and care settings. But we can compare the findings of small Canadian studies with those of U.S. studies. We can assume that the well-established link between quality and compensation established in the U.S. studies is applicable in the Canadian context.

In Canada, the recent research project, *You Bet I Care!* included studies of the quality of child care centres (Goelman, Doherty, Lero, LaGrange, & Tougas, 2000) and regulated family child care homes (Doherty, Lero, Goelman, Tougas, & LaGrange, 2000). The media release for the quality study stated that "while safe environments with supportive adults are the norm for child care in Canada, fewer than 1 in 3 preschoolers and 1 in 4 infants are in programs that stimulate the child's social, language and thinking skills, say two comprehensive studies on child care quality released today in Toronto and Vancouver" (University of Guelph Centre for Families, Work, and Well-Being, 2000). The centre-based study looked at the relationships between centre quality and centre characteristics (such as size of centre and auspice—nonprofit or commercial); program staff wages and working conditions; and program staff characteristics and attitudes (Goelman et al., 2000). The study found that the majority of programs provided safe environments with caring adults. But less than half (44.3 percent) of the preschool rooms and just over a quarter (28.7 percent) of the infant/toddler rooms were providing environments that were stimulating and supportive of children's optimal early development. For further discussion, see Chapter 3.

The study of regulated family child care homes considered the relationship between quality and the child care provider's characteristics and attitudes; child care provider's income levels and working conditions; and the child care provider's use of resource programs and networking and professional development opportunities (Doherty et al., 2000). The results showed just over one-third of the family child care homes provided environments that would stimulate children's development.

Both the centre- and home-based studies of quality found that the provider's or staff's level of income and level of education predicted the quality of the environment. That is, higher-quality environments were more likely when there were higher income and educational levels. Also higher levels of satisfaction were found more often in the higher-quality settings. Both studies found that compensation directly influenced the level of quality.

The Canadian Child Care Sector Study (Beach, Bertrand, & Cleveland, 1998) and the follow-up report (Beach et al., 2004) reviewed Canadian research studies, consulted with caregivers and early childhood educators in all types of early child development settings across Canada, and interviewed government officials, representatives from early childhood education/child care organizations, and experts in the field. Both studies report that the research, consultations, and interviews identified concerns and questions about the quality of child care in regulated and unregulated settings.

> Research from other countries suggests many child care settings in Canada are not providing optimal environments for young children. There is a considerable body of U.S. research which finds high turnover rates, poor compensation, and a lack of related caregiver education qualifications are associated with poor quality child care [reported in Doherty, 1996]. These problems exist in the Canadian context and it is reasonable to assume that they have a similar influence on the quality of care (Beach et al., 1998, p. 35).
>
> Reports of quality child care [in Canada] indicate that some regulated child care centres and family child care homes support optimal early child development, but many others offer mediocre, custodial services that meet only children's basic physical needs (Beach et al., 2004, p. 123)

In 1989, the National Child Care Staffing Study reported some significant findings relating quality in child care to variables in the adult work environment. The study found that the education of child care staff and the arrangement of their work environments are essential determinants of the quality of programs for children. As you might expect after reading the earlier discussions in this text, early childhood educators provided more responsive and appropriate care for children if they have had formal training in early childhood education at the college level, earned higher wages and better benefits, and worked in centres whose budgets used a higher percentage of their funds for early childhood educator salaries and benefits. The most important predictor of the quality of care children receive, among all the variables related to adult work environments, is staff wages. Better-quality centres had higher wages for early childhood educators and, consequently, lower rates of teaching staff turnover.

The problem persists in Canada and the United States. Early childhood educators employed in child care programs continue to earn low wages, especially considering

1985
The report of the government's Task Force on Child Care recommends a national system of child care in Canada.

NAEYC establishes a voluntary accreditation system for centres.

1986
The report of the federal government's Special Committee on Child Care recommends increased tax credits for families, continuation of child care subsidies to low-income families, and small operating grants to child care programs.

1987
NAEYC publishes its position statement on developmentally appropriate practice, revised from a preliminary statement in 1984.

The Canadian Child Day Care Federation (later the Canadian Child Care Federation) is established.

the fact that they have higher levels of formal education than the average Canadian worker. In 2000, about 75 percent of early childhood educators and assistants have a certificate, diploma, or degree compared to 57 percent of the all workers in all occupations (Beach et al., 2004). The average annual full-time income for early childhood educators and assistants with a college or university qualification was $23 600 compared to $41 619 across all occupations.

RESEARCH INTO PRACTICE

Quality, Compensation, Qualifications, and Turn Over

The turnover rate of early childhood educators in child care centres is high compared to other sectors. Higher rates of staff turnover have a negative impact on quality (Shonkoff & Phillips, 2000). Overall, staff turnover in full-time child care centres in 1998 was 21 percent across Canada (Doherty et al., 2000). This was less than the turnover rate of 26 percent reported in 1991 (CCCF & CCAAA, 1992). Consider the table below. Turnover rates vary across Canada and would appear to be related to compensation, qualification levels, and quality, although other provincial factors play a role.

Overall, turnover rates increase as the percentage of staff with ECE qualifications decreases. But there are exceptions that are probably related to differences in provincial policies. For example, in New Bronswick the percentage of staff with ECE qualifications and the turnover rate are lower than elsewhere in Canada. Because government funding does not provide additional funding for more than the minimum number of qualified staff, there is little incentive to increase the overall numbers of early childhood educators beyond the minimum.

TABLE 9.1

ECE Turnover Rates in Child Care Settings 1998

Jurisdiction	*Turnover Rate (%)*	*Staff with ECE Credential (%)*	*Average ECERS (quality measure)*	*Average Full-time Salary ($)*
Alberta	45	64	5.1	17 000
Saskatchewan	32	59	4.1	21 000
New Brunswick	26	57	4.0	14 400
Newfoundland	24	80	N/A	13 600
British Columbia	24	91	5.6	23 500
Nova Scotia	22	84	N/A	17 400
Ontario	18	89	4.9	26 500
Quebec	17	82	4.7	20 700
Manitoba	17	67		18 700
Prince Edward Island	15	84		16 000
CANADA	22	82	4.7	22 700

1989
The Canadian government passes a resolution to eliminate poverty among Canadian children by the year 2000.

There are 943 000 poor children in Canada.

Keep in mind that the issue of low wages for early childhood educators is receiving considerable attention and there are some signs of improvement:

- Overall, salaries for child care staff (qualified early childhood educators and other staff) increased more between 1990 and 2000 than salaries did for all occupations for the same period of time: 40 percent increase for child care staff compared to 35 percent increase across all occupations (Beach et al., 2004).
- In several provinces, salary grants have improved average salaries since 2000, particularly for child care staff who are qualified early childhood educators. For example, the government of Manitoba is committed to increasing child care salaries by 10 percent between 2002 and 2007 (above cost of living increases). The government of Quebec has raised salaries by 30 percent between 1999 and 2003. In 2004, the annual salary for a qualified early childhood educator employed full-time in a child care centre was $30 000 (Friendly & Beach, 2005).
- Overall early childhood educators who are qualified and working in any type of early child development programs earn more than those who do not have post secondary qualifications. Those with university degrees earn 15 percent more than those who have college certificates and degrees. (See figure Annual Income and Education Levels for Early Childhood Workforce in 2000.)

A Canadian review (Bertrand et al., 2004) of published studies related to the child care workforce found a mismatch between current compensation levels for the child care workforce, and public, parental, and professional expectations for quality, early childhood environments that support optimal child development. While increased educational qualifications seem desirable across all levels of the child care workforce, there are few financial incentives available and postsecondary education or professional development opportunities are often difficult to access. Over the past decade, educational levels of child care staff have increased and larger numbers are qualified early childhood educators. However, compensation has not made the increases that school teachers and other professionals have made (Beach et al., 2004).

FIGURE 9.1

Annual Income and Education Levels for Early Childhood Workforce in 2000

Full-time Occupation	Overall	Post Secondary Certificate or Diploma	University Degree
ECE and Assistants in Centre-based Programs	$22 000	$22 500	$25 800
ECE and Assistants in Family Child Care	$15 000	$14 900	$15 200
Kindergarten Teachers	$46 500	$39 000	$47 000
Educational Assistants	$21 000	$21 000	$27 000
In Home Child Care	$15 900	$17 400	$17 400

Source: Beach et al., 1998; Statistics Canada 2001; Beach et al., 2004; Friendly & Beach 2005.

Early childhood educators' habit of caring for others extends even to this form of sacrificing their own incomes. But awareness has been growing that this sacrifice hurts those whom teachers have been trying to protect in the long run—children and families—through the staff turnover that results from early childhood educators' dissatisfaction.

Canadian studies report a connection between compensation levels and staff turnover (the number of staff leaving the centre in that year, divided by the total number of staff employed). In *You Bet I Care!* (Doherty et al., 2000), the annual average turnover was 21.7 percent in 1998. The most common reason for leaving a centre voluntarily was dissatisfaction with pay. In an earlier study, *Caring for a Living* (Canadian Day Care Advocacy Association and Canadian Child Day Care Federation, 1992), the total turnover rate averaged 26 percent across child care centres. An analysis of the *Caring for a Living* data (Beach et al., 1998) finds that low wages significantly increase the probability of turnover. Another compensation factor that affects turnover is pensions. In centres where pension plans (either partially or fully paid by employers) are available, staff was much less likely to indicate that they planned to leave.

High-quality infant child care is linked to low staff turnover.

Clearly, there is a connection between low wages and staff turnover. In too many communities, early childhood educators discover they cannot pay all their bills on the salaries they earn as early childhood educators, and discover they need to take on additional jobs to meet their financial responsibilities. Working with young children all day long is already physically exhausting, and emotionally and cognitively challenging; to have to then go on to a different job puts heavy burdens on early childhood educators, to say nothing of strains on their personal lives. And there is more to it than that: the low salaries imply a lack of societal support and respect for the importance of what early childhood educators do, which ultimately eats away at self-esteem and a sense of professional worth.

One early childhood educator who chose other career directions after five years of working with four-year-olds said, "I got tired of always being broke days before my next paycheque. And hoping against hope that I wouldn't get sick enough to have to go to a doctor, let alone take time off my job, since sick days weren't one of our centre's benefits. And most of all I got tired of seeing the friends I had gone to college with be able to go on trips and stuff that I knew I'd never be able to do if I stayed in that job. I miss the work and the kids, but I decided if changes were coming, they weren't coming soon enough to suit me." It is not hard to imagine the feelings of frustration, hurt, and disappointment that lie behind such words, and behind such a final act as leaving the early childhood profession. The American study, *Cost, Quality, and Child Outcomes in Child Care Centres* and the Canadian study, *You Bet I Care!* document that quality suffers with these high rates of early childhood educator turnover. Several characteristics of quality are directly related to the issue of compensation. The study found that high-quality centres shared these characteristics: small groups of children were assigned to each adult; college-educated early childhood educators worked competently with children,

1990s
There are 320 288 day care spaces in Canada.

The average annual salary for an early childhood educator working in a child care centre is $11 639; the average salary of a teacher in a kindergarten program is $32 501.

basing their actions on their knowledge of child development; experienced administrators managed the programs; staff were stable, resulting from the programs' ability to recruit and retain good staff; and mechanisms existed to meet high standards, such as strong licensing requirements and voluntary accreditation.

Training is important, but it is quite unreasonable to expect a high level of professional preparation without the matched levels of compensation. When trained early, childhood educators cannot be recruited. Administrators who are desperate to hire staff to at least maintain the adult-child ratios may lower their standards for early childhood educators, with a resulting drop in the quality of experiences for children. In centres without well-trained staff, children's development suffers, as is clearly shown in all the studies.

Even when staff have appropriate training, if they are inadequately compensated, children and families still suffer because of the high rates of staff turnover. When children are left in the care of adults other than their parents, it is critical that they be able to form trusting, warm relationships with those caregivers. Learning and stimulation, as we have said, occurs within the context of relationships, with teaching embedded in interaction. Learning to feel safe and secure with adults is an important developmental task for young children. It is impossible to accomplish this task when a young child's question is, "Mommy, who's going to be my teacher today?" (Whitebook and Granger, 1989). The disruptions in style of care and in routines are disturbing to children's security, especially that of younger children.

Just consider all the changes children must adapt to when an early childhood educator leaves. The daily schedule may be different; there are likely new rules and expectations; the new early childhood educator will not know, at least for some time, each child's needs, likes, and style; and the songs she sings or the things she says are unfamiliar to the young child. The security of the daily rituals, and the person who was associated with them are gone, shaking children's sense of safe belonging. And for parents who are already struggling with turning the care of their children over to others, having to learn to trust still another adult takes time, energy, and a feeling that it may not be worthwhile to invest much in building yet another relationship. This is an attitude that will inhibit the comfortable communication that benefits children, parents, and early childhood educators. The centre as a whole is disrupted when staff members leave, with those who remain having to take on additional responsibilities, including orienting another new early childhood educator, while wondering how much longer they can remain or grow in this context of continual disruption. The dilemma, to paraphrase Marcy Whitebook, is that many early childhood educators cannot afford to stay, while the children cannot afford to have them leave (Whitebook, in Whitebook and Granger, 1989).

The issues related to inadequate compensation are pervasive and completely counterproductive to overall quality, professional growth, and development of individuals. As we have seen, there is a vicious cycle at work here: there are many factors related to compensation that push early childhood educators out of the field, which results in replacing them with less-qualified staff, therefore diminishing the quality of programs for children. When the public perceives this poor quality—and reads headlines such as those we saw earlier, which reported the recent study without seeing the complexity and interrelatedness of factors that result in quality—their response is to devalue the work of early childhood educators. Then we're right back to the problem of low status, one of those factors that relate to compensation and to a decreased sense of professionalism in the first place!

RESEARCH INTO PRACTICE

The Quality–Compensation–Accessibility Link

Early Learning and Care in the City was a joint initiative of the Centre of Early Childhood Development at George Brown College and the Atkinson Centre for Society and Child Development at Ontario Institute for Studies in Education of University of Toronto. *Early Learning and Care in the City* audited current early learning and care policies and practices at George Brown College and in Toronto.

A program evaluation indicates that the child care programs operated by George Brown College offer significantly higher quality environments than is typically found in Ontario centres. The study measured the quality of programs for four- and five-year-old children using the *Early Childhood Environment Rating Scale.* Revised (ECERS—R) (Harms, Clifford & Cryer, 1998). Overall quality rating was 6.2 compared to the 1998 study of child care centres that found overall quality rating of 4.9 (Goelman et al., 2000).

The study found that early childhood educators working in the George Brown College child care centres have higher educational credentials, receive better compensation and are less likely to seek other employment opportunities than their counterparts in community child care settings.

George Brown College's expenditures for its eight lab centres were approximately $4.3 million in 2003. More than 90 percent is allocated to salaries and benefits. The college receives almost $600 000 in fee subsidies, $3.1 million from parent fees, and $593 000 in wage grants. In 2003, the college absorbed a $163 000 deficit. George Brown College is committed to supporting the childcare and absorbs this deficit. The college

FIGURE 9.2
Early Childhood Education Rating Scale—Revised

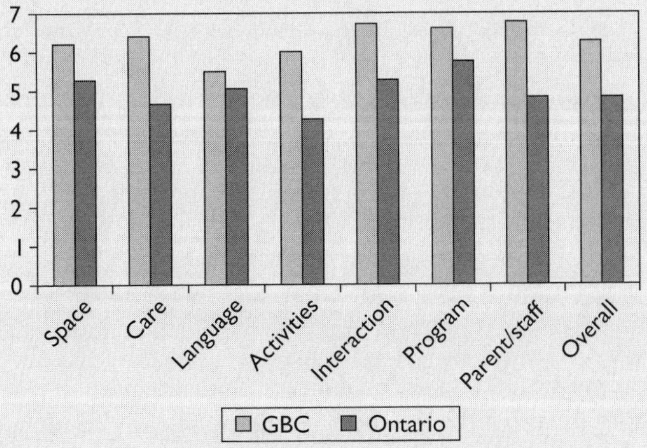

(cont'd)

The Quality–Compensation–Accessibility Link (cont'd)

TABLE 9.2

Early Childhood Educators

	Early Childhood Educators	
Average Full-time Salary, 2003	*George Brown College*	*Non-profit Toronto Community Child Care Centres (City of Toronto, 2004)*
All full time program staff	38 000	26 000
ECE Diploma/Degree	39 500	29 143

Sources: Adapted from Johnson, Lero, & Rooney (2001); Beach, Bertrand, Michal, Forer, & Tougas (2004); Friendly & Beach (2005).

FIGURE 9.3

The Cost of Quality

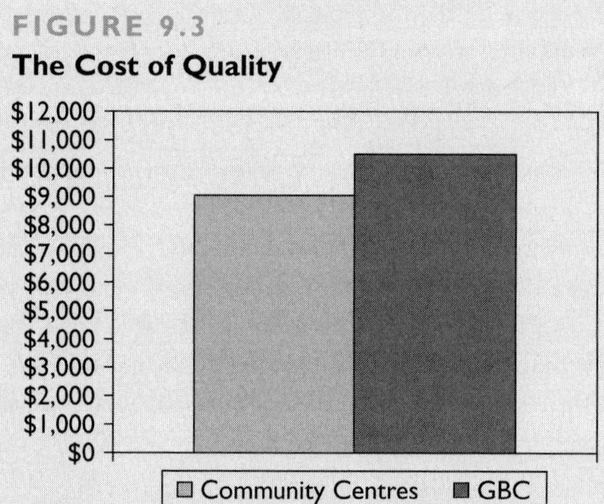

and its partners who provide space contribute approximately $300 000 in physical plant costs (lost rent and maintenance services).

While the George Brown College child care centres cannot make quality programs available to everyone, it has managed to keep the parent fees about 20 percent lower than the full cost of quality would demand.

Source: Cooke, M., Keating, D., & McColm, M. (2003). *Early Learning and Care in the City.* Toronto: George Brown College and Atkinson Centre at OISE/UT.

Compensation and accessibility. The compensation levels of early childhood educators are also linked to the accessibility of early childhood education and care programs to families. The issue of affordability (which determines accessibility) for families is directly tied to the issue of early childhood educators' compensation.

In nonprofit child care programs, by far, the largest percentage of the budget that drives parent fees is the salaries and benefits for the professional staff. Another aspect of child care budgets that affects compensation costs is the adult-child ratio, or the number of children that are cared for by one adult. Obviously, lower adult-child ratios are more costly, as well as more effective for quality programs.

Let's consider the phrase **full cost of quality.** Although parents find their budgets strained by the cost of their child care, they—and policymakers—do not realize that child care costs more than is apparent from the fees that parents pay. The full cost includes hidden costs, such as goods and services that may be donated, occupancy of the facility, donations, and, most importantly for this discussion, **foregone annual wages** and benefits—that is, the difference in wages between the actual wage received as an early childhood educator and the amount the individual could have earned in another occupation. Foregone wages amount to nearly 20 percent of the full cost of quality. By accepting low wages, child care professionals are, in fact, subsidizing the child care costs of the families in their communities.

Quality and accessibility. The third link is between the quality of an early childhood education and care program and its accessibility to children and their families. As quality of early childhood programs increases, their availability and affordability often decrease. Families base their child care decisions on what they can afford and on what is available in a given geographic area; the level of quality that they can afford depends on the choices available.

The result? Parents who cannot afford the fees of high-quality child care programs will choose lower-quality and less-expensive services or they may not use any service at all. If high-quality child care programs that meet individual children's and families' needs do not exist within a reasonable travel distance, again, parents will choose to not use child care or to use a lower-quality form of child care.

Doherty-Derkowski reports that studies in both Canada and the United States "indicate that children from less stressed families with higher socioeconomic status are more likely to be enrolled in high quality early childhood programs than are their peers from stressed and/or low socioeconomic status homes" (1995, p. 175). Stressed families are likely less able to seek out child care programs that may be within the availability circle of less-stressed families. Families of low socioeconomic status clearly are less able to pay for quality child care.

This focus on the issue of quality may bring parents into the battle for fair compensation as co-supporters, in ways that have not yet happened with other initiatives. For some time now, it has seemed to many early childhood educators that they were going to have to "face the harsh reality of the economic marketplace. No one else is going to solve our problem for us. We must become more and more assertive on our own behalf. It is child care employees themselves who hold the key to improving compensation" (Morin, 1989, p. 18).

The expanded understanding that we now have is that the link between increasing compensation and increasing parent fees can, and must, be broken. Consumers simply cannot bear the burden of an appropriate income for all early childhood educators. Serious commitments of public and private funds will be essential, and recent efforts show progress in this direction. By removing the link between early childhood educator salaries and parent fees, both early childhood

1991

The first Worthy Wage Day in the United States, organized by the Child Care Employee Project, is held on April 9.

The federal government introduces a ten-week parental leave benefit, in addition to the existing fifteen-week maternity leave benefit, as part of the Unemployment Insurance program.

1992

Caring for a Living, a national report on child care centre staff working conditions and wages, is released.

The Live-In Caregiver Program is introduced by the federal government.

educators and parents, unhindered by the need to protect personal vested interests, will be able to focus on the idea that quality for early childhood educators means corresponding quality for children and programs.

Public Policy Options

The cycle must be broken if there are to be viable futures for all of us, including you, who are just entering the profession. And the cycle must be broken because the healthy future of children and families also depends on it. Actually, the headlines *should* read, as Marcy Whitebook (1995) said, "What's Good for Child Care Early Educators Is Good for Our Country's Children." In the past, early childhood educators have been reluctant to lobby for their own interests, thinking it made them appear less professional and more self-centred, rather than focused on serving others and concerned about the increased costs of care for parents. But the studies discussed earlier make it clear that it is necessary to lobby for changes in policies and conditions that affect quality for children and themselves, simultaneously. In addition, because parents have a clear interest in obtaining the highest possible quality of care for their children, they should understand that supporting early childhood educators' efforts to establish higher standards in regulations and finding access to extra resources beyond parent fees will benefit their own children.

MAKING IT HAPPEN

Unions Advocate for Child Care

The trade union movement in Canada has a thirty-year history in supporting public policies that help ensure the provision of high quality early childhood programs. Unions have always linked high quality child care to improved wages, benefits, and working conditions for child care staff. Many unions (both those that represent child care staff and those that do not) have policies stating that child care should be publicly funded, universally accessible, of high quality, and regulated. They are involved in child care advocacy activities and organizations, locally, regionally, and nationally. Often unions who represent early childhood educators in child care centres have child care committees that move issues forward internally and externally. In other cases unions work on the issue through their equality or women's committees.

A few collective agreements in Canada contain provisions for child care facilities or family support, and those with provisions are concentrated in the public sector, universities and the automotive industry. The Canadian Auto Workers and the Canadian Union of Postal Workers are examples of unions that have bargained with employers for improved early child development programs.

The Canadian Auto Workers In 1987 the Canadian Auto Workers (CAW) negotiated a child care fund from the Big Three auto makers—Ford of Canada, Daimler-Chrysler Canada and General Motors of Canada. Extended bargaining won capital funds that helped support child care centres in Windsor, Oshawa, and Port Elgin, Ontario. In order to meet the needs of other members, the Big Three contract negotiated in 1999 included a child care subsidy of $10 per day per child to a maximum of $2 000 per year, paid directly to a licensed non-profit child care provider. The contract also included $450 000 to assist existing child care centres to better serve the needs of employees covered under the agreements, including expanding operating hours for shift-working parents. Child care workers at CAW-sponsored centres receive above-average industry wages and benefits. The CAW has joined forces with CEOs of General Motors of Canada and Daimler-Chrysler to jointly urge the federal government, working with the provinces, to provide a national child-care program. The CAW's child-care provisions dovetail with the union's social agenda for a national child-care program. In 2000, CAW joined other funds to support Toronto First Duty, a demonstration project to study the integration of early childhood programs into a new delivery model.

The Canadian Union of Postal Workers In 1981 the Canadian Union of Postal Workers (CUPW) bargained for paid maternity leave for its members. After going on strike over the issue they won a top-up to federal maternity benefits of 93 percent of wages for seventeen weeks. Following on the CUPW precedent, many other unions followed suit. CUPW put child care on the bargaining table with Canada Post in the 1980s. CUPW was successful in achieving a child care fund to help postal worker parents balance work and family. The fund helps members who have the most trouble finding or affording high quality child care. The fund is used for projects to provide child care and related services to CUPW families, provide child care information programs, and undertake needs assessments and child care research. Canada Post contributes to the child care fund every three months; the union develops the programs and administers the fund. CUPW believes that quality child care should be a right of all children. As part of the union's overall commitment to universal social programs, the union is working alongside advocacy groups to press for a government funded, universally accessible, high quality child care system. The union has also developed a one week in-residence educational program for postal workers on child care.

Source: J Kass & B. Costigiola, 2003; Beach et al., 2004; Cleveland et al., in press.

The quality, compensation, accessibility triangle is at the crux of the challenge facing early childhood educators. The Introduction identified the range of public policies that shape early child development programs in Canada today. These policies are caught in four interrelated contradictions:

1. Government policies at the federal and provincial/territorial level see the benefits of early education for all children, but the costs seem prohibitive. Governments move to provide early childhood development opportunities to the targeted groups of children and families who are likely to benefit the most.
2. The federal versus provincial/territorial jurisdiction of child care continues to thwart both government's attempts and resolve to address early child development policy.
3. Canada is ambivalent about whether early childhood education and care is a public or private responsibility. The ambivalence about women's equality, preferred family structures, and the rights and obligations of parents all come into play. Are early childhood education and care programs a public right to Canada's youngest citizens, or is it the responsibility of their parents to care for and educate children until they reach school age?
4. For some, the primary purpose of early childhood education and care programs is to promote children's optimal development, whereas others view programs as services that enable parents to participate in the labour force or prepare for labour force participation.

1993

The Perry Preschool Project publishes its data on the now 27-year-olds who were once in its preschool programs, showing the continued benefits in social adjustments and proving economic effectiveness of preschool education.

The Manitoba Child Care Association initiates the Worthy Wage Campaign.

Policymakers and government officials often seem captive to these dilemmas and are unable to address the quality, compensation, accessibility dilemma. Child care advocates must open their minds to put forward a range of policy options to meet the needs of children, their families, and early childhood educators. Policy options that fail to improve all three problems of quality, compensation, and accessibility will not be real improvements. Increasing the amount of child care at prices affordable to parents, without ensuring reasonable wages for competent early childhood educators, is not a solution. Increasing wages and benefits for early childhood educators by increasing the cost of programs to families is not a solution either. Nor is improving requirements for early childhood educator qualifications and reducing adult-child ratios, while passing on the increased costs to parents.

Below is a shopping list of the public policy options often put forward to address early childhood education and care issues. Many were introduced in Chapter 1 when you reviewed the public policy that now shapes early childhood education and care programs in Canada. Consider how each measures up to the task of addressing the quality, compensation, accessibility dilemma. Policies that cannot measure up in addressing all three issues are not solutions and may become part of the problem. As you consider each policy, ask the following questions:

- Does the policy support improved quality by increasing the knowledge and abilities of early childhood educators and reducing turnover?
- Does the policy support improved compensation for early childhood educators?
- Does the policy ensure that higher-quality early childhood education and care programs, with better compensated early childhood educators, will be more available to families and more affordable?

Integration of children/family services. In Canada, provincial/territorial public policy initiatives and programs for children and their families tend to be divided across health, education, and social service ministries. In most jurisdictions, governments are moving toward a more integrated approach, which either moves responsibilities for child and/or family services into one ministry or establishes a children's secretariat to coordinate related policy and services. This direction offers the potential to bring together various early childhood education and care services, such as kindergarten programs in schools that are part of education; early intervention programs, which are operated by health ministries; and regulated child care services in social service ministries.

Expand early childhood education and care programs located in the schools. Many out-of-school programs, child care centres, nursery schools, and family resource programs are located in school buildings. Early childhood educators often share information, resources, and expertise with educators in the school system and may receive low-cost or rent-free space.

Integrate early childhood education and care programs into the education system. Kindergarten programs are offered as part of the school system and could be expanded to full-day programs. The school system could also expand full-day programs to younger children, as well as operate out-of-school programs for school-age children. The Quebec, Nova Scotia, and New Brunswick governments have extended full-day programs for kindergarten.

MAKING IT HAPPEN

Public Policy for an Early Child Development System in Quebec

Quebec's child care system is unique in Canada. In 1997, Quebec revised its family policy away from sizeable payments to parents on the birth of children to a multi-pronged approach: maternity/parental leave for employed and self-employed parents covering up to 75 percent of salary, a progressive child allowance, and, low cost child care. The latter two initiatives are now in full operation. Funding disputes between the Federal and Quebec governments led to a delay in the implementation of the maternity leave policy. This has only now been resolved and the new plan is moving forward.

Maternity and Parental Leave

The changes to maternity and parental benefits are significant, including a change to the eligibility criteria so benefits are more accessible to working parents in non-standard forms of employment (e.g., part time, self-employed) and an enhanced amount of payable benefits.

Under this legislation, parents who qualify would be eligible for:

- up to a maximum of 18 weeks of maternity benefits;
- up to a maximum of 5 weeks of paternity benefits;
- up to a maximum of 32 weeks of parental benefits; or
- up to a maximum of 37 weeks of adoption benefits.

Quebec is the only jurisdiction that designates a period for the parent that did not give birth (5 weeks). The intention is to encourage fathers to become active participants in child rearing.

Parents would have two choices in regards to payment of benefits:

- 70 percent of their average weekly earnings for the first 25 weeks and 55 percent of their earnings for the rest of the period (25 weeks); or
- 75 percent of their average weekly earnings for a maximum of 40 weeks.

The maximum insurable earnings would be at $52 500, compared to $39 000 under the federal EI program making maximum payments in Quebec $757 a week compared to $413 in the rest of Canada.

Under the current EI, eligibility criteria for maternity and parental benefits are based on having worked a minimum of 600 hours in the previous 52 weeks, or since the beginning of the last benefit period. Under Quebec's plan, eligibility would be based on a minimum level of gross earnings ($2 000 during the qualifying period). There would be no waiting period, compared to the two-week waiting period required under the federal EI program.

Network of Child Care Programs

Funding for its network of over 900 child care programs is also exclusive to Quebec. Programs receive 87 percent of their funding from government; parents pay a flat fee of $7 per day (originally $5). Children of parents on social assistance are entitled to free enrollment for 22.5 hours a week. The policy objectives are to facilitate work-family balance, encourage the labour force participation of parents on social assistance and provide children, no matter the financial status of their parents, with high-quality early childhood education and care that fosters their social, emotional, and cognitive development as well as readiness for school.

The system, fueled by high demand, has gone through a rapid expansion and now serves nearly 235 000 children, in 178 000 spaces. Another 35 000 kids are waiting for spots to open up. The goal is 200 000 spaces by 2008. About 63.4 percent of young children were in regulated child care in 2003–04.

(cont'd)

Network of Child Care Programs (cont'd)

Ministry jurisdiction is divided by age groups. Children 0–4 are the responsibility of the Ministry of the Family. Children in this age group are served by *Centres de la petite enfance*, or CPEs. Each CPE provides both group and family child care for a geographic area where 300 families reside. The majority of programs (80 percent) are operated by parent boards (at least two-thirds must be parent users). A new government elected in 2003 included for-profit operators in its expansion plans.

At age five, children begin school full time. When twelve or more parents request child care, the education ministry requires school boards to establish before and after programs. The main focus for school age children is to provide recreation and assistance with school assignments.

Staff/child ratios are higher in Quebec than in most other Canadian jurisdictions. For example, infant ratios (0–18 months) are 1:5; preschool 1:8 and school age 1:20.

Quebec has taken steps to improve quality by establishing curriculum expectations and by raising staff qualifications. Previously only 1 in 3 staff required a diploma, now two-thirds of staff in non-profit programs must have a college or university ECE degree. For-profit programs operate under the old guidelines.

A series of labour actions in 2000 led to the establishment of a province-wide wage scale negotiated between the government and the CPE association. Program supervisors now average $30/hour; trained staff earns $19/hour. A pension plan has been established. The government reneged on a promise to adjust salaries through pay equity evaluations leading to rotating strikes which are ongoing.

Challenges to ECD System Building

A new government took office in 2003, determined to restructure the system. Parent fees were raised by $2 a day; $40 million was cut from the $1.3 billion budget; centres were not allowed to build up reserve funds and a preference was shown for commercial centres and family child care. In addition to the labour strife, Quebec's child care is now showing other signs of stress.

- The original vision for CPEs included plans to forge links with CLSCs (community health and social service centres) in local neighbourhoods. CLSCs provide direct health care, pre- and post-natal supports, family supports, and early identification and intervention programs. However, their funding is now being curtailed and except for a few isolated situations, these links are not happening.
- ECE college programs are under-enrolled pointing to an ongoing staff recruitment challenge.
- CPEs are posting deficits as parents default on fee payments.
- Programs are refusing children with special needs because funding does not cover costs.
- Quality is deteriorating. A study (Jappel & Tremblay, 2005) shows only a quarter of programs are meeting objectives. Quality is most problematic in for-profit centres, 27 percent of which were graded inadequate as opposed to 7 percent of non-profit.
- Children from low-income families are less likely to attend *any* kind of child care. There is also a significant quality gap: children from poorer families are more likely to be in for-profit child care settings that are of inferior quality (20 percent vs. 9 percent of children from well-off families).

The latter problem is exacerbated by the service design. It is difficult to establish and maintain parent-run programs in low-income and transient communities; therefore, for-profit operators are filling the gap. CPEs are refusing expansion funding saying it is no longer adequate to provide quality programming. Commercial programs are taking up the unallocated dollars.

The government also has, under active consideration, a new type of family daycare provider that will operate outside the support monitoring of the CPEs. These new providers will be individually licensed and monitored by a self-regulatory agency.

Promising Signs

For all the difficulties the program is showing its value.

- Quebec's maternal labour force participation has gone from below the national average to above. Quebec women with children under six are far more likely to be in the job market than other women across Canada.
- Quebec women are not just in the traditional sectors. Women outnumber men in post-secondary education and are the majority of graduates from medical and law schools.
- Tax revenues from mothers' increased labour force participation now covers 40 percent of the cost of the child care program, expected to rise to 50 percent within five years (Baker & Milligan, 2006).
- Quebec's child poverty rates have dropped 5 percentage points—more than any other province indicating factors beyond overall economic performance (Campaign 2000, 2006).

Entrepreneurship. The private sector could be encouraged to operate more early childhood education and care programs as businesses, based on market demand.

Work-related child care. Workplace child care centres, child care information and referral services, and support to employees who use neighbourhood early childhood education and care programs are all considered work-related child care. In Canada, a survey of all child care centres located on or near the work site reported that they account for less than 3 percent of licensed child care spaces (Beach, Friendly, & Schmidt, 1993). The survey findings noted that most work-related child care centres charge comparable fees to other programs and receive few funds from employers.

Work-related centres can meet the needs of young children and their families.

National early child development system. Many advocates in Canada recommend that the federal government establish a national policy with broad principles and cost-share funding with provincial/territorial governments that pulls together all forms of early childhood education and care programs, family support programs, and early years community initiatives.

Direct or block grants to early childhood education and care. Funding for programs may be targeted to specific operating costs, such as salaries or in-service training. Direct grants can also be used for the overall operating costs, reducing, or even eliminating, fees to parents.

Child care tax deductions/benefits. Income tax deductions and benefits direct public funds to parents who are paying fees for early childhood education and care programs. The Child Care Tax Deduction now in effect allows parents to deduct up to $7 000 for their child care fees for children under seven years. The deduction must be claimed by the parent with the lowest income, and a receipt from a family child care provider or an early childhood education and care program must be provided. The resulting reduction in income tax is greater for higher-income earners. An income tax benefit could be targeted to lower-income families.

1994
Fisher Price Toy Company sells $800 million worth of toys.

Loris Malaguzzi, founder of the schools in Reggio Emilia, Italy, dies, while the philosophy of his schools continues to influence programs around the world.

2000 1950 1900 1850 1800 1750 1700 1650

Complementary work and family policies. Early childhood education and care programs cannot address all of the supports families need to raise their children and earn a living. Families need work policies (such as flexible hours and family responsibility leave) that help parents balance work and family life.

Taking Action

There is no simple solution or quick policy fix for early childhood education and care and its workforce. Despite the obstacles, the prospects have never been brighter to finally make the early childhood workforce a well-recognized and well-rewarded profession (Bellm et al., 1994, p. 168). Early childhood educators are powerful advocates who can take action. The first step is identifying policy options to meet the objectives of quality, compensation, and accessibility. The next step is to take action.

Worthy wage campaigns. Worthy wage campaigns draw attention to early childhood educators' inadequate compensation and to the value of the work itself. Often, not even parents and family members are aware of the wages and benefits early childhood educators actually receive. Campaigns inform the public of the wide discrepancies between the responsibilities and skills required and the compensation levels. Often a worthy wage campaign begins with a survey of wages and benefits. The campaigns use innovative actions to publicize the information and to celebrate the early childhood workforce. The purpose is to mobilize support for improvements to compensation levels, which will also support quality but not reduce accessibility by raising the fees that parents must pay.

You can clearly see the importance of the compensation issue to the profession, to children, families, and communities, and to you. Progress is being made, albeit slowly. Nevertheless, these efforts will not succeed unless all early childhood educators make it their business to understand the issues and the solutions and to recruit others, both parents and early childhood educators, to join in the effort. Make it your concern, now as a student and later as an early childhood educator, to find out about Worthy Wage campaign efforts in your community.

Position papers and presentations. Local, provincial/territorial, and federal governments need to hear from early childhood educators. Task force committees, commissions, and public hearings present opportunities to communicate your policy recommendations and to respond to government policy initiatives and budget announcements. This is one way to influence government policy and to draw attention to the challenges facing early childhood education and care programs.

The following steps outline how to prepare a position paper, which outlines your perspective and recommendations on a particular issue or policy (Bertrand, 1990):

1. Identify who you are representing—perhaps yourself, a group of early childhood educators, a particular early child development program, an early childhood organization, or a coalition of organizations and programs.
2. Briefly state your position.
3. Define the issue. Clearly state the problem or concerns you are addressing in the position paper. It may be useful, here, to review key points in a government initiative or to relate a series of events in chronological order to help identify the central problem or concern.

4. Support the position. Find common ground with the government's policy and state your differences. Provide specific arguments or reasons to back up your position. Include examples of support and agreement from the community or from other government officials.
5. Conclude with strength. Restate your position and include an optimistic view about the positive outcome that is likely if your recommendations are followed.

Building coalitions. Coalitions build the base of support for public policy changes at the local, provincial/territorial, and national level. They often include child care programs, parents, early childhood educators, community associations, child welfare organizations, trade unions, teachers' federations, child care resource groups, human service agencies, women's groups, and early childhood educator students.

Media. Television, radio, newspapers, and the Internet are the most effective, powerful tools in maintaining a sustained advocacy campaign. Appearing daily to a broad cross-section of the population, the media provide an opportunity to reach many people outside committed supporters and confirmed opponents. The media are an important part of a strategy to bring about significant change.

Contact members of the media in person, on the telephone, or through press releases. It is helpful to cultivate contacts with particular media persons who seem to have an interest in the issue and will put forward a fair position.

MAKING IT HAPPEN

Ontario Coalition for Better Child Care

The Ontario Coalition for Better Child Care (OCBCC) brought together child care activists, early childhood educators, trade unions, teachers' federations, women's groups, social policy organizations, First Nations, Francophones, anti-poverty groups and parents in 1981 to form a coalition of interests and organizations at the provincial level.

Since its beginning, the OCBCC has been a powerful force in the campaign for more affordable, accessible, high-quality child care in that province. It has also spearheaded a number of initiatives to improve the compensation of early childhood educators, including provincial wage grants and pay equity legislation and grants. The OCBCC continues to play an important role in Ontario's and Canada's struggle for a system of early learning and child care.

The OCBCC promotes a single comprehensive system to replace the present fragmented collection of policies and services. Such a system would simultaneously provide healthy development opportunities for children and supports for parent to work, study, and parent-effectively. These services would be non-compulsory but available to all children to the extent their parents wish to use them and regardless of their parents' employment status.

Source: Beach et al., 2004; Friendly & Beach, 2005; OCBCC, 2006.

1995
There are 1 472 000 poor children in Canada.

In Canada, approximately 3 million children under the age of twelve have parents who work in the labour force or are pursuing further education and training. There are 474 969 regulated child care spaces.

For a major issue or event, a press conference can be assembled. You might organize a press conference when you want to respond to a particularly critical situation or when you are initiating a major campaign, such as a local Worthy Wage Campaign.

Unionization. Unionization of early childhood educators and other staff members in early childhood education and care settings can raise wages, improve working conditions, and contribute to better-quality care and education. Although many early childhood educators have been reluctant to form unions to lobby on their own behalf, unionization is a clear strategy to improve compensation and working conditions, as well as to improve the quality of the early child development programs.

The labour movement in Canada has been involved in organizing the early childhood workforce and bargaining for better compensation and working conditions since the 1970s (Beach et al., 2004). To date, less than 20 percent of early childhood educators employed in child care or other early child development programs, are members of trade unions in Canada (Doherty et al., 2000; Beach et al., 2004). Employment structures and funding present barriers for the organization of early childhood educators. In centre-based child care programs, it is difficult to organize relatively small staff groups into collective bargaining units. Demands for increased compensation are immediately faced with the ability of parents to afford increased fees. Early childhood educators employed in programs which are operated within larger institutions (such as municipalities in Ontario or community colleges) may be included as a small proportion of a broad bargaining unit and it may be difficult to address issues specific to the child care workforce (Beach et al., 1998).

Rates of unionization do vary across Canada. For example:

- While the overall level of unionization of full-time staff in regulated child care centres is low, the rate in Quebec is over 30 percent (Beach et al., 2004).
- A 1997 survey of school age child care staff found that unionization rates across Canada ranged from 96 percent in Quebec to 22 percent in British Columbia, 21 percent in Nova Scotia, 17 percent in Saskatchewan, 11 percent in Ontario, 10 percent in Manitoba, and 7 percent in Alberta (Jacob, Mill & Jennings, 2002).

Early childhood educators and other staff working in child care centres that are unionized earn higher pay and better benefits than staff in other settings. On average, child care staff earns 8.3 percent more in unionized centres. They are also more likely to receive benefits such as disability insurance, extended health care, life insurance, employee top-up of maternity and parental leave benefits and pensions (Beach et al., 2004).

Informational advocacy. Because of their education and experience, early childhood educators can lead the way in advocating for children and families. Those who have knowledge of child development have an obligation to share their expertise with others to help them make informed decisions. Often in the name of accountability, fiscal economy, and efficiency, policies are made that can be harmful to children's development.

Informational advocacy, most often in the form of public education, is a powerful force early childhood educators can use to counter these policy directions. Many of the activities discussed in the earlier section on public advocacy will also serve to inform and educate the general public. As well, early childhood

MAKING IT HAPPEN

Unions and Early Childhood Educators

Unions that represent the early childhood workforce in Canada include:

- Canadian Union of Public Employees (CUPE). In Quebec, CUPE is a member of the Quebec Federation of Labour.
- Fédération de la Santé et Services Sociaux (FSSS/CSN), and the Fédération des employées et employés de services publics (FEESP/CSN), two federations which are members of the Confederation des syndicats nationaux (CSN).
- Fédération du personnel de soutien scolaire (FPSS/CSQ) and the Fédération des intervenantes en petite enfance du Québec (FIPEQ/CSQ), members of the Centrale des syndicats du Québec (CSQ).
- Fédération indépendante des syndicates autonomes (FISA)
- B.C. Government and Services Employees Union (BCGEU), Saskatchewan Government and General Employees Union (SGEU), Ontario Public Service Employees Union (OPSEU), and Manitoba General Employees Union (MGEU) are all components of the National Union of Public and General Employees (NUPGE).
- Service Employees International Union (SEIU).
- Health Sciences Association (HSA).
- Public Service Alliance of Canada (PSAC).
- Canadian Auto Workers (CAW).
- Union of Needletrades, Industrial, and Textile Employees (UNITE).
- United Food and Commercial Workers (UFCW).

educators can build awareness about what ECEC is and why it is important to young children by

- taking part in information sessions at conventions, shopping malls, or entertainment events;
- early childhood environments using photographs, videos, multimedia presentations, three-dimensional models, and children's own art work; and
- seeking out and recognizing individual early childhood educators whose work with young children is an inspiration to others.

Talking About Early Child Development

As we discussed in the previous chapter, early childhood educators have a specialized knowledge base. We have an understanding of children's early growth and development, and the skills on how to connect, engage, and interact with young children. Early childhood educators can be powerful communicators about young children, families, and early child development programs. But sometimes we use too much jargon and we are not very effective. Or we use phrases like "children learn through play," or "our children are the future," without explaining what that means. To be effective in talking about early child development:

- Use everyday language as much as possible and explain what you mean by terms like *cognitive development* or *gross motor skills*. Better yet, try to talk about children learning to think, and use symbols such as pictures or words to represent ideas and objects rather than *cognitive development*.
- Avoid scare tactics such as "invest in early child development or children will become deviant" arguments. Early child development is a foundation of later development but it does NOT determine later actions.
- Always remember that parents are the experts about their own child. You have much to learn from them. Early childhood educators can contribute their knowledge and expertise about young children in general; parents and other primary caregivers are the experts in how your general knowledge will benefit their specific child.
- Practice speaking and writing about early child development. It will force you to be precise and clarify concepts that are fuzzy. Your communications with parents and other professionals will be informed and your input will be valued.

Essentials for Early Childhood Educators

Having decided that working with young children is the career for you, you will now continue in a planned program preparation at a college or university. This course of study has been designed to offer you both the knowledge base that you will need to provide developmentally appropriate responses, environments, and learning activities for the children you will work with, and the opportunities to develop your skills in supervised practica. The path through your course work has been designed quite clearly for you, to offer the most appropriate sequence of learning experiences.

But how you travel that path is up to you. As an advocate for young children and their families, for quality early childhood education and care programs, and for the early childhood workforce, you must start with a commitment to being a competent, learning early childhood educator.

It is important to understand that the same principles we recognize as optimal for children's learning apply equally well to adults. We know that children learn best when they take initiative, make choices among interesting possibilities, act on materials, and interact with people. So, too, adults construct their increasingly sophisticated new ideas by interaction with the concepts and experiences they encounter. Whether your past learning environments have encouraged you to play this active role of a learner or not, allow yourself now to assume an active role. You will become an advocate for yourself, the young children and families whom you will work with, and for the early childhood workforce.

If you are to be a successful early childhood educator, you must invent your own way of teaching; you will use the knowledge and experience you gain, and you will reflect on your own meanings and experiences. You will come out of your professional preparation program ready to assume your own identity as an early childhood educator, only if you have done more than passively meet the assigned requirements, by creating your own knowledge and increasing your self-understanding.

Begin inventing your own way of teaching now, by framing some of your own questions and using some of the additional resources suggested at the end of each chapter to delve further into the material. Use every encounter and opportunity to create your expanded understanding of what it means to be an early childhood educator, and how you will do it.

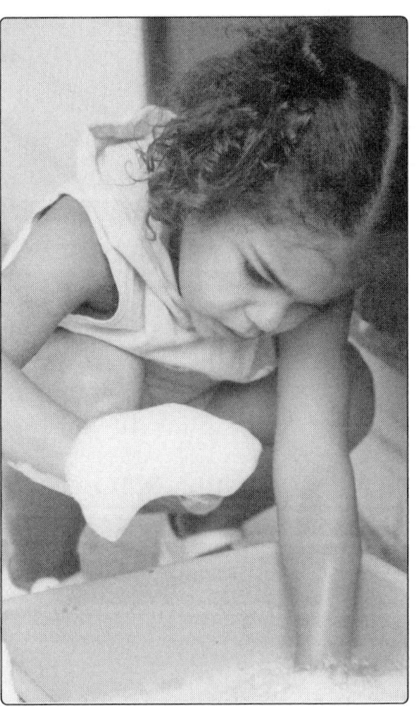

Young children rely on reflective practitioners who will advocate for their best interests.

Attitudes and Dispositions

The attitudes and dispositions that you now begin to form will guide you as you become an effective professional early childhood educator. In general, you will need to have a positive attitude toward yourself, the children you work with, their parents, your supervising teachers and other administrators, and your colleagues, now, as a student, and later, as an employee. This positive attitude allows you to see the potential in any situation or person, rather than narrowly focusing on limits and restrictions. Early childhood educators who nurture this perspective find less frustration and greater pleasure in their working situations.

In acknowledging that there is no one right way to teach and that there are always unknowns, the disposition of remaining open to new ideas and possibilities develops. It is important that you realize that completing a professional preparation program is not the end of something, but only another step along the path. So many students seem to feel that graduation means the learning part of their career is over, and they are now moving into the practice aspect. It is vital that you understand continual learning comes from the practice, if, as an early childhood educator, you are to remain able to grow and adapt to new demands. Learning becomes a passion for open, growing teachers. "The exceptional teachers I know are passionate about learning. . . . They see connecting points everywhere" (Perrone, 1991, p. 117).

Along with this disposition to remain open to insights and learning goes the disposition of risk-taking. You must dare to try new things, to risk the mistakes and failure that sometimes accompany new directions, and to learn from what you have risked. These are characteristics that you will want to cultivate. Students are often unnecessarily hard on themselves, expecting the polished performances they see when visiting the classrooms of mentor teachers. Recognize now that much of your learning as a student will come in evaluating experiences afterward and figuring out what you will do differently the next time. Mistakes and less-than-positive experiences are a necessary part of this learning.

Closely related to risk-taking is the disposition of restlessness: the inability to accept and drift with the status quo. For your healthy professional future, it is important that you avoid being pulled into any rut and maintain a perspective of restless searching for what step, idea, or experience comes next—for you and for your early childhood program.

Another disposition to develop is what Van Arsdell (1994) describes as "seeing themselves less as managers of learning and more as witnesses to learning" (p. 94). Being able to see the excitement in others' active learning, and not to feel one has

1996 The Canada Health and Social Transfer (CHST) block grant, which combines funding for social services (including child care subsidies), social assistance, health care, and post-secondary education, replaces the Canada Assistance Plan.

The National Crime Prevention Council identifies early child care and education programs as essential components of an integrated approach to reduce the long-term incidence of crime.

The National Forum on Health calls for a broad, integrated child and family strategy.

2000 1950 1900 1850 1800 1750 1700 1650

to control the directions of that learning, allows teachers to retain true excitement about children's learning and growth.

Perhaps the most important disposition is the capacity to be passionate about what you do. To retain the edge of excitement and freshness, early childhood educators develop strong convictions about what is appropriate for children's healthy growth. That underlying passion propels teachers with determination that doesn't falter, even in the face of frustrating circumstances. Care about what you do, and keep caring. These attitudes and dispositions will be indispensable as you travel your professional path.

Collegiality and Connection

Your growth and learning as a professional will have to be in the context of dialogue with others in the early childhood workforce. For those of you planning to do family child care, this will be harder than for the others, but the principle remains the same. It is within those professional relationships that you will find the support, the challenges, the ideas that you will need. When you find yourself within a community of others who care about common issues, as well as for each other's welfare, you will be encouraged in the difficult periods and fortified in the good times of teaching. Where are you going to find these connections?

First, deliberately seek employment in a setting that values collegiality. You will be able to tell if this is so by asking questions about staff meetings and staff development opportunities, by looking at the staff bulletin board, reading job descriptions, and talking with teachers. Some programs make collegiality and **team teaching** a vital part of their day-to-day life, and it is evident in the relationships of the co-workers.

When newly employed, convey an attitude of openness to others by asking for their assistance and opinions about issues that will occur. New early childhood educators are often so anxious to prove themselves and their competence to others that they put up invisible barriers that prevent them from getting the support and assistance they really need. Seek out the experienced early childhood educators whose programs you admire, and let them know you would value their ideas and help in designing your practice. Find out if there are formal mentoring programs in your program; many communities have designed such pairings to support new early childhood educators in their first year or two of teaching. If there is such a system, volunteer to become involved. Not only will this relationship foster your developmental growth as an early childhood educator but also will benefit the experienced colleague. If such systems do not exist, read about and promote discussion of mentoring systems.

Make sure you become involved in whatever local early childhood organization is available to you. Here you will find a ready-made group of individuals who have similar interests and commitment to children's issues. You will find members with a cross-section of experience, job description, and training; within such diversity you will find others to support you. Take the initiative to seek out what you need. If you gain more by talking with experienced early childhood educators, do so. Or if it is more helpful to talk with other novice early childhood educators who are undergoing the same kinds of adjustments to working with young children that you are, create these opportunities.

There are several ways to form early childhood educator support groups. If a number of graduates from your program are working in the same area, you may be able to form the core of a group for regular meetings to discuss common concerns. Or the professional association may offer such options. Both new and experienced early childhood educators benefit from the exchange of questions and ideas in such a group. Sometimes groups read and discuss a common book; others simply raise issues of personal or program concern. Sometimes such groups work on community early childhood issues, finding a common voice together, but for beginning teachers, their main benefit is support for professional growth. Whatever form it takes, teachers who expect to grow and learn, through good times and bad, will discover that they must find ways of **networking,** or making connections with colleagues.

Reflective Teaching

Throughout this text, you have been encouraged to discover the importance of reflection on your relationship to teaching and caring for young children. **Reflective teaching** is the process of thinking about your daily interactions with young children. As you move into early childhood settings, it will continue to be important for you to use your daily experience as material for you to consider, muse, meditate, and speculate upon. "The basic and comprehensive question during reflection is, 'What am I doing and why?'" (Valverde in Cruickshank, 1987, p. 3).

Many early childhood educators find that recording events and questions to reflect upon in a personal journal allows them to gain different perspectives for approaching their work. Finding a few minutes when children are napping or at the end of the day may seem too difficult for new early childhood educators, who are overwhelmed with program plans, material preparations, and physical environment maintenance. But it is likely one of the most important things you can do to help keep your focus on your professional development. Through using a reflective journal, early childhood educators record their "experiences within and outside of the classroom that bear directly on classroom life" (Cruickshank, 1987, p. 10). This record of thoughts, actions, beliefs, and attitudes will help teachers learn much from the children and the classroom. When ideas and experiences are recorded, they provide a frame of reference for early childhood educators to refer back to and see growth, or see patterns of questions that will identify needs for additional research. Make it your resolution to begin a journal on the first day of your new job, and to record in it regularly. Keeping a journal forces an early childhood educator to assume the posture of reflection. The early childhood educator asks: "How did I come to do it this way? What might I do differently?" Early childhood educator growth and development lie in the answers.

Fine-Tuning Skills and Deepening Knowledge Base

As has been stated, completing a program of professional preparation at a college or university is a beginning. During the early years of your practice, you will discover there are many classroom skills that you will need to fine-tune. There are many things you learned in theory, and likely had limited opportunities to practice, in your early education courses and practica.

1997

The federal and provincial/territorial governments agree to develop a National Children's Agenda, which is intended to be a comprehensive strategy to improve the well-being of Canada's children.

The Quebec government announces major child care and education reforms, which will expand the provision of early childhood education and care programs in that province.

1998

The federal and provincial/territorial governments introduce the National Child Benefits System.

The child care sector report, *Our Child Care Workforce: From Recognition to Remuneration*, is released.

1999 Developmental *Health and the Wealth of Nations*, by Daniel Keating and Clyde Hertzman, is published.

2001 The federal/provincial/territorial Early Child Development Agreement is signed.

2002 Maternity and Parental Leave and Benefits extended to one year in Canada.

2003 The MultiLateral Framework Agreement between the federal, provincial, and territorial governments directs new dollars to early learning and child care.

2005 A universal family allowance is made available to all families in Quebec.

2006 Ontario introduces a College of Early Childhood Educators.

2000 1950 1900 1850 1800 1750 1700 1650

However, it is only through regular and frequent use of these skills in the context of your own early childhood education program that you will become comfortable, confident, and proficient in their use, and that you will discover what additional knowledge you need. Instead of purely concentrating on survival during your first months and years in the early childhood setting, you will benefit from consciously identifying skills you need to develop, and setting small goals for each on a regular basis. For example, you will likely need to develop your skills of observation, organization of your record-keeping, communication, and decision-making.

A beginning early childhood educator might set the goal of recording an observation on every child at least once a week. Recognizing that the early childhood educator preparation program was just a beginning, good early childhood educators continue to develop their own goals and skills.

From our discussions of the developments of the profession in this chapter, and the issues facing the profession in Chapter 6, you know that your knowledge must grow in these two areas in order to remain current.

Self-Evaluation

One of the most difficult things for many new early childhood educators is to develop the skill of self-evaluation (Duff, Brown, & Van Scoy, 1995). Perhaps because so many life experiences depend on others' telling us how well (or not) we are doing, most beginning early childhood educators have had little experience in evaluating their own performance. Any well-run program will provide you with evaluation from your supervisor, but usually such feedback is so occasional that teachers must, instead, rely on their own evaluation of their performance to determine their strengths and to set their own goals for improvement. Your personal reflections and your journal can be helpful in starting this process. You will likely discover a number of evaluation tools in the course of your studies and as you visit various centres. The questions at the end of each chapter in Carol Hillman's *Teaching Four-Year-Olds* (1988) act as useful informal self-evaluation guides on the various aspects of an early childhood educator's practice. Don't hesitate to evaluate yourself honestly and fairly; your professional growth depends on it.

Personal Philosophy of Education

To evaluate how close you are keeping to your personal pathway, it is important that you have a guideline of your personal philosophy of early childhood education. As your last act in this preliminary examination of early child development, organize your thoughts on what you believe about teaching and learning into a written statement. No doubt, this document will grow and be adapted as you proceed through subsequent course work in your professional preparation. Plan to review it at the end of each semester or year, and take it with you, making it something you refer to and reflect on as you complete each year, evaluation session, or some regular period in your professional life. As you evaluate your day-to-day practice in the light of your vision and philosophy, you may be able to keep your ideals and realities aligned.

Rhythms of Working with Young Children

New skills, new insights, new growth—the daily life of an early childhood educator!

As is true of so many things in life, there is a rhythm, pacing, and pattern to working with young children, ranging from the exhilaration of the first experiences, to the plateaus of sameness and day-to-day duties, to the depths of frustration. Recall the stages of early childhood educator development that we discussed in Chapter 5, and give yourself the benefit of time to grow, to develop, to become. Be aware that the first year of working in an early childhood setting is generally recognized as difficult for most new early childhood educators. Don't be afraid to admit your dissatisfactions and disappointments and to seek the help and support you need during this difficult time. As you will be patient with your children's progress, so, too, be patient with your own. You won't be the same early childhood educator in the first month that you will be in your twelfth and then in your twentieth. Know that your decision was right and good, find the supports you need, and watch your own growth and development as an early childhood educator. Don't let discouragement take you from the field. Stay, for all the reasons that brought you here.

The early childhood workforce is a challenging profession with many wonderful aspects. It provides a way to stay young at heart, to maintain a lifetime of active learning, to be a special part of the world of the present *and* the future, while having opportunities to delve into the past. It is, in every respect, a profession of hope (Perrone, 1991, p. 131).

A story is told of two men visiting an ocean. They saw, much to their amazement, that a storm had tossed thousands, perhaps, millions, of starfish up on the shore. As far as the eye could see, piles of starfish lay there out of the water in the sunshine; it was obvious that very soon, they would begin to die. One of the men stooped down and began to pick up starfish and throw them back into the water. "What are you doing?" cried his friend. "Don't you see that it is hopeless? There are millions of starfish here, and they are all going to die!" Picking up another and throwing it back into the waves, the first man replied, "Not that one." Keep your eyes firmly fixed on the lives you can touch.

SUMMARY

Many issues are part of dialogue and study in early child development programs today. The role of advocacy continues to be important in addressing the challenges of compensation, quality, and accessibility. Early childhood educators can take on personal, public, and informational advocacy roles and learn to be effective voices in raising both the awareness of, and support for, quality early education and child care opportunities for children and their families in Canada.

The first step in being an advocate is to be the best possible early childhood educator you can be. You are just beginning the journey.

REVIEW QUESTIONS

1. Discuss the relationships between early childhood educator compensation, quality, and accessibility of programs for children.
2. Identify the Worthy Wage Campaign. How does it influence increasing professionalism?
3. Identify and discuss personal and collective approaches to advocacy in early child development.

STUDY ACTIVITIES

1. Visit the Web site www.ece.nelson.com and note the current issues and challenges facing the early childhood workforce in your region.
2. Do some informal research on the relationship between factors associated with quality in your community.
   a. Determine the adult-child ratios in each child care facility. Compare the salaries and benefits paid to early childhood professionals. Try to compare positions that might be similar, such as lead teachers or assistant teachers. Learn if there is a different wage paid to professionals with training or advanced degrees.
   b. Through conversations, try to learn how long early childhood educators have been in their positions at the centre. You may want to cooperate on gathering this information with other students and combine your data. Draw up a table to allow you to juxtapose this information. Do your findings support the correlations found in the studies referred to in this chapter?
3. Discover whether there is a Worthy Wage Campaign in your community. If there is, find out how you can become involved.
4. Prepare a short presentation about a child development issue that you think would inform parents. Try it out with parents in your next field placement.

KEY TERMS

advocacy: Defending or stating the cause of another. In early education, supporting the ideas and issues of the profession.
foregone annual wages: Additional amounts that practitioners, given their education, could have earned annually in another occupation.
full cost of quality: An initiative promoted by NAEYC, to help parents and policymakers understand the hidden subsidy provided in child care by the inferior wages of practitioners.
quality, compensation, and accessibility: An initiative sponsored by NAEYC to draw attention to correlations between staff compensation and the factors that produce quality in programs.
networking: Making connections with others in the profession for mutual support and information, and for professional development and advancement.
reflective teaching: Process of thinking back over daily experiences with young children to form questions, set goals, and grow as a practitioner.
team teaching: Status and responsibility of early childhood educators in an early childhood setting are equal, rather than hierarchical.

SUGGESTED READINGS

Canadian Child Care Advocacy Association. (1993). *Children: Our hope, your future.* Ottawa: CDCAA.

Bloom, Paula Jorde. (1993, March). But I'm worth more than that! *Young Children,* 48 (3), 65–68.

———. (1993, May). But I'm worth more than that! Implementing a comprehensive compensation system. Part 2. *Young Children,* 48 (4), 67–72.

Cleveland, G., & Krashinsky, M. (1998). *The benefits and costs of good child care: The economic rationale for public investment in young children.* Toronto: Childcare Resource & Research Unit.

Doherty, G., & Dunster, L. (2000). Guide to self-reflections for practitioners in child care settings. In *Partners in quality: Tools for practitioners in child care settings.* A project of the Canadian Child Care Federation.

Doherty, G., Lero, D., Goelman, H., Tougas, J., & LaGrange, A. (2000). *You Bet I Care! Caring and learning environments: Quality in regulated family child care across Canada.* Guelph: Centre for Families, Work and Well-Being, University of Guelph, Ontario.

Doherty, G., & Forer, B. (2003). *Unionization and quality in early childhood programs.* Ottawa: Canadian Union of Public Employees.

McCuaig, K. (2004). *From patchwork to framework: A child care strategy for Canada.* Toronto: Child Care Advocacy Association of Canada.

Modigliani, Kathy. (1988, March). Twelve reasons for the low wages in child care. *Young Children,* 43 (3), 14–15.

NAEYC. (1993, January). The effects of group size, ratios, and staff training on child care quality. *Young Children,* 48 (2), 65–67.

———. (1990, November). NAEYC position statement on guidelines for compensation of early childhood professionals. *Young Children,* 46 (1), 30–32.

Ontario Coalition for Better Child Care. (1997). *A guide to child care in Ontario.* Toronto: OCBCC.

Russell, Sue. (1993, July). Linking education and compensation: A wholistic model. *Young Children,* 48 (5), 64–68.

References

Ade, W. (1982, March). Professionalization and its implications for the field of early childhood education. *Young Children,* 37 (3), 25–32.

AECEO. (2005). *Common table for childhood development and care in Canada.* Toronto: AECEO.

———. (1997). Meet the affiliates. The Association of Early Childhood Educators, Ontario (AECEO). *Interaction* (Spring), 3.

Alberta Child Care Accreditation. (2004). *Child care accreditation.* http://www.child.gov.ab.ca/whatwedo/childcareaccreditation/page.cfm?pg=index

Allen, Jeannie. (1991). Caregiver's corner. *Young Children,* 46(6), p. 18.

Almy, M. (1988). The early childhood educator revisited. In Bernard Spodek, Olivia N. Saracho, & Donald L. Peters, (Eds.), *Professionalism and the early childhood practitioner.* New York: Teachers College Press.

———. (1975). *The early childhood educator at work.* New York: McGraw-Hill.

Anderson, C., & Bushman, B. (2001). Effects of violent video games on aggressive behavior, aggressive cognition, aggressive affect, physiological arousal and prosocial behaviour: A meta-analytic review of the scientific literature. *Psychological Science,* 12, 353–359.

Arnup, K. (1994). *Education for motherhood: Advice for mothers in twentieth-century Canada.* Toronto: University of Toronto Press.

Association of Canadian Community Colleges (ACCC). (1997). *Canadian training inventory.* www.accc.ca/english/programs/ecce/institutions.cfm

Astington, J. W. (1993). *The child's discovery of the mind.* Cambridge, MA: Harvard University Press.

Ayers, William. (1993). *To teach: The journey of a teacher.* New York: Teachers College Press.

———. (1989). *The good preschool teacher.* New York: Teachers College Press.

Baker, Amy C. (1992, July). A puzzle, a picnic, and a vision: Family day care at its best. *Young Children,* 47 (5), 36–38.

Baker, M., Gruber, J. & Milligan, K. (2006). *What can we learn from Quebec's universal child care program?* Vancouver: C. D. Howe Institute. Retrieved June 16, 2006 at http://www.cdhowe.org/pdf/ebrief_25_english.pdf.

Ball, J. (2005). Early childhood care and development programs as hook and hub for inter-sectoral service delivery in First Nations communities. *Journal of Aboriginal Health,* 1 (2), 36–50.

Balaban, Nancy. (1992, July). The role of the child care professional in caring for infants, toddlers, and their families. *Young Children,* 47 (5), 66–71.

Barnett, S., Yarosz, D., Thomas, J., & Hornbeck, A. (2006). *Educational effectiveness of a Vygotskian approach to preschool education: A randomized trial.* New Jersey: National Institute for Early Education Research.

Beach, J. (1999). Community colleges and the delivery of professional development to the early childhood care and education sector. *Research Connections Canada,* 2, 101–140.

Beach, J., & Bertrand, J. (2000). *More than the sum of the parts: An early child development system for Canada.* Occasional Paper No. 12. Toronto: Childcare Resource and Research Unit, University of Toronto.

Beach, J., Bertrand, J., Forer, B., Michal, D., & Tougas, J. (2004). *Working for change: Canada's child care workforce.* Prepared for the Child Care Human Resources Sector Council. Ottawa: Child Care Human Resources Sector Council.

Beach J., Friendly, M., & Schmidt, L. (1993). *Work-related child care in context: A study of work-related child care in Canada.* Occasional Paper No. 3. Toronto: Childcare Research & Resource Unit, University of Toronto.

Beach, Jane, Bertrand, Jane, & Cleveland, Gordon. (1998). *Our child care workforce: From recognition to remuneration.* Ottawa: Child Care Human Resources Steering Committee.

Behrmann, Michael M., & Lahm, Elizabeth A. (1994). Computer applications in early childhood special education. In *Young children: Active learners in a technological age.* Washington, DC: NAEYC.

Bellm, Dan, Gnezda, Terry, Whitebook, Marcy, & Breunig, Gretchen Stahr. (1994). Policy initiatives to enhance child care staff compensation. In Julienne Johnson & Janet B. McCracken (Eds.), *The early childhood career lattice: Perspectives on professional development.* Washington, DC: NAEYC.

Benner, A. (1999). *Quality child care and community development: What is the connection?* Ottawa: Canadian Child Care Federation.

Bennett, J. (2004). *Starting strong: Curricula and pedagogies in early childhood education and care.* Paris: Directorate for Education, OECD.

Beretier, C. (1972). An academic preschool for disadvantaged children. In J.S. Stanley (Ed.), *Preschool programs for the disadvantaged: Five experimental approaches to early childhood education.* Baltimore: Johns Hopkins University Press. 1–21.

Bergen, D. (2002). The role of pretend play in children's cognitive development. *Early Childhood Research and Practice.* Spring 2002, Volume 4, Number 1.

Bergmann, B. (1996). *Saving our children from poverty: What the United States can learn from France.* New York: Russell Sage Foundation.

Berk, Laura, & Winsler, Adam. (1995). *Scaffolding children's learning: Vygotsky and early childhood education.* Washington, DC: National Association for the Education of Young Children.

Bernhard, J., Pollard, J., Eggers-Pierola, C., & Morin, A. (2000). Infants and toddlers in Canadian multi-age child care settings: Age, ability and linguistic inclusion. In *Research Connections Canada,* 4, pp. 79–154. Ottawa: Canadian Child Care Federation.

Berton, P. (1991). *The Dionne years.* Toronto: McClelland and Stewart.

Bertrand, J. (2001). *Summary of research findings on children's developmental health.* Ottawa: Canadian Institute of Child Health & Canadian Child Care Federation.

———. (1990). *Child care management guide.* Toronto: Ontario Coalition for Better Child Care.

Bertrand, J., Beach, J. Michal, D., & Tougas, J. (2004). *Working for a change: Canada's child care workforce. Literature review.* Labour Market Study. Ottawa: Child Care Human Resource Council.

Blades, C. M. (2002). Full-day kindergarten: "A blessing or a bane for young children?" in *CBE mild and moderate full-day kindergarten project* (2001–2002). Calgary, AB: Calgary Board of Education.

Bloom, B. (1964). *Stability and change in human behaviour.* New York: Wiley.

Bowman, B., & Beyer, E. (1994). Thoughts on technology and early childhood education. In *Young children: Active learners in a technological age.* Washington, DC: NAEYC.

Bradshaw, D. (1997). Front Line Profile, *Ideas,* Volume 4 (2) (December 1997), 19.

Bredekamp, S. (1995, January). What do early childhood professionals need to know and be able to do? *Young Children,* 50 (2), 67–69.

———. (1992, January). Composing a profession. *Young Children,* 47 (2), 52–54.

Bredekamp, Sue, & Willer, Barbara. (1993, March). Professionalizing the field of early childhood education: Pros and cons. *Young Children,* 48 (3), 82–84.

Broere, A. Supervisor, Rural Roots Children's Centre front line profile. (1995, December). *Ideas: The Journal of Emotional Well-Being in Child Care,* 1 (3), 15–16.

Bronfenbrenner, U. (1979). *The ecology of human development.* Cambridge, MA: Harvard University Press.

Brooks-Gunn, J. (2003). Do you believe in magic: What we can expect from early childhood intervention programs. *Social Policy Report XVII*(1): 3–7

Burts, D. C., Charlesworth, R., & Fleege, P. O. (1992). Observed activities and stress behaviors in developmentally appropriate and inappropriate kindergarten classrooms. *Early Childhood Research Quarterly,* 7, 297–318.

Cameron, C., Moss, P., & Owen, C. (1999). *Men in the nursery: Gender and caring.* London: Paul Chapman Publishing.

Canadian Child Care Federation. (2000). *Tools for practitioners in child care settings.* Ottawa: CCCF.

______. (1997). *Partners in quality survey.* Ottawa: CCCF.

———. (1991). National Statement on Quality Child Care. Ottawa.

Canadian Council on Social Development. (2006). *Growing up in North America.* Ottawa: CCSD.

Canadian Day Care Advocacy Association & Canadian Child Day Care Federation. (1992). *Caring for a living: Final report: A study on wages and working conditions in Canadian child care.* Ottawa: Author.

Canadian Education Association. (1999). *Education in Canada.* Toronto: CEA.

———. (1993). *Admission to faculties of education in Canada: What you need to know. A report from the canadian education association.* Toronto: author.

Carew, D. (1980). Observation study of caregiver and children in day care homes. Paper presented at the Society for Research in Child Development meeting. San Francisco, California.

Carnegie Commission on Educational Television. (1967). *Public television: A program for action.* New York: Carnegie Corporation.

Carson, Linda. (1978). Notes from a municipal day care worker. In K. G. Ross (Ed.), *Good day care: Fighting for it, getting it, keeping it.* Toronto: The Women's Press.

Carter, M., & Curtis, D. (1994). *Training teachers: A harvest of theory and practice.* St. Paul, MN: Redleaf Press.

Caruso, J. (1977, November). Phases in student teaching. *Young Children,* 32 (1), 57–63.

Chandler, Phyllis A. (1994). *A place for me: Including children with special needs in early care and education settings.* Washington, DC: NAEYC.

Chera, P., & Wood, C. (2003). Animated multimedia "talking books" can promote phonological awareness in children beginning to read. *Learning and Instruction,* 13, 33–52.

Child and Youth Officer for British Columbia. (2005). *Special report: Healthy early childhood development in British Columbia.* Victoria: Government of British Columbia.

Christie, James F., & Enz, Billie. (1992). The effects of literacy play interventions on preschoolers' play patterns and literacy development. *Early Education and Development, 3*(3), 205–220.

City of Toronto. (2004). *Toronto Report Card on Children* (Vol. 5, Update 2003). Toronto: City of Toronto, Children's Services Division, Children and Youth Advocate.

Clarke-Stewart, K. (1987). In search of consistencies in child care research. In D. Phillips (Ed.), *Quality in child care: What does the research tell us?* 105–120. Washington, DC: National Association for the Education of Young Children.

Clements, Douglas. (1994). The uniqueness of the computer as a learning tool: Insights from research and practice. In *Young children: Active learners in a technological age.* Washington, DC: NAEYC.

Cleveland, G., & Krashinsky, M. (1998). *The benefits and costs of good child care: The economic rationale for public investment in young children.* Toronto: Childcare Resource & Research Unit.

Cleveland, G., Corter, C., Pelletier, J., Colley, S., Bertrand, J., & Jamieson, J. (In press.) *Early childhood learning and development in child care, kindergarten and family support programs.* Toronto: Atkinson Centre at OISE/UT.

Cleverley, J., & Phillips, D. (1986). *Visions of childhood: Influential models from Locke to Spock.* New York: Teachers College Press.

Colley, S. (2005). *Integration for a change: How can integration of services for kindergarten aged children be achieved?* Toronto: Institute for Child Study at OISE/UT.

Combs, Arthur W., Blume, Robert A., Newman, Arthur J., & Wass, Hannelore L. (1974). *The professional education of teachers: A humanistic approach to teacher education* (2nd ed.). Boston: Allyn and Bacon, Inc.

Cooke, K. et al. (1986). *Report of the Task Force on child care.* Ottawa: Government of Canada.

Cooke, M., Keating, D., and McColm, M. (2005). *Early learning and care in the city: Update, June 2005.* Toronto: Atkinson Centre at the Ontario Institute for Studies in Education of the University of Toronto and Centre of Early Childhood Development at George Brown College.

Corbett, Barbara. (1989). *A century of kindergarten education in Ontario.* Mississauga: The Froebel Foundation.

Corson, P. (2005). Multi-age grouping in early childhood education: An alternative discourse. *Research Connections Canada,* 13, 93–108.

Corter, C., Bertrand, J., Pelletier, J., Griffen, T., McKay, D., Patel, S., & Ioannone, P. (2006). *Toronto First Duty phase 1 summary: Evidence-based understanding of integrated foundations for early childhood.* Toronto: Atkinson Centre at OISE/UT. http://www.toronto.ca/firstduty.

Cruickshank, Donald R. (1987). *Reflective teaching: The preparation of students of teaching.* Reston, VA: Association of Teacher Educators.

Cryan, J. R., Sheehan, R., Wiechel, J., & Bandy-Hedden, I. G. (1992). Success outcomes of full-day kindergarten: More positive behavior and increased achievement in the years after. *Early Childhood Research Quarterly. Special Issue: Research on Kindergarten,* 7(2), 187–203.

Da Costa, J. L, & Bell, S. (2003). *Full-day vs. half-day kindergarten: Narrowing the SES gap.* Paper presented at the annual meeting of the Canadian Society for Studies in Education, Halifax, NS.

deJong, M., & Bus, A. (2002). Quality of book-reading matters for emergent readers. *Journal of Educational Psychology,* 94, 144–155.

Deloitte & Touche. (2000). *États Généraux sur la Petite Enfance.* Report to the Ontario Ministry of Education, Toronto.

Derman-Sparks, Louise. (1989). *Anti-bias curriculum: Tools for empowering young children.* Washington, DC: NAEYC.

Diamond, Karen E., Hestenes, Linda L., & O'Connor, Caryn E. (1994, January). Integrating young children with disabilities in preschool: Problems and promise. *Young Children,* 49 (2), 68–73.

Doherty, G. (2003). *Occupational standards.* Ottawa: Canadian Child Care Federation. http://www.cccf-fcsge.ca/subsites/training/pdf/occupational-final-e.pdf.

———. (2000). Issues in Canadian child care: What does the research tell us? *Research Connections Canada* 5, pp. 5–106.

______. (1998). Elements of quality. *Research Connections Canada* 1, pp. 1–20.

———. (1997). Zero to six: The basis for school readiness. Research paper, Applied Resources Branch. Ottawa: Human Resources Development, Canada.

Doherty, G., Friendly, M., & Beach, J. (2003). OECD thematic review of early childhood education and care: Canadian Background Report, Canada.

Doherty, G., Lero, D., Goelman, H., LaGrange, A., & Tougas, J. (2000). *You bet I care! A Canada-wide study on: Wages, working conditions and practices in child care centres.* Guelph: Centre for Families, Work, and Well-being, University of Guelph, Ontario.

Doherty, G., Lero, D., Goelman, H., Tougas, J., & LaGrange, A. (2000). *You bet I care! Caring and learning environments: Quality in regulated family child care across Canada.* Guelph: Centre for Families, Work and Well-Being, University of Guelph, Ontario.

Doherty, G., & Stuart, B. (1996). *A profile of quality in Canadian child care centres.* Guelph: University of Guelph.

Doherty, Gillian. (1997, July). Credentialing as a strategy for promoting quality in child care. Draft. Ottawa: Canadian Child Care Federation.

———. (1996). *The great child care debate: The long-term effects of non-parental child care.* Occasional Paper No. 7. Toronto: University of Toronto, Child Care Resource and Research Unit.

Doherty-Derkowski, Gillian. (1995). *Quality matters: Excellence in early childhood programs.* Reading, MA: Addison-Wesley Publishers Ltd.

Doxey, Isabel (Ed.). (1990). *Child care and education: Canadian dimensions.* Toronto: Nelson Canada.

Drew, M., and C. Law. (1990). Making early childhood education work. *Principal* *69*(5, May): 10–12. EJ 410 163.

Duff, R. Eleanor, Brown, Mac H., & Van Scoy, Irma J. (1995). Reflection and self-evaluation keys to professional development. *Young Children,* 50 (4), 81–88.

Edwards, Carolyn. (1994). Partner, nurturer, and guide: The roles of the Reggio teacher in action. In Carolyn Edwards, Lella Gandini, & George Forman (Eds.), *The hundred languages of children: The Reggio Emilia approach to early childhood education.* Norwood, NJ: Ablex Publishing Corporation.

Einarsdottir, Johanna. (2000). Incorporating literacy resources into the play curriculum of two Icelandic preschools. In Kathleen A. Roskos & James F. Christie (Eds.), *Play and literacy in early childhood: Research from multiple perspectives* (pp. 77–90). New York: Erlbaum.

Elicker, J., & Mathur, S. (1997). What do they do all day? Comprehensive evaluation of a full-day kindergarten. *Early Childhood Research Quarterly, 12, pt. Index Issue*(4), 459–480.

Elkind, D. (1988). *Miseducation: Preschoolers at risk.* New York: Alfred A. Knopf.

———. (1983, January). Montessori education: Abiding contributions and contemporary challenges. *Young Children,* 38 (2), 3–10.

Epstein, Ann S. (1993). *Training for quality: Improving early childhood programs through systematic inservice training.* Ypsilanti, MI: High/Scope Educational Research Foundation.

Ferguson, E. (1998). *Caring in practice: Child care substitute youth internship program. A synopsis.* Halifax: Child Care Connection-NS.

Ferguson, Elaine E. (1997). *Child care administrator credentialing: A work in progress.* Halifax: Child Care Connection-NS.

———. (1995). *Child care . . . becoming visible.* Halifax: Child Care Connection-NS.

Frede, E., & Ackerman, D. (2002). *Curriculum decision-making NIEER.* Retrieved April 2, 2006. http://nieer.org/resources/research/CurriculumDecisionMaking.pdf.

Friendly, M. (2000). *Child care and Canadian federalism in the 1990s: Canary in a coal mine.* Toronto: Childcare Resource and Research Unit, University of Toronto.

Friendly, M., & Beach, J. (2005). *Early childhood education and care in Canada 2004.* 6th edition, May.

Friendly, M., Doherty, G., & Beach, J. (2006). *Quality by design. . . . What do we know about quality in early learning and child care and what do we think? A literature review.* Toronto: Childcare Resource & Research Unit, University of Toronto. Available at http://www.childcarequality.ca, accessed 15 May 2006.

Frontline Profile. (1997, December). *Ideas: The Journal of Emotional Well-Being in Child Care, 4* (3), p. 19.

Gaffield, C. (1991). Children, schooling, and family reproduction in nineteenth-century Ontario. *Canadian Historical Review,* LXXII:2 (June 1991), 157–191.

Galant, Kim, & Hanline, Mary Frances. (1993). Parental attitudes toward mainstreaming young children with disabilities. *Childhood Education,* 69 (5), 293–297.

Galinsky, E., Howes, C., Kontos, S., & Shinn, M. (1994). The study of children in family child care and relative care—key findings and recommendations. *Young Children,* 50 (1), 58–61.

Gandini, Lella. (1993, November). Fundamentals of the Reggio Emilia approach to early childhood education. *Young Children,* 49 (1), 4–8.

Gersten, R., & Keating, T. (1990). Long-term benefits from direct instruction. In M. Jensen & Z. Chevalier (Eds.), *Issues and advocacy in early education.* Boston: Allyn and Bacon.

Gestwicki, C. (2006) *Developmentally appropriate practice: Curriculum and development in early education.* (3rd Ed.). Albany, NY: Delmar Publishers Inc.

———. (1996). *Home, school, community relations* (3rd ed.). Albany, NY: Delmar Publishers.

Giles, T. E., & Proudfoot, A. J. (1994). *Educational administration in Canada* (5th ed.) Calgary, Alberta: Detselig Enterprises Ltd.

Gladwell, M. (2002). *The tipping point.* Boston: Little, Brown & Co.

Goelman, H., Doherty, G., Lero, D., LaGrange, A., & Tougas, J. (2000). *You bet I care! Caring and learning environments: Quality in child care centres across Canada.* Guelph: Centre for Families, Work and Well-Being, University of Guelph, Ontario.

Goelman, H., & Pence, A. (1987). Effects of child care, family and individual characteristics on children's language development: The Victoria day care research project. In D. Phillips (Ed.), *Quality child care: What does research tell us?* Research monograph, Vol. 1. Washington, DC: National Association for the Education of Young Children.

Gonzalez-Menza, J. (1993). *Multicultural issues in child care.* Mountain View, CA: Mayfield Publishing Co.

Gopnik, A. (2005). *The philosophical baby.* New York: Houghton Mifflin; London: Weidenfeld and Nicolson.

Gopnik, A., Meltzoff, A. N., & Kuhl, P. K. (1999). *The scientist in the crib: Minds, brains, and how children learn.* New York: William Morrow.

Goss Gilroy. (1998). *The family child care provider survey.* Ottawa: Canadian Child Care Federation.

Goulet, M. (2001). *Handout #5: Curriculum development.* Toronto: George Brown College.

———. (1995). Building responsive relationships in infant care. *IDEAS* (2), 1, pp. 9–13.

Greenberg, Polly. (1990, January). Why not academic preschool? (Part 1). *Young Children,* 45 (2), 70–80.

Griffin, S. (1994). *Professionalism: The link to quality care.* Ottawa: Canadian Child Care Federation.

Griffin S., & Case, R. (1998). Re-thinking the primary school math curriculum: An approach based on cognitive science. *Issues in Education,* 4 (1), 1–51.

Guy, K. (1997). *Our promise to children.* Ottawa: Canadian Institute of Child Health.

Harms, T., & Clifford, R. (1980). *Early childhood rating scale.* New York: Teacher's College Press.

Harms, T., Clifford, R. M., & Cryer, D. (1998). *Early childhood environment rating scale.* Revised edition. New York: Teachers College Press.

Hebrew Univ. of Jerusalem (Israel). National Council of Jewish Women Research Inst. for Innovation in Education. (1993). *HIPPY: Home instruction program for preschool youngsters* (p. 48). Proceedings of the HIPPY International Research Seminar (1st, Jerusalem, Israel, December 16–19, 1991).

Helburn, S., Culkin, M., Morris, J., Morcan, N., Howes, C., Phillipsen, L., Bryant, D., Clifford, R., Cryer, D., Peisner-Feinberg, E., Burchinal, M., Kaga, S., & Rusticic, J. (1995). *Cost, quality & child outcomes in child care centres.* University of Colorado, University of California, University of North Carolina, and Yale University, Bloomington, IN: Phi Delta Kappa Educational Foundation.

Herman, Barry E. (1984). *The case for the full-day kindergarten.* Fastback 205. Bloomington.

Hill, Patty Smith. (1987, July). The function of the kindergarten. *Young Children,* 42 (5), 12–19.

Hillman, Carol. (1988). *Teaching four-year-olds: A personal journey.* Bloomington, IN: Phi Delta Kappa Educational Foundation.

Hohmann, C., Carmody, B., & McCabe-Branz, C. (1995). *High/Scope buyer's guide to children's software* (11th ed.). Ypsilanti, MI: High/Scope Press.

Holmes, C. T., & McConnell, B. M. (1990, April). *Full-day versus half day kindergarten: An experimental study.* Paper presented at the annual meeting of the American Educational Research Association, Boston.

Housden, T., and R. Kam. (1992). *Full-day kindergarten: A summary of the research.* Carmichael, CA: San Juan Unified School District.

Houston, A. (2004). In the new media as in old, context matters most. *Social Policy Report XVIII, IV*(4).

Howe, N., Jacobs, E., & Fiorentino, L. (2000). The curriculum. In L. Prochner, & N. Howe (Eds.), *Early childhood care and education in Canada.* Vancouver: UBCPress.

Human Resources Development Canada. (1994). *Child care and development: A supplementary paper.* Ottawa: Government of Canada.

Human Resources Development Canada, and Indian & Northern Affairs, Canada. (2001). *Federal/Provincial/Territorial early childhood development agreement: Report on government of Canada activities and expenditures 2000–2001.* Ottawa: Minister of Public Works and Government Services Canada.

Humphrey, Jack W. (1983). *A longitudinal study of the effectiveness of full-day kindergarten.* Evansville, OH: Evansville-Vanderburgh School District.

Hunt, J. McVicker. (1961). *Intelligence and experience.* New York: Ronald.

Hyson, Marion C. (1982, January). Playing with kids all day: Job stress in early childhood education. *Young Children,* 37 (2), 25–31.

Irwin, S. (1995). *Charting new waters.* Wreck Cove, NS: Breton Books.

Irwin, S., Lero, D., & Brohpy, K. (2004). *Inclusion: The next generation in child care in Canada.* Wreck Cove, NS: Breton Books.

Isenberg, J., & Quisenberry, N. (1988). Play: A necessity for all children. *Childhood Education,* 64 (3), 138–145.

Jacobs, E., Mill, D., & Jennings, M. (2002). *Quality assurance and school age care.* Final Report for the National School-Age Care Research Project 1997–1999. Montreal: Concordia University.

Janmohamed, Z. (2001). Unpublished paper. Toronto: George Brown College, 20–27.

Janus, M., & Offord, D. (2000). Readiness to learn at school. *Isuma,* 1 (2), 71–75.

Japel, C., & Tremblay, R. (2005). *Quality counts.* Montreal: Institute for Research on Public Policy.

Japel, C., Tremblay, R. E., & Côté, S. (2005). La qualité, ça compte! Résultats de l'Étude longitudinale du développement des enfants du Québec (ÉLDEQ) concernant la qualité des services de garde. Montreal: Institute for Research on Public Policy.

Joffe, C. (1977). *Friendly intruders.* Berkeley, CA: University of California Press.

Johnson, L., & Mathien, J. (1998). *Early childhood services for kindergarten-age children in four Canadian provinces: Scope, nature and models for the future.* Ottawa: The Caledon Institute of Social Policy.

Johnson, K., Lero, D., & Rooney, J. (2001). *Work-life compendium 2001: 150 Canadian statistics on work, family & well-being.* Guelph: Centre for Families, Work and Well-Being, University of Guelph.

Johnson, J., Christie, J., & Wardle, F. (2005). *Play, development and early education* Boston: Pearson/Allyn and Bacon.

Johnson, D. L., & Walker, T. (1991). A follow-up evaluation of the Houston parent-child development center: School performance. *Journal of Early Intervention*, 15(3), 226–236.

Jones, E. (Ed.). (1993). *Growing teachers: Partnerships in staff development.* Washington, DC: NAEYC.

Jones, E., & Nimmo, John. (1994). *Emergent curriculum.* Washington, DC: NAEYC.

Johnson, J. & McCracken, J. (Eds.) (1994). *The early childhood career lattice: Perspectives on professional development.* Washington: NAEYC.

———. (1988, May). Dealing with our ambivalence about advocacy. *Child Care Information Exchange*, (61), 31–34.

Kaiser, J., & Rasminsky, S. (1991). *The good day care book.* Toronto: Little, Brown & Company (Canada) Ltd.

Kamii, C. (Ed.). (1990). *Achievement testing in the early grades: Games grown-ups play.* Washington, DC: NAEYC.

Katz, L. (1995). *Talks with teachers: A collection.* Norwood, NJ: Ablex Publishing Corp.

———. (1995). *Talks with teachers of young children.* Norwood, NJ: Ablex Publishing Corporation.

———. (1993). *Five perspectives on quality in early childhood programs.* Perspectives from ERIC/EECE. [Monograph series, 1]. Urbana, IL: ERIC Clearing House on Elementary and Early Childhood Education.

———. (1991). Ethical issues in working with young children. In Lillian Katz & Evangeline Ward (Eds.), *Ethical behaviour in early childhood education.* (Expanded ed.). Washington, DC: NAEYC.

———. (1984, July). The professional early childhood teacher. *Young Children*, 39 (5), 3–10.

Katz, Lilian G., Evangelou, Demetra, & Hartman, Jeanette Allison. (1991). *The case for mixed-age grouping in early education.* Washington, DC: NAEYC.

Keating, D., & Hertzman, C. (1999) *Developmental health and the wealth of nations.* New York: Guilford Press.

Keating, D. (1998). Enhancing learning readiness: The family and the preschool child. *Transition*, pp. 13–14.

Kellerman, Maureen. (1995). *The 1995 report on family resource programs across Canada.* Ottawa: Canadian Association of Family Resource Programs.

Kershaw, P., Irwin, L., Trafford, K., & Hertzman, C. (2006). *The British Columbia atlas of child development.* 1st Edition. Vancouver: Human Early Learing Partnership

Kilbride, K. (1997). *Include me too! Human diversity in early childhood education.* Toronto: Harcourt Brace.

Kraft, K. C., & Berk L. (1998). Private speech in two preschools: Significance of open-ended activities and make-believe play for verbal self-regulation. *Early Childhood Research Quarterly, 13*, 637–658.

King, A., & Peart, M. J. (1990). *The good school.* Toronto: Ontario Teacher's Federation.

Kipnis, Kenneth. (1987, May). How to discuss professional ethics. *Young Children*, 42 (40), 26–30.

Kochendorfer, Leonard. (1994). *Becoming a reflective teacher.* Washington, DC: National Education Association.

Kyle, I., & Kellerman, M. (1998). *Case studies of Canadian family resource programs. Supporting families, children and communities.* Ottawa: Canadian Association of Family Resource Programs.

Lafreniere-Davis, N. (2005). *Early childhood in Canada's francophone minority communities: A transformative analysis.* Ottawa: Commission nationale des parents francophones.

Lazer, I., & Darlington, R. (1982). Lasting effects of early education: A report from the consortium for longitudinal studies. *Monographs of the Society for Research in Child Development* 47, 2–3.

Lero, D., Irwin, S., & Darisi, T. (2006). Partnerships for inclusion—Nova Scotia: An evaluation based on the first cohort of child care centres. Guelph: Centre for Families, Work and Well-being, University of Guelph.

Liebert, R., Sprafkin, J. (1988). *The early window: Effects of television on children and youth.* New York: Allyn and Bacon.

Love, J. M., Kisker, E. E., Ross, C. M., Schochet, P. Z., Brooks-Gunn, J., & Paulsell, D. et al. (2002, October). *Making a difference in the lives of infants and toddlers and their families: The impacts of early head start: Volume 1: Final technical report.* Princeton, NJ: Mathematica Policy Research, Inc.

Lyon, Patricia, & Canning, Mary. (1995). *The Atlantic day care study.* St. John's, NF: Memorial University of Newfoundland.

Malaguzzi, L. (1993, November). For an education based on relationships. *Young Children,* 49 (1), 9–12.

Malaguzzi, L. (1993). History, ideas, and basic philosophy. In C. Edwards, L. Gandini, & G. Forman, (Eds.), *The hundred languages of children: The Reggio Emilia approach to early childhood education,* 41–89. Norwood, NJ: Ablex.

Mathien, J. (2001). Children, families and institutions in late 18th century and 20th century Ontario. Unpublished master's thesis, Ontario Institute for Studies in Education, University of Toronto.

———. (1990). School programs for young children in Ontario and Toronto. (Unpublished manuscript).

McCain, M., & Mustard, J. F. (1999). *Early years study.* Toronto: Ontario Children's Secretariat.

Meisels, S., & Shonkoff, J. (1990). Preface. In *Handbook of early interventions,* S. Meisels and J. Shonkoff (Eds.). New York: Cambridge University Press.

Melhuish, E. C., Mooney, A., Martin, S., & Lloyd, E. (1990a). Type of childcare at 18 months— I. Differences in interactional experience. *Journal of Child Psychology and Psychiatry,* 31 (6), 849–859.

Melhuish, E. C., Mooney, A., Martin, S., & Lloyd, E. (1990b). Type of childcare at 18 months—II. Relations with cognitive and language development. *Journal of Child Psychology and Psychiatry,* 31 (6), 861–870.

Millichamp, D. (1974). Epilogue to *The adult and the nursery school child,* by Margaret Fletcher. Toronto: University of Toronto Press.

———. (1944). *Toronto day nurseries.* Toronto: Institute of Child Study

Modigliani, K. (1988, March). Twelve reasons for the low wages in child care. *Young Children,* 43 (3), 14–15.

Moss, P. (2000). Workforce issues in early childhood education and care. Prepared for consultative meeting on International Developments in Early Childhood Education and Care, May 11–12, 2000. New York: Columbia University.

Moss, P. (2004). *Setting the scene: A vision of universal children's spaces.* London: Day Care Trust.

NAEYC. (1995). *Guidelines for preparation for early childhood professionals associate baccalaureate, and advanced levels. Position statement.* Washington, DC: NAEYC.

———. (1991a, November). Early childhood teacher certification: A position statement of the association of teacher educators and the National Association for the Education of Young Children. *Young Children,* 47 (1), 16–21.

———. (1991b, September). NAEYC to launch new professional development initiative. *Young Children,* 46 (6), 37–39.

National Research Council. (2001). *Eager to learn: Educating our preschoolers* (Committee on Early Childhood Pedagogy of the Commission on Behavioral and Social Sciences and Education). Washington, DC: The National Academies Press.

Neuman, Susan B., & Roskos, Kathy. (1992). Literacy objects as cultural tools: Effects on children's literacy behaviors in play. *Reading Research Quarterly, 27*(3), 202–225.

NICHD Early Child Care Research Network. (2000). Characteristics and quality of child care for toddlers and preschoolers. *Journal of Applied Developmental Science, 4,* 116–135.

Nicholson, Simon. (1974). How not to cheat children: The theory of loose parts. In G. Coates (Ed.), *Alternate learning environments.* Stroudsberg, PA: Dowden, Hutchinson and Ross.

OECD (2004). *Early childhood education and care policy: Canada: Country note,* OECD Directorate for Education, 2004.

———. (2001). *Starting strong: Early childhood education and care.* Paris: OECD.

Olds, D., Henderson, C. R., Chamberlin, R., & Tatelbaum, R. (1986). Preventing child abuse and neglect: A randomized trial of nurse home visitation. *Pediatrics, 78*(1), 65–78.

Osborn, D. (1991). *Early childhood education in historical perspective* (3rd ed.). Athens, GA: Education Associates, Div. of The Daye Press, Inc.

Paley, Vivian Gussin. (1990). *The boy who would be a helicopter.* Cambridge, MA: Harvard University Press.

Pence, A. (2005). Horton and the worlds of ECD: Hearing and supporting other voices. *Research Directions Canada,* 13. Ottawa: Canadian Child Care Federation.

———. (1990). The child care profession in Canada. In Isabel Doxey (Ed.), *Child care and Canada.* Toronto: Nelson Canada.

Penn, H. (1999). *Values and beliefs in caring for babies and toddlers.* Toronto: Childcare Resource and Research Unit, University of Toronto.

Perrone, V. (1991). *A letter to teachers: Reflections of schooling and the art of teaching.* San Francisco: Jossey-Bass Publishers.

Perry, B. (1996). Neurodevelopmental adaptations to violence: How children survive the intragenerational vortex of violence. In *Violence and childhood trauma: Understanding and responding to the effects of violence on young children.* Cleveland: Gund Foundation.

Peters, R. (2001). *Developing capacity and competence in the better beginnings, better futures communities: Report summary.* Kingston: Research Coordination Unit, Queen's University.

Phillips, C. (1991). At the core: What every early childhood professional should know. In Julienne Johnson, & Janet B. McCracken (Eds.), *The early childhood career lattice: Perspectives on professional development.* Washington, DC: NAEYC.

Pollard, J. (1996). Student and sponsor-educator relationships during early childhood education practicum. Unpublished master's thesis, the School of Child and Youth Care, University of Victoria.

Prentice, S. (2001). *Changing child care: Five decades of child care advocacy and policy in Canada.* Halifax: Fernwood Publishing.

Prochner, L. (2000). A history of early education and child care in Canada, 1820–1966. In L. Prochner, & N. Howe (Eds.), *Early childhood care and education in Canada.* Vancouver: UBCPress.

———. (1996). Quality in care in historical perspective. *Early Childhood Research Quarterly,* 11, 5–17.

Rasmussen, J. (2000). Personal Communication.

Raymond, Jocelyn. (1991). *The nursery years.* Toronto: University of Toronto Press.

Rideout, V., Vandewater, E., & Wartella, E. (2003). *Zero to six: Electronic media in the lives of infants, toddlers and preschoolers.* Menlo Park, CA: Kaiser Family Foundation.

Robinson, B. (1988, September). Vanishing breed: Men in child care programs. *Young Children,* 43 (6), 54–57.

Roskos, K., & Christie, J. (2004). Examining the play-literacy interface: A crticial review and future directions. In E. Ziegler, D. Singer, & S. Bishop-Josef (Eds.), *Child's play: The roots of reading.* Zero to Three, 95–124.

Royal Commission on Learning, *For the love of learning.* Toronto: Government of Ontario.

Rubenstein, J., & Howes, C., (1983) Caregiving and infant behaviour in day care and in homes. *Developmental Psychology,* 15 (1), 1–24.

Rubenstein, J., & Howes, C. Social-emotional peers and individual differences. In S. Kilmer (Ed.), *Advances in early education and day care* (Vol. 3, pp. 13–45). Greenwich, CT: JAI.

Schulz, Patricia. (1978). Day care in Canada: 1850–1962. In *The good day care book.* Toronto: The Women's Press.

Schweinhart, L., & Weikart, D. (1993, Summer). Changed lives, significant benefits: The High/Scope Perry Preschool project to date. *High/Scope Resource,* 10–14.

Schweinhart, Lawrence J., & Weikart, David P. (1986, January). What do we know so far? A review of the head start synthesis project. *Young Children,* 41 (2), 49–55.

Schweinhart, L., Weikart, D., & Larner, M. (1986). Consequences of three preschool curriculum models through age 15. *Early Childhood Research Quarterly,* 1, 15–45.

Searls, D. T., Mead, N. A., & Ward, B. (1985). The relationship of students' reading skills to TV watching, leisure time reading, and homework. *Journal of Reading 29,* 158–162.

Segal, M. (2004). The roots and fruits of pretending. In E. Ziegler, D. Singer, & S. Bishop-Josef (Eds.), *Child's play: The roots of reading.* Zero to Three, 33–48.

Seifert, Kelvin. (1988). Men in early childhood education. In Bernard Spodek, Olivia N. Saracho, & Donald L. Peters (Eds.), *Professionalism and the early childhood practitioner.* New York: Teachers College Press.

Sherry, J. (2001). The effects of violent video games on aggression: A meta-analysis. *Human Communication Research, 27,* 409–431.

Shonkoff, J., & Meisels, S. (Eds.). (2000). *Handbook of early childhood intervention* (2nd ed.). Cambridge: Cambridge University Press.

Shonkoff, J. & Phillips, D. (2000). *Neurons to neighborhoods. The science of early childhood development.* Washington: National Science Council.

Siegler, R. (1994) Cognitive variability: A key to understanding cognitive development. *Current Directions in Psychological Science,* 3, 1–5.

Silin, Jonathan G. (1985, March). Authority as knowledge: A problem of professionalization. *Young Children,* 40 (3), 41–46.

Singer, J., & Lythcott, M. (2004). Fostering social achievement and creativity through sociodramatic play in the classroom. In E. Ziegler, D. Singer, S. Bishop-Josef (Eds.), *Child's play: The roots of reading.* Zero to Three, 77–94.

Singleton, C. (1997). The development and implementation of a reflective mentoring program for early childhood educators. Unpublished master's thesis, Memorial University of Newfoundland.

Social Development Canada, Public Health Agency of Canada and Indian & Northern Affairs Canada. (2005). *Early childhood development and early learning and child care activities and expenditures 2003–2004.* Ottawa: Government of Canada. http://www.socialunion.ca.

Smart Start Evaluation Team. (2003). *Smart Start and preschool child care quality in North Carolina: Change over time and relationships to children's readiness.* Chapel Hill, NC: FPG Child Development Institute, University of North Carolina at Chapel Hill.

SpeciaLink. (1996). Provincial and territorial early intervention directory, SpeciaLink Supplement.

Spodek, Bernard. (1994). The knowledge base for baccalaureate early childhood teacher education programs. In Julienne Johnson & Janet B. McCracken (Eds.), *The early childhood career lattice: Perspectives on professional development.* Washington, DC: NAEYC.

Spodek, B. & Saracho, O. (1991). *Issues in early childhood curriculum. Yearbook in Early Childhood Education.* Vol. 2. Troy, New York: Educators International Press.

———. (Eds.). (1988). *Professionalism and the early childhood practitioner.* New York: Teachers College Press.

Stanton, J. (1990). The ideal nursery school teacher. Reprinted in *Young Children,* 45 (4), 19. Used with permission of New York State AEYC. Originally published in *New York Nursery Education News* (Winter 1954).

Statistics Canada. (1992). *National child care study: Introductory report.* Cat. No. 89–526. Ottawa: Author.

Stone, S., & Christie, J. (1996). Collaborative literacy learning during sociodramatic play in a multiage (K-2) primary classroom. *Journal of Research in Childhood Education, 10*(2), 123–133.

Surbeck, Elaine. (1994, Summer). Journal writing with preservice teachers. *Childhood Education,* 70 (4), 232–35.

Sure Start Research Team. (2005b). *National evaluation report: Early impacts of sure start local programmes on children and families.* London: Queen's Printer.

Sutherland, N. (1976). *Children in English-Canadian society: Framing the 20th century consensus.* Toronto: University of Toronto Press.

Sylva, K. (1994). School influences on children's development. *Journal of Child Psychology and Psychiatry,* 35 (1), 135–70.

Thomas, B. (1998). *Family literacy in Canada.* Welland, ON: Soleil Publishing.

Tremblay, R., & Craig, W. (1995). Developmental crime prevention. In M. Tonry & D. P. Farrington (Eds.), *Building a safer society: Strategic approaches to crime prevention.* Chicago: University of Chicago Press, 151–239.

Tzelepis, A., Giblin, P. T., & Agronow, S. J. (1983). Effects of adult caregiver's behaviours on the activities, social interactions, and investments of nascent preschool day care groups. *Journal of Applied Developmental Psychology,* 4, 201–216.

United Nations. (1989). *Convention on the rights of the child.* Ottawa: Human Rights Program Department of Canadian Heritage.

United States Department of Commerce. (2002). *A nation online: How Americans are expanding their use of the Internet.* Washington, DC: U.S. Department of Commerce.

U.S. Census Bureau. (2001). *Table 4. Preprimary school enrollment of people 3 to 6 years old, by control of school, mother's family income, race, and Hispanic origin: October 2000. In School enrollment-social and economic characteristics of students: October 2000* (PPL-148). Washington, DC: Author. Retrieved May 31, 2006, from www.census .gov/population/socdemo/school/ppl-148/tab04.txt.

Vander Ven, K. (1994). Professional development: A contextual model. In J. Johnson & J. McCracken (Eds.), *The early childhood career lattice.* Washington, DC: National Association for the Education of Young Children and National Institute for Early Childhood Professional Development.

———. (1988). Pathways to professional effectiveness for early childhood educators. In Bernard Spodek, Olivia N. Saracho, & Donald L. Peters (Eds.), *Professionalism and the early childhood practitioner.* New York: Teachers College Press.

Watson, J. (1928). *Psychological care of infant and child.* London: Allen and Unwin.

Weiss, A. M. D. G., & Offenberg, R. J. (2002, April). *Enhancing urban children's early success in school: The power of full-day kindergarten.* Paper presented at the annual meeting of the American Educational Research Association, New Orleans, LA.

Welsh, J. (2002). *Full-day kindergarten a plus.* Pioneer Press. Minneapolis Public Schools.

Whitebook, M., Phillips, D., & Howes, C. (1990). *Who cares? Child care teachers and the quality of care in America.* Final report of the National Child Care Staffing Study. Oakland, CA: Child Care Employee Group.

Whitebook, Marcy. (1995, May). What's good for child care teachers is good for our country's children. *Young Children,* 50 (4), 49–50.

Whitebook, Marcy, & Granger, Robert C. (1989, May). Mommy, who's going to be my teacher today? Assessing teacher turnover. *Young Children,* 44 (4), 11–14.

Whitebook, Marcy, Hnatiuk, Patty, & Bellm, Dan. (1994). *Mentoring in early care and education: Refining an emerging career path.* Washington, DC: National Center for the Early Childhood Work Force.

Whitebook, M., Phillips, D., & Howes, C. (1993). *The national child care staffing study revisited: Four years in the life of center-based child care.* Oakland, CA: Child Care Employee Project.

Willer, B. (1994). A conceptual framework for early childhood professional development. NAEYC position statement. In Julienne Johnson & Janet B. McCracken (Eds.), *The early childhood career lattice: Perspectives on professional development.* Washington, DC: NAEYC.

Willer, Barbara, & Bredekamp, Sue. (1993, May). A new paradigm of early childhood professional development. *Young Children,* 48 (4), 63–66.

———. (1990, July). Redefining readiness: An essential requisite for educational reform. *Young Children,* 45 (5), 22–24.

Willms, J. D. (2000). Three hypotheses about community effects relevant to the contribution of human and social capital to sustaining economic growth and well-being. Report prepared for the Organization for Economic Cooperation and Development and Human Resources Development Canada. Fredericton, NB: Canadian Research Institute for Social Policy, University of New Brunswick.

Wright, M. (2000). Toronto's Institute of Child Study and the teachings of W. E. Blatz. In L. Prochner and N. Howe (Eds). *Early childhood care and education in Canada.* Vancouver: University of British Columbia Press. Pp. 96–114.

Wright, J. C., & Huston, A. C. (1995). Effects of educational TV viewing of lower income preschoolers on academic skills, school readiness, and school adjustment one to three years later: A report to Children's Television Workshop.

Wright, J., & Shade, D. (Eds.). (1994). *Young children: Active learners in a technological age.* Washington, DC: NAEYC.NEL.

Wright, J., Huston, A., Vandewater, E., Bickham, D., Scantlin, R., Kotler, J., Caplovitiz, A., Lee, J., Hofferth, S., & Finkelstein, J. (2001). American children's use of electronic media in 1997: A national survey. *Journal of Developmental Psychology, 22,* 31–47.

Yonemura, M. V. (1986). *A teacher at work: Professional development and the early childhood educator.* New York: Teachers College Press.

Youcha, Geraldine. (1995). *Minding the children: Child care in America from colonial times to the present.* New York: Scribner.

Young, N. (1994). *Caring for play: The school and child care connection.* Toronto: Exploring Environments.

Ziegler, E., Singer, D., & Bishop-Josef, S., (2004). *Child's play: The roots of reading.* Zero to Three.

Photo Credits

p. xxi: FTP Getty Images; **p. 6:** Play and Learn; **p. 8:** Yes I Can! Nursery School; **p. 17:** Play and Learn; **p. 19:** Play and Learn; **p. 39:** Eglinton Public School; **p. 42:** Ingrid Crowther; **p. 45:** Play and Learn; **p. 52:** Ingrid Crowther; **p. 64:** Shutterstock; **p. 72:** George Brown College; **p. 78:** Ingrid Crowther; **p. 82:** George Brown College; **p. 91:** George Brown College; **p. 113:** George Brown College; **p. 115:** Photos.com; **p. 117:** George Brown College; **p. 119:** Yes I Can! Nursery School; **p. 121:** George Brown College; **p. 129:** Ingrid Crowther; **p. 133:** George Brown College; **p. 139:** Alwynn Pinard; **p. 146:** Red River Community College; **p. 155:** Yes I Can! Nursery School; **p. 157:** Ingrid Crowther; **p. 161:** George Brown College; **p. 165:** Ingrid Crowther; **p. 173:** Play and Learn; **p. 178:** Can. Archives; **p. 185:** Archives and Museum, Toronto Board of Education; **p. 189:** Ontario Archives; **p. 192:** Metropolitan Reference Library, Special Collections Centre; **p. 196:** Thomas Fisher Rare Book Room, University of Toronto; **p. 211:** Photos.com; **p. 214:** George Brown College; **p. 220:** George Brown College; **p. 229:** Ingrid Crowther; **p. 235:** Alwynn Pinard; **p. 239:** Shutterstock; **p. 245:** George Brown College; **p. 255:** Ingrid Crowther; **p. 261:** Ingrid Crowther; **p. 265:** George Brown College

Index

D

E

F